12/06/99
16
ABH-0714

P9-DJL-949

FREUD
AND
BEYOND

OTHER BOOKS BY STEPHEN A. MITCHELL

Hope and Dread in Psychoanalysis (1993)

*Relational Concepts in Psychoanalysis:
An Integration* (1988)

Object Relations in Psychoanalytic Theory
(with Jay Greenberg, 1983)

FREUD
AND
BEYOND

A History of Modern
Psychoanalytic Thought

STEPHEN A. MITCHELL
MARGARET J. BLACK

BASIC
BOOKS

A Member of The Perseus Books Group

Copyright © 1995 by Stephen A. Mitchell and Margaret J. Black.
Published by BasicBooks, A Member of The Perseus Books Group

All rights reserved. Printed in the United States of America. No part of this book
may be reproduced in any manner whatsoever without written permission except in
the case of brief quotations embodied in critical articles and reviews. For information, address BasicBooks, 10 East 53rd Street, New York, NY 10022-5299.

Designed by Elliott Beard

Library of Congress Cataloging-in-Publication Data
Mitchell, Stephen A., 1946–
    Freud and beyond : a history of modern psychoanalytic thought / Stephen A.
Mitchell, Margaret J. Black.
        p.   cm.
    Includes bibliographical references and indexes.
    ISBN 0–465–01404–6 (cloth)
    ISBN 0–465–01405–4 (paper)
    1. Psychoanalysis. 2. Psychoanalysis—History. 3. Freud, Sigmund, 1856–1939.
I. Black, Margaret (Margaret J.). II. Title.
BF173.M546   1995
155.19'5—dc20   95-8972
                                                                  CIP

    99 00 ❖/HC 9

For Caitlin and Samantha

Those who know ghosts tell us that they long to be released from their ghost life and led to rest as ancestors. As ancestors they live forth in the present generation, while as ghosts they are compelled to haunt the present generation with their shadow life.

—*Hans Loewald*

CONTENTS

7: CONTEMPORARY FREUDIAN REVISIONISTS:
OTTO KERNBERG, ROY SCHAFER,
HANS LOEWALD, AND JACQUES LACAN
170

8: CONTROVERSIES IN THEORY
206

9: CONTROVERSIES IN TECHNIQUE
229

ACKNOWLEDGMENTS

This book grew out of our shared excitement about the teaching of psychoanalytic ideas, a process that has involved us for over twenty-five years: first as students and supervisees, then as teachers, supervisers, and consultants and educational administrators. We have seen psychoanalytic concepts taught well, and we have seen them taught poorly. "Everything you do," declared an early teacher to start his course, "is determined by forces inside you of which you are totally unaware." This kind of approach makes psychoanalytic ideas seem esoteric and alien, the claims made by psychoanalytic theorists arrogant and ominous. When taught well, psychoanalytic concepts have the capacity to enrich rather than deplete, to empower rather than diminish, to deepen experience rather than haunt it. It is with this ideal in mind that we have approached the writing of this book, hoping that the reader will find the concepts contained in it stimulating, challenging, and fundamentally graspable.

Our subject matter is vast. Only a portion of all the existing concepts could be presented, and only a portion of the relationships among them explored. We were regularly confronted with impossible choices: whether to fill out and make accessible a particularly difficult concept, or whether to use the space to discuss the work of one more person we felt had made a valuable contribution to psychoanalytic understanding. We know that we will never be fully reconciled to all the choices we made, but console ourselves with the hope that if we succeeded in presenting what we *could* include in an engaging enough manner, the book could provide for the reader an entrée into the psychoanalytic literature (where everything is available).

Many colleagues read and commented on various portions of various versions of this manuscript. This is not to imply that they agree with all we have written. The selection and the manner of presentation were, ultimately, our choices. We are very grateful for the imput of: Neil Altman, Lewis Aron, Diane Barth, Anthony Bass, Martha Bernth, Phillip Bromberg, Jody Davies, Sally Donaldson, James Fosshage, Kenneth Frank, Jay Greenberg, Adrienne Harris, Irwin Z. Hoffman, Frank Lachmann, Clem Loew, Susan McConnaughy, John Muller, Sheila Ronsen, and Charles Spezzano.

Those to whose generosity we are most indebted are our patients, whose willingness to allow us to explore their lives with them is the foundation for all the thoughts and concepts developed here. It is a great irony indeed that, because of confidentiality, patients can never be thanked by name. We are also deeply grateful to our many supervisees whose openness and generosity with their own work, both in moments of despair and in moments of mastery, have allowed us to better illustrate the constructive impact of psychoanalytic theory on the clinical process.

We both also feel extremely fortunate to have had the opportunity to teach psychoanalytic ideas to interested students in many settings. The selection of concepts presented here and the way they are developed were honed by the reactions and challenges of our students. It is no secret that the best way to learn anything is to muster the temerity to teach it, and we are grateful to the students and supervisees who have shared that kind of learning experience with us.

I (MB) would like to express my thanks to the National Institute for the Psychotherapies, where, as a member of the board of directors and as director of continuing education, I have had the privilege of being intimately involved in the shaping of psychoanalytic education in a community that fosters intellectual freedom and creative thinking. Many of my thoughts, about effective teaching as well as meaningful learning, have crystallized in these experiences. I have had the additional pleasure of serving on the faculty there as well as at the Postgraduate Center for Mental Health, the Institute for the Psychoanalytic Study of Subjectivity, and the Psychoanalytic Institute of Northern California, all institutes that give a great deal of careful thought to the teaching of psychoanalytic ideas.

I (SM) want to thank the William Alanson White Institute and the New York University Postdoctoral Program, on whose faculty I have served for many years. They have provided me with exciting intellectual communities and an academic freedom that has made possible the development of my own thought. I also have appreciated the opportunities for teaching at: the National Institute for the Psychotherapies; the doctoral program at Teachers' College, Columbia University; the Washington School of Psychiatry; and various local chapters of Division 39 (Psychoanalysis) of the American Psychological Association, in Boston, Denver, New Haven, San Francisco, Seattle, and Toronto. Most of all, I am indebted to the members of the reading groups with whom I have been meeting weekly or biweekly for years to discuss psychoanalytic ideas and the challenges of clinical work.

Jo Ann Miller at Basic Books was encouraging and helpful throughout, and Deborah Rosenzweig's meticulous eye was a great help and reassurance in the preparation of the manuscript.

Most of all, we would like to express our gratitude to our daughters, Caitlin and Samantha, whose spirit and good humor have always served as a source of inspiration for us.

PREFACE

What is psychoanalysis?

Movies and cartoons offer images of a patient lying on a couch, speaking endlessly into a vacuum, while a silent, colorless, older gentleman with a beard takes notes. Many people who are unfamiliar with psychoanalysis fear it as a coward's way out, an admission of defeat, a ceding of control and authority to a stranger.

But what of those who have benefited from or who practice psychoanalysis? Their voices are not often heard. The problem is that psychoanalytic concepts derive from and are concerned most fundamentally with the *experience* of the analytic process, an intensely emotional, highly charged, deeply personal experience for both participants. From the *inside,* in the eyes of those who practice and study psychoanalysis as well as those who have undergone a "successful" (i.e., personally meaningful) analysis, the world of psychoanalysis is a rich and intriguing place. Its basic concepts and modes of thought are imbued with an experiential vividness, a conceptual clarity, and a continual practical applicability to the day-to-day conduct of their lives. Psychoanalytic thought helps knit together different domains of experience: past and present, waking and sleeping, thinking and feeling, interpersonal events and the most private fantasies.

To the psychoanalytically informed mind, analytic concepts provide useful tools for expanding, consolidating, and enriching one's own life and one's relationships with others. Yet it is hard to convey this to someone who has not experienced it. To those for whom psychoanalysis is not a lived reality, psychoanalytic concepts can seem odd, abstract, alien, and out of reach. It is sometimes hard to believe they are, themselves, derived from actual human experience.

But there is more to it than that. Answering the question "What is psychoanalysis?" is more complicated than it would otherwise need to be because of four major myths about psychoanalysis that have wide currency in both the popular and scholarly spheres. Psychoanalysts themselves have contributed greatly to the perpetuation of these misleading notions.

Myth #1: Psychoanalysis Is Largely the Work of One Man.

For the first five decades in the history of psychoanalytic thought (up until Freud's death in 1939), it would have been tenable to argue that psychoanalysis *was* largely the invention of Freud's singular genius. Freud regarded psychoanalysis as a form of treatment, but also as a new branch of science. He carefully tended his creation, and it grew up around him. Those taught and analyzed by Freud were justifiably impressed with his early discoveries; they admired him and let him take the lead. Freud also regarded psychoanalysis as a quasi-political movement, and proved himself a dominant leader, wary of opposition, often reading others' creativity and originality as signs of disloyalty.

Alfred North Whitehead's claim that Western philosophy is a series of footnotes to Plato was an interpretive leap. But Freud's presence so infused early psychoanalysis that it has become tradition among many psychoanalytic writers to begin articles with a devout account of the ways Freud had already covered or believed or certainly would have believed the very ideas the author is about to develop. Thus authors of highly original contributions have often presented their work literally as mere footnotes to Freud. And major figures in the early decades of psychoanalysis—Jung, Adler, Ferenczi, Rank—were expelled from the Freudian mainstream as their ideas diverged significantly from established doctrine.

But since 1939, there has been no Freud to adjudicate competing claims concerning the truly psychoanalytic. Consequently, psychoanalytic thought has been released to flow more naturally. Where there was one channel, now there are many. Where there was one tradition, now there are multiple schools, technical terminologies, and forms of clinical practice. Psychoanalysis is no longer the work of one individual.

Myth #2: Contemporary Psychoanalysis, in Both Theory and Clinical Practice, Is Virtually the Same as It Was in Freud's Day.

Psychoanalysis *is* sometimes presented as if it were fundamentally unchanged since Freud's time. Because of their deference to Freud and psychoanalytic tradition, some analytic authors write as though caught in a time warp, oblivious to the burgeoning innovative literature of psychoanalytic theory and technique. Others, more aware of contemporary developments but still maintaining their loyalty to tradition, publicly advance a version of psychoanalysis that no longer reflects their actual clinical practice.[1] And many dismissive critics of psychoanalysis believe that knocking Freud, or taking easy shots at outdated features of his thought, is equivalent to demolishing psychoanalysis in its entirety.

The startling reality is that very little of the way Freud understood and practiced psychoanalysis has remained simply intact. The major pillars of his theorizing—instinctual drives, the centrality of the Oedipus complex, the motivational primacy of sex and aggression—have all been challenged and fundamentally transformed in contemporary psychoanalytic thought. And Freud's basic technical principles—analytic neutrality, the systematic frustration of the patient's wishes, a regression to an infantile neurosis—have likewise been reconceptualized, revised, and transformed by current clinicians.

The popular image of the isolated supine patient endlessly free-associating and surrendering to the analyst's superior authority has evolved into revised versions of psychoanalytic treatment that embrace flexibility of both form (on the couch or sitting up) and process. They rely for their impact not on the presumption of the analyst's authority, but on the development of a collaborative inquiry between analyst and analysand. And with a deeper understanding of the subjective nature of experience, today's analyst does not naively presume to be the arbiter of reality as much as the guide on a mutually undertaken journey.

Thus the contemporary psychoanalytic world can only be meaningfully characterized as post-Freudian. Anyone who thinks that a familiarity with Freud's work is equivalent to an understanding of psychoanalysis is out of touch; it is like believing that contemporary physics is contained in the work of Newton, or contemporary biology in Darwin's opus. Freud's oeuvre will always represent one of the most impressive personal achievements of Western intellectual history and culture, but it hardly represents contemporary psychoanalytic thought and clinical practice. The living impact of the revolution Freud provoked has expanded, changed, and flowered into concepts, methods, and understandings that would have scarcely been imaginable to Freud and his contemporaries.

Myth #3: Psychoanalysis Has Gone Out of Fashion.

This myth is based on a partial truth. Orthodox, classical Freudian psychoanalysis *is* going out of fashion. That is because orthodox psychoanalysis is not of our time; its methods and its understandings were fashioned almost a hundred years ago. As the world around psychoanalysis has changed, psychoanalysis itself has changed, in the settings in which it is applied, the forms through which it is practiced, and the understandings it generates.

With the proliferation of many other forms of psychotherapy and of psychiatric medication, as well as the increasing control of the insurance industry and government over payments leading inevitably to less frequent and much shorter modes of treatment, psychoanalysis has certainly lost the near monopoly it once enjoyed as a psychological treatment. Although the number of both psychoanalysts and psychoanalytic patients has been steadily increasing (Panel, 1978; Michels, 1988), the briefer, problem-oriented, symptomatic treatments are appealing to many people. In our modern world, with its frantic rate of change, its emphasis on cost effectiveness, its relentless demands for profit and productivity, the languorous timelessness and deep reflectiveness of psychoanalysis *can* seem as dated as Freud's Victorian chaise longue draped with Oriental throw rugs.

At the same time, the past decade has witnessed a psychoanalytic expansion of striking proportions. Most of the wide range of psychotherapies outside psychoanalysis proper have derived from and are continually influenced by both classical and more contemporary psychoanalytic concepts. In particular, psychoanalytic object relations theories and psychoanalytic self psychology have been among the most important influences on casework within the field of social work and on virtually all forms of psychotherapy practiced today (family therapy, couples therapy, cognitive and behavioral approaches, Gestalt psychotherapy, and short-term dynamic psychotherapy).

The extension of psychoanalysis beyond the clinical setting has been even more impressive. Throughout Freud's often lonely and combative lifetime, psychoanalysis occupied, even at its most influential, a beleaguered minority position in relation to society and culture at large. Today, Freud's contributions are so broadly accepted, so tightly woven into the fabric of our culture and our experience of ourselves, that, in the broadest sense, we are all "Freudians."

Psychoanalysis is not only a professional and scientific discipline *within* our culture, but a form of thought, an approach to human experience, that has become *constitutive* of our culture and pervades the way we have come to experience ourselves and our minds. Major features of Freud's own contributions that were highly controversial in his time have become commonplace ideas in our world: unconscious motivation and meaning, the infinite variability of forms of sexuality, the formative power of early events, the centrality of oedipal themes in family life, the sexual and sensual dimensions of infantile and childhood experiences, the efficiency of the mind in disavowing unpleasant truths, and so on.

From a literary point of view, the critic Harold Bloom (1986) has argued that Freud's "conceptions . . . have begun to merge with our culture, and indeed now form the only Western mythology that contemporary intellectuals have in common." And in the very different but equally contemporary world of artificial intelligence, Douglas Hofstadter and Daniel Dennett (1981) point to Freud as the pioneer whose vision of mind has led in directions never imaginable in his day:

> [W]hen Freud initially hypothesized the existence of *un*conscious mental processes, his proposal met widely with stark denial and incomprehension. . . . Freud's expansion of the bounds of the thinkable revolutionized clinical psychology. It also paved the way for the more recent development of "cognitive" experimental psychology. We have come to accept without the slightest twinge of incomprehension a host of claims to the effect that sophisticated hypothesis testing, memory searching, inference—in short, information processing—occurs within us though it is entirely inaccessible to introspection. (p. 11)

It seemed fitting that as the Soviet Union lurched into modern Western culture, one of the first important signs of intellectual awakening was a new interest in psychoanalysis (Barringer, 1988).

Similarly, psychoanalytic contributions to modern experience and culture did not end with Freud's death. Harry Stack Sullivan's methodology of participant observation and his interpersonal field theory have had an enormous impact on contemporary methodology in all the social sciences and on current concepts of social constructivism. Erik Erikson's epigenetic approach to the life cycle and his concept of identity have influenced anthropology, history, and biography. Melanie Klein's startling vision of infantile fantasy life and Margaret Mahler's powerful, romantic depiction of the psychological birth of the child from a symbiotic embeddedness with the mother have had a broad effect on the way parents and researchers think about children, their struggles, and their developmental requirements. John Bowlby's compelling and well-documented theory of attachment has spawned an industry of research into infant–mother bonding and parent–child separations, which has contributed to the political and social debate about the needs of our children (cf. Fraiberg, 1977). Donald Winnicott's evocative and innovative understanding of the origins of subjectivity and the place of the "holding environment" in the mother–infant dyad have had a pervasive (if sometimes unacknowledged) impact on the experience of parenting for an entire generation. And Winnicott's concepts of the "transitional object" and "transitional experience" have been taken up by early-childhood educators and philosophers of creativity, culture, and aesthetic experience.

Contemporary revisionist Freudian approaches have had a central and often dramatic influence on literary criticism. Roy Schafer's application of the concept of "narratives" to psychodynamics and psychoanalytic life stories and Jacques Lacan's provocative and elusive account of the unconscious in terms of contemporary linguistics and structural anthropology are both widely cited. Heinz Kohut's compelling study of the vicissitudes of narcissism and the self have been picked up and developed by interpreters of literature, history, and culture in general. For example, in his influential book *The Culture of Narcissism* the scholar Christopher Lasch drew heavily on the theories of narcissism developed by both Kohut and Otto Kernberg.

A rich and complex cross-fertilization has also taken place between psychoanalysis and feminism. Many early feminists justifiably used Freud's patriarchal and condescending view of women as a target. But as chapter 8 notes, the feminist critique from outside the field of psychoanalysis was paralleled by critical revision within it. Psychoanalyst/feminist writers have played an important role in the most innovative current thinking about gender and sexuality. Thus post-Freudian developments in psychoanalytic ideas have filtered into and profoundly shaped contemporary life and thought.

Therefore, the portrayal of psychoanalysis as slipping into irrelevance is far from accurate. The dominant concerns within the contemporary analytic literature and current analytic practice—the nature of subjectivity, the generation of personal meaning and creativity, the embeddedness of the subject in cultural, linguistic, and historical contexts—are, in fact, the predominant concerns of our time.

Myth #4: Psychoanalysis Is an Esoteric Cult Requiring Both Conversion and Years of Study.

Freud was a great prose stylist, and his brilliant manner of argumentation allows anyone willing to work at it to follow along in the development of his ideas. Most of the post-Freudian texts are written in a style that encourages a view of psychoanalysis as an esoteric, impenetrable world unto itself, its self-proclaimed riches accessible only to a select few. The language is dense, thick with jargon and complex argumentation. A considerable familiarity both with previous psychoanalytic literature and with clinical process is generally presumed. As postclassical psychoanalysis has fragmented into competing schools and traditions, the insights and contributions in any individual work are generally presented with the major political schisms in mind. Any particular author is likely to be arguing against one or more other authors or positions, often unnamed. New language is sometimes invented to convey old ideas, so that differences can be exaggerated in claims to originality. Old language is sometimes stretched to convey new ideas, so that similarities can be exaggerated in claims to continuity. All this makes it difficult for anyone who has not spent years studying the history of psychoanalytic ideas to pick up any individual psychoanalytic work and to grasp its contribution.

Politics and economics have also played an important part in the inaccessibility of psychoanalytic ideas. Despite Freud's own wishes, psychoanalysis, particularly in the United States, was thoroughly medicalized up until recently. The American medical establishment laid claim to psychoanalysis and ran it monopolistically. Thus the impression that psychoanalytic ideas were by their nature esoteric, highly technical, and accessible only to the officially initiated partially reflected the political elitism and financial interests of those who benefited from maintaining the impression that psychoanalysis was a highly technical medical specialty.

The last two decades have witnessed a social revolution in the practice and training of psychoanalysts in the United States. Newer institutes training psychologists and social workers have proliferated and flourished in many cities, the content of their curriculum not constrained by the politics of loyalty to Freud or to the medical model; they teach more directly and openly the invigorating infusion of the ideas of more contemporary writers into the conceptual explorations and clinical practice of psychoanalysis. A restraint-of-trade lawsuit, successfully undertaken against the medically dominated American Psychoanalytic Association, has forced the opening of formally medical institutes to nonmedically trained professionals. All this has begun to effect a reversal of the traditional elitism and contrived obscurantism of psychoanalytic writing. Psychoanalysis is in the process of modernization; its ideas need to be made available to all who are interested.

Freud and Beyond: A History of Modern Psychoanalytic Thought is based on our conviction that psychoanalytic ideas, from their origins in Freud's work to the current diverse array of competing schools, can and ought to be made accessible both to practicing clinicians who have not undergone years of formal study and to any interested reader. This conviction has developed during our many years of teaching psychoanalytic ideas to students on different levels. Effective teaching has always involved finding a way to help the student see past jargon and political packaging to the experiential kernel of theoretical concepts. Each psychoanalytic formulation is an effort to grasp and portray some piece of human experience, some aspect of the workings of the mind. Each formulation refers to real people, their way of organizing experience, their difficulties in living, their struggle to shape and maintain a personal self in relation to other people.

This book presents the central ideas of the major contributors to contemporary psychoanalytic thought. We are not aiming to be comprehensive. A full consideration of each of the major figures and his or her theoretical perspectives would require an entire book of its own. We are also not aiming for a full and detailed tracing of sources and influences, sequences and progressions. Delineating the historical relationships of contemporary psychoanalytic schools to one another is a different and monumental project, presupposing a technical acquaintance with the inner workings of those schools themselves.

The historical perspective we provide is largely for purposes of comparison—to survey and consider in relation to one another the major currents and patterns of contemporary psychoanalytic thinking. We begin with Freud, not only because of his historical significance, but because he is still *the* major point of reference for the generation of new perspectives: understanding each theorist's relationship to Freud is crucial to placing them vis-à-vis each other.

Our aim is to *introduce* each system. Presuming no familiarity on the reader's part, we provide an entry into each theoretical tradition by selectively explaining its fundamental sensibility and some of its basic concepts, wherever possible, through clinical illustrations of the human struggles they attempt to illuminate. The clinical examples are drawn, for the most part, not from the major theorists themselves, whose illustrations (presented for polemical purposes and by now thoroughly picked over by scholars) often have a dated, remote quality for contemporary students and readers, but from our own clinical work and that of clinicians we have supervised and taught. Some of the cases, like Angela in chapter 2, Eduardo in chapter 6, and Harvey in chapter 9, describe a relatively new and inexperienced psychoanalyst's encounter with clinical problems for which the theoretical innovations explored in those chapters were extremely useful. (The extended illustrations are composites of work with several different patients, disguised and drawn together to preserve confidentiality.) Despite the fact that psychoanalytic theories have been developed by authors in many different countries at many different points in history and cultural evolution, we want to highlight the applicability of psychoanalytic ideas to real people living real lives with real problems in our current world.

The story is sometimes told that in the last years of his life one of the most important innovators in post-Freudian psychoanalysis had taken to bringing a gun with him when he presented his work at more traditional institutes. He would place it on the lectern without comment and proceed to read his paper. Invariably someone would ask about the gun, and he would say, in a pleasant voice, that the gun was for use on the first person who, rather than addressing the ideas he was presenting, asked instead whether they were "really psychoanalysis." Whether that story is true or not, it captures a great deal of the tenor of the contemporary psychoanalytic world, in which psychoanalysis has been struggling to expand and redefine itself. In this book, we consider a vast array of ideas, sometimes competing, sometimes complementary, that are all "really psychoanalysis," because they derive from the in-depth, textured, detailed psychoanalytic exploration of human experience.

1

SIGMUND FREUD AND THE CLASSICAL PSYCHOANALYTIC TRADITION

Very deep is the well of the past. . . . For the deeper we sound, the further down into the lower world of the past we probe and press, the more do we find that the earliest foundations of humanity, its history and culture, reveal themselves unfathomable.

—*Thomas Mann*

In 1873, when Freud was seventeen, the German archaeologist Heinrich Schliemann put together clues from fragmentary historical and literary sources and located the ancient city of Troy on the coastal plain of what is now Turkey. Perhaps no other event so fired the imagination of Freud, who tended to draw his inspiration from ancient heroes such as Moses and Hannibal. Later, Freud's consulting room came to resemble the office of an archaeologist, filled with primitive sculptures and relics. The site of Freud's dig was not the earth but the minds of his patients; the tools he used were not a shovel and brushes but psychoanalytic interpretations. The exhilaration was the same, however. Freud felt he had discovered an important site and had fashioned the necessary technology for exposing the underlying structure of the human mind and for unearthing the archaic history of both the individual patient and all humankind.

1

The historical development of Freud's theories is extremely intricate and complex. Since our focus is not intellectual history per se, but an explication of the concepts Freud bequeathed to contemporary psychoanalysis, we will not examine that development in any detail. Yet a broad sketch of the chronological unfolding of Freud's major concepts is essential to appreciating their origin in the clinical problems his patients presented to him. Unlike Schliemann, who knew precisely what he was looking for, Freud stumbled across his route to the "well of the past," his access to the depths, as he went, while trying to address his patients' difficulties in living in the present and on the surface.

FROM BRAIN TO MIND

Freud graduated from medical school at a time when the study of the physical structure of the brain was in its burgeoning infancy. The neuron, the individual nerve cell, had recently been isolated; techniques were being developed for tracing neural pathways; the enormous complexity of the brain was just beginning to be sensed. Freud started out as a researcher in neurophysiology, and when he switched from research to clinical practice, he treated patients suffering from what were understood to be neurological conditions, victims of damaged or weakened nerves. The dramatic demonstrations of the renowned neurologists Jean-Martin Charcot and Hippolyte Bernheim he witnessed during a stay in France sparked his interest in unconscious ideas, fatefully shifting his focus from brain to mind.[1]

For example, "glove anaesthesia," the lack of feeling in the hand, makes no sense neurologically. The nerves in the hand extend up the arm; if the nerves themselves were damaged, the numbness would not be limited only to the hand. But glove anaesthesia makes sense psychologically. The *idea* the patient has of his hand is central to the functional disability. It is not the nerves themselves that are damaged; something is disordered in the patient's thoughts, thoughts about his hand. The patient may have no direct access to these thoughts; they may be absent from the conscious portion of his mind. Yet they have a powerful effect and result in a physical phenomenon.

Charcot demonstrated not only that ideas, rather than damaged nerves, were responsible for conditions like glove anaesthesia and hysterical paralysis and blindness, but that ideas could also effect (generally temporary) cures. Charcot would place patients in hypnotic trances and, through hypnotic suggestion, induce hysterical symptoms that hadn't been there before. He might say something like, "When you awake, you will be unable to see, unable to walk." And, even more startling, he would use hypnotic suggestion to temporarily remove symptoms, to make the hysterically blind see, the hysterically paralyzed walk.

The problem is not in the flesh—the hand, the eyes, the legs are intact. The problem is an idea, out of awareness—the idea that the patient cannot feel, cannot see, cannot walk. That pathogenic idea is counteracted by another idea, the hypnotist's injunction to feel, to see, to walk. That idea, introduced into the mind of the subject by the hypnotist, can control experience and behavior, despite the fact that it seems to be wholly unknown and inaccessible to the subject herself.

Before Freud, hysterics—patients who suffered from physical disabilities but evidenced no obvious actual physical impairment—were regarded as malingerers, morally suspect fakers, or victims of a generally weakened nervous system that produced random, meaningless disturbances in functioning. Freud, following Charcot, Bernheim, and other practitioners of medical hypnotism, demonstrated that hysterics suffered a disease not of brain but of mind. It was ideas, not nerves, that were the source of trouble.

Why would certain ideas become so different from ordinary ideas in the mind? How do some ideas become inaccessible? How do they develop the capacity for wreaking such havoc?

Some progress was made toward answering these questions by Freud's first collaborator, Josef Breuer, a highly respected Viennese internist. In 1880 Breuer was treating a brilliant young woman named Bertha Pappenheim, who later became a pioneer in the discipline of social work. While nursing her sick father, Pappenheim had developed a wide array of dramatic symptoms, including paralyses and speech dysfunctions. Breuer tried placing her in a hypnotic trance and, using the experimental procedures of Charcot and others, removing the symptoms through posthypnotic suggestion. Although this attempt proved ineffective, Pappenheim, while in the hypnotic trance, fell into talking about her various symptoms. Breuer, evincing the qualities that were to become crucial in a psychoanalyst—curiosity and a willingness to follow the patient's lead—allowed her simply to talk. With some encouragement on his part, her associations would lead back to the point at which the symptom originally appeared, inevitably some disturbing, stressful event. Pappenheim and Breuer discovered that this talk and the emotional discharge produced when the memory of the original disturbing incident emerged had a curative effect. Through this process, which she called "chimney sweeping," the symptoms disappeared (Freud & Breuer, 1895, p. 30).

At one point, for example, Pappenheim found herself unable to drink liquids; she had no idea why, but they had suddenly become repugnant to her. She became dehydrated and began to be seriously ill. Employing the proce-

dure they had developed together, Breuer placed her in a trance and prod-
ded her into talking about her disgust. She felt disinclined to talk about its
onset. He pushed her. Overcoming a strong resistance, she remembered
recently walking into her room to discover the dog of her "English lady-
companion, whom she did not care for" lapping water from a glass (p. 34).
She recounted the scene with great anger that, wanting to be polite, she had
held back at the time. She then emerged from the trance, and requested a
glass of water.

Breuer told an eager Freud about these experiences, and in 1893 the two
published the first psychoanalytic essay, "A Preliminary Communication,"
which stated, "Hysterics suffer mainly from reminiscences" (Freud & Breuer,
1895, p. 7). Hysteria was caused by trapped memories and the feelings
associated with them, they argued. Those memories and feelings had never
been lived through in an ordinary way; they had become split off from the
rest of the mind, only to fester and rise to the surface in the form of disconcerting and seemingly inexplicable symptoms. If those symptoms were
traced to their origins, their meanings would become apparent and the feelings would be discharged in a cathartic burst. Then the symptoms would
disappear. Freud and Breuer added fuller theoretical chapters and extended
case histories (including that of Bertha Pappenheim, whom they called
Anna O.)[2] and published *Studies on Hysteria* in 1895.

Perhaps the most important question raised by these initial clinical discoveries was: Why do certain experiences generate feelings that become dissociated, split off from the rest of the mind? In this first psychoanalytic
work, Freud and Breuer actually wrote separate theoretical chapters, suggesting two very different hypotheses. Breuer argued that the experiences
that became dissociated and therefore problematic were those that took
place during altered states of consciousness, which he called "hypnoid
states." Pappenheim, for example, was exhausted and overstressed from
nursing her sick father. The disturbing events could not be integrated into
her ordinary mental processes because they were registered in an altered
state of mind, when she was already not herself. By placing her in a trance
and encouraging her to relive the memories, the split was healed, normal
processing of emotions took place, and the mind was made whole once
again. Perhaps, Breuer thought, certain people were more prone to hypnoid
states than others and therefore more likely to become hysterics.

Freud introduced a very different hypothesis: The pathogenic memories
and feelings were dissociated not because of a prior altered state of consciousness but because the actual *content* of those memories and feelings
was disturbing, unacceptable and in conflict with the rest of the person's
ideas and feelings. It was not that they just happened to be recorded in a

different way, to have fallen into a different part of the patient's mind—they were incompatible with the rest of consciousness and were therefore actively kept out of awareness. The difference between these early hypotheses of Breuer and Freud highlights the features that would become characteristic of Freud's understanding of mind throughout his subsequent career. Whereas Breuer saw hysterics as people susceptible to altered states of consciousness, to being "spaced out," Freud saw hysterics as people rent with conflicts and harboring secrets, from themselves as well as from others.

FROM HYPNOSIS TO PSYCHOANALYSIS

From 1895 to 1905 Freud produced a burst of creative theorizing and innovative clinical technique perhaps unrivaled in the history of ideas. The theory was always stimulated by and grounded in his clinical efforts; the theory often led to technical innovations that in turn generated new clinical data, which invariably stimulated more theoretical advances. During this ten-year period, psychoanalysis emerged from hypnotism and became a distinct methodology and treatment in its own right; many of the basic concepts that guide psychoanalytic thought to this day were established.

Freud began to find hypnosis less helpful in gaining access to pathogenic memories and feelings than he and Breuer had initially perceived it to be. As his clinical experience grew, Freud realized that what was most crucial to a permanent removal of symptoms was for the objectionable, unconscious material to become generally accessible to normal consciousness. (For Pappenheim, for example, the unconscious thought might be something like "I hate this woman's loathsome dog and it angers me that she lets it drink from my glass.") Troublesome "reminiscences" that emerged during a hypnotic trance slipped beyond reach again as the patient came out of the trance. There was a resistant force in the patient's mind, which Freud called the *defense*, that actively kept the memories out of awareness. (A well-bred young woman of Pappenheim's time and class would not have such unseemly rage about the dog.) The hypnotic trance artificially circumvented the defense, gaining access for the analyst to the festering secrets. But the patient was the one who needed to know, and the patient could not know because the resistance to that particular memory (and similar associatively linked memories) was reinstated when the trance ended. Simply being informed of the secret by the analyst after the trance would give the patient only intellectual, not experiential, awareness of it. (Pappenheim would know, based on her faith in the analyst, that she must hate the dog and possibly the governess too, but she doesn't *feel* the hatred and disgust.)

The Topographic Model

Freud's struggle with this clinical problem led to crucial theoretical and technical advances. In terms of theory, he began to envision a *topographical model* of the mind, dividing it into three different realms: an *unconscious,* containing unacceptable ideas and feelings; a *preconscious,* containing acceptable ideas and feelings that are capable of becoming conscious; and the *conscious,* containing those ideas and feelings in awareness at any particular time.

The theoretical advances represented in the topographical model were accompanied by technical innovations. The clinical task shifted from the discovery of the hypnotized patient's secrets by the analyst to the removal of the defenses against those secrets in the patient's own mind. Freud struggled to find a method that would dismantle or dissolve the defenses rather than temporarily lull them as hypnosis did. Around the turn of the century, he settled on the method of *free association,* the basic procedure that has been the backbone of psychoanalytic technique ever since.

Free Association

Free association retained some of the trappings of hypnotism. The patient lies comfortably on a couch in a quiet, peaceful setting, a situation intended to induce a state of mind midway between normal waking consciousness and a trance. The analyst is behind the head of the couch, out of direct vision. The patient says whatever comes into her mind, with no effort to screen or select thoughts, and is encouraged to become a passive observer of her own stream of consciousness: "Act as though . . . you were a traveler sitting next to the window of a railway carriage and describing to someone inside the carriage the changing views which you see outside" (Freud, 1913, p. 135).

As a strategic device, free association helps the analyst discern the patient's secrets, the unconscious wishes, *while* the defenses remain active and can be addressed. By encouraging the patient to report on all fleeting thoughts, the analyst hopes to get the patient to bypass the normal selection process that screens out conflictual content. Yet the patient is fully awake and can be shown that her unintended flow of thoughts contains disguised ideas and feelings that she has been keeping out of awareness.

Transference and Resistance

Free association is impossible to do for very long, Freud discovered. The defenses block the emergence of thoughts too closely linked to the repressed secrets. Furthermore, conflictual thoughts and feelings that constitute the center of the patient's difficulties are soon transferred to the person of the analyst, who becomes an object of intense longing, love, and/or hate. The patient refuses to speak of embarrassing or seemingly trivial thoughts, particularly because those thoughts often pertain to the analyst; the patient often finds she has no thoughts at all. The resistance to particular free associations is the very same force, Freud began to speculate, that drove the original memories out of consciousness in the first place. It is precisely this *transference* and this *resistance* that need to be exposed, identified, and dissolved. By analyzing the patient's free associations and resistances to free associations, Freud believed, he could gain access to both sides of the pathogenic conflict: (1) the secret feelings and memories and (2) the defenses—the thoughts and feelings rejecting those secret feelings and memories.

We can see this conflict in the case of Gloria. A lawyer in her twenties who grew up in an upper-middle-class family in a large Western city, she sought analytic treatment because she was paralyzed in trying to decide whether to marry the man she had been living with for some time. "I just don't know if he is Mr. Right," she said. Marriage was not the only area in which Gloria was indecisive, analytic inquiry began to reveal. Although she herself had never quite articulated it, even to herself, a pervasive doubt shadowed all important areas of her life. Virtually every activity seemed to expose her to lurking dangers. It was very difficult for her to allow herself to act spontaneously in any circumstances, and her life was consequently constricted and fretful. Each step of the way, she envisioned the worst possible scenario, and then combed her world for clues as to its likelihood.

In the initial months of analysis, these doubts, ruminations, and fears were traced increasingly further back in her childhood. She remembered being very worried that something disastrous would happen to her parents and other relatives. She would make up games with imagined predictive powers: if an even number of cars came around the corner in the next two minutes, everything would be all right; an odd number meant disaster was sure to strike.

Gloria agreed to begin her analytic sessions in much the same way Freud's patients began theirs—by reporting on whatever she found herself experiencing. This soon became problematic, however. She had great difficulty in knowing what it was she felt she "should" talk about; she headed off the horrifying possibility of having nothing to say by preparing detailed agendas for the sessions ahead of time. Sometimes she stopped speaking altogether. With some coaxing on the part of the analyst, she revealed that she had begun to feel anxious because she was having trouble grasping and using whatever the analyst said back to her. The analyst's questions and statements seemed complicated and confusing; his responses seemed "too big" and her mind seemed too small.

Among Freud's most important clinical observations was that the patient's difficulties in the analytic situation (the resistance and transference) are not an obstacle to the treatment but the very heart of it. Over the course of many months, it became apparent that Gloria's fears about free-associating and the analyst's interpretations derived from the same fears that had dominated her childhood and underlay her anxious, inhibited adulthood. If she allowed her ideas simply to flow, she was convinced, dangerous and deeply conflictual thoughts and fantasies would emerge. Her feelings, her bodily processes, her imagination—these were dangerous, likely to get out of control; they needed to be reined in at all costs. Without realizing it, she was constantly monitoring and scrutinizing her experience and inhibiting her mental processes.

What was most helpful to patients like Gloria, Freud found, was not circumventing her defenses (through hypnotism) to discover her secrets, but exploring those very defenses as they manifested themselves in the analytic situation. The central focus of the analytic process shifted to the analysis of transference (the displacement onto the analyst of the patient's conflictual feelings and wishes) and the analysis of resistance (the impediments to free association).

DREAMS

Among the associations generated by Freud's patients were their dreams. Freud treated dreams like any other associations: they were likely to contain hidden thoughts and links to earlier experiences.

Freud himself was a prolific dreamer. He also had certain troublesome neurotic symptoms. Soon, his most important patient became himself. He immersed himself in the new technique he had created, associating to the elements in his own dream life and communicating his self-discoveries in feverish letters to a physician friend in Berlin, Wilhelm Fliess, who functioned, at that considerable distance, as Freud's quasi-analyst. By 1895, Freud felt he had grasped the secret of dream formation.

Dreams are disguised fulfillments of conflictual wishes, Freud became convinced (Freud, 1900). In sleep, the dynamic force (the defenses) that ordinarily keeps forbidden wishes from gaining access to consciousness is weakened, as in a hypnotic trance. If the wish were simply represented directly in the dream, sleep would likely be disrupted. A compromise is struck between the force that propels the wish into consciousness and the force that blocks access to consciousness. The wish may appear in the dream only in a disguised form, an intruder dressed up to look as though he belongs. The true meaning of the dream (the *latent dream thoughts*) undergoes an elaborate process of distortion that results in the dream as experienced (the *manifest content* of the dream). Condensation, displacement, symbolism—all are employed in the dream work to transform the unacceptable latent dream thoughts into acceptable, although apparently meaningless, disconnected images, which are strung together into a story (*secondary elaboration*), to throw the dreamer even further off the track.

The technique for interpreting dreams follows from this conception of their formation. Each element of the manifest content of the dream is isolated and associated to. The associations to the various elements lead in different directions, exposing the different memories, thoughts, and feelings that had created them (through condensation, displacement, and symbolization). Eventually the various lines of association coalesce in the nodal latent dream thoughts. Dream interpretation reverses the process of dream formation, tracing the path from the disguised surface to the hidden secrets lying beneath.

The form that Freud delineated in his theory of dreams became the central structural pattern for his understanding of all important psychic phenomena. The structure of neurotic symptoms, slips of the tongue (Freudian slips), and motivated errors in general are all identical to the structure of the dream: a compromise is struck between an unacceptable thought or feeling and the defense against it. The forbidden material is allowed access into conscious experience only in disguised form.

An early dream of Gloria's can be analyzed from this perspective.

She dreamed that she was five years old, waiting with great excitement for her father to return home from work. When he arrived, it was discovered that he had something disgusting on his shoe, probably some dog feces he had stepped in. But there was something ominous about whatever this was he had brought in. The dream ended with a feeling of spooky uneasiness (rather like the feelings generated by the alien pods of the movie *Invasion of the Body Snatchers*).

As with all important dreams, new associations and meanings emerged repeatedly over the course of the analysis. Some of Gloria's associations with particular relevance to Freud's early theories of dream formation include the following:

When she was five years old a brother was born. She remembered having a vague understanding of her father's role in impregnating her mother and eventually remembered feeling quite jealous of the father's having given the mother, rather than her, a baby. She had many memories of baby dolls, which she valued highly, and also many horrible memories of her early relationship with her brother, whose arrival she came to regard as a virtual disaster.

Viewed from the perspective of Freud's theory of dream formation, the dream might be understood as follows:

As a little girl, and even as a grown woman, Gloria was intensely attached to her father and his penis. (The erotic excitement of her relationship to her father is condensed into the image of his eagerly awaited return home, and her interest in his penis is displaced onto and symbolized by his shoe.) Her brother was a piece of shit, she believed, and his arrival marred her erotic relationship with her father. She was unable to blame her father directly for this event that deeply enraged her, so she tended to regard it as an accident outside his control. The manifest content of the dream, a puzzling, odd story, conceals the latent dream thoughts beneath: childhood wishes, rage, and fears. The dream is a disguised composite of her deepest childhood wishes and her defenses against those wishes, woven together (through "secondary elaboration") into a bizarre narrative.

CHILDHOOD SEXUALITY

The other fateful discovery during those same years when Freud was establishing the significance of dreams concerned the *type* of memories and disturbing secrets he was reaching in his psychic excavations. As his clinical experience expanded, Freud found that symptoms thought to have been removed with the cathartic method (adapted from Breuer's treatment of Pappenheim) often returned. When he inquired into these symptoms further, it turned out that the event that was considered to be the origination of the symptom concealed an *earlier* unpleasant experience. Unless the symptom was traced to the earlier episode, the symptom was likely to recur. Often there was a series of associatively linked episodes, beginning in early childhood, all of which needed to be exhumed. Current conflicts and symptoms were invariably tied, Freud began to suspect, to events in early childhood.

Freud found that many of his patients, not just hysterics, were suffering from troubling memories of earlier experiences. If each exposed memory was examined to see whether it concealed earlier prototypes, all symptoms could be traced to traumatic incidents during early childhood (before the age of six). Even more surprising, these incidents invariably had to do with a precocious involvement with sexuality.

Gloria and her analyst gradually discovered the central importance of Gloria's early relationship with her father, whom she found both exciting and terrifying. She had many memories, which emerged over the course of treatment, of her father's flaunting his semi-nakedness. She was both fascinated and repulsed by his penis, which seemed huge and demonic. In her early struggles with the information she had been able to gather about sexuality and reproduction, she could not imagine how her small vagina could ever accommodate such a penis. Sexuality in general and her father in particular seemed both intensely exciting and profoundly dangerous. The analytic situation itself, like all important and anxiety-provoking areas of her life, was organized (in the transference) around this central, traumatic configuration: the analyst's interpretations, like her father's penis, seemed huge, both intensely exciting and extremely dangerous; her mind, like her vagina in childhood, was small and vulnerable; she longed to take in the interpretations, but was afraid they would destroy her.

A final aspect of Freud's early clinical discoveries was even more startling: If the memories of childhood sexuality were systematically peeled back to their troublesome core, they were invariably connected to an actual sexual encounter of one sort of another. These discoveries led Freud to the controversial theory of *infantile seduction:* The root cause of all neurosis is the premature introduction of sexuality into the experience of the child.[3] The child, whose natural innocence allows her no way to process the experience, becomes victimized by it again when her own sexuality naturally blossoms at puberty. The new, intense feelings of adolescence rekindle the earlier memories and feelings, trapped in their unprocessed form beneath the surface of the child's mind, creating a powerful pressure that produces neurotic symptoms.

This early theory would suggest that Gloria's memories of her feelings and fears with respect to her father must conceal an actual instance of seduction by the father. And indeed, Gloria had many memories not of explicit molestation, but of what she perceived as her father's frightening, intense interest in her sexuality: he would barge into her room despite her demands for privacy, noting and commenting on her physical maturation in a way she found extremely uncomfortable and embarrassing.

Freud expanded and developed his theory of infantile seduction, despite considerable criticism from his medical colleagues. At the same time, he wrestled, through the interpretation of his dreams, with his own past.

In 1896, his father died, and Freud had a series of dreams that revealed feelings about his parents which were surprising to him. Freud had wondered about the possibility of a sexual encounter in his own childhood. If all neurosis begins with seduction, and he himself had neurotic symptoms, he himself must have been seduced. Yet he had not uncovered any such memories. The dreams about his father seemed to suggest something else: As a small boy, he'd had sexual longings for his mother; he had regarded his father as a dangerous rival; he felt a triumph in connection with his father's recent demise. It seemed as if Freud had not been seduced as a child, but rather, he had longed to be seduced!

Freud's surprising self-discoveries were coterminous with his growing doubts about the theory of infantile seduction. Neurotic symptoms were very common. Was it possible that so many upper-middle-class Viennese children were routinely abused by their caretakers? Ironically, the more data Freud accumulated in support of his theory (the more patients recovered what appeared to be memories of childhood sexual experiences), the less probable the theory appeared. Putting these strands together, Freud arrived at the momentous conclusion, which he announced in a letter to Fliess in 1897, that many of the encounters probably had never taken place, that what he had taken for memories of events were memories of wishes and longings (Freud, 1985, pp. 264–66).[4]

It was a particular hallmark of Freud's genius to turn apparent setbacks into opportunities for further exploration. The collapse of his theory of infantile seduction forced him to grapple with his clinical data in a very different way. He had shared the general assumption of his day that children, left to their own devices, were sexually innocent. Sexuality was something that emerged in the hormonal changes of puberty. The theory of infantile seduction had seemed so compelling because it accounted for the introduction of sexuality into the innocence of childhood by an adult seducer. But if the seductions never happened, if analysis was uncovering not memories of events but memories of wishes and longings, the whole assumption of childhood innocence needed to be rethought. The collapse of the theory of infantile seduction led in 1897 to the emergence of the theory of infantile sexuality. The impulses, fantasies, and conflicts that Freud uncovered beneath the neurotic symptoms of his patients derived not from external contamination, he now believed, but from the mind of the child itself.

Freud became increasingly convinced that intensely conflictual sexuality dominates the childhood not only of future neurotics, but of all men and women. Further, the sexuality hidden in the symptomatology of neurotics is not limited to conventional heterosexual intercourse but is more like the sexuality of perversions. Body parts other than the genitals, such as the mouth and the anus, and bodily processes other than coitus, such as sucking, defecating, and even looking, are involved. This wide array of interests and activities characteristic of the sexuality of both neurosis and perversion can be traced, Freud increasingly felt, to the natural sexuality of childhood. But why is sexuality such a powerful motivator of difficulties in living? Freud's clinical discoveries led him to rethink the nature of sexuality and its role in the mind in general.

The Theory of Instinctual Drive

The theory of sexuality that Freud developed over the next several years (1905b) is based on the notion of instinctual *drive*, which became Freud's fundamental building block for all his subsequent theorizing.

The mind, Freud reasoned, is an apparatus for discharging stimuli that impinge upon it.[5] There are two kinds of stimuli, external (such as a threatening predator) and internal (such as hunger). External stimuli can be avoided; internal stimuli keep mounting. The mind becomes structured so as to contain, control, and, if possible, discharge internal stimuli.

Central among the internal stimuli are the sexual instincts. These appear as a broad array of tensions arising from different body parts, demanding activity to effect their discharge, Freud believed. Thus, for example, oral libido arises in the oral cavity (its *source*), creates a need for sucking activity (its *aim*), and becomes targeted toward and attached to something (generally external to the person) such as the breast (its *object*), which is required for satisfaction. The source and aim are inherent properties of the drive, Freud believed; the object is discovered through experience. Thus in feeding for purposes of self-preservation, the infant discovers that the breast is a source of libidinal pleasure; hence, through experience, the breast becomes the first libidinal object.

The concentration of nerve endings in particular organs underlies their function as the source of libidinal drives. These "erogenous zones" always have the potential for sexual excitation, but at different points during childhood one or another zone has prominence, Freud believed, and activity involving that zone becomes the central organizing focus of the child's emotional life. Freud proposed a sequence of psychosexual stages, through which one or another body part and its accompanying libidinal activity assumes prominence: oral, anal, phallic, and genital.[6]

If psychoanalysis in general was like an archaeological dig, the development and elaboration of Freud's vision of human sexuality had all the intensity and excitement of the expeditions of early explorers searching for the source of the Nile. Freud began with the main channel, adult sexuality and its central and obvious role in human experience. But where does it begin? What does it look like at its source? Freud's patients' associations to their present experience and the progressively earlier memories they revealed provided Freud with the vessel he needed to move backward in time, to earlier and earlier experiences, fantasies, wishes. The main channel divided repeatedly. There was not a singular beginning of sexuality, in either a sudden awakening or a specific trauma (as the theory of infantile seduction had suggested). Sexuality has many, many tributaries (Freud called them "component instincts"). It does not begin as genitality, but in a diffuse sensuality, located in many different body parts, stimulated through the many different activities in the first years of life.

The impulses of childhood sexuality survive in adulthood disguised (neurotic symptoms) and undisguised (sexual perversions), Freud believed. Some of them persist as foreplay, having been subsumed under the ultimate goal of genital intercourse. But most of the pieces of infantile sexual experience are objectionable to the socialized adult mind. Under the best of circumstances they are channeled into *sublimated, aim-inhibited* forms of gratification. Many of the drive impulses are too objectionable to be allowed any gratification at all; elaborate defenses are built to keep them repressed or to divert them into harmless activities. Thus the river of adult experience is composed of the continuous flow from its infantile sources, now merged, disguised, blended together into what appears to be a transparent whole.

Consider anal eroticism. The anus, with its aggregate of nerve endings and its central role during the years of toilet training, is an important erogenous zone. The child has intense wishes to defecate when and where he wants, to maximize the sensual pleasures of elimination, to manipulate and stimulate the anus, to mess, and to generate fecal odors. Socialization requires a complex set of inhibitions and restrictions of these wishes. Defecation must be regulated and controlled; it is permissible only in specific circumstances. Some degree of tidiness must become established; basic principles of bodily hygiene are developed.

What happens to anal erotic impulses? Freud came to the conclusion that there is a continuous flow of anal as well as oral and phallic impulses into adult experience, and that a great deal of adult functioning is constructed either to provide disguised forms of gratification or effective defenses or, most often, complex combinations of gratification and defense.

There are people, for example, who are expert at spreading disorder. They cannot tolerate tidiness, which they experience as repressive and suffocating. As guests, they always leave your house a good deal messier than when they arrived. In terms of Freud's theory of infantile sexuality, they are perpetually finding outlets for slightly disguised anal erotic impulses to soil, to smell up.

Their counterparts are those whose lives are dedicated to order and tidiness, who cannot tolerate mess. These are the people for whom everything has a place. "Where does this go?" is their perpetual question. Dinner dishes are washed, dried, and out of sight before food is digested. Surfaces are all scrubbed. As guests, they always leave your house a bit more organized than when they arrived. (Places have been found for things that had no regular place.) In terms of Freud's theory of infantile sexuality, they are dedicated to shoring up defenses against anal erotic impulses. Departures from their regime are dangerous. If dirt or mess is tolerated at all, defecation will no longer be containable in the bathroom, and an explosive nightmare will result.

The Oedipus Complex

The centerpiece of Freud's theory of development was the Oedipus complex. Freud believed that the various elements of sexuality converge around the age of five or six in a genital organization, in which the component pregenital instincts (such as orality and anality) are subsumed under a genital hegemony. The aim of all the child's desires becomes genital intercourse with the parent of the opposite sex. The parent of the same sex becomes a dangerous, feared rival. (Later Freud [1923] introduced the concept of the *negative Oedipus complex,* in which the child takes as her object the parent of the same sex and the parent of the opposite sex becomes the rival.) Like Sophocles's Oedipus, each child is destined to follow her desires and thereby become caught in a powerful, passionate drama with no easy resolution. The coloration of the Oedipus complex for each child depends considerably on the course of the earlier, pregenital organizations. For the child with a strong oral fixation, genitality will take on oral themes (sexuality becomes infused with dependency issues). For the child with a strong anal fixation, genitality will take on anal themes (sexuality is pervaded with images of domination and control).

The Oedipus complex is resolved, Freud believed, through the threat of *castration anxiety.* A boy wants to remove the threat posed by his rival by castrating him, and assumes that his father will punish him in like fashion. It is only because of the threat of castration that the child's oedipal ambitions are renounced. In 1923, Freud introduced the concept of the *superego*, a key component of which is the *ego-ideal,* as "the heir of the Oedipus complex" to account for the internalization of parental values that accompanies the resolution of the oedipal struggle and holds infantile sexuality in check. Freud had a great deal of difficulty accounting for the resolution of the Oedipus complex and the establishment of the superego in girls, for whom, presumably, castration would pose less of a threat. (We will consider the issue of differential developmental pathways for boys and girls more fully in chapter 8.)

The details and texture of the Oedipus complex depend on both constitutional and experiential factors and differ for each individual. But for all of us, Freud suggested, the central themes of childhood sexuality become organized in the Oedipus complex, and that organization becomes the underlying structure for the rest of life. As the psychoanalytic scholar Jay Greenberg (1991) has put it,

For Freud, the Oedipus complex was both the nodal event of normal development and the core conflict of the neuroses; the interplay of psychic forces in both mental health and psychopathology becomes comprehensible in its context. It is an extraordinary analytic invention, a framework for conceptualizing family dynamics and their residue in the psychic life of the child. (p. 5)

The Oedipus complex has always been the concept most widely associated with Freudian psychoanalysis. Greenberg (1991) has argued that the meaning of this concept has changed remarkably over decades of psychoanalytic theorizing and that Freud's vision of sexual possession and rivalry has been vastly broadened to include an array of different kinds of motivations and various constellations of family dynamics. However, the identity of a "Freudian" is generally contingent on the integration of various theoretical and technical innovations into an expanded vision of the Oedipus complex. Thus even a theoretician as critical of classical drive theory as Roy Schafer (see chapter 7) notes that "*for us* the most adaptable, trustworthy, inclusive, supportable, and helpful storyline of them all [is] the Oedipus complex in all its complexity and with all its surprises" (1983, p. 276).

Psychic Conflict

The terms Freud introduced in presenting his theories of the unconscious, infantile sexuality and instinctual drive have become so commonplace, it is difficult to appreciate just how revolutionary his understanding of the psyche was and how striking it remains today. What we experience as our minds, Freud suggests, is merely a small portion of it; the rest is by no means transparent to our feeble consciousness. The real meaning of much of what we think, feel, and do is determined unconsciously, outside our awareness. The mind has elaborate devices for regulating the instinctual tensions that are the source of all motivation and that exert a continuous pressure for discharge. The apparent transparency of mind is an illusion; the psyche and the personality are highly complex, intricately textured layers of instinctual impulses, transformations of those impulses, and defenses against those impulses. Freud wrote:

What we describe as a person's "character" is built up to a considerable extent from the material of sexual excitations and is composed of instincts that have been fixed since childhood, of constructions achieved by means of sublimation, and of other constructions, employed for effectively holding in check perverse impulses which have been recognized as being unutilizable. (1905, pp. 238–39)

For Freud, the very stuff of personality is woven out of impulses and defenses.

In Gloria's analysis it became apparent that some of the central issues she had struggled with in childhood involved conflicts over wishes and impulses, which subsequently became embedded in her adult personality in different ways.

Gloria's childhood emerged with increasing vividness over the first several months of treatment. She began to realize that her first full-blown neurotic symptom had appeared around the age of eleven or twelve, when her widespread obsessive ruminations became quite troubling and evolved into a disturbing compulsion. Gloria would lie awake at night, ruminating on patterns of hot and cold. She would go into the bathroom and turn on the hot and cold faucets in sequence: hot-cold-hot-cold; hot-hot-cold-cold; hot-cold-cold-hot-hot-cold-cold-hot. She would be tormented by the problem of how to end the sequence with a sense of finality. Each sequence seemed to have no natural ending; each could be extended in endless repetitions. She would go on and on, searching for closure, until she gave up in a state of unsettled exhaustion.

The onset of Gloria's symptom coincided with the onset of puberty, when her body, her reactions, and her feelings were changing in ways she found quite frightening. Her developing breasts and her initial menstrual periods attracted great attention from her father, who would make frequent excited, congratulatory comments about both. Her own enhanced capacity for sexual excitement was extremely problematic, because sexuality was so bound up for her with frightening images of damaging surrender to bigger, stronger, intimidating male figures. Perhaps the flow from the faucet represented the eruption of her womanhood and her sexuality, and the hot-cold of the water represented the hot-cold of her feelings. Within Freud's understanding of symptoms as disguised compromise-formations, Gloria's struggle with the water faucets was a displaced and camouflaged enactment of her intense conflicts over wanting to be turned on and wanting to turn herself off, her wish to surrender to the natural processes surging in her body and her desperate efforts to gain control and mastery over them.

What happened to this central conflict, this struggle between forbidden impulses and defenses against those impulses, as Gloria grew older? Sex itself had been largely unpleasurable and sometimes painful. It was as if the adult experience of sex was organized along the lines of her childhood fantasies, and the actual discomfort made it an experience to be avoided as much as possible. However, the exciting features of sex were contained in masturbatory fantasies involving abductions, constraints, and domination.

Sex as painful surrender was too frightening to give herself over to in actuality; the controllable fantasy (where she turned herself on and off) of sex as painful surrender was safe enough to allow very intense enjoyment.

But it was not only in adult sexuality that the traces of Gloria's childhood conflicts were discovered. Gloria's whole life could be understood as a battle that pitted her emerging intelligence, talents, self-expression, and vitality against her desperate efforts to control everything. One of the most vivid examples of this central and pervasive struggle was her difficulty in growing plants. She would buy plants from a nursery and care for them effectively for a while. When new growth began, however, she could not resist a compulsion to manually open the new shoots, thereby stunting all development. Similarly, virtually every area of her own life was constricted by her conviction that she needed to watch and vigilantly control all her natural physical and emotional expressions less they grow out of control and endanger her.

THE AGGRESSIVE DRIVE

From the point at which he abandoned the theory of infantile seduction until 1920, Freud regarded the sexual drive as the source of all conflict and psychopathology. He wrote about other drives besides sexuality (e.g., the self-preservative instincts), but it was, he felt, the impulses and wishes deriving from the sexual drive, in all its complexity and urgency, that created self-fragmentation. Issues involving aggression, sadism, and power found an increasingly important place in Freud's clinical descriptions during the 1910s; yet in terms of theory, he regarded aggression and sadism as pieces of sexuality, components of the sexual drive (as, for example, in oral sadism or anal sadism).

In 1920 Freud introduced what has come to be known as his *dual-instinct theory*, which granted aggression equal status with sexuality as a source of the basic instinctual energy that drives mental processes. This was no minor addition. The way a theorist understands motivation, the underlying goals of behavior, imparts a crucial cast to his portrait of the mind and human activity. In his early writings (e.g., 1908) Freud conjured up a vision of people struggling with impulses and wishes that had become forbidden largely because of social conventions concerning sexuality, some of which he regarded as unnecessarily severe and constrictive. He envisioned the products of successful analysis as individuals constructively free of repression, able to use their manifold component sexual instincts for their own pleasure and satisfaction.

Increasingly, and especially after 1920, Freud's view of human nature darkened.[7] What is repressed are not just harmless sexual wishes, he came to believe, but a powerful, savage destructiveness deriving from a *death instinct*. With this crucial shift in the way Freud envisioned the instincts came an important reformulation of the way he and the early generations of psychoanalysts understood the relation between the individual and society. Repression is not imposed unnecessarily by a restrictive society; repression is a form of social control that saves people from themselves and makes it possible for them to live together without perpetually killing and exploiting one another. Ideal mental health does not entail an absence of repression, but the maintenance of a modulated repression that allows gratification while at the same time preventing primitive sexual and aggressive impulses from taking over. The turn toward a darker vision of instincts brought a more appreciative attitude toward social controls, which he now regarded as necessary to save people from themselves. Freud thus moved from an early implicit political philosophy that was Rousseauian in tone to one more darkly Hobbesian. In his most widely read book on culture, *Civilization and Its Discontents* (1930), Freud painted a picture of man requiring culture for survival but, because of the instinctual renunciation it entailed, necessarily always being dissatisfied in some fundamental fashion.[8]

FROM TOPOGRAPHY TO STRUCTURE

Another major innovation, introduced in 1923, concerned the basic categories into which Freud distributed various pieces of experience.

From his earliest differences with Breuer on the cause of repressed memories, Freud regarded conflict as *the* central clinical problem underlying all psychopathology. His favorite metaphors for the mind (and the analytic process) were military. One part of the mind was at war with another part of the mind, and the symptoms were a direct, although masked, consequence of this hidden, underlying struggle. Freud's theoretical models of the psyche were all efforts to portray the patient's conflict, which was at the heart of analytic treatment.

By the early 1920s, the topographical model (of the unconscious, with its inaccessible, repressed wishes, impulses, and memories, at odds with the more acceptable conscious and preconscious) was proving insufficient as a map of conflict. Growing clinical experience and conceptual sophistication led Freud to theorize that the unconscious wishes and impulses are in conflict with the defenses, not with the conscious and preconscious, and that the defenses cannot possibly really be conscious or accessible to consciousness. If I know I am keeping myself from knowing something, I must also know what it is that I am keeping myself from knowing. Freud's patients not only did not know their own secrets, they also did not know that they *had* secrets. Not just the impulses and wishes were unconscious, but the defenses seemed to be unconscious as well.

Freud had discovered something else in the unconscious: guilt, prohibitions, self-punishments. Gloria's masochistic longings for her father, for example, were linked with a sense of self-blame—she deserved the punishment she imagined herself receiving at the hands of her fantasied abusers. Her unconscious contained not just forbidden wishes, but also defenses against them, as well as self-accusations and punishments for them.

As Freud's early notion of the unconscious had become increasingly complex, everything that was interesting, certainly everything involved in psychodynamic conflict, could be assigned a place there. When Freud began to perceive the basic conflictual seam in the psyche as not *between* conscious and unconscious but *inside* the unconscious itself, a new model, the structural model, became necessary to delineate the primary constituents of mind.

The structural model puts all the major components of the self in the unconscious, and the significant boundaries are between the *id, ego,* and *superego.* These are not topographical regions, but rather three very different kinds of agencies: The id is a "cauldron full of seething excitations" (1933, p. 73) of raw, unstructured, impulsive energies; the ego is a collection of regulatory functions that keep the impulses of the id under control; the superego is a set of moral values and self-critical attitudes, largely organized around internalized parental imagoes.

Drawing heavily on the Darwinian metaphors of his day, Freud portrayed humankind as only incompletely evolved, as torn by a fundamental rift between bestial motives and civilized conduct and demeanor, between an animal nature and cultural aspirations. And the very process of socialization entailed self-alienation and self-deception. Consistent with Freud's understanding of animal nature (drawn from the zoology and animal psychology of his day) was his view of people as "driven" to seek pleasure in a single-minded and rapacious fashion. In order to become acceptable, both to others and to oneself, one has to conceal from oneself these purely hedonic motives. The ego, with the aid of the internalized parental presences in the superego, represses and regulates bestial impulses in the id to maintain safety in a world of other people, Freud proposed. The result is a mind largely unknown to itself, filled with secrets and disavowed impulses, sexual and aggressive. It is the pressure of those impulses in the "return of the repressed" that creates the neurotic symptoms whose code Freud felt he had broken.

FREUD'S LEGACY

Freud always regarded his discovery of the meaning of dreams to be his greatest contribution. This is because hidden in the story of the dream are secrets that pertain to human subjectivity in general. Subsequent psychoanalytic authors were to demonstrate that all the stories we tell ourselves about ourselves are secondary elaborations, woven from a broad and varied range of fragments of past and present psychic life: wishes and longings, fantasies and perceptions, hopes and dreads.

Freud kept close watch and a tight rein on psychoanalysis as a quasipolitical movement, as well as a science (Grosskurth, 1991). There were several important theoreticians whom Freud broke with (or who broke with Freud) early on, including Alfred Adler, Carl Jung, Otto Rank, and Sandor Ferenczi. Many of their concepts and sensibilities, although developed outside the Freudian mainstream, found their way back into psychoanalytic thinking decades later, generally without credit to the pioneer dissidents. For example, Adler's early claim for the primacy of aggression and power was picked up by Freud himself in his introduction of the aggressive drive, and Adler's emphasis on social and political factors anticipated important developments by "culturalists" such as Harry Stack Sullivan, Erich Fromm, and Karen Horney. Jung's early concern with the self has been continued in the fields of self psychology (chapter 6) and object relations (chapters 4 and 5) over the past several decades. Jung's other major concern, spirituality, was reviled for decades within Freudian theory because of Freud's repugnance toward religion (1927). But it has returned in a form of contemporary psychoanalytic theorizing that integrates psychodynamics and spirituality (Sorenson, 1994). Rank's groundbreaking work on the will strongly anticipated more current explorations of agency (see chapter 7). And Ferenczi's radical thought and clinical experimentation both greatly prefigured and, in some cases, actually influenced recent developments in interpersonal psychoanalysis (chapter 3) and object relations theories (chapters 4 and 5).

Cosmologists believe that slight variations emerged in the extraordinarily compact density of matter in the initial moments following the big bang. Without those variations, the universe would necessarily always be uniform and evenly distributed. They made possible the congealing of matter into sep-arate galaxies and the worlds that developed within them. Freud's discover-ies gave birth to the universe of psychoanalysis just as exclusively and com-pletely as the big bang gave birth to the universe we find ourselves in. Freud's contributions were remarkably rich and dense, and second-generation the-orists developed different facets of them. These were slight variations in their day, but, fortunately for us, these kinds of differences evolved into the fertile abundance of schools of contemporary analytic thought that we will consider in the chapters that follow.[9]

2

EGO PSYCHOLOGY

The child is father of the man.

—*William Wordsworth*

Man can be defined as the animal that can say "I," that can be aware of himself as a separate entity.

—*Erich Fromm*

Freud saw himself as the discoverer of a previously unknown world (the unconscious). He'd had to make his way through complex expanses of psychic territory to expose the crucial unconscious infantile wishes and fears that deeply fascinated and excited him. What Freud wanted to find were the secrets, not the more ordinary levels of mental life within which the secrets were concealed. Like Schliemann intent on unearthing his long-buried city, Freud noted and identified a variety of more commonplace finds in the course of his exploration, but his passion for discovering remote and exotic relics inevitably shifted his attention back to the dig, propelling him beyond them into what he felt were the deeper, primitive recesses of human experience.

As Freud continued his investigation, however, some of his followers gathered around the site became intrigued with the more ordinary features of mental life that Freud had unearthed and set aside as he pursued darker infantile secrets. Freud's excavation had opened up dramatic cross-sectional perspectives on the inner structure and developmental stratification of the psyche. These newly exposed vistas prompted an explosion of investigations into the early history of the human psyche and its functioning. The tradition known as ego psychology germinated in the 1930s in Vienna, was dispersed via the war into England, and eventually took firm root in America.

Before 1923 Freud had used the term *ego* in a loose, unsystematic fashion to refer to the dominant, largely conscious mass of ideas from which the repressed was split off. In 1923, in *The Ego and the Id,* he began to use *ego* to represent one of the three fundamental psychic agencies of the mind (in addition to the id and the superego). The ego's major functions were to represent reality and, through the erection of defenses, to channel and control internal drive pressures in the face of reality (including the demands of social convention and morality). The kinds of questions that became central to the ego psychologists were natural extensions of Freud's vision of the mind as structured around drive impulses and defenses: Are there phases, a kind of progressive ability, to accomplish the ego's defensive tasks? Is this progression an inherently predetermined process, one that inevitably unfolds, or do environmental factors aid or inhibit its development? Although initiated well before the crucial oedipal phase, is the development of the ego, like that of the superego, affected by contact with and internalization of aspects of caregivers? Although depicted as functionally opposed to and controlled by the ego, do the libidinal and aggressive drives play any part in the initial development of ego capacities? Interest in these more "ordinary" features of the psyche also included attention to the differences in drive organization and expression over the course of development and a better understanding of how the superego becomes consolidated and its constructive functions established.

Ultimately, attention to these questions produced an expanded understanding of normal psychological functioning and psychopathology that in turn both refined and invigorated psychoanalytic theory and significantly broadened its therapeutic range. As we shall see, the ego psychologists shared many concerns with other schools of psychoanalytic thought: interpersonal psychoanalysis, object relations theories, and self psychology. All these theoretical traditions that branched off from Freud's opus began to address, in one fashion or another, problems of normal development and the impact of the environment and early relationships. What distinguishes the ego psychology approach from other lines of thought is the careful preservation of Freud's drive theory that underlies it.

ANNA FREUD: THE BUILDING BLOCKS OF DEFENSE THEORY

Sigmund Freud's early topographical model depicted a clash between conscious and unconscious mental functioning in which id impulses pushed against ego defenses erected to contain them. The success of psychoanalytic treatment was seen as depending on the innate pressure within id impulses to seize the moment and gain expression once the patient temporarily suspended defensive operations by obeying the "fundamental rule" of free association. The structural model, introduced in 1923, depicted a more complex psyche containing a struggle among three internal agencies: ego, id, superego. According to this model, neurosis is the result of a compromise-formation worked out unconsciously among these fundamentally antagonistic parties: the id, pressing to gratify infantile wishes; the superego, striving to prevent this morally forbidden gratification; and the ego, mediating among the claims of the id, the superego, and the outside world. Displaying some sympathy for the id, the ego works out a strategy that allows a certain amount of instinctual gratification but channels this gratification through a complex system of clever defenses. The ego disguises the appearance of the id's impulses, thereby both preventing social censure and keeping the impulses under careful regulation. For the neurotic person, these compromises between forbidden impulses and defenses result in complex, uncomfortable symptoms and a constriction of functioning (often involving sexual inhibitions or an inability to work and compete successfully). One has to pay a price for maintaining and pursuing, even in disguised forms, socially unacceptable infantile longings. This inherent punishment is negotiated by the ego to satisfy the demands of the superego.

Anna Freud (1895–1982), Freud's devoted daughter and a pioneer of child analysis, was a crucial figure in the further exploration of the ego. Pondering her father's 1923 structural model of the psyche, Anna Freud detected a strategic technical problem: If the crucial battle line of psychic conflict was no longer between unconscious impulses and conscious defenses but among three psychic agencies, each of which carried out significant aspects of its functioning unconsciously, then the clinical process by which these unconscious aspects of the patient's psychic life could be revealed needed to be reevaluated. The topographical model had explained that the id's impulses would seek expression in the treatment for purposes of gratification. But why would it be in the interest of the unconscious portions of the ego and the superego, the other two contributors to this conflict, to make themselves known to consciousness in the analytic situation?

The patient's ego might be able to comply with the analyst's instruction to free-associate and hold back conscious objections to reporting all that comes to mind. However, the ego also contains complex unconscious defensive arrangements that have evolved to satisfy the demands of neurotic compromise, ways of thinking that keep repressed impulses out of conscious awareness in an ongoing way. Unlike unconscious id impulses that respond with enthusiasm to the prospect of liberation in making their presence felt in the analytic hour, unconscious ego defenses gain nothing from being exposed. Their unobtrusive, seamless presence in the patient's psychic life is perfectly acceptable (ego syntonic) to the patient; they often function as a central feature of the patient's larger personality organization.[1]

Consider the defense of *reaction formation,* whereby the ego obscures unacceptable hostile impulses by transforming them into their opposite. The angry person becomes overly nice, often insistently helpful, even suffocatingly kind; he may be regarded by many (including himself) as a pillar of the community. To undo this carefully crafted solution by unmasking the defensive aspect of it, to tell the patient that his niceness is actually a clever cover for his nastiness, is not just to release id impulses from the clever defensive constraints of the ego, but to threaten a whole way of life. The ego, charged with the daunting task of keeping the peace between warring internal parties and ensuring socially acceptable functioning, works more effectively if it works undercover. The psychoanalyst, whose interest is in making unconscious experience conscious, is the longed-for liberator to unconscious id impulses, but a menace to the embattled ego and its unconscious, characterological defenses. If psychoanalysis was still to be conceived of as a battle, it had become less a rescue mission to release captives behind the lines and more a full-scale attack against a culture.

Sigmund Freud had abandoned hypnotism because he had learned that it was not enough to lull the defenses into temporary inactivity; they needed to be directly, consciously engaged and interpreted. But Anna Freud's exploration of the ego followed its defensive operations from specific, circumscribed, clearly discernible symptoms to its infusion into the entire character; aspects of one's basic style of personality functioning could be rooted in defensive processes. If these unconscious defensive processes are not decisively brought out into the open, Anna Freud came to believe, the therapeutic impact of psychoanalysis was severely curtailed. Simply bringing id impulses into consciousness is like a Cold War rescue of a few East Berliners, which fails to address the continuing existence of the Wall and the remaining intricate security system. Freeing some has little impact on the fate of others approaching the same border; the guards themselves must be won over, the defensive machinery dismantled.

Anna Freud's study of the complexities of the ego and its characterological defenses led to a redefinition of the role and the focus of the analyst in
the therapeutic process. Free association was increasingly viewed as an
unavoidably compromised activity from the start, at best a goal of the analytic process rather than the immediately available vehicle it had been
naively assumed to be. As much as the patient tries to be cooperative in
choosing to suspend ego attitudes and conscious objections for some period
of time, unconscious defensive patterns and corresponding unconscious
superego attitudes are always operating, outside the patient's awareness
and control. This revised understanding of unconscious psychic activity
necessitated a shift in the analyst's role. As Anna Freud reconceptualized it,

> It is the task of the analyst to bring into consciousness that which is
> unconscious, no matter to which psychic institution it belongs. He directs
> his attention equally and objectively to the unconscious elements in all
> three institutions . . . when he sets about the work of enlightenment, he
> takes his stand at a point equidistant from the id, the ego, and the super-
> ego. (1936, p. 28)

In the case of defenses, then, rather than waiting until the patient's free
associations were blocked and then interpreting the presumed underlying id
content, the analyst needed to more actively discern subtle workings of defensive operations *within* the associations themselves, which compromised and
distorted them. At such points, the analytic focus needed to turn from the
pursuit of id impulses, concentrating instead on the out-of-awareness workings of the ego. Yet it is not always so easy to distinguish between defended
and undefended communication. "We are aware of it only subsequently,"
observed Anna Freud, "when it becomes apparent that something is missing"
(1936, p. 8).

In the defense of *isolation of affect,* for example, conflictual ideas are
allowed into consciousness in an intellectualized form; the disturbing feelings associated with them are blocked. The ego may permit a flow of ideas
that looks like "free" associations, but the ideas are separated from their
corresponding feelings. A patient might speak of intense sexual encounters,
for example, but in a detached, dispassionate manner. Or, using the defense
of *projection,* a patient might deny feelings of anger but be very sensitive to
and preoccupied with angry feelings in others around her. The patient
might seem to be talking "freely," but it is the impact of the unconscious
defense as much as it is the impact of the instinctual pressure that shapes
the verbalizations.

Anna Freud's book *The Ego and Mechanisms of Defense* (1936) was a partial response to this problem. It became a psychoanalytic field marshal's handbook, documenting and illustrating various unconscious defensive strategies of the ego, alerting the clinician to telltale signs of their operation in the patient's psyche. Reorienting analysis from its concentration on tracking down id derivatives, Anna Freud defined the proper analytic attitude as "neutral," an evenhanded oscillation in attention among all three parties in the neurotic construction, the id, the ego, and the superego.

Reports from the consulting room documented the value of this theoretical reorientation. Ernst Kris (1900–1957), a graduate of the Vienna Institute who moved to New York in 1940, was one of the most astute and subtle developers of the new ego psychology sensibility. He offered an account of his reanalysis of a young man who had undergone an earlier psychoanalytic treatment along more traditional lines. The first analysis, which had restricted interpretations to revealing the id aspects, the unconscious infantile longings inherent in the patient's neurotic struggle, had produced improvements, but had not significantly affected the paralyzing constriction in the patient's professional life.

The patient, a capable scientist in his early thirties, was concerned about his inability to publish his research, which was impeding his professional advancement. In his first analysis he had learned that fear and guilt kept him from being productive. He became aware of a constant pressure to use other people's ideas as his own, in particular those of a well-known scientist friend with whom he spent long hours in conversation. The first analyst had interpreted the symbolic meaning of the problem by identifying and exposing the infantile instinctual wish that propelled it, seeing the wish to plagiarize as representing the patient's hidden wish to steal and aggressively devour someone else's ideas. Eventually the analyst exposed the earliest and most defended form of this unconscious instinctual current: primitive oral aggression.

Kris, content with the first analyst's identification of the id aspects of the problem, turned his attention to the ego's unconscious defensive operations. Since the patient's work inhibitions had not been resolved, were there unconscious ego defenses still at work? Was the patient's very account of what was happening itself skewed by unconscious defensive operations that made things seem different from how they actually were? Kris undertook an "extended scrutiny," inquiring into the texts the young man feared plagiarizing, learning about his research ideas and about the specific interchanges in the conversations he had with his friend. Eventually Kris discovered something quite startling. Rather than being a potential plagiarist, it was actually the patient himself who had introduced, in discussion with his distinguished friend, ideas that the friend then eagerly used as his own, developing and eventually publishing them, giving no credit to the patient in the process. Later, upon reading the friend's writings, the patient was unaware of his part in creating them and was under the mistaken impression that he was encountering, for the first time, an idea crucial to his own point of view, but one he could not claim without being guilty of plagiarism. He wasn't a plagiarist, but a ghostwriter!

Behind this complex defensive distortion, Kris discovered a persisting boyhood wish to admire and learn from a disappointing father whose own inhibitions prevented *his* professional success. In his unconscious efforts to redress this childhood disappointment and create an impressive father worthy of admiration, the patient infused his older friend with his own intellectual substance, sabotaging his own progress. Using the defense mechanism of projection, he had attributed his own abilities to his friend, whom he then regarded with awe and admiration.

Subsequent oedipal conflicts further complicated this patient's life. His attempts to get something from an admired man by building him up over time evoked competitive feelings and the unconscious and prohibited oedipal wish to steal the father's penis, a wish that, so long as it survived even in symbolic action, had to be punished. Unavoidably and painfully, this guilt-ridden patient was sentenced to play out an experience in relation to his friend that sapped him of his own ideas and resulted in mortifying accusations of stealing, effectively preventing him from publishing his own work.

Kris (1951) described the shift in technique that made his inquiry successful. Beyond revealing the instinctual conflict unearthed in the previous, more traditionally Freudian analysis, he had added a detailed analysis of the ego's operations and the surface behavior of the patient.

> The second set of interpretations ... implemented [those from the first analysis] by its greater concreteness, by the fact that it covered a large number of details of behavior and therefore opened the way to linking present and past, adult symptomatology and infantile fantasy. The crucial point, however, was the "exploration of the surface." The problem was to establish how the feeling, "I am in danger of plagiarizing," comes about. The procedure did not aim at direct or rapid access to the id through interpretations; ... [rather,] various aspects of behavior were carefully studied. (p. 86)

In chapter 1 we noted the ways Freud himself had become increasingly interested in defenses as well as the secrets they were protecting. Anna Freud greatly extended this shift in clinical focus by cataloging and studying various defensive operations of the ego, noting both their modus operandi as well as locating them, in terms of appearance and operational sophistication, along a developmental continuum. Her investigations produced interesting observations on aspects of defensive functioning that had not received careful attention. While internally arising conflict and ensuing superego guilt had been offered as the common formula for prompting the ego's defensive activity, Anna Freud clarified that defenses, such as denial, can also be called into action by displeasure that has its source in the external world. She also observed that while this defense had been generally associated with severe psychopathology (e.g., psychotic delusions), her work with children gave evidence of the early developmentally normal appearance of this kind of defensive operation. Children regularly simply "get rid of unwelcome facts" (1936, p. 83) by negating their existence, while their overall reality testing remains unimpaired. Her work suggested that the use of denial, as well as that of projection and introjection, signaled, in the adult, disturbances that were rooted in developmentally early phases of childhood.

Depicting the pervasiveness of ego processes throughout all areas of personality functioning, Anna Freud established the ego itself as an object of psychoanalytic inquiry worthy of study in its own right. At the same time, she expanded the range of applications of psychoanalytic ideas from symptoms to character style and from psychopathology to varieties of normal personality functioning.

The experiences of an analyst with a difficult patient illustrate the impact of ego psychology on clinical issues. Angela, a twenty-three-year-old bank teller, was at a crisis point in her life; her usual style of ignoring her feelings and keeping herself under control was failing her. A friend had advised her that her behavior at work was increasingly inappropriate. She was seen as inconsistent, often snapping at her coworkers with no provocation and with little warning. Angela said she cared for no one and felt dead inside. She had recently been attending wild all-night parties, where she had her first sexual experiences with partners she later could not identify.

In the midst of the initial consultation, following the analyst's expression of concern, Angela exploded and attacked the analyst as inept. She demanded to know her credentials and what she planned to do with her. This ineptitude, she went on, reminded her of her mother, who had been no help to her at all and whom she "should have told to fuck off a long time ago." Her mother had had too many children, had no time for her, and expected her to be another mother instead of a child. Angela described her rage at her mother's repeated pregnancies; she remembered how she had hoped, at age six, that the hot coffee her mother drank would burn and kill the fetus then growing inside her.

The following session began with Angela's concern about what would happen if she really "got into things" in therapy. She seemed tentative and anxious. To be in therapy required trust in another person; that, she felt, was too much for her. Her manner then abruptly changed. She announced that whatever the analyst wanted to know, she couldn't tell her, because she was "behind a wall"; no one could get in, and she couldn't get out. "Go ahead," she taunted, "try and get me to talk."

Angela is a dramatic example of a resistant patient; far from freely revealing "all that comes to mind," she was unwilling to report anything at all. The analyst's initial tack, along classical Freudian lines, had been to think of her behavior as a kind of (transference) resistance: perhaps she was circumventing the (verbal) analytic process by engaging the analyst in some interaction that would gratify an instinctual pressure. A fight with the analyst would allow hostile feelings originating in her relationship to her mother to be played out with the analyst rather than described and analyzed. This interpretation fell on deaf ears.

Clinical problems encountered in efforts to help difficult patients such as Angela came to represent a new frontier of psychoanalysis for ego psychologists eager to implement Anna Freud's directive to study the ego "in its own right." This focus encouraged a clinical approach that more directly engaged the patient; it placed less emphasis on uncovering hidden secrets and more on assessing psychic structure.

With Angela, the analyst ignored her provocativeness, commenting instead that there seemed to be something about having the wall between them that felt important; she encouraged Angela to tell her about the wall. Rather than interpreting her (id) aggression, the analyst described and expressed interest in Angela's (ego) need to protect herself. Assured that this crucial aspect of her psychic makeup was respected by the analyst, very gradually, Angela allowed a dialogue to develop.

Angela's wall appeared whenever she felt anxious, often after someone was "too nice" to her, or when she was very angry and feared a loss of self-control. Behind the wall she felt protected, but at a price, because the wall made her feel distant from people and not a part of life. Her earliest memory of the wall-like experience was at age five, when she started school and was frightened to be close to the other children lest she throw something at them. During that year she began to feel there was a large hazy circular space all around her. Once this sensation began, Angela felt paralyzed and unable to move or to respond. Her increasing social withdrawal apparently went unnoticed. She began to feel she was "an idea in someone else's head."[2]

Angela's mother was a chronically frustrated, overworked, and emotionally volatile woman. In her youth something of a radical, she had left her native Italy, where cultural expectations severely limited her aspirations. In her new country, she had been fiercely intent on developing a career, but because religious beliefs precluded birth control, she felt overwhelmed and defeated by her steadily increasing family and its accompanying obligations. "When you were little," Angela's mother once commented to her daughter, "all I did was scream at you." Angela reported one occasion when her mother pulled a sharp knife from the kitchen drawer, thrust it into the hands of her terrified daughter, and commanded, "Go ahead, get it over with quickly, instead of killing me with all these little things." As a child, Angela was convinced that her inevitable shortcomings in completing household chores accounted for her mother's erratic, frightening behavior.

While quiet and obedient, trying to be Mother's perfect helper, Angela developed an intense and active fantasy life. She recalled her internal world becoming peopled, somewhere between the ages of three and seven, with what were to become certain familiar presences. There was a "fat and greedy" baby, wanting things "to be there forever," who was easily frustrated and could "rip people's eyes out if they left" her. There was a man "who lives in the basement and is just waiting for me to do something wrong so he can come up and hurt me." This man ordered a sequence of punishments for wrongdoings, however minor, that took the form of inescapable preoccupying fantasies of initially physical and later sexual torture. Deeply envious of the care and attention other children were given, Angela often wished them ill, fantasizing horrible accidents or cruel punishments. When one such highly envied schoolmate was hit by a car and killed, Angela became terrified that her hostile thoughts had caused the tragedy. Subsequently the man in the basement upped the ante, demanding actual experiences of torture and self-mutilation whenever Angela made a "mistake." She began to secretly mutilate her body in an effort to exert more control over her thoughts.

An Assessment of Psychic Structure

Let us compare Angela's clinical picture to that of Kris's scientist patient. From the perspective of the structural model, neurosis is a long-standing compromise arrived at by the psychic agencies of id, ego, and superego. The analytic process envisions inviting this triumvirate to the negotiating table. By maintaining a balanced interest in each side of the story (Anna Freud's "neutrality"), the analyst can help the patient achieve a more serviceable resolution among the competing claims.

Successful negotiations at this summit depend heavily, of course, on the participants, and here the ego psychologists' ability to assess psychic structures (id, ego, and superego) in terms of the quality of their functioning becomes crucial. Consider the appearance and quality of the cast of characters who emerged for the anticipated negotiations in Angela's analysis in comparison to those of Kris's patient. The latter's infantile (id) wish to deprive his father of his penis had been smoothly integrated into his personality, obtaining gratification only in highly disguised, symbolic forms. It was consciously available only after years of interpretation by two different analysts. By contrast, Angela's equally unacceptable murderous (id) fantasy of snuffing out the life of her anticipated sibling rival took no hard work to uncover; it was conscious and readily reported by her at the very outset of treatment.

The superego objection to the oedipal plot of Kris's patient is easily detectable in his telltale feeling of guilt; this superego made certain that a morally unacceptable wish was effectively held in check and that the punishment for the wish was integrated into the patient's personal experience through a troubling professional inhibition. Angela, by contrast, felt no guilt signaling an internalized, functioning moral code. Her "man in the basement," the part of her experience most suggestive of superego functioning, was envisioned as not really part of her at all, but as an aggressive "other," who had taken up residence inside her. More a sadistic tyrant than a reasoned standard-bearer, he brought no defined code of ethics, no better course of action to recommend. Although post hoc explanations were supplied by Angela, no clear pattern could be found in his censure to serve as a guide for personal improvement.

Kris's patient's ego successfully mediated the conflict between infantile longing and the superego's moral code, instituting a clever system of defenses utilizing symbolism, displacement, and projection to hide the conflict and seamlessly absorb it into ongoing personality. Angela's wall, an aspect of her ego functioning called into play to protect her throughout childhood (and in the analysis as well), seemed both primitive and obvious. Allowing none of the camouflaging fluidity of Kris's patient's defenses, it announced itself glaringly and desperately, interrupting anything remotely resembling smooth functioning. Noteworthy also was the difference in the quality of emotional expression between these two people, an issue that was to become of increasing importance as a dimension of clinical assessment. Kris's patient's wish to castrate his father was somewhat remote for him, coming to him, even after he accepted Kris's crucial interpretation, more as an upsetting yet compelling idea. The murderous wish when conscious was intrinsically conflictual, because Kris's patient valued and appreciated his father. Angela's wishes have a very different feel to them. Intense and powerful, primitive and uninhibited, when Angela was angry she seemed unconcerned about hurting or damaging others; she spoke as though she had no positive feelings for them at all.

Angela's analyst was charged with renegotiating compromises among the claims of her ego, superego, and id. There was compelling evidence to suggest, however, that in this case, the three psychic agencies each needed remedial work before meaningful negotiations could proceed. Should, for example, Angela's ego defenses against her id impulses be encouraged to relax a little? Was it best to convince these guards that their services were no longer needed, or was returning them to boot camp for additional training more the issue? Angela's "summit" was most striking, not the complexity of issues struggled over, or the eloquence of competing claims, but for the shabby demeanor of its participants. Improving, not removing, seemed the task at hand.

Prior to the development of ego psychology, the clinical goal of psychoanalysis had been the release of trapped, unconscious energies. Freud had stressed a nondirective, nonsuggestive approach. Removing the debris clogging the stream was the task, not strengthening the channel through which it flowed. Improving defenses and encouraging the development of ego functions for patients like Angela required an engineering blueprint of the basic architecture of the channel, including a documentation of the materials it was made of so that it could be repaired.

HEINZ HARTMANN: THE TURN TOWARD ADAPTATION

The person most responsible for developing this kind of blueprint was Heinz Hartmann (1894–1970), who came to be known as the father of ego psychology. Like Anna Freud, Hartmann was intrigued by the unexamined psychic artifacts Sigmund Freud's excavation had unearthed in his pursuit of infantile aims and longings. The ancient spearhead Hartmann cradled in his hand did not, however, evoke images of battle and a fascination with defensive strategies, as it had for Freud's daughter. Rather, Hartmann moved beyond conflict and pondered what might be considered the broader technological implications of the discoveries themselves. How had the spearhead been crafted? The metal melded? Who participated in this creation? What other abilities did they have? Did they meld coins as well? How did the community function on a day-to-day basis? One cannot understand a country by studying only its wars. And with that seemingly simple shift in focus, Hartmann powerfully affected the course of psychoanalysis, opening up a crucial investigation of the key processes and vicissitudes of normal development.

Hartmann's contributions broadened the scope of psychoanalytic concerns, from psychopathology to general human development, from an isolated, self-contained treatment method to a sweeping intellectual discipline among other disciplines. This was not an easy task. Hartmann had to maintain a delicate balance between extending psychoanalysis to problems outside its original purview and preserving what Freudians considered essential to a distinctly psychoanalytic approach. Sullivan and the interpersonalists (see chapter 3) stressed, like Hartmann, the shaping influence of the environment on personality, but Sullivan had abandoned Freud's drive theory and thus his contributions were not considered psychoanalytic within the Freudian mainstream. Hartmann, on the other hand, carefully and ingeniously developed his innovations as extensions and elaborations of Freud's basic vision.

Heinz Hartmann was well suited for the pivotal expansive role he would play in the field of psychoanalysis. His Viennese family of origin was renowned for its scholarly and artistic achievements. His father was an eminent historian and ambassador to Germany, his mother a sculptor. Noted musicians, philosophers, physicians, politicians, and intellectuals from Vienna and the world beyond streamed through the family home, exposing young Heinz to a panoply of cultures, ideas, and points of view. Trained as a physician and a psychiatrist, he was deeply respectful of Freud and his contributions; in 1934, at Freud's invitation, he entered analysis with him. He was, however, similarly stimulated and intrigued by the world of science outside psychoanalysis and also pursued wide-ranging interests in psychology, history, music, and philosophy.

Hartmann's groundbreaking book, *Ego Psychology and the Problem of Adaptation* (published in German in 1937), was highly abstract and largely nonclinical. However, it provided others with the conceptual framework to support clinical exploration, experimental studies, and eventually new and powerful therapeutic approaches aimed not so much at revealing repressed primitive impulses within the human psyche as at repairing structural dimensions of the psyche itself.

Sigmund Freud, Anna Freud, and Wilhelm Reich had all attributed an increasing complexity to the ego's operations. Yet, prior to Hartmann, the ego's functions were still perceived as being embedded in psychic conflict. Sigmund Freud regarded the baby as initially and fundamentally self-absorbed, preoccupied with internal tensions and sensations and not oriented toward external reality. The baby only slowly begins to realize that hunger pangs remain unquelled by dreamy pleasure-seeking fantasies. He must, regretfully, deal with what Freud called the "brick wall of reality," forcibly reorienting himself. Like the traditional slap on the bottom jolting the newborn into taking account of the necessity of breathing, the rude exigencies of the external world ultimately force the infant to become aware of external reality. Freud saw purposive action and higher-order thinking (*secondary process,* as opposed to the *primary process* of fantasy-based wish fulfillment) as eventually developing out of this unwelcome encounter. The infant has to think and respond realistically to avoid the discomfort of mounting instinctual pressures. This model of psychic development had provided the conceptual underpinnings for the design of the classical therapeutic approach. Nongratification (e.g., not answering the patient's questions) and interpretive confrontations were aimed at forcing the id-generated fantasies to seek gratification out in the open, exposing them to conscious scrutiny and analytic interpretation, thereby transforming them into more realistic, mature ways of thinking, generating increased ego functioning. "Where id was, there ego shall be. It is a work of culture—not unlike the draining of the Zuider Zee" (Freud, 1933, p. 80).

Hartmann's vision of human development radically challenged this picture. Like Freud, Hartmann took his inspiration from Darwin's theory of the evolution of the species, but Hartmann drew on a different dimension of Darwin's account.

Freud had derived from Darwin the notion, commonplace today but stunning to those living in the nineteenth century, that having evolved from other species, humans were not wholly different creatures from other animals. Much of Freud's vision of the instinctual source of human motivation, the primitive forces of infantile sexuality and aggression, could be traced to this Darwinian view. Hartmann put his emphasis on the notion that animals were designed, through the process of survival of the fittest, to be highly adapted to their surroundings, so that there would be a continual "reciprocal relationship between the organism and its environment" (1939, p. 24).

If humans, like all organisms, are intrinsically designed to fit into their environment, this must also be true of not just their physical but their psychological self, Hartmann reasoned. Conversely, the natural environment must be, by design, specifically suitable to humans' psychological existence. Consequently, Hartmann envisioned not a dreamily drifting baby who is suddenly forced to get to work, but a baby who arrives with built-in ego potentials, waiting, like the seed awaits the spring rains, for the proper "average expectable" environmental conditions to spark their growth.

Rather than being forged in conflict and frustration, certain "conflict-free ego capacities" were seen as intrinsic potentials, part of people's birthright, functions that would emerge naturally in a suitable environment, enabling them to fit into their surround. These capacities included language, perception, object comprehension, and thinking.

While retaining an appreciation of the established psychoanalytic understanding of conflict, Hartmann launched an investigation into nonconflictual adaptive development. He began sorting out and labeling ego operations in terms of their origin, their current and changing function, and the specificity of their relationships with one another. He noted that an adaptive apparatus of primary autonomy (speech, for example) could become secondarily entangled in conflict (stuttering). And defenses originally born in conflict could eventually become autonomous by evolving an adaptive capacity.

Reaction formation, for example, is a defense called into play to keep one consciously unaware of the continuing, socially unacceptable pleasures involved in bathroom activities; the toddler's original fascination with his bowel movements is transformed into a conscious attitude of disgust. Yet reaction formation, originating in conflict, may eventually serve a highly adaptive function in the overall personality as genuine pleasure in good hygiene and tidiness and thus graduate into a role outside of conflict, becoming "secondarily autonomous." Similarly, the defense of intellectualization, which employs abstract thinking in an effort to prevent awareness of conflictual emotions, is often the predominant defense of highly intelligent people, whose capacity for abstract thinking has significant adaptive uses. For the analyst to interpret only the defensive aspect ("You intellectualize rather than feel") is to risk leaving the patient with the sense that there is something wrong with his or her capacity to think. Hartmann's precise distinctions offered clinicians greater specificity in pinpointing both conflictual and adaptive aspects of psychic functioning.

But Hartmann's depiction of "conflict-free" ego functions also posed a problem. Where do these functions get their energy? If the mind is primarily fueled by libido and aggression, which manifest themselves in conflictual demands for largely forbidden gratification, what fuels adaptive processes such as perception and capacities for learning?

Freud had struggled with the same problem in different terms, in his efforts to reconcile higher cultural pursuits (such as literature and the arts), which he deeply loved, with a motivational theory that regarded all intentions as fundamentally sexual and aggressive. Freud's solution was the concept of *sublimation,* a quasi-defensive process that harnesses the power of the sexual impulse and channels it into acceptable, productive pursuits. Thus a voyeuristic fixation might be transformed into a talent for photography.

But even when drives are sublimated, they retain, in a disguised form, their sexual and aggressive qualities. If the ego's conflict-free functions are truly autonomous, they seem to require an energy without such qualities. Hartmann proposed a process he termed *neutralization,* through which the ego strips the drives of their sexual and aggressive qualities. Unlike sublimation, neutralization actually changes the nature of the drives themselves, much as a hydroelectric plant transforms the raging, muddy river into clean, usable electrical energy.

Hartmann's notion of a child born with an innate potential that unfolds naturally in a receptive environment opened up a host of questions that were pursued by subsequent developmental ego psychologists. How might we envision this necessary environment to which the human child is born preadapted? What elements are intrinsic to the "average expectable environment" on which psychic development depends? Are there factors in children's early relationship with their environment that facilitate the process of drive neutralization, toning down instinctual conflicts and making that energy source available to fuel the ego's nonconflictual activities?

DEVELOPMENTAL EGO PSYCHOLOGY: RENÉ SPITZ

René Spitz's heartbreaking publication *Hospitalism* (1940) played a seminal and dramatic role in deepening the interest in issues of environment. It left no doubt that whatever inborn psychological potential humans may have, its realization is doomed in the absence of emotional connectedness with another person. Spitz (1887–1974) studied children left, from birth, in a foundling home, whose physical needs were adequately met but who were deprived of any ongoing nurturing interaction. They invariably became depressed, withdrawn, and sickly. If this emotional starvation continued beyond three months, eye coordination deteriorated and motor retardation developed. The infant became increasingly listless, the mattress in her crib progressively hollowing out in a little groove cradling her quiet body. By the end of the second year, one-third of these children had died. By the time the survivors had reached their fourth year, few could sit, stand, walk, or talk. If, however, the mother returned within the first three months of life, this deteriorating course reversed itself. While Freud had heralded deprivation as a stimulant to ego development that forced the crucial turn toward reality, Spitz's study of "failure to thrive" infants dramatically suggested that the "brick wall of reality" is deadly in the absence of a loving caregiver's touch.

The question remained, however, as to the exact nature of the tragedy Spitz had witnessed. If food and other physical needs were not the crucial elements, what exactly *does* involvement with a nurturing person provide? Hartmann had offered that an average expectable environment is essential to the emergence of ego capacities such as object comprehension and perception, but what are the essential features of this environment? How does what is outside affect what develops inside?[3]

The Libidinal Object

Spitz devoted much of his professional life to these questions. Using methodology borrowed from experimental psychology, he conducted what many would regard as the first analytic research on *object relations* between infants and their primary caregivers, carrying out a systematic large-scale study of controlled, direct observations of infants and mothers over a span of many years. Spitz watched, he filmed, he interviewed, he tested, tracking the transformation of the biologically adaptive tie between infant and mother into complex psychological resources for the child. In so doing, he fundamentally recast the basic psychoanalytic concept of the *libidinal object.*

Freud had introduced the term *object* to refer to the target of instinctual impulses, through which the instinctual tension is discharged. This object could be a person, but it could also be inanimate. A shoe is a libidinal object for the fetishist, for example, as it provides the opportunity for expression of his or her sexual impulse. In this schema, the libidinal object itself has no intrinsic value. It is tacked on to the drive through experience because of its functional utility in reducing drive tension. Thus, in the beginning, the mother as person has no singular importance to the child, but is grouped in the "variable" category of object only to the extent that she functions as one of the "thing(s) in regard to which or through which the instinct is able to achieve its aim" (Freud, 1915, p. 122). The mother becomes important because she provides gratification, he believed; human love is built on both direct and disguised (aim-inhibited) gratifications, as the ego finds ways to repress, sublimate, and refine instinctual impulses so they find a place in more complex object relations.

Freud did not assume that libidinal connections with others are sought in their own right. Consider his approach to *identification,* the process through which the child makes someone or an aspect of someone a part of himself. Children become a great deal like their parents, and this identificatory process greatly facilitates learning to live in the world and culture to which they are born. But why and how does identification take place? As with so many of Freud's developmental explanations, the process of identification was conceptualized not as primary but as defensive in nature, a psychical maneuver attempting to soften the frustrating experience of loss. One may take on some qualities of a loved one following her death; the five-year-old identifies with his father's moral code in response to the oedipal frustration of being denied mother as a sexual partner. As long as gratification is available via objects in the real world, identification is irrelevant. When gratification is interrupted, when the object is lost or becomes unavailable because of conflict, the object is internalized to permit fantasy gratification. Identification with an object, for Freud, is a second-best solution, a compensation reluctantly accepted when instinctual gratification is itself not possible.

Spitz cut a conceptual course for theory-building midway between Freud's drive theory and radical object relations theories (see chapter 5). Spitz preserved Freud's notion that libido itself is pleasure-seeking, but added new dimensions to pleasure-seeking that deepened and filled out Freud's vision of development of early relations to objects. Spitz added to the id's libidinal purposes a set of capacities that originate and develop in the ego, parallel to the libido's pursuit of pleasure, that allows for the unfolding of a sense of caring and a deeply gratifying personal connection. In Spitz's system, having a libidinal object is not a given, something easily obtained with even the most impersonal experience of gratification. Rather, having a libidinal object is a developmental achievement reflecting the complex psychological capacity to establish a selective, very personal attachment that is retained even in that person's absence. Spitz's libidinal object is not simply a means to an end, drive discharge, nor the consequence of defensive internalization, but fundamentally important in its own right. The libidinal object provides the essential human connectedness within which all psychological development occurs.

Psychological Fusion

Hartmann had characterized the immature psyche as internally "undifferentiated," to suggest that at birth, the ego, superego, even the basic drives of libido and aggression are not yet articulated and distinguishable from one another. Spitz reoriented psychoanalytic focus on early life by describing the infant as initially both undifferentiated (a term reflecting the state of the infant's individual psyche) and nondifferentiated (a term recasting the basic image of crucial developmental concern from that of the infant alone to a new image of "infant-with-mother").

Spitz envisioned the infant as extending the physiologically parasitic relationship with the mother in the womb into a state of psychological fusion with the mother after birth. Like a conjoined twin who depends on the life flow between self and partner, the infant is in grave danger if abruptly separated from the mother or in any way deprived of the gradual process that eventuates in his acquiring the capacity for independent functioning. The mother, with her more developed psychical capacities, is the environment for the essentially helpless, vulnerable baby. Spitz likens the newborn to a blind person whose sight is restored. Far from being overjoyed, the newborn, like the newly sighted, is initially overwhelmed by a maelstrom of meaningless stimuli that he cannot process. The mother mediates this encounter. Processing the experience, she functions as the baby's "auxiliary ego," regulating the experience, soothing him, shielding him from disorganizing overstimulation, until he develops the ego capacity to process and regulate experience on his own.

Spitz was particularly interested in how the infant acquires the capacities that the environment-mother initially provides. Exactly how do Hartmann's primary autonomous ego functions develop, thereby enabling the infant to cull out and recognize what is meaningful in the flood of experience? Spitz concluded that complex interactional patterns develop between infant and mother, a kind of "dialogue," a "sequential action-reaction-action cycle within the framework of the mother–child relations . . . that enables the baby to transform step by step meaningless stimuli into meaningful signals" (1965, pp. 42, 43).

This dialogue takes place initially outside the verbal and gestural channels of adult communication that rely on the capacity for symbolic understanding. Through physical contact, body tension, posture, motion, rhythm, and tone, the mother communicates with her baby using a "total sensing system." The infant is *re*ceptive to expressive signals, rather than *per*ceptive; that is, he soaks up the sense of the mother's message, which is strongly shaped by the affective climate she creates with him: Is it safe? Is it good? Is it food? Is it frightening? Through expression, tone, and touch she mediates every perception, every action, every piece of experience, in repetitive patterns, gradually building up recognizable systems of meaning out of the chaos of stimulation, laying the groundwork for what will be the infant's emerging perceptual capacity.

Spitz brought to life Hartmann's principle of adaptation, detailing the psychic plasticity between mother and infant as they fit together, reciprocally influencing each other. Exquisitely sensitive to her infant's nonverbal messages, the "good" mother empathically divines the needs of her baby with near clairvoyant accuracy, relying on her capacity to regressively revive in herself this early communication channel that, Spitz felt, is lost to most adults. She senses why her infant is crying, a mystery to others, and is able to respond correctly. Each accurate reading and satisfying intervention—picking him up, feeding him, jostling him, soothing him—becomes another interaction in the essential cycle of meaning-making. Spitz saw these repetitions as also helping the infant sort out feeling states into discernible, sequential categories with beginnings and endings (for example: I was upset, then I felt better), contributing to the laying down of memory traces of recognizable experience. Thus Spitz offered psychoanalysis a very different kind of developmental progression, adding to the unfolding psychosexual sequence of drive discharge (from oral to anal to phallic to oedipal) the increasing structuralization of ego capacities which emerge, in the first year of life, within crucial transformations in the relationship to the libidinal object.

Noting that certain predictable shifts take place in the infant's behavioral attitudes toward others, Spitz concluded that these external manifestations, which he called "indicators," were signposts of increasing internal psychological complexity, marking critical developmental turning points, which he called "organizers of the psyche." The first indicator is the baby's first social response, the smiling response which occurs predictably at three months of age. Babies of this age will smile at mother, at Uncle Oscar, at the bank teller, as well as at a properly configured mask of a human face, but still show a clear preference for the gestalt of the human face over other things in their environment.

Gradually this response specifies and deepens; by eight months, the infant not only recognizes the mother's face, distinct from all others, but reacts with anxiety and retreats from a stranger's face. This external indicator of the second organizer of the psyche Spitz labeled "stranger anxiety." He reasoned that this emotional retreat was based not simply on what the infant *was* seeing, but also on what the infant was *not* seeing. Since the baby, now capable of storing memory traces, had had no bad experience with this total stranger, his distress must be caused by the contrast to his now internally held image of his mother. The stranger's presence alerts him to his mother's absence. For Spitz, this behavioral reaction signaled the attainment of psychological capacities that make a singular, personal attachment possible. "There is no love until the loved one can be distinguished from all others" (1965, p. 156).

Spitz's third organizer of the psyche, the mastery of the "no," encouraged a consideration of the developmental aspects of superego formation, a topic taken up more fully by Edith Jacobson. In 1936, Anna Freud had introduced a defensively motivated process, *identification with the aggressor,* to account for the internalization that had conceptually accounted for the establishment of the superego (i.e., Father the aggressor prohibits me from taking Mother as a love object; I will give up my quest for gratification and become like him instead). Spitz likened the child's acquisition of "no," which occurs at about fifteen months, to this phenomenon later in development, noting that once the child acquires locomotion, the mother must function increasingly as a prohibitor, curbing his intentions. For Spitz, the child's "no" is the external indication of a deeply enriching preoedipal identification with her, also evidencing dramatically enhanced psychic capacities, including those for judgment and rudimentary abstract conceptualization.

Thus Spitz demonstrated that virtually every aspect of early psychic development is mediated through the maternal environment. This revised conceptualization shifted attention to issues concerning the infant's emergence from psychological embeddedness with the mother and establishment of a personal sense of separate identity. How did an infant, psychically merged with his mother, grow into an autonomous child? Were there predictable phases and pitfalls in this developmental process?

DEVELOPMENTAL EGO PSYCHOLOGY:
MARGARET MAHLER

Margaret Mahler (1897–1985), a child analyst and former pediatrician who trained in Vienna before moving to New York, shed considerable light on the normal and abnormal features of this process. She carried the framework Spitz developed into some of the darker corners of childhood experience: families and hospitals that housed psychotic children. While psychoanalysis had creatively grappled with the knotty complexities of neurotic conflict, psychosis had remained largely outside the reach of psychoanalytic treatment.

First, the demands of the treatment process itself seemed to screen out those with more severe disorders. A patient in psychoanalysis must be able to lie on the couch, suspend ego functioning, detach herself from "reality" concerns, and say whatever occurs to her, no matter how illogical it may sound. Once having thus "regressed," the patient must be able to bounce back to normal functioning at the hour's end. The psychotic seems lost in her own world of fantasy and illogical thought from the start. Since the capacity for normal reality-testing is already compromised, encouraging selective regression in which reality-testing is abandoned altogether seemed therapeutically pointless, if not dangerous. While some analytic pioneers like Carl Jung, Paul Federn, and many followers of Melanie Klein explored therapies for more disturbed patients, in general psychotics were not candidates for psychoanalytic treatment.

Second, Freud envisioned the therapeutic action of the analytic process as provided by the patient's transference of unconscious libidinal longings, originally directed toward forbidden infantile objects, onto the person of the analyst. Freud assumed that in its earliest form libido was directed toward objects in the outer world. In his efforts to stretch libido theory to account for schizophrenia as well as neurosis, in 1914 Freud revised this conceptualization now depicting early libido as inwardly directed (primary narcissism). In the mind of the psychotic, libido was understood to have secondarily withdrawn back into this state of self-contained pool of narcissism, its most primitive condition, detached completely from external objects, even from memories or unconscious longings for childhood objects. Hence, in psychosis, it was believed, there is nothing to transfer onto the person of the analyst, no unconscious longings for gratification from others discoverable in the analytic process, because all energy is bound up in narcissistic self-absorption. (This problem will be revisited in the section on self psychology in chapter 6.)

Psychoanalytic theory offered few compelling explanations for this massive unavailability of productive psychic energy. Treatment prospects for psychotics, including psychotic children, were at best grim. "Childhood autism," the psychiatric diagnosis then given to most severely disturbed children, was more a verdict than a contribution to understanding. But Mahler, extending Spitz's emphasis on the crucial role of early relationships, initiated a more constructive exploration of severe disturbances of childhood.

For example, Stanley, a six-year-old psychotic boy described by Mahler (1968, pp. 82–109), responded with a "total emotional reaction" to his experience. His behavior alternated between complete listlessness and uninterrupted frenetic action. All feelings seemed to overwhelm him; he often cried uncontrollably. Presented with a picture book, he would confuse the picture of a baby behind the slats of a crib with the picture on the facing page of a panda in a cage. Seemingly caught by the visual similarity of the vertical lines in both pictures, he appeared unable to perceive the obvious differences; the two images became fused and were used interchangeably.[4]

Perhaps, Mahler speculated, the kind of massive problem evidenced in children like Stanley is not best formulated in terms of the direction of libidinal energy. What appears to be psychotic self-absorption might more meaningfully be described as a failure in the basic formation of the self, a profound confusion about who one is: what is self and what is other. Through Mahler's eyes, Stanley seemed not so much detached from objects as caught between powerful early needs for others and a sense of grave danger in having those needs met, a consequence of a disturbance in the expectable and necessary boundary between himself and his object world.

If Spitz was correct that a sense of identity develops out of a crucial early merger experience with the mother, perhaps specific failures in this early experience or in its resolution could be linked with specific kinds of disturbance in the formation of personal identity.

What disrupts the normal developmental passage through and healthy emergence from symbiotic relatedness? Mahler continued to consider hereditary and constitutional factors and the impact of early traumatic experience as key in symbiotic dysfunctions. Stanley, for example, had suffered from an inguinal hernia, causing severe, unexpected, and unrelievable attacks of pain from six months on. When exposed to painful shocks that cannot be patterned or avoided, experimental mice become catatonic. Mahler described the similar impact of this kind of unmanageable pain on the immature psyche: Selective repression is impossible and the child is driven inward, away from developing any capacities that would help him order and make sense of his experience.

But, like Spitz, Mahler also emphasized the importance of the human environment. The infant needs "an optimal level of pleasure" to secure "safe anchorage" (p. 17) and psychic growth within the symbiotic orbit. The mother provides for her infant's immature ego the crucial "mirroring frame of reference" (p. 19). If she is unpredictable, unstable, anxious, or hostile, the frame will be compromised and eventual independent functioning of the child is less likely. As an infant, Stanley could not regulate or protect himself from his environment. His intense distress was considered a dangerous risk to further complications. Although functionally present, his mother was emotionally detached and preoccupied with issues in her own life, seeming to have trouble really connecting with him emotionally. She attempted to interrupt his violent crying and distract him, for example, by force-feeding him while he was in pain. Stanley, Mahler concluded, "did not experience her ministrations as a real and efficient rescuing from the traumatic situations that suffused his 'rudimentary ego'" (pp. 93–94). Safe anchorage was impossible. His mother was unable to create a strong enough presence as his desperately needed auxiliary ego, as a stimulus regulator, helping him sort out and eventually identify different kinds of experiences and laying the groundwork for what would have been his perceptual capacity. Her force-feeding interventions only added to his experience of being assaulted by unprocessible, distressing stimulation.

Unable to use the symbiotic experience as a safe milieu in which to grow, Stanley was instead trapped in a developmental phase beyond its appropriate time. His psychic states, reflected in his external behavior, oscillated between lapses into a kind of personal formlessness and desperate attempts to establish a sense of his own separate identity. When his attention was not externally engaged, he would typically drift into a completely listless state apparently devoid of any aim or focus. Then he would suddenly wrench himself into action, purposefully touching his therapist's arm to prompt a kind of "switching on" of agitated energy expressed in paroxysms of jumping, twisting, and cramping. Because Stanley lacked a reliable experience of himself as a discrete entity when not externally engaged, Mahler felt, he lapsed into an internal state of symbiotic merger in which he experienced himself dissolving into total psychical nonbeing. "At those times," Mahler observed, when Stanley was quiet, "he seemed to be no more than a quasi-part of the environment . . . in a state of cohesion with it and undifferentiated from it" (p. 87). Feeling himself psychically disappearing, he was compelled to call on external mechanisms for reassurance, trying to establish some *outside* definition containing some *inside* substance. Mahler saw the touching of the therapist as a deliberate attempt to flood himself with intense directionless excitement, revving himself into agitated action and thus forcibly contriving a feeling of distinctness, a boundary feeling, "as if to defend against his apathetic state, as if to ward off the danger of symbiotic fusion, through which his entity and identity would otherwise become entirely dissolved into the matrix of the environment" (pp. 87–88).

Separation–Individuation

Documenting the devastating impact of severe symbiotic disruption, Mahler at the same time was conducting a systematic investigation into the intricacies of these earliest phases of development. Drawing on extensive observation of both normal and disturbed infants and their mothers, as well as of toddlers and older children, Mahler began by reformulating the nature of the early phase of life that Freud had characterized as essentially objectless, the stage labeled "primary narcissism." Within these earliest months, Mahler argued, the child breaks out of an "autistic shell," entering into the earliest of human connections, "normal symbiosis." She delineated the normal progression in the complex yet powerful interplay among the child's physical and cognitive maturation, his psychological evolution, and the crucial function of the maternal partner in his evolving identity.

Mahler subdivided the overarching process, which she defined as *separation–individuation*, into identifiable subphases, each with its own onset, normal outcome, and risks. *Hatching*, the first subphase, is signaled by the infant's increased alertness and "prototypical biphasic visual pattern" (p. 16), the regular alteration in the gaze, now more outwardly directed, now checking back to the mother as a point of orientation. This phase culminates at about nine months, when active locomotive capacities and physical development usher in the *practicing* subphase. Now an increasingly capable toddler launches himself into the world, elated with his new abilities, infused with a sense of omnipotence: despite actual moving away from his mother, he experiences himself, psychically, as still at one with her, sharing in her perceived omnipotence.

During *rapprochement,* which occurs between fifteen and twenty-four months, the child experiences a crucial psychic disequilibrium, Mahler theorized. Now psychological development catches up with physical maturation, bringing the distressing awareness that this very mobility demonstrates psychic separateness from the symbiotic union with the mother. Previously fearless in action, the toddler may now become tentative, wanting his mother to be in sight so that, through action and eye contact, he can regulate this new experience of apartness. The risk is that the mother will misread this actually progressive need as regressive and respond with impatience or unavailability, precipitating an anxious fear of abandonment in the toddler, who does not yet possess the psychic capacities to function as an independent agent. Mahler reported that a basic "mood predisposition" may be established at this point: a "significant lack of acceptance and 'emotional understanding' by the mother during the rapprochement subphase" contributes to an ongoing "proclivity to depression" (1966, pp. 157, 161, 166).

In breaking down the developmental journey through successive states of psychic organization, Mahler enabled clinicians to understand more deeply and treat more effectively children and adults who came to be officially diagnosed as *borderline* patients, whose severe pathology fell between the classifications of neurosis and psychosis.

Such problems were categorized as *preoedipal* in nature, to distinguish them both in origin and in dynamic composition from maturationally later pathology. Oedipal dynamics emphasize competitive sexual and aggressive conflict, exploring primarily the role of the father as the little girl's longed-for oedipal object and the little boy's feared oedipal rival. Preoedipal dynamics center on the role of the mother, and consider developmental disruption in the formation of the psychological structures that would eventually play a part in these oedipal struggles.[5] If defective, these structures can, in their own right, contribute to a host of earlier, often crippling disturbances.

Preoedipal pathology manifests not so much in discrete symptoms or guilty, conflictual indecision as in more pervasive disturbances of psychological function: intense, unregulatable feeling states, extreme fluctuation in images of self and/or other, impaired capacity for steady relatedness—disturbances that characterize pathology like masochism and severe depression.

But the contributions of Spitz and Mahler had a relevance far beyond their application to psychopathology. They provided what amounted to a new myth of origin for the human psyche. The baby Freud had envisioned is a creature filled with untamed instinctual tensions, a prehuman beast, that is brought under control, only incompletely, by social regulation. The unconscious, Freud stressed, is timeless; these infantile instincts always remain in a state of tension beneath the social veneer of adults. The baby envisioned by the developmental ego psychologists emerges sequentially out of a symbiotic union with the mother. The psychological birth of this baby is not coincident with his physical emergence from the womb. The mother's care contains his fragile psyche in much the same manner as her body contained his fetal development. This vision of the symbiotic prehistory of human development that emerged in Freudian ego psychology has provided a new vantage point for understanding many features of human experience. For example: Ernst Kris (1952) understood the creative freedom of the artist as reflecting a regression to less structured preoedipal states "in service of the ego"; Martin Bergmann (1973) has explored the episodic return to symbiotic fusion that characterizes some of the deepest aspects of mature romantic love.

A REVISED THEORY OF INSTINCTUAL DRIVE: EDITH JACOBSON

The rich account of the early years of life formulated by Hartmann, Spitz, and Mahler posed increasingly knotty problems for existing Freudian theory. In particular, the emphasis on the formative impact of very early relations with caregivers was in direct conflict with some of Freud's established tenets.

Two of the particularly problematic classical concepts in this regard were Freud's closely related notions of the death instinct and primary erotogenic masochism, both introduced in 1919. Freud was stunned and deeply saddened by the scope of human destructiveness displayed in World War I; he had also struggled in the consulting room with certain masochistic patients who seemed impervious to help, seemingly relentless in their pursuit of pain and suffering. The apparent attraction of painful experience posed a challenge for the fundamentally hedonic framework of Freud's libido theory, according to which the mind operates on the *pleasure principle* (always reducing pain and seeking pleasure).

We noted in chapter 1 that Freud's view of human instinctual endowment turned darker in 1919, when he concluded that aggression was a second instinctual drive equal in importance to libido. Libido, in Freud's account, begins as inwardly (narcissistically) directed, and is only secondarily directed toward objects. Freud used this pattern as a template for understanding the aggressive drive as well. Thus he suggested that aggression also begins as inwardly directed, derived from a *death instinct*. The baby begins life with both self-directed love and self-directed destructiveness. This revised Freudian infant, now infused with both sexual and aggressive energies, is often in a state of heightened tension, within which she may be indiscriminately aroused, stimulated by both libidinal and aggressive feelings, pleasure and pain. From Freud's perspective, the masochism of patients like Angela derives from a permanent psychic channel (a phenomenon he termed *primary erotogenic masochism*) that is often employed for disguised oedipal gratification as it allows pain to feel sexually stimulating.[6]

When Freud encountered intractable problems, he often fell back on constitution as an explanation. His formulation of the death instinct and primary erotogenic masochism derived these early, fundamental energic channels wholly from constitutional sources, largely unaffected by the infant's relationship to the human environment. Yet the developmental ego psychologists viewed the infant as psychically merged with the primary caretaker, continually receptive to and dependent on the mother's psychological participation. Is masochism a basic instinctual state or a consequence of problematic caretaking? How can vulnerability and receptivity to environmental impact be reconciled with an overarching theory that depicts the human psyche in fundamentally constitutional terms?

Edith Jacobson (1897–1978), originally a member of the Berlin Psychoanalytic Society, arrived in New York in 1938 shortly after her release from a Nazi prison and her escape from Germany. A courageous woman of strong convictions, she had returned to Germany from safety to defend a former patient who was in trouble with the Nazis. There she was imprisoned by the Gestapo for refusing to give information on the political activities of her patients (Kronold, 1980). Despite her exposure to these horrifying forms of human behavior, once out of Germany Jacobson was instrumental in revising the darker cast Freud's late revisions had lent to the psychoanalytic depiction of human nature.

How could Freud's emphasis on the constitutional be reconciled with the developmentalists' emphasis on the environmental? Biology and experience, Jacobson proposed, mutually influence each other and are in ongoing interaction throughout development. Drawing on the contributions of many, including Anna Freud, Hartmann, Spitz, and Mahler, and without heralding her innovations as fundamental revisions, Jacobson, in *The Self and the Object World* (1964), effectively reworked the entirety of Freud's energy theory, his account of the psychosexual stages of development, and his conceptualization of id, ego, and superego.

In agreement with Hartmann, Jacobson proposed that instinctual drives are not "givens" but rather are biologically predetermined, innate *potentials*. While responsive to internal maturational factors, their distinctive features are acquired in the context of early relationships. Experience is, from the start, registered in terms of how it *feels* to the baby and is organized by what Spitz had termed "affective perception"; memory traces cluster, like iron filings in a magnetic field, around the distinctive poles of feeling good or feeling bad. Normally, the baby's experience is predominantly satisfying; libido gradually emerges from a collection of good experiences into a strong, solid motivating force in the infant's life. Ideally, aggression is present in lesser levels. Early experience can, however, shift this balance. If it is largely frustrating and registers negatively, a more powerful and intense aggressive drive will consolidate that distorts the still vulnerable normal developmental processes.

Because experience is *subjectively* processed, Jacobson stressed, there is no such thing as simply "good" mothering, in some objective sense, only mothering that *feels* good to this particular baby. Issues of temperamental predisposition (e.g., an easily frustrated infant), fit or misfit (e.g., a calm baby and an excitable mother), affective matching or mismatching (e.g., a happy baby and a depressed mother), and the mother's capacity to sense and respond to her baby's changing developmental needs—these will all be crucial in determining what affect is elicited in the infant at any given time. Ultimately, the basic drive constitution that finally emerges depends on the collective impact of many moments.

Jacobson's model thus offered a description of the interplay between actual experience and drive development. Further, she argued that the balance in the subjectively registered feeling tone of earliest experience not only contributes to the consolidation of libido and aggression as drives, but also lays the groundwork for ongoing tendencies in the ways we feel about ourselves and others. This aspect of experience was felt to be represented in features of psychic development termed *self images* and *object images*. Following Hartmann, Kris, and Loewenstein (1946), and in agreement with Spitz, Jacobson proposed that when experiences feel good, images of a loving, giving mother and a happy, contented self accumulate in the infant's psyche; conversely, when experiences feel frustrating or upsetting, images of a frustrating, unloving mother and an angry, frustrated self accumulate. Since the newborn is at first unable to distinguish self from other, Jacobson believed that these earliest images are often fused and confused rather than distinct, self-contained units. Just as drives emerge from the registering of good and/or bad experience, so is one's deepest subjective sense of self and others an eventual outgrowth of the consolidation of these earliest images, providing a set of lenses through which subsequent experience is continually filtered.

By about six months of age, the infant is maturationally capable of distinguishing images of himself from images of others, and more realistic depictions of each become possible. He is now capable of picturing his mother as a discrete presence who is gratifying but also sometimes frustrating, and similarly, of experiencing himself as generally feeling good and loving but also capable of feeling bad and angry. This integration of good and bad *images* (i.e., the same mother who is bad and frustrating is also good and loving) must, Jacobson observed, facilitate the capacity to integrate conflictual *feeling states*. In this fusion of loving and hating feelings (a concept introduced by Hartmann), the raw primitive nature of the earliest forms of both drives (the demanding neediness of infantile libido and the violent eruptiveness of infantile aggression) is toned down. As a consequence, the affective singularity of intense love alternating with intense hate is replaced with more varied and subtle feeling states.

The attainment of affectively integrated images of self and of other allows a greatly increased capacity for more complex experience: an ability to register and to tolerate differences between one's emotional state and that of an important other; gradations in emotional response enhancing capacities to think and to learn that are jeapordized by unqualified acceptance or complete rejection; the ability to be disappointed by someone but still love her; and tolerance of anger without an internal collapse and a loss of a sense of one's being worthwhile or loving.

Jacobson's new model deftly rendered Freud's conceptualizations of primary erotogenic masochism and the death instinct logical impossibilities. If the newborn arrives with libido and aggression only as unformed, undirected potentials and without a distinct, articulated self, libidinal and aggressive drives cannot be initially self-directed. Into the conceptual vacancy created by removing key energic building blocks of Freud's drive metapsychology, Jacobson inserted new ego psychology formulations, detailing a fascinating interplay between richly elaborated processes of psychic development and the human environment within which they evolve. This included an expanded vision of the development of the superego. Jacobson described the superego as evolving over a long period of time, during which the child's experience of the human environment is continually internalized, transforming the child's drive-derived impulses and wishes. According to Jacobson (elaborating Spitz), early preoedipal experiences with the mother have two kinds of broad impact on the development affecting superego formation. Experiences of gratification and frustration shape the formal consolidation of the drives themselves, and experiences of maternal constraints and prohibitions leave behind early images as precursors around the which the later (oedipal) superego is formed. The formation of the superego was thus rendered more broadly dependent on the complex interpenetration between passions and experiences with others.

Jacobson not only revised Freud's derivation of libido and aggression, but also extended the functional impact of the drives. Freud had, in his later writings (e.g., 1940), described libido as a synthetic force that brings things together, aggression as a force that undoes connections. Jacobson applied these sensibilities to the recently articulated processes of separation and individuation which the ego psychologists had found to be so fundamental in early development. Libido, in Jacobson's account, provides the psychic glue in developmental processes, integrating, for example, opposing images of good and bad objects and a good and bad self. Aggression, in developmental processes, energizes an awareness of differences, promoting separation and the establishment of differentiated images of self and other.

For Jacobson, libido and aggression function as indispensable counterbalances to each other. Libido (evoked in moments of gratification) encourages pulling close, taking in; aggression (evoked in moments of frustration) prompts pushing off, moving out.[7] Both libido and aggression figure cyclically in the evolution of a stable identity, an achievement that ultimately depends on one's capacity to function autonomously, building up and continually enriching oneself by taking in from one's environment.

Jacobson felt that the libidinally motivated yearning to merge remains highly gratifying throughout life. Merger fantasies are evocative at all stages of psychic development, although the quality of one's ego boundaries greatly affects one's subjective experience of them. Normally, in later life, with boundaries between self and others clearly delineated, fusion fantasies can provide one of the deepest sources of gratification. They are an important dimension, for example, of the satisfaction experienced in sexual intercourse. For one newly launched into self-definition, however, or for whom ego boundaries are not clearly delineated, fusion fantasies are dangerous and deadly, a powerful regressive pull toward psychic dissolution. Aggression-evoking experiences of frustration and limit-setting can function constructively here, balancing against the regressive pull. They remind the young voyager with necessarily weak ego boundaries of her separateness, encouraging her to push off from destructive indulgence in experiences of gratification and the ego-undermining shoals of fusion fantasies.

Evoking aggression can function similarly in emotionally vulnerable adults who, when confused or depressed, pick fights with others in order to experience greater psychic clarity. Aggression operates here not as a drive per se, but as an experience actively called up in the self to promote self-delineation. Such temporary relief is, however, not always to be had. For aggression to come to function in this capacity, it must have consolidated in an atmosphere modulated by sufficient gratifying libidinal experience. If this balance is lacking the aggression evoked will feel too powerful, over-whelming and disrupting the attempt at self-delineation with fears that one has been too hurtful or destructive in the interaction.

CLINICAL APPLICATIONS OF
DEVELOPMENTAL EGO PSYCHOLOGY

Freud regarded the repression of conflictual impulses as the core of neuro-sis. The ego psychologists, as we have seen, came to pay increasing atten-tion to disruptions in developmental processes that were felt to result in a broad range of problems in the structuralization of the psyche itself. Freud's focus was on *oedipal* conflict, organized in the more mature cognitive and linguistic schemata of later childhood. The ego psychologists investigated *preoedipal* disturbances, those that often take place prior to the emergence of language. But how would an adult patient in analysis recall experience that occurred before language was available to define it? How could the analytic process identify and constructively engage these early distur-bances?

Freud viewed the transference as the centerpiece of the analytic process, providing access to the patient's hidden and forbidden wishes as she expressed and tried to gratify them with the analyst. The ego psychologists began to view the analytic relationship in broader terms. Particularly with more disturbed patients, the transference came to be understood not only as expressive of forbidden longings but as an arena within which remnants of ill-fated attempts at building normal psychic structure could be discerned in particulars of the relationship that the patient established with the ana-lyst. By attending to specific features of the experiences and images that emerge in this relationship, and using them as indicators of the fate of important developmental processes, the analyst could determine which aspects of psychic structuralization had been compromised and, with the patient, develop a verbal account of what went wrong in the patient's early experience, using this very processing as an aspect of repair.

But how can an analyst determine from the transference whether the patients' problems are oedipal or preoedipal in nature? In contrast to oedi-pal transferences, which generally unfold slowly and only with analytic clarification come to center on some specific emotionally charged experi-ence in relation to the analyst, the preoedipal transference is more fre-quently characterized by a kaleidoscopic presentation of images of self and other, dominated by intense emotional immediacy. This qualitatively different presentation is well illustrated by specific features of the transference of Angela, the patient described earlier in this chapter.

From the outset, Angela expected the analyst to scream at her, to attack her and to disappear; the gripping intensity of these anticipations was apparent in her cowering fearfulness. Alternatively, she would become manifestly transformed, fearless, eyes glittery, face contorted in a cruel smile, as she contemptuously berated the analyst for a broad range of failings. These shifting images and affective states, indicating a failure in consolidation of positive and negative self and object images, proved a distorting lens through which life was viewed, and precluded, as Jacobson had predicted, Angela's ability to develop any consistent, reliable perspective on herself or others in her life.

Other experiences seemed suggestive of unprocessed, preverbal memories reflecting developmentally traumatic aspects of her early life. For example, Angela persistently experienced the analyst as emotionally disconnected and uninterested in helping her, "just watching" her. This experience, characterized by near-frantic anxiety, seemed to represent not a frustration of instinctual longing, but a chronic sense of being anxiously adrift in an ambiguous, unresponsive environment.

Sometimes Angela would offer her own explanation for this unbearable experience of aloneness: she was bad, too needy and ugly, undeserving of the analyst's concerned attention. For a patient such as Angela, this kind of transference expression would suggest disruption of the early maternal environment, where empathic sensitivity and containment of the child's emotional experiencing are crucial elements of "safe anchorage" within the symbiotic experience. A chronic emotional misattunement in Angela's early environment would have precluded her building up a store of safe, gratifying experiences around which a solid libidinal drive could consolidate. Early experiences that register as frightening or anxiously unproccessable mobilize, as Jacobson had described, a stronger aggressive drive which itself becomes a dominant factor in the child's ongoing attempts at meaning-making. If one is often anxious, frustrated, and angry, one might well feel unlovable, perpetuating a cycle of continuing negative experience of self and other. These understandings of the meaning of Angela's transference experience would, within Mahler's developmental schema, suggest a disruption in the fundamental process of separation-individuation and a resulting disturbance in the ability to maintain a reliable sense of individual identity which would continue to compromise experience into adulthood.

Consider a nightmare reported by Angela following her expressing more positive feelings for the analyst.

> Someone called me into a castle. He was in an upstairs window. It was impressive and beautiful. I get inside. I can't find him. Then there are hands reaching out to me. I move closer, but then I see the hands are on arms coming out of the walls. They reach around my neck and are trying to pull me into the wall. I am terrified and try to fight. I don't want to disappear.[8]

With this dream, Angela had been able to visualize the nameless terror that haunted her, making intimate relationships impossible. While Mahler had speculated that a fear of disappearing into one's environment lay behind the behavior of young children like Stanley, this dream of Angela's expresses such a terror in clear and unambiguous terms.

If she let herself feel warmly for someone, she feared she would disappear into the other, and enter a marginal, formless world, part human, part inanimate. Here hands, symbolic for her of human connectedness, reached out to her to lure her into a nonhuman nightmare.

Jacobson emphasized that to be used for constructive projects, such as efforts at separation or boundary establishment, aggression must be available to the child's psyche in a manageable form.[9] One cannot put a wild bronco in harness and hope for a comfortable ride through Central Park. The toning down of aggression is an outcome of the developmental accomplishment of tolerating separateness and then of simultaneously holding good and bad feelings for self and for other. How difficult this is to do depends on the relative strength of each set of feelings. If the aggression is too powerful, bringing it together with loving feelings risks the internal experience of destroying those loving feelings and the loved person altogether.

Angela's aggression had a raw and eruptive quality. When someone upset and angered her, she experienced them as totally bad, devoid of any redeeming features, herself now a singularly destructive person with unmitigated power to damage. At times, she felt convinced she had destroyed the analyst "with the hate in my eyes." She expected to return and find "you wouldn't be here, and no one would have heard of you." Angela was not simply describing the feeling "I could kill you"; she envisioned her aggression as annihilating, effecting a complete psychic erasure of the analyst as well as any internal record of her existence.

Freud had depicted the ego as arbitrator in a high-level conference with

strong and competitive participants. The ego psychologists offered a different vision of the central struggle in severe psychopathology: How does one
function with defective equipment? How does one get close, move away,
pursue pleasure, regulate feelings, do the things that most people take for
granted, if fundamental psychological structures are not in place?
Hartmann's principle of adaptation became a standard feature of the clinical version of ego psychology, applied not just to normal functioning but to
pathological structures. Angela's "wall" can be understood as her ego's
attempt to force a psychic boundedness when a more naturally evolving
separation between herself and others was impossible. Angela's sadomasochistic masturbatory fantasies can be viewed similarly. In her fantasies, Angela pictured herself tied on a conveyer belt, passing helplessly
through a variety of strangely stimulating sexual tortures, while Mega, the
one in charge, sadistically, methodically thrust hot pokers into her vagina.

Although Angela's sadomasochistic fantasies were sexual in content,
from an ego psychology perspective they reflect a more fundamental and
formidable psychological dilemma. From this perspective, she was not
sneaking forbidden oedipal gratification by disguising it as pain. Rather,
she was struggling with how she might satisfy her need for human contact
and pleasure when it led to a terrifying sense of psychic dissolution,[10] trying to construct a barrier against the threat of disintegrating merger when
the very act of pushing away required her calling on aggressive forces
within herself that seemed murderous in potential. Her sadomasochistic
masturbatory fantasy offered a kind of makeshift yet creative structure in
the face of this dilemma, allowing and regulating needed contact with others, while simultaneously expressing and containing her aggression.

In this fantasy, there was pleasure and there was contact; she could reach
orgasm and was not totally alone. The pleasure, however, was always
mixed with pain. This formula would keep her ever on guard, never comfortable, the conveyer belt imagery further underscoring how strongly she
needed to defend against any awareness of herself as voluntarily moving
toward another person. And the aggression she so needed to draw on to
help maintain boundaries was not out of control but channeled through a
personification, who reminded her, by title and action, that there was a
greater authority to whom she must answer. For Angela, the sadistic quality of the punishment seemed reassuringly appropriate, as it provided the
necessary counterforce to the intensity of her negative feelings; a wimpy
controller would be no match for the rageful, murderous person she felt
herself to be. And, as Angela would later conclude, the harsh and hurtful
tone of this controller's communication reminded her very much of her

mother's forceful, aggressive ways of "curbing and prohibiting" which, as predicted by Jacobson, had contributed powerfully in the formation of this superego presence.[11]

Developmental Transformation in the Transference

For ego psychologists, the experience between patient and analyst becomes an occasion to understand the nature of the patient's psychic disruption and her adaptive efforts to compensate. The analytic relationship also has powerful transformative potential, the transference providing an opportunity for reworking early disruptions, for the patient to use the analyst to try to fill unmet developmental needs, for the patient now as an adult to verbalize and experience with the analyst early fears and terrors that had, in childhood, seemed overwhelming.

These opportunities can manifest in a variety of forms. At one point, for example, Angela became increasingly passive and provocatively reluctant to talk. "Go ahead," she taunted the analyst, "you get me into it." Angela eventually acknowledged that she longed for the analyst to aggressively push her into things because this kind of interaction had been one of the few ways she had felt any sense of her mother's interest in her. After both the sexual and aggressive dimensions of this request were addressed, attention turned to what it was Angela felt she needed to be pushed into and how the analyst might be with her in this experience. (Spitz had seen as crucial the impact on the child's perceptual development of the mother's jointly processing, organizing, and making sense of his early chaotic experience.) Angela began to articulate the underlying fears that had infused her experience: fears that thoughts could kill; fears that closeness meant disappearing.

Over time Angela found the process of naming and clarifying feelings with the analyst increasingly comforting and tolerable. She had begun treatment describing herself as a "nervous wreck" with "no idea of what my problem is." Helping her track and articulate her experience, putting it into words that made sense, encouraged a greater sense of self-definition and gave her more insight into her feeling states. Eventually, she could call up feeling states from memory rather than finding herself precipitously infused and controlled by them.

Angela's increasing reservoir of good experience both of the analyst and of herself bolstered her confidence in bringing negative feelings into the analytic relationship, where they could be examined. Analyst and patient explored the ways Angela's child's mind had processed certain traumatic experiences, such as the death of her envied classmate, confusing aggressive fantasies with responsibility for actual events. In this context, they also learned how Angela's experience with her mother, who seemed always on the verge of emotional collapse and too fragile to grapple with aggression in any meaningful way, deprived her of an important opportunity to process her worrisome fantasies and greatly contributed to her isolation. Angela's stubbornness was explored, not as aggressive resistance needing removal, but as reflecting a wish to "come up against" the analyst, thus reaffirming her own self as separate, her ideas as different. Aggressive transference expressions with the analyst ("I wish I had a big knife, and I would cut you into pieces") were accepted as expressions of Angela's frustration, and she was encouraged to try to put the specific frustration into words. She was interpretively reminded, when deeply involved with a "totally bad" image of the analyst, of previously shared better moments in the treatment when she had felt helped or cared about. (Recall Jacobson's emphasis on the crucial ability to bring together, in a single experience of another, both good and bad feelings.) In this way, the analyst functioned in the transference as a kind of container for both positive and negative experience, repeatedly demonstrating to Angela that the good could survive exposure to the bad, eventually helping her tone down her singularly aggressive emotional state and develop more balance in her emotional life.

CONCLUSION

The psychoanalytic process can be, and has been, conceptualized in many different ways. The metaphors that are chosen to illustrate principles of clinical technique often provide the best indication of the underlying assumptions of each analytic model. Freud's metaphors all have an adversarial quality: war, chess, hunting wild beasts. As the ego psychologists shifted the focus from the id to the ego, from the repressed to the central nexus of psychological processes, their models of the analytic process also began to change. Initially, in taking on the analysis of the unconscious aspects of the ego's defensive functioning, analysts came to appreciate that what had been identified as the broader functions of the ego, evidenced in the patient's self-observation, reflection, and the maintenance of a reality orientation, could be put to good use in this project.

Much as early explorers came to appreciate the invaluable advantage of engaging natives as scouts and trappers, analysts became increasingly appreciative of the patient's potential as a therapeutic ally in the process of documenting and revealing unconscious conflict. Calling upon her ego capacities, the patient could reveal to the analyst the "inside story" on crucial psychic terrain, enabling the analyst to more effectively discern the competing psychic claims and crafty defensive strategies of neurosis. As a consequence, techniques were developed aimed at encouraging the patient to enter into what would eventually be called a "working alliance," within which analyst and patient could share the work (see Zetzel, 1958, and Greenson, 1965). Although cure itself was still understood in terms of making the unconscious conscious, the process was now envisioned as occurring within a dyadic context, within a metaphoric partnership rather than a battle.

A second fundamental change in understanding the analytic process came with the growing realization that for the patient, the experience of working in this kind of partnership could prove therapeutic in its own right. Operating as an effective scout, the patient *developed* her abilities to better observe herself, to be reflective rather than simply reactive, to delay gratifying herself (for Hartmann, a process synonymous with drive neutralization) in favor of describing what she needed, to work toward anticipating consequences rather than leaping to action.

Finally, a deepening understanding that psychic structure itself consolidated within a human partnership spawned innovation in clinical technique aimed at attempts to reactivate, between patient and analyst, some form of the early developmental reciprocity that existed between mother and infant. In her early treatment efforts with children, Mahler began looking to the treatment experience itself as a potential corrective, symbiotic experience. In the treatment of adult depressives, Jacobson stressed not the power of accurate interpretation, not the content of the analyst's words, but the crucial role of emotional resonance. "There must be a continuous, subtle, emphatic tie between the analyst and his depressive patients," she observed, to that end encouraging the analyst, for example, to "adjust to the slowed-up emotional and thought processes of such patients," to "not let empty silences grow," and "not to talk too long, too rapidly, or too emphatically" (1971, p. 299). Thus, as developmental ego psychologists further explored the role of parental functions in building strong and healthy psychic structure, depictions of the patient as an effective ally began to shade into images of dyadic analytic provisions that might remedy faulty parental imput. The analytic process came to be understood not only as a partnership with work to be done, but also as a growth experience in its own right, the relationship with the (quasi-parental) analyst providing opportunity to rework early developmental experience.[12]

3

HARRY STACK SULLIVAN AND INTERPERSONAL PSYCHOANALYSIS

It is correct (and a great improvement) to begin to think of the two parties to the interaction as two eyes, each giving a monocular view of what goes on and, together, giving a binocular view in depth. This double view *is* the relationship.

—*Gregory Bateson*

Without wearing any mask we are conscious of, we have a special face for each friend.

—*Oliver Wendell Holmes, Sr.*

Interpersonal psychoanalysis was born in the 1920s in the clinical encounter of the American psychiatrist Harry Stack Sullivan with patients on the extreme end of the mental-health continuum: schizophrenics. Sullivan (1892–1949) grew up in rural Chenango County, in upper New York State. He studied medicine in Chicago, in the days when the pragmatist "Chicago School" dominated American intellectual life, particularly the social sciences. At St. Elizabeths Hospital in Washington, D.C., he worked under William Alanson White, who, along with Adolf Meyer, was a dominant presence in American psychiatry and sparked Sullivan's early interest in working with schizophrenics.

Freudian psychoanalysis had some presence in the clinical thinking and practice of American psychiatry at that time, but the theoretical system that dominated the field was the traditional psychiatric approach to schizophrenia, fashioned by the German psychiatrist Emil Kraepelin in the late nineteenth and early twentieth centuries. Perhaps the most important distinguishing feature of schizophrenia (Kraepelin's term was "dementia praecox") is the disconnection from ordinary channels of relationship with other people. Schizophrenics have disordered thought and live in their own world. They adopt postures (like catatonic stupor) and behaviors (like hebephrenic feces-smearing or paranoid rages) that dramatically discourage any efforts by others to reach them. Kraepelin's approach cast schizophrenia as a neurophysiological disease, a physically based disorder that worsens inexorably over time and ends in total deterioration.

Sullivan felt that these concepts were strikingly inapplicable to his own experience with schizophrenic patients, whom he found to be extremely sensitive and responsive to their interpersonal environment. Although their communications were often oblique and disguised, they were exquisitely aware, often painfully so, of other people.

The kinds of clinical experiences that led Sullivan to begin to fashion an interpersonal approach to psychological processes were reported four decades later by the British psychiatrist R. D. Laing (together with Aron Esterson), who, like Sullivan, and influenced by Sullivan's work, had come to doubt the traditional understanding of schizophrenic symptomatology as random sputterings of a deteriorating physiological system.

Laing and Esterson (1970) worked with several regressed schizophrenic patients from the back wards of hospitals who suffered from symptoms thought to be intractable and meaningless indications of their deteriorated physiology. A patient they called Maya Abbott, for example, had auditory hallucinations, felt unreal and detached, wooden and withdrawn; she spoke of experiencing herself as a machine rather than a person, lacking any control of her own mind, with her thoughts and feelings being controlled externally by others. Encountered as an individual, Maya could be persuasively understood to be suffering from a spontaneously arising, completely autonomous, deteriorative internal process. Laing and Esterson brought Maya together with her parents and observed how they interacted.

One small part of family interplay seemed particularly relevant to one of Maya's psychotic symptoms, characteristic of paranoid schizophrenia, *ideas of reference:* convictions that things going on around you, unrelated to you, are really about you (for example, that events on a television program are personal messages to you).

An idea of reference that she had was that something she could not fathom was going on between her parents, seemingly about her. Indeed there was.

When they were all interviewed together, her mother and father kept exchanging with each other a constant series of nods, winks, gestures, knowing smiles, so obvious to the observer that he commented on them after twenty minutes of the first such interview. They continued, however, unabated and denied. (1970, p. 40)

Laing and Esterson were struck by the mystifying impact of Maya's parents' quite public and obvious behaviors, perceived by her, yet denied by them.

> Much of what could be taken to be paranoid about Maya arose because she mistrusted her own mistrust. She could not really believe that what she thought she saw going on was going on. Another consequence was that she could not easily discriminate between actions not usually intended or regarded as communications, e.g. taking off spectacles, blinking, rubbing nose, frowning, and so on, and those that are—another aspect of her paranoia. It was just those actions, however, that were used as signals between her parents, as "tests" to see if Maya would pick them up, but an essential part of this game the parents played was that, if commented on, the rejoinder would be an amused, "What do you mean?" "What wink!" and so on. (p. 40)

Maya's behavior, which seemed clearly bizarre and meaningless when she was encountered as an individual, took on obvious, understandable meaning when she was observed in the original interpersonal context within which that behavior had arisen.

Harry Stack Sullivan's formative clinical experiences in the 1920s were the same as Laing's in the 1960s. (Laing, of course, had the benefit of Sullivan's writings, which he acknowledged as the only helpful work on schizophrenia he had found.) To understand psychopathology, Sullivan became increasingly convinced, the individual is simply not the unit to study. Human beings are inseparable, always and inevitably, from their interpersonal field. The individual's personality takes shape in an environment composed of other people. The individual is in continual interaction with other people. The personality or self is not something that resides "inside" the individual, but rather something that appears in interactions with others. "Personality . . . is made manifest in interpersonal situations and not otherwise" (1938, p. 32), Sullivan suggested. Personality is "the relatively enduring pattern of recurrent interpersonal situations which characterize a human life" (1940, p. xi).

The principle that the field, not the individual, is the most meaningful unit of study sounds simple, but it has profound implications for thinking about personality, psychopathology, and psychoanalysis. From the interpersonal perspective, focusing on the individual without considering past and present relationships wrenches the object of study from the context that makes it understandable, like studying animal behavior by observing an animal in a cage rather than its natural habitat. Sullivan came to feel that human activity and human mind are not things that reside *in* the individual, but rather are generated in interactions among individuals; personalities are shaped to fit interpersonal niches and are not understandable unless that complex, interactive honing process is taken into account.

Although he began his work with schizophrenics, Sullivan came to feel that less disturbed patients are just as embedded in their interpersonal contexts and that to try to understand them outside those contexts is a serious mistake.

For example, Sullivan described a young man whose life had been centered around a series of "grand passions" for women: "he has fallen deeply in love with one woman after another for years and years past but, shockingly enough, nothing has ever come of it" (1956, p. 46). The patient knew something was distinctly wrong with his approach to relationships, but he had no idea of what it was or how it worked. A traditional Freudian psychoanalyst, using the intrapsychic approach, would generate certain kinds of hypotheses about dynamics *inside* the patient: The ill-fated romances are likely to be entangled with oedipal dynamics, conflictual wishes to win the mother. The kind of data relevant to testing such hypotheses would include the patient's fantasies about these women and the patient's fantasies about his mother. The failed romances would be found to both express and preserve the patient's tie to the oedipal parent.

Sullivan was interested in very different data. He wanted to know *what happens* between this man and these women: "there must be something in his relationship with these women—something in the pattern of his behavior toward them—that makes each love object unwilling to continue to be a love object" (p. 47). Whereas the Freudian analyst is looking for repressed wishes and fantasies, Sullivan is looking for unattended interactions.

In the classical analytic setup, the analyst waits silently for the hidden wishes to appear in disguised form in uncensored free associations and then interprets them. In Sullivan's approach, the analyst actively inquires into interactions; the relevant data will not simply appear, because the patient (without awareness) leaves out what is most important. "So we settle down

with this patient and want as much as we can get of what he can recall of
the current events in his relationship with the love object" (p. 49).

Sullivan went after details: Who is this other person? How was she
selected? What happened? Who said what to whom? When precisely did
the emotional climate in the relationship change? For Sullivan to get the
data he needed, he had to know more than what the patient thought, felt,
and fantasized about. He sought details about what actually happened, and
it is only that interactional context, Sullivan suggested, that yields an
understanding of the ways the patient was re-creating his fate over and
over.

In this case, Sullivan found that

> this man works so diligently at investing each of his feminine love objects
> with rare and desirable qualities which she obviously does not have and
> devotes so much attention to expressing his profound admiration for these
> qualities which she does not have that she cannot overlook the fact that
> she is not the person that he is in love with. (p. 49)

It is only through a highly textured exploration of what was said and done
in several of these love relationships that the pattern of subtle rejection,
under the guise of great passion, emerged.

> He has a way of discouraging each love object about any illusions that she
> may have that she will do, and he fits the practice to the personality. For
> example, if the woman is very docile and self-effacing, he will find in her
> the fine aggressive certainty of herself which is so very dear to him. And if
> she is quite domineering, then he will find in her an extraordinary consid-
> eration for other people's feelings. (pp. 49–50)

Sullivan was also interested in the past, but not primarily the impulses
and wishes of the past, which were, he believed, small segments of larger
interpersonal configurations; looking at them in isolation entailed a violent
decontextualization that destroyed any possibility of meaningfully understanding them. Rather, he looked at the interactions of the past. In this
example, Sullivan placed primary emphasis on identifying something
important about what was taking place between the patient and women in
the present: he approached women by falling in love with inflated misrep-
resentations of them. Sullivan would next want to understand the origins
of that interaction in the patient's early history: How did he learn to destroy
love in this fashion? Was he loved in this fashion? Were significant others
in his early life reachable only in this way?

ANXIETY AND MOTIVATION

Sullivan's study of interpersonal processes increasingly focused on anxiety as the crucial factor determining the way the individual shapes his experience and his interaction with others.

While other features, such as dramatic and disturbing symptoms, can seem more prominent, Sullivan came to feel that they often are distractions from, and techniques for the management of, underlying points of anxiety. Oscar, a man in his mid-thirties, sought treatment because of a chronic dread that he might be gay, which had tortured him since his mid-adolescence. He had been in psychotherapy before and had seen several other symptoms and problems improve, but his agonizing doubts about his sexual orientation had remained. He had a great many relevant notions about his sexuality, his fears of intimacy, and his family dynamics, but they did little to dispel his concerns.

The interpersonal analyst became interested in the last time these thoughts had arisen. Oscar had spent the previous weekend with an old girlfriend. The first night, they had made passionate love; the next morning, he approached her sexually again and she declined. "How about a blow job then?" was his response, and she became angry. He explained that oral sex had long-standing political dimensions between the two of them. She considered his request a demand for submission. He felt his support of feminism and her interests in general were above reproach and sex should be something free and open between them, without concerns of political correctness. He became depressed at the rapid resurgence of their old sexual/political struggle and withdrew. He found himself wondering about a man he had seen the day before at the office. If he were in a sexual situation with this man, would he get aroused? He pictured the man naked and felt a mild degree of excitement. That alarmed him in the now familiar way, and he became caught up in a tense, ruminative preoccupation about whether he was gay and whether he would ever be happy in an intimate relationship with a woman.

From an interpersonal point of view, what is important about this sequence of events is not the sexual content per se, but the way mental content (sexual and otherwise) is moved around in the service of managing anxiety. Upon inquiry, the analyst and Oscar learned that he had felt both elated and anxious following the previous evening's sexual encounter. Things going well with this woman frightened and confused him. What would happen? Would this mean a commitment he felt ill-prepared to make? In reflecting on his request the next morning for oral sex, it became clear to Oscar that there was an absolute certainty his girlfriend would be antagonized and that their characteristic political debate would follow. The purpose of his request seemed not to draw them closer or obtain sex; the purpose of the request was to create distance. He had been anxious about their intimacy; he was seeking the familiar ground of their distancing conflict. Similarly, he knew that he was capable of being excited by both women and men, and that if he evoked the image of the man and imagined a sexual situation, he would feel a mild degree of arousal. He knew further that that arousal would serve as the basis for self-torture and the by now comfortable confusion he lived in most of the time. The sense of power and success he had felt after the sexual intimacy with his girlfriend had frightened him. His provocative request the following morning helped him rid himself of the anxiety connected to intimacy and potency, and the homosexual reverie further established him securely (even if also anxiously) as unmanly and deferential. Rather than being the causal motivating factor, sexuality seemed rather a means for managing anxiety about closeness and distance, novelty and familiarity.

How do anxiety and its management come to play such a central role in psychopathology? Sullivan introduced a developmental theory in which anxiety is the key pathological factor in shaping the self and regulating interactions with others.

Sullivan portrayed the newborn as oscillating between a state of more or less complete comfort and a state of tension in which needs of various sorts are demanding attention. Most of the tensions that arise for the newborn are not problematic, as long as a reasonably responsive caregiver is present. The baby's needs are matched by complementary responses in the caregiver. The expression of physical needs for food, warmth, absence of irritation; emotional needs for safety and tenderness; intellectual needs for play and stimulation—all these tend to call out a satisfying reciprocal response in the caregiver, thereby reducing the tension.

Sullivan called these needs *integrating tendencies* because their essential nature is to draw people together in mutually satisfying ways. The nursing interaction between baby and mother is the most vivid example of the complementarity of integrating tendencies. The baby is hungry and needs to feed. The breasts of the lactating mother are full of milk—she needs to nurse. They are drawn together in a mutually gratifying integration.

These *needs for satisfaction* generate reciprocity with others not just for the newborn but all throughout life, Sullivan believed; various needs in adults tend to evoke complementary needs in other adults. Given a reasonable amount of patience, flexibility, and tact, various emotional, physical, sexual, and intellectual needs can generate mutually satisfying integrations with others.

In contrast to Freud, Sullivan envisioned human needs as unproblematic in themselves. We are not born with asocial, bestial impulses needing to be tamed and socialized only through great threat and effort, Sullivan argued; rather, we have evolved into social creatures who are wired in a way that draws us into interactions with others.

But if needs for satisfaction operate so smoothly as integrating tendencies, why then are human interactions so filled with dissatisfactions, conflicts, clashes? As Sullivan saw it, the fly in the ointment of nearly all human endeavors is anxiety. Needs for satisfaction arise spontaneously within the baby, but anxiety is something visited upon the baby from the outside.

Sullivan distinguished between fear and anxiety. If a loud noise occurs, if hunger is unaddressed, if tensions of any sort increase, the baby becomes afraid. Fear actually operates as an integrating tendency; as it is expressed in crying and agitation, it draws the caregiver into an interaction that will soothe the baby and address the problem. Anxiety, in contrast, has no focus and does not arise from increasing tension in the baby herself. Anxiety is picked up from other people.

Feeling states are contagious. Someone who is jittery tends to make other people jittery; someone who is sexy tends to evoke sexual feelings in others, and so on. Babies are particularly sensitive to other people's feeling states, Sullivan believed. Their own state is greatly affected by the emotional tone of the people around them. Sullivan termed this contagious spread of mood from caregivers to babies the *empathic linkage.*

If the caregiver is relaxed and comfortable, the baby oscillates gently between a euphoric ease and states of tension generated by arising needs, which are more or less smoothly responded to. But what if the caregiver is anxious?

Sullivan believed that anxiety in the caregiver is picked up by the baby and experienced as a formless tension with no focus, no apparent cause. Unlike needs for satisfaction, the tension of anxiety does not serve as an integrating tendency, *cannot* serve as an integrating tendency, because the potential rescuer from the tension of anxiety is the very person who has caused it in the first place.

Consider a devoted caregiver who is worried about something altogether unrelated to the baby. The baby picks up the anxiety and experiences it as a tension, demanding relief. He cries, in the same way he responds to tensions created by various needs for satisfaction. The caregiver moves toward the baby, concerned and hoping to comfort him. But as she moves closer in her effort to soothe, the caregiver also brings her own anxiety closer to the baby. Most likely she is even more anxious now, precisely because of the baby's distress. The closer she gets, the more anxious the baby becomes. Unless the caregiver can find a way to pull both herself and the baby out of their anxious state, the baby experiences a snowballing tension with no possible relief.[1]

In Sullivan's vision, anxiety becomes a nightmarish condition for the infant that has a profound impact on early experience. Not only is anxiety stressful, frightening, and inescapable in itself, it also operates as a *disinte*grating tendency with respect to all the infant's needs for satisfaction. When the infant is anxious, she is unable to feed, to cuddle, to sleep. Anxiety in adults likewise interferes with thinking, communicating, learning, sexual performance, emotional intimacy, and so on. Anxiety, for Sullivan, is the monkey wrench in a complexly evolved, otherwise harmonious system of interpersonal and social mutual regulation.

Because anxiety is so strikingly different from other states, Sullivan believed, the first basic differentiation in the infant's experience is not between light and dark, or between mother and father, but between anxious states and nonanxious states. Because it is the caregiver who generates the anxiety in the child, Sullivan terms this first distinction "good mother" (nonanxious) states vs. "bad mother" (anxious) states. Experiences with various caregivers (not just the biological mother) when they are anxious are all joined together into the child's experience of "bad mother"; experiences with various caregivers when they are not anxious (and therefore able to respond effectively to needs for satisfaction) are all joined together into the child's experience of "good mother." The fact that these are actually different people is irrelevant to the infant, for whom the only important distinction is between anxious and nonanxious. Similarly, the fact that each of these people is sometimes anxious and sometimes not anxious is irrelevant; the difference in their impact on the child in these two states is so dramatic that they are, as far as the child is concerned, two different people.

Sullivan assumed that the infant originally experiences his states of mind passively; whether "good mother" or "bad mother" reigns, with their enormously different impact on him, is beyond his control. Little by little, however, the infant gains control over his fate. He begins to learn that he can predict whether it is "good mother" or "bad mother" who is approaching. Facial expression, postural tension, vocal intonation become reliable predictors of whether the baby will find himself in the hands of someone who calmly responds to his needs, or at the mercy of someone who draws him into a maelstrom of unrelievable stress.

A second crucial step comes with the child's discovery that whether "good mother" or "bad mother" appears has something to do with him. He arrives at the startling realization that some of his own activities and gestures make his caregivers anxious, while some of his activities and gestures have a calming effect and elicit approval. Of course, putting a slowly evolving process into language like this is very misleading. Sullivan envisioned a gradual building-up of connections.

Some of the child's activities (e.g., touching the genitals or fussing) may make a particular caregiver anxious; that anxiety is communicated to the baby, who then begins to connect touching the genitals or fussing with an anxious state of mind. Some of the child's activities (e.g., resting quietly) may make a particular caregiver relax and generate approval; that approval is likewise communicated to the baby, who then begins to connect resting quietly with a peaceful, approved-of state of mind. In this way, Sullivan speculated, different areas of the child's experience take on different valences. The activities of the child that tend to generate approval (and therefore, through the empathic linkage, a relaxed state in the child) are organized together under a generally positive valence ("good me"). The activities of the child that tend to generate anxiety (and therefore an anxious state in the child) are organized together under a generally negative valence ("bad me").

Activities of the child that provoke *intense* anxiety in the caregivers (and therefore, through the empathic linkage, intense anxiety in the child) are of a different order. Sullivan believed that intense anxiety is extremely disruptive and generates points of amnesia for the experience immediately preceding it. Thus activities that regularly provoke intense anxiety in the particular surrounding adults are not experienced as versions of the child at all—they become "not me," dissociated states which are not organized into any form that the child, and later the adult, recognizes as himself.

The Self-System

The final and crucial step in the child's assumption of some degree of control over his own experience comes with the realization that he can shape his own activities in a direction which will make it more likely that "good mother" will appear and less likely that "bad mother" will appear. A more active set of processes (the *self-system*) develops, allowing access to awareness largely to "good me" and excluding "not me" altogether. The self-system steers activities away from gestures and behaviors associated with rising anxiety in the child's caregivers (and therefore also in himself) and toward gestures and behaviors associated with decreasing anxiety in his caregivers (and therefore also in himself).

Gradually and incrementally, but inevitably, the self-system shapes the child to fit into the niche supplied by the personalities of his significant others. The myriad potentialities of the child become slowly and inexorably honed down, as he becomes the son of this particular mother, the son of this particular father. The outline of the child's personality is sharply etched by the acid of the parents' anxiety.

Sullivan regarded the self-system as conservative but not fixed: As the child develops, the self-system selectively steers experience in the direction of the familiar, the known. Because anxiety in infancy is so nightmarish in its impact, we all become frightened of, phobic about, anxiety itself. If there has been a great deal of anxiety in the first years of life and the self-system has developed rigid controls, genuinely new experience is virtually precluded.

Nevertheless, Sullivan felt, the major developmental epochs of childhood and early adulthood are precipitated by the emergence of a powerful need for a new form of relatedness with others (a new need for satisfaction): the need for peer relations at four or five, replacing the more or less exclusive involvement with adults; the need for a single close friend, the "chum" in preadolescence; and the need for sexual satisfaction and emotional intimacy in adolescence. Each time a new need emerges, the constraints of the self-system are loosened, making possible a new, healthier integration. Old anxieties may be overridden by the force of the new pull toward interpersonal integration on a higher level.

Sullivan never devised a comprehensive theory of development or a theory of healthy functioning. His formulations were explicitly concerned with the development of psychopathology and the response of the self to difficulties in living. Thus his formulations concerning the self all pertain to processes designed to keep anxiety at a minimum. (He termed these anti-anxiety processes *needs for security* to distinguish them from needs for satisfaction.) When anxiety is not a threat, the self-system fades into the background; needs for satisfaction emerge and operate as integrating tendencies, drawing the individual into mutually satisfying interactions with others. When anxiety is looming, the self-system dominates: controlling access to awareness, producing interactions that have been successful in minimizing anxiety in the past, selectively shaping the individual's impressions both of herself and of others she is dealing with.

Like Freud, Sullivan envisioned human experience as playing itself out in a tension between pleasure (Sullivan's "satisfactions") and the defensive regulation of wishes for pleasure (Sullivan's "security"). Yet there are several very basic differences between traditional Freudian theory and Sullivan's interpersonal approach to motivation, early development, and psychic structure:

Whereas Freud regarded sexuality and aggression as inherently asocial and inevitably conflictual, Sullivan believed that particular areas of experience become conflictual only if they tend to arouse anxiety in significant caretaking others. What is conflictual in one family may work very smoothly to generate mutual satisfaction in another. The source of difficulties is not in the inherent nature of the impulses themselves, but in the response of the human environment.

Whereas Freud regarded the intensity of conflict largely as a property of the impetus behind the drives (the amount of libido or aggression one is born with), Sullivan suggested that levels of anxiety in an individual are a direct product of levels of anxiety in their early environment. The more anxious the caretakers, the more areas of experience become tinged with anxiety for the child (there is more "bad me" and "not me").

Although there is a marked difference in terminology and sensibility between Sullivan's work and the tradition of Freudian ego psychology, there is some interesting overlap in the ways these two traditions approached theorizing about mind and development. The ego psychologists, like Sullivan, broadened the framework of analytic concern beyond Freud's focus on the individual mind and its intrapsychic interior to the interactions between the individual and the environment. The ego psychologists, like Sullivan, regarded the vicissitudes of early caretaking and the relative health or character pathology of the caretakers as crucial to the development of the child. However, the ego psychologists, as we noted in chapter 2, built their concepts alongside of or in conjunction with Freud's drive theory. They viewed mind as built up from two interpenetrating constituents: constitutional drives and an ego shaped through interaction. Sullivan, on the other hand, envisioned mind as thoroughly social. There may be constitutional differences, but the psychological valences and meanings they accrue are all derived from the way significant others respond to them.

Security Operations and the Point of Anxiety

Sullivan used the term *suave* to describe the processes of a well-functioning self-system. Each of us moves through life exquisitely sensitive to rising anxiety, developing complex, extremely rapid, covert *security operations* to steer us from points of anxiety back onto familiar footing. One of the central techniques of the interpersonal psychoanalyst is to increase awareness of the operations of the self-system by asking questions and encouraging self-reflection, so that crucial, rapid sequences can be observed, understood, and, through understanding, gradually altered.

The use of detailed inquiry marks a stark contrast between Sullivan's clinical methodology and that of Freudian psychoanalysis. In the strictest applications of the classical method, the analyst does not ask questions, and within the logic of the classical model, this is as it should be. The patient's conflicts emerge within free associations, and free associations need to be uninfluenced by any direction supplied by the analyst. The nondirectedness of the classical method is the central safeguard of the patient's autonomy and guarantees that the deepest levels of the patient's conflicts are being accessed. The analyst's function is to interpret the underlying dynamics embedded in the patient's free associations, to reveal the latent thoughts hidden therein. Of course, interpretations themselves might be viewed as directives, having an impact on subsequent associations, but it is a clear, intentional and deepening impact, sparse and off-set by long silences, that is clear and intentional. Asking questions gums up and muddies the clarity of the emerging associations without making clearly identifiable interpretive statements.

Sullivan saw the clinical situation very differently, and this difference reflects important contrasts in understanding the human mind and, particularly, language. In Sullivan's view, each of us uses language in a largely idiosyncratic fashion. The meaning of words is embedded in the original interpersonal contexts in which they were learned. It takes a long time for one person to understand the real meaning of words used by another person, particularly if what is being discussed involves intensely affective and deeply personal matters. For the analyst to assume she knows what the patient means by the words he is using and to make interpretations based on that assumed understanding is, for Sullivan, to greatly compound confusion and lose any hope of meaningful insight. The only way for the analyst to know what the patient is really talking about is to ask detailed questions. Further, the only way for the analyst to get the relevant information about the situations the patient is describing is to direct the inquiry, at least part of the time. Because of the smoothness through which the self-system steers the person away from the threat of anxiety, a patient can systematically ignore the very details and features of his experience that might be most relevant.

This inattention is clearly evident in Fred, who sought psychoanalysis because he was deeply discontented with his wife; she didn't seem to understand him, and they fought continually. He thought of her fondly during the day, and would go home from work each evening determined to make his marriage better. Yet despite their best efforts, they would fall into their customary sniping at each other, and Fred soon became discouraged.

The interpersonal analyst would be very interested in the details of what takes place between Fred and his wife. When did the fighting start last night? What does he mean when he speaks of his fondness for her? His discontent? When did Fred notice the change in his attitude toward his wife?

Fred, like most analysands beginning treatment, was a poor observer of his own psychic processes and the full range of his interactions with others. The interpersonal analyst would try to find a way to get Fred interested in those processes and interactions through an individually styled, tactful, detailed inquiry designed to broaden his field of perceptual consciousness.

What happened when he first got home on a particular evening? What sort of mood was he in? How did his wife respond? Who said what to whom? It may take many weeks of detailed inquiry for Fred to become an effective enough observer to be able to pinpoint the crucial moments in their interactions. On the evening in question, Fred and his wife both began with what seemed to be an enthusiasm for each other. She responded to his recounting of his day with an affectionate comment. He noticed the similarity of her comment to her mother's favorite manner of expressing herself, which he pointed out with some disdain. She backed off and found something critical to say about his family. They were now on familiar ground, settling comfortably into what Sullivan called a *hostile integration*.

How and why did this shift take place? If one could videotape such an interaction, the camera might pick up a flicker of vulnerability in Fred's facial expression when his wife responded tenderly to his approach to her, right before he found an opportunity to criticize her. That flicker of vulnerability is a *point of anxiety*, which, Sullivan suggested, always precedes security operations. Of course, videotapes of family interactions are generally not available to the interpersonal psychoanalyst, so she relies both on the detailed inquiry into outside events and her own experiences in interacting with the patient. The latter (countertransference) would become increasingly important in the interpersonal tradition, as we shall see.

Fred came from a family in which everyone sniped at everyone else from a position of suspicious isolation. He was very comfortable with simmering low-grade hostility. He spent his childhood and adolescence longing for someone he would not fight with, who would understand and accept him. He had many girlfriends, all of whom eventually disappointed him. The early relationship with his wife seemed more promising, but their initial intimacies soon deteriorated into the chronic bickering that drove him into treatment. Moments of tenderness between Fred and his wife make him feel anxious, vulnerable, unprotected. Feelings of tenderness in his original family had been systematically crushed. He had learned to transform any tender impulse (a need for satisfaction) rapidly and unwittingly into a posture of critical superiority, a position from which he felt quite secure and no longer vulnerable.

The interpersonal analyst uses detailed inquiry to slow down and stretch out time. Fred began treatment knowing only that despite his best intentions, he always found himself at odds with his wife. He became aware, little by little, of the way he himself used his critical superiority to push his wife away. He became sensitive to the gradations of his emotional state: his excitement; the way that excitement would turn into an anxious vulnerability; his feeling of security when he arranged things so that he could once again feel comfortably discouraged. The greater awareness of his own security operations made more constructive choices possible.

Sullivan viewed security operations as purchasing a short-term reduction in anxiety at the price of a long-term maintenance of the anxiety-causing situation. Security operations always work. As soon as Fred begins to think his wife is defective, he becomes less anxious; yet in the long run he is stuck with this defective woman. It is their immediate effectiveness that makes security operations so tenacious, amenable to change only through a great deal of hard analytic work. The effectiveness of security operations draws on the same principle as the old joke about the man who snaps his fingers to keep the tigers away. "But there aren't any tigers around here," his companion points out. "See how well it works," answers the omnipotent finger-snapper. Security operations are the self-system's anxiety-reducing maneuvers for warding off anticipated threats, overgeneralized from earlier interpersonal situations.

The more the patient understands about the workings of the self-system in its efforts to avoid anxiety, the more easily that patient can make different choices, Sullivan believed. The kind of change Sullivan regarded as the goal of treatment has something in common with insight, as Freud understood it. But change for Sullivan was not just *conceptual*, it was largely *perceptual* (Bromberg, 1980, 1989), as awareness of both internal processes and also sequences of interpersonal actual events expands. Fred became aware of the ease with which he bailed out of points of intimacy and therefore vulnerability with his wife. To stay in the situation would make him more anxious in the short run but enhanced the chances for resolving his chronic marital unhappiness in the long run. The magic of the finger-snapping (disparagement of his wife), although extremely tempting, came to be understood as a distraction that removed him from the underlying causes of his doubts and unhappiness.

SULLIVAN'S APPROACH TO OBSESSIONALS

Some of Sullivan's most important contributions were developed in his clinical work with obsessionals, people who tend to be extremely controlling of both themselves and others: stingy, competitive, fastidious, and mired in paralyzing detail. Freud thought about them originally in terms of an anal fixation, as struggling with anal libidinal wishes to mess up, to defy the regimes of toilet training and social cleanliness. He saw their controlling character traits as complex defenses (reaction formations) against, or disguised expressions of, these impulses to mess and defy. Freud later noted the importance of sadism in the dynamics of obsessionalism, and this theme was developed further by Wilhelm Reich. Obsessionals were portrayed as sadistic and power-hungry. Their controlling personality characteristics were understood as an expression of their wish to gain and maintain power over others, or, alternatively, as an expression of efforts to defend against those wishes through deference and obsequiousness.

Sullivan developed a very different understanding. He regarded the obsessional's need for control not as reflecting anal eroticism, a primary sadism, or concern with power, but rather as a preemptive defense against anticipated humiliation and profound anxiety. Obsessionals, Sullivan found, were raised in families of hypocrites. They were brutalized, either physically or emotionally, while at the same time being told they were loved, that the beating or the humiliation was done for their own good, out of caring for them. Obsessionals, in Sullivan's view, are deeply confused, mystified. They dread engagements with other people, because they anticipate ending up feeling bad and helpless without understanding why or how. Their power maneuvers are motivated by a need to disarm others, to remove them as threats to their sense of security.

The intrapsychic framework of Freudian psychoanalysis casts the patient as rent by a fierce internal battle. Dangerous impulses are pushing for expression; sturdy defenses are erected against those impulses. The enervating struggle between these internal forces drains energy from possibilities for more satisfying living. The scene of the action is in the patient's internal world. In Sullivan's interpersonal framework, the patient is viewed as striving to maintain security in her dealings with others. Past relationships have resulted in deep pain and humiliation; security operations have developed to ward off those dangers in present relationships. The scene of the action is in the patient's interactions with others.

The analyst's role, as Sullivan understood it, is to increase the patient's awareness of her ways of participating in those interactions. The patient begins to notice significant features that she has been studiously avoiding. She comes to appreciate the extent to which her effective efforts to control anxiety in the short run preclude a more satisfying life in the long run. The patient's relationship with the analyst is often a powerful medium for demonstrating the self-limiting features of characterological security operations. Sullivan pointed to the inevitability of the patient's enacting important interpersonal patterns in that relationship. But he did not make an exploration of the analytic relationship itself a central feature of his technical approach. That was left to subsequent interpersonal theorists.

The analysis of Emily, an extremely resourceful and extremely obsessional young woman, illustrates how a patient's pattern of relating can be played out with the analyst. Emily came to treatment because of her difficulties in establishing satisfying relationships with other people, both men and women. She tended to put people off for reasons she did not understand; she found herself irritated and impatient with others. She was talented and successful in many areas of her life, in all of which she worked on her own. She tended to feel that in most of her activities—in her work, around her house, sexually in her bed—she could do it better by herself than relying on others. She was so good at what she did that the wisdom of this approach seemed to be substantiated again and again.

Emily began to pursue the analytic work in her characteristically efficient fashion. She identified problem areas, worked hard to present and explore relevant material, both past and present, and came up with interesting and often helpful insights. The work seemed to be going so well that it took the analyst a while to realize he felt somewhat extraneous to the process, that he felt discouraged by Emily from saying much. When he did speak, Emily would address his contribution and seemed to make good use of it. But he became increasingly aware that he always felt he was interrupting something he perhaps should be staying out of. He became interested in this process and began to pick up the subtle ways Emily managed to convey this impression: the prepared agenda she brought to each session, the focused thoroughness with which she pursued that agenda, the way she eventually worked her responses to the analyst back around to her original concerns.

The analyst asked Emily about her experience at the point at which he began to speak: he had the impression that she always felt somehow interrupted. Emily at first quickly rejected this observation, as if to reassure the analyst that his efforts were appreciated. Eventually Emily was able to reflect more fully on these moments, and she began to realize how at odds she was with herself regarding the analyst's potential contributions. On the one hand, she came for treatment because she knew she needed help and felt a great regard for the analyst's professional abilities. On the other hand, she did operate in the analysis as she operated in all interpersonal situations: with a deep conviction that she could do whatever needed to be done better by herself. She did feel that she had been thrown off the track whenever the analyst spoke. As she was talking about her concerns and offering her associations to various topics, it was if she were chugging along productively. When the analyst began to speak, it meant she had to deal with *him, his* thoughts, which could only be a distraction from her own focus, her own sense of where she needed to go. Of course, she was there because she wanted to know his thoughts, so she made every effort to listen to and consider them. But without really being aware of it, she felt a powerful internal pressure to work herself free of his thoughts as soon as she could so that she could once again make her customary progress on her own.

What was the paradigm for the security operations Emily and her analyst were delineating in her present patterns of relating? Emily's parents were both extremely emotional, anxious, intense. The father, a businessman who moved through cycles of great successes and cataclysmic failures, was extremely self-absorbed and had little time to focus on his children. Of Emily's three siblings, two had gone into the father's business; their own personal concerns seem to have been swallowed up by the maelstrom generated by the father's activities and anxieties. Emily's mother was treated as imbecilic and incompetent. Constantly panicked about the ups and downs of the father's business activities, from which she was excluded, she continually turned to Emily tearfully for reassurance. Neither parent seemed capable of attending to Emily's needs; they broke into her world only when they needed something from her.

As these processes in the present and their roots in the past became clearer and more available for Emily to think about, the analyst asked whether she could imagine the possibility that he might introduce a thought that would take her somewhere useful that neither of them had previously envisioned. Of course, Emily could have answered yes reflexively to such a question. But the analytic inquiry into her manner of maintaining security by controlling the access of others to her own thought processes had made her more deeply aware of how she operated. As she thought about that question more reflectively, she became aware of how little she really allowed for the possibility of getting anything terribly useful from anyone else, and of how her self-controlling manner of directing her own experience made such a possibility extremely unlikely. Maintaining security in the present undermined her chances of broadening her security-enhancing network of relationships in the long run.

CONTEMPORARY INTERPERSONAL PSYCHOANALYSIS

The person most responsible for shaping interpersonal psychoanalysis in its contemporary form was Clara Thompson (1893–1958). She had been trained in classical Freudian analysis at the New York Psychoanalytic Institute and had been analyzed in Budapest by Sandor Ferenczi, the most experimental and controversial of the major figures surrounding Freud. Ferenczi broke with Freud over the issue of sexual abuse of children by adults, believing actual incidents to be the cause of neuroses, in contrast to Freud's emphasis on instinctually based fantasy. Ferenczi also felt the analyst had to be more than a detached observer of the patient's dynamics; the analyst's deep and genuine caring was essential to overcome the trauma caused by early abuse.

Thompson found a close compatibility between Ferenczi's emphasis on the importance of actual relationships, past and present, and Sullivan's interpersonal theory. To complete the amalgam that Thompson fashioned into her version of interpersonal psychoanalysis she added Erich Fromm's "humanistic psychoanalysis." Fromm (1900–1980) had repositioned much of Freud's account of psychodynamic forces within a broader Marxist conception of history and an existentialist vision of human nature.

Human beings develop different character types at various points in history, Fromm reasoned, because different types of societies require particular types of people to perform specific socioeconomic functions. We are profoundly social creatures who dread isolation above all else; there is thus a tremendous pressure for all people to shape themselves according to social need. The separation of experience into conscious and unconscious realms is determined, therefore, not by the inherent primitivity of instinctual drives, but by the social selection of desirable and undesirable traits from the broad range of human possibilities. In Fromm's view, the unconscious is a social creation, maintained because of the deep abhorrence each of us has of our own freedom and the social isolation we fear may result from a fuller expression of our authentic, personal experience.[2]

Thompson wove Sullivan's interpersonal theory (which he always considered a school of psychiatry, not psychoanalysis) with strands from Ferenczi and Fromm into the loose fabric of interpersonal psychoanalysis, less a comprehensive, integrated theory than a common set of theoretical emphases and a clinical methodology. Two broad developments in the interpersonal tradition from Sullivan's early contributions to current interpersonal practice greatly reflect the impact of Fromm's thought.

First, the emphasis has shifted markedly from the past to the present, from the there and then to the here and now. Sullivan placed great importance on the patient's personal history, suggesting that treatment begin with an exhaustive investigation of the patient's background and all significant developmental phases. In order to understand what was happening in the current interpersonal field, Sullivan felt, it was necessary for the therapist to have a firm sense of the illusory personifications, shaped in the past, with whom the patient was interacting in the present. A full understanding of a patient's current security operations depended on the analyst's knowing how they had come into being in their original interpersonal contexts.

Contemporary interpersonal analysts (like many contemporary Freudians; see chapter 9) have tilted the balance between past and present more toward the present. The concept of "character," central to the contributions of both Thompson and Fromm, became increasingly important. What mattered was not so much a reconsideration of the patient's early, formative relationships but the manner in which those relationships shaped an approach to living in the present. The crucial scene of the action was felt to be the patient's way of integrating relationships with others (and the relationship with the analyst was regarded as the key arena in which this could be observed). A preoccupation with the past was in many cases regarded as a distraction from (sometimes an avoidance of) dealing with real issues taking place in the present between patient and analyst.

In a second and closely related development, the personal experience of the analyst came to be regarded as much more activated by and embedded in the analytic situation; *countertransference* (the analyst's personal experience of the patient) was now regarded as a crucial feature of the analytic process.[3]

Sullivan described the analyst's way of engaging the patient as "participant observation." The patient attempts to draw the analyst into his characteristic forms of interaction. The analyst, like a sensitive instrument, uses her awareness of these subtle interpersonal pulls and pushes to develop hypotheses about the patient's security operations. But Sullivan did not regard it as helpful for the analyst to get deeply personally involved with the patient. The analyst was an expert at interpersonal relations, and her expert status would keep her from getting drawn into pathological integrations. She needs to be aware enough of minor eruptions of anxiety within herself to avoid engaging in security operations of her own. The competent analyst would not need anything interpersonally from the patient and therefore would have no strong or turbulent feelings for the patient.

Contemporary interpersonal analysts tend to position the analyst differently. The patient's interpersonal gambits are regarded as powerful inducements to join the patient in his relational patterns. The analyst is regarded as having interpersonal needs, anxieties, and security operations that are inevitably evoked in interactions with the patient. Because the present is given relatively more weight than the past, the analyst is seen less as a semi-detached observer of the patient's operations and more as a full participant in interpersonal patterns they create and maintain together.

Edgar Levenson (1972), the most influential of contemporary interpersonal theorists, has used the term *isomorphic transformations* to describe the way the same fundamental interactional patterns that constitute the patient's personality are repeated in all important areas of his life: in the past, in current relationships outside the analytic situation, and in the analytic relationship itself.

Let us reconsider Emily's treatment from a more contemporary interpersonal perspective. We had noted that she had learned, in her relationship with her parents, that other people were not likely to contribute anything positive to her experience, but required careful handling and deflecting. The analyst was able to describe to Emily her characteristic mode of operating with others and the way it functioned at cross-purposes with her seeking help from the analyst. But how did the analyst arrive at this understanding?

The important relationships in Emily's life all reflected the same pattern. She kept her parents, her close friends, her boyfriends at a measured distance from the center of her life: her own intense, isolated productivity. She would check in with others, ascertain what they seemed to need from her, and provide it effectively. She tended to regard the men she became involved with as excessively dependent and clingy, and, according to her descriptions, they indeed seemed to be. She experienced everyone she was involved with as somehow wanting a great deal from her and was proud of her facility for being helpful to them. She was always genuinely surprised when lovers or friends broke off relationships with her because they somehow felt a lack of commitment on her part.

The analyst experienced himself as being treated by Emily with officious respect. Her job involved periodic, unplanned trips out of town, necessitating occasional phone calls to cancel and reschedule sessions. Returning Emily's phone calls entailed dealing with her secretary, who handled the analyst the way she handled Emily's clients, properly guarding the time of her important employer, with a slight air of condescension toward those who would intrude upon it.

As noted above, the analyst felt Emily could drive the sessions along largely on her own. Nevertheless, he generally found some way to engage her that seemed productive. What he began to notice, however, was an odd discontinuity between his experience at the end of each session and the beginning of the next. He would generally end sessions with a sense of accomplishment and connection with Emily. On her return for the next session she always seemed somehow remote and a bit perplexed about what she was doing there. She often had no memory of the previous session and would sometimes begin by saying something like, "Well, what shall we talk about today?" as if arriving at a meeting whose agenda was organized by

someone else. When it was established that the analyst did not having anything to propose, it became apparent that Emily invariably did have something to work on, and worked productively. This way of beginning sessions
increasingly struck the analyst as having an odd, almost ritualized quality,
the effect of which was to create the impression that she was meeting the
analyst for the first time.

The analyst became increasingly aware of several features of his experience of Emily. Despite his efforts to maintain his professional dignity, he felt
put off by the way Emily and her secretary treated him, by the continual
reminders that her time, indeed, her very existence, was more important
than his. He also became aware of a subtle but increasingly discernible
pressure to make himself useful to Emily, to break into her self-contained
labors, to be important to her. He began to realize that the ritualized beginnings of sessions and the discontinuity in emotional connectedness between
one session and the next were designed to negate him and his impact. It was
as if the value of his previous efforts had evaporated, and he had to begin
all over again.

These self-observations and reflections led the analyst to an understanding of Emily's patterns of interacting with others. She was handling the analyst in the same manner she handled others: she expected nothing terribly
useful, discerned what he needed, took care of that, and went on her way.
The analyst was able to use his reactions to Emily (the countertransference)
as a source of hypotheses about the ways she was structuring her relationship with him along characteristic lines.

The analyst began to describe his sense that Emily kept him at a distance,
let him contribute only reluctantly, and had dispersed his input by the time
she returned for the next session. He of course did not lay this on her all at
one time, but rather, little by little, with what he felt was a sympathetic
regard for her underlying anxiety and the historical need for these security
operations. Emily responded in two ways: Sometimes she was hurt and genuinely puzzled about how the analyst could possibly feel diminished by her
when she had been so conscientious in her efforts as a patient. Sometimes
she reacted in an "understanding" and concerned fashion, as if to reassure
the analyst that he really had something to offer. It gradually became apparent that there were many ways that Emily experienced the analyst as similar to her friends and lovers—as someone who needed to feel wanted, was
excessively demanding, and needed reassurance.

How should we understand Emily's beliefs about the analyst's vulnerabilities and the necessity for her careful handling of them? Were they transference? In the classical Freudian model they would be considered tempo-
ral displacements, pieces of the patient's history infused with sexual and

aggressive aims that were superimposed on the present experience with the analyst. Sullivan would understand them similarly as displaced fragments of earlier interpersonal integrations, sensed by the analyst through his own participation in the present.

A contemporary interpersonal analyst would begin with the assumption that Emily's beliefs about the analyst were likely to be grounded in her actual interactions with him in the present. Although shaped according to the patterns derived from the past, the patient's transference is seen as a living reaction to the analyst's actual presence and behavior, and the analyst's countertransference is seen as a living reaction to the patient's actual presence and behavior.

Within this frame of reference, Emily's lofty self-sufficiency and productive superiority have had an inevitable impact on the analyst's experience with her, undermining his sense of what he had to offer. He tried to deal with his own anxiety by pressing to find an opening into her solitary labors, to make himself useful. She experienced this pressure in him the way she experienced pressure for contact in the people around her—as a needful demand for her to make the other person feel reassured so that she could get on with her important activities.

From the point of view of the Freudian and classical interpersonal traditions, the analyst's emotional involvement in these interactions with Emily reflected a departure from what the analyst should be doing: observing and then either interpreting or asking questions from an emotionally neutral position. From a contemporary interpersonal point of view, there *is* no emotionally neutral position. The analyst will get caught up in the patient's dynamics no matter how hard he tries not to. The very idea that he might be free of the interactional mix itself is a problem, because it blinds the analyst to his own involvement and requires the patient to collude in that denial. Thus if Emily's analyst was not aware of the extent to which she had gotten under his skin, he would be likely to make interpretations or ask questions that had a punitive, retaliatory, or beseeching quality. Emily in turn would be likely to experience the interpretations or questions in precisely that way. Because Emily was convinced that the analyst, like everyone else she was close to, was exceedingly vulnerable and needy, this would be the last thing in the world she would want to talk about. She believed it to be true, and therefore had to believe that the analyst would not want to be confronted with it. If the treatment continued, it would be built on a collusion between analyst and analysand, an implicit agreement to pretend that what they were understanding in the patient's relationships with all the important figures in her life was not happening between them.

In the contemporary interpersonal framework, the analyst assumes that, despite his best intentions, he and the patient will end up playing out the characteristic dynamic patterns of the patient's inner life. As these patterns are identified in other relationships, the analyst looks for the ways they are also emerging in his experience and in the interaction of the analytic relationship.

What does the analyst do with this more interactive perspective? There are several possibilities. Levenson speaks of the analyst gradually "resisting transformation." Understanding the ways the analyst has been induced into the repetitive scenario in itself opens up the possibility of a different sort of presence with the patient. As the analyst reflects on and becomes clearer about his own participation, that exploration itself creates a different form of participation. Some of that exploration may go on solely in the mind of the analyst. Some of it may involve confronting the patient with her side of the interaction. Some of it may entail a judicious disclosure to the patient of the analyst's own experience.

In working on these issues with Emily, her analyst had a fantasy that he ended up sharing with her, which became a point of reference for the two of them. He told her he imagined himself as a door-to-door salesman of vacuum cleaners who would show up every few days and try to interest her in his product. She was always surprised to see him, and treated him as if they had never met before. Despite her skepticism, he demonstrated his cleaner and she was interested. He should come back again, she suggested, but when he did, she acted as though he was arriving for the first time, and they would begin all over again. Meanwhile, she was getting her house cleaned.

What was at stake in acknowledging the possibility that the analyst might actually help her? Did it involve a concession that her house was dirty? A humiliating and dangerous admission that she cannot do everything herself? If she exposed herself to the unfamiliar dependence on another's help, did she fear being enslaved forever, either by her own needs or by having to reciprocate and take care of the other in a total and terrifying fashion? Could she sustain the uncertainty at the point of anxiety long enough to allow for something else to happen? These are the kinds of questions that characterized subsequent analytic inquiry.

A rich set of controversies concerning technical implications and clinical options has been generated by the interpersonal view of the analytic process in which the analyst's participation is taken more fully into account. We will consider these issues further in chapter 9. It should be noted here that there has been a broad movement across all the major psychoanalytic traditions in the direction of a more interactive approach to the analytic situation. The interpersonalists have served, in effect, as pioneers who opened up a radical (and still controversial, undeveloped, and problematic) conceptual territory that other settlers have moved into at a more cautious pace.

Sullivan's work has been prescient with respect to other recent trends in psychoanalytic thought and contemporary intellectual culture. Psychoanalysis has played a major role in the development of a complex, decentered, contextualized understanding of what it means to be a person.[4] We noted in chapter 1 that Freud's exploration of unconscious processes challenged the belief, held for centuries, that the mind is transparent to itself, and that conscious experience is the center of initiative and meaning. Although written in a very different technical language, Sullivan's work represents a radical extension of that theme. The person one takes oneself to be, the self-system, is a construction, Sullivan suggested, whose purpose is to invent illusions to dispel anxiety.[5] Although we experience ourselves as *having* a self as a quasi-object inside us, we partially construct ourselves variably through memories and anticipations in the moment, depending on the interpersonal context we find ourselves in. Although we experience ourselves as singular, we actually operate through multiple self-organizations that are keyed in to experiences of the other(s) with whom we find ourselves interacting.

In contrast to Freud's notion of the self as organized vertically, with conflictual areas buried by repression, Sullivan introduced a vision of the self as organized and partitioned horizontally, with incompatible areas separated through dissociative processes. (See Bromberg, 1991, 1993, for a recent development of this approach to the self.) This understanding of self as decentered, multiple, and contextualized is central to the ways subjectivity and experience have been explored in many areas of contemporary philosophy, literature, and social criticism.

4

MELANIE KLEIN AND CONTEMPORARY KLEINIAN THEORY

Now that my ladder's gone,
I must lie down where all ladders start,
In the foul rag-and-bone shop of the heart.

—W. B. Yeats

If you hate a person, you hate something in him that is part of
yourself. What isn't part of ourselves doesn't disturb us.

—Hermann Hesse

Melanie Klein (1882–1960) has had
more impact on contemporary psychoanalysis than any other psychoanalytic writer since Freud. Klein's intent, which she continually reaffirmed throughout her long and productive career, was to merely validate and extend Freud's hypotheses through direct observation and clinical work with children.[1] Yet her discoveries led to a vision of mind that is strikingly different from Freud's in many basic respects.

Klein made enormous contributions to psychoanalysis; psychoanalysis (according to Klein's biographer, Phyllis Grosskurth) seems to have saved Klein. Melanie Reizes Klein's early adulthood in Vienna was dominated by a suffocating relationship with her mother and a troubled, deeply unsatisfying marriage. She suffered severe depressions and seems to have been rapidly deteriorating into the life of a psychological invalid when, in 1914, she discovered Freud's work on dreams "and realized immediately that was what I was aiming at, at least during those years when I was so very keen to find out what would satisfy me intellectually and emotionally" (quoted in Grosskurth, 1986, p. 69).

Klein, who had moved to Budapest, entered psychoanalysis in 1914 with Sandor Ferenczi, one of Freud's closest and most influential disciples, and began writing psychoanalytic papers on her observations of and clinical work with children (initially her own two sons and daughter) in 1919. Her work quickly captured the interest of Karl Abraham, another key figure in the early decades of psychoanalysis. He invited her to Berlin, where she had a brief analysis with him before his untimely death in 1925. In 1926 Klein was invited by the Freud translator and biographer Ernest Jones to move to England (Jones's interest in Klein was partly as an analyst to his own children), where she lived and did her controversial work till her death in 1960.

By the late 1920s Klein and her followers had already begun to clash with the more traditional Freudians, dividing the psychoanalytic world into the "London school" and the "Viennese school." The initial issues on which Klein and Anna Freud differed concerned technical problems with regard to analyzing children. Klein took the position that children were analyzable, much in the way adults are, as long as their play is interpreted the way an adult analysand's free associations are interpreted. Anna Freud argued that small children are not analyzable because the weak and undeveloped ego cannot handle deep interpretations of instinctual conflict. She recommended a quasi-educational approach to children with emotional problems.

Shortly after Sigmund Freud and his daughter, Anna, finally left Vienna and moved to London in 1938, barely escaping the Nazis, the battle between the Kleinians and (Anna) Freudians culminated in a series of vituperative discussions within the British psychoanalytic society on what had developed into wide-ranging differences in both theory and technique. The result was a splitting of the society into different groups, which still exist to this day. (A third group, the independents, was formed around the contributions of Fairbairn and Winnicott.) The schism within the British society broadened into a deep rift within the contemporary international psychoanalytic community, dividing Kleinian from Freudian psychoanalysts ideologically, politically, educationally, and clinically.

Up until the 1980s, the dominant ideology within American psychoanalysis was Freudian ego psychology, which, as we noted in chapter 2, was greatly shaped by the work of Anna Freud. The schism within the British society between the (Anna) Freudians and the Kleinians resulted in a lingering antipathy in the American tradition toward the contributions of Klein.

Consequently, Kleinian theory was either largely ignored or summarily dismissed by psychoanalysts in the United States, and Kleinian authors also became insulated from developments in other theoretical traditions.[2]

Political loyalties and the common use of technical terms can make it difficult to grasp clearly just how different Klein's understanding of mind is from Freud's.

Sigmund Freud saw the central neurotic conflict as concerned with secrets and self-deceptions. The core of this conflict is formed in the culmination of infantile sexual life, the oedipal phase, during which the five- or six-year-old struggles with intense and dangerous incestuous wishes, Freud believed. Klein became interested in earlier processes. She found what she felt was evidence that Freud's hypotheses about the older child (five or six years old) could apply to the much younger child (two or three years) and even to the infant. In extending Freud's theories to earlier developmental phases, Klein argued that fantasies of both incestuous union (Oedipus complex) and terrifying self-punishments (superego) are present from a very young age, although in more "primitive," frightening forms. Yet to read Klein as merely extending Freud backward in developmental time misses the dramatic difference between the mind as Freud saw it and the mind as Klein came to see it. The elaboration of oedipal conflicts in the mind of the infant began to take on a very different quality from the oedipal drama Freud had depicted.

Freud's patients were adults, with coherent, if conflictual and tormented, lives. Klein's patients during the 1920s and 1930s, the patients who most influenced the development of her thought, were children, many of them extremely disturbed and terrified. Freud's patients were neurotic; he considered psychosis inaccessible to analytic treatment, because the totality of emotional withdrawal it entailed made impossible a transference of repressed oedipal wishes and fears onto the person of the analyst. During the 1950s and 1960s Klein and her followers applied techniques and understanding gained from work with young children to psychotic adult patients. Their withdrawal and bizarre behavior were understood by Klein as desperate efforts to ward off the terrors she had witnessed in the play of children.

For Freud, the psyche is shaped through the oedipal conflict into stable and coherent structures, with hidden recesses and illicit designs. In an increasingly dramatic although unannounced fashion, Klein substituted for Freud's vision a portrayal of mind as a continually shifting, kaleidoscopic stream of primitive, phantasmagoric images, fantasies, and terrors. For Klein, the psyche, not just of the small child but of the adult as well, remains always unstable, fluid, constantly fending off psychotic anxieties. For Freud, each of us struggles with bestial wishes, fears of retribution, and guilt. For Klein, each of us struggles with the deep terrors of annihilation (paranoid anxiety) and utter abandonment (depressive anxiety).

The issues that created the early divergence between Melanie Klein and Anna Freud around the accessibility of the child's mind to analytic inter- pretation have had remarkable staying power. Klein came to regard the adult mind in the same way she understood the child's—as beset with deep, psychotic-like terrors, as unstable, dynamic, and fluid, and as always responsive to "deep" analytic interpretations. The ego psychological tradi- tion (which we traced in chapter 2) is based on a view of the adult mind as highly structured and stable, stratified by layers of ego capacities and defenses. According to the ego psychologists, for adults in analysis, deep interpretations of intrapsychic conflict can come only from layer-by-layer interpretive work, from the surface down. The Kleinians tend to view ego psychology as concerned with shallow dimensions of emotional life. The ego psychologists tend to view the Kleinians as wildly interpretive, over- whelming patients with concepts they cannot possible understand or use (Greenson, 1974). It is only in the last several years that there has appeared the beginning of a rapprochement between contemporary Kleinian authors and some American writers who have emerged from the ego psychology tradition (Schafer, 1994).

Klein's most important and abiding contribution to the development of psychoanalytic thought was her depiction of what she termed the "para- noid-schizoid" and "depressive" positions. To grasp what Klein meant by these two positions requires an appreciation of several basic features of her theory. So let us consider a piece of clinical experience and the way it might be understood in Kleinian terms, particularly with respect to the paranoid- schizoid and depressive positions.

THE PARANOID-SCHIZOID POSITION

After several years in analysis, Rachel, a waitress in her mid-twenties, recalled with great vividness an experience, not thought about for years, that had dominated both her waking and dream life as a child. As far back as she could remember, she had felt tormented by two vivid and intense images and their relationship to each other. She couldn't remember whether these images had begun as parts of a dream and then had been taken up in her waking fantasy, or whether they had begun as a daydream and infil- trated her dream life. The first image was of tiny, extremely delicate flow- ers. The second image was of enormous humanlike figures, menacing, with- out features, composed entirely of feces. The two images were bound together in a way she did not understand but felt compelled somehow to resolve. She would think of the flowers and then the shit people, then the flowers, then the shit people.

The images were as opposite as could be imagined, yet Rachel felt they belonged together. She wanted them to merge, to be integrated in some fashion, but she couldn't figure out how to do it. It was as if there were a magnetic force drawing them together, but an even more powerful force, as with magnets of the same pole, keeping them apart. Central to her sense of the impossibility of their merger was her dread that such an integration would result in the destruction of the delicate, vulnerable flowers; they would be submerged and buried forever under the massive, ominous shit people. The longing to merge these two images would return again and again with great urgency, both in her waking and in her dream life, but she could never resolve the tension posed by their intense polarity.

The drama of these images became a central, organizing theme of Rachel's analysis and came to be understood as containing and representing a great deal of information about the structure of her subjective world. She had had an absolutely wretched childhood, beginning with a sequence of experiences that would likely have completely crushed someone with less native intelligence and resourcefulness.

Rachel's father had died during her first year of life and her mother became progressively physically and mentally debilitated and unable to care for her. Rachel was raised by a cousin of her mother's in a rural area. This surrogate mother was striking in her inconsistency. She took care of Rachel and sometimes seemed affectionate toward her; at other times she would turn on her in a vicious, paranoid fashion. There was ample evidence in Rachel's memories to suggest that this surrogate mother suffered from a schizophrenic condition. The woman's husband, a chronic alcoholic, provided little refuge; he was at times emotionally available and caring but more often remote or simply absent from the home.

In her analysis, Rachel began to realize that the two images, the flowers and the shit people, were so important because they represented in a collapsed but extremely vivid way the experiential quality of her life, especially her childhood, but her adult life as well. It was as if she had two very different kinds of experiences, and they had virtually nothing to do with each other.

A good deal of the time, she felt a dark, ominous heaviness about herself and other people. She felt she was filled with ugly destructiveness, a hate that was directed toward everyone, including herself, that knew no bounds, that, if unleashed, would destroy both herself and those around her. In this shit world, other people were experienced as being menacing and hateful toward her as well. Everything was clear and consistent. No relief, no escape was possible. There were no surprises. The hatred she felt in the world outside herself was deeply connected to her experience of her own inner nature.

At other times Rachel felt a very different kind of experience, in isolated, circumscribed moments with some of her acquaintances (she had no real friends), and especially when listening to music or reading poetry. The general sense of bleakness and darkness would lift and she would have a warm feeling, both from herself toward the other person and from the other person toward her (the other most often consisted of long-deceased poets and composers). The experiences with poetry and music had a relative consistency to them; they could be evoked by her and seemed to be a reliable basis on which she developed and shaped relationships to poets and composers over time. When these experiences happened in relation to real people, they seemed moving but dangerous, totally unpredictable; it was very important not to anticipate them, long for them, try to make them happen.

The images of the flowers and the shit people were crystallizations of these two pervasive modes in which Rachel's experience was generated, these two strikingly different worlds in which she lived. She longed to bring them together, to lighten the gloom, to have a greater sense of continuity, to feel that positive connections and loving moments could be a consistent feature of her relationships with real, live other people. Yet to do that, to really count on another for something important, to anticipate it, to try to make it happen, risked being disappointed, provoking her explosive rage and hatred. To integrate the two types of experiences risked destroying even the filaments of light that fleetingly relieved her darkness. So it seemed crucial to keep the good experiences separated as far as possible from the bad, the loving feelings from the hatred. It was essential that she experience the moments of connection as arbitrary and circumscribed, having nothing at all to do with the general sense of distance, distrust, and malevolence she experienced between herself and other people.

In Kleinian terms, the nature of these two images and their relationship to each other, central to the personal struggles of this extremely deprived young woman, reflects a universal organization of experience (the paranoid-schizoid position) that we all share in our early months and years—and that we maintain, at least episodically, throughout life. Klein derived her understanding of the ways experiences become organized from Freud's formulations, particularly his concept of instinctual drive and the dual-instinct theory, but she applied Freud's concepts in her own fashion.

As we noted in chapter 1, Freud's idea of instinctual impulse was a borderline concept between the physical and the psychical. He portrayed the impulse as beginning in an accumulation of substance in somatic tissues, outside the mind, which then generates a psychical tension in the mind, a "demand on the mind for work." "Objects" are "accidentally" discovered in the external world, such as the breast during feeding, which are found to be useful in eliminating the libidinal tension of the drive, and these objects are thereby associatively linked to the impulse.

Klein never departed from the language of Freud's instinct theory. All her contributions derive from and are framed in terms of Freud's postulation of libidinal and aggressive energies as the basic fuel of mind, and the gratification of and defense against libidinal and aggressive impulses as the underlying drama of mental life. Yet Klein's formulations markedly altered these conceptual building blocks.

For Freud, the instinctual impulse was discrete and distinguishable both from the mind from which it demands gratification and from the object to which it becomes serendipitously associated. Klein gradually extended the concept of the impulse on both ends, both in terms of the source from which it arises and in terms of the aim toward which it is directed.

Klein's instinctual impulse, although embedded in bodily experience, was much more complex and personal. She saw libidinal and aggressive impulses not as discrete tensions, but as entire ways of experiencing oneself, as "good" (both loved and loving) or as "bad" (both hated and destructive). Although libido and aggression are expressed in terms of body parts and substances, they are generated by and reflect more complex organizations of experience and senses of self, Klein believed.

For Freud, the *aim* of the impulse was discharge; the object was the accidentally discovered means toward that end. Klein regarded objects as built into the experience of the impulse itself. To experience thirst, even prior to drinking, was to long for, in some vague and inchoate fashion, the object of that thirst. The object of desire was implicit in the experience of desire itself. The libidinal impulse to love and protect contained, embedded within it, an image of a lovable and loving object; the aggressive impulse to hate and destroy contained, embedded within it, an image of a hateful and hating object, Klein believed.

Freud's account of the workings of the structural model conjures up an image of a cohesive and integrated ego, now dealing with a specific libidinal impulse, now dealing with a specific aggressive impulse. Klein's account of early experience conjures up an image of a discontinuous ego, vacillating between a loving orientation toward loving and lovable other people and a hateful orientation toward hating and hateful other people. Rachel's flowers and shit people are not merely vehicles for libidinal and aggressive discharge; they represent more complex relationships between a particular kind of self and a particular kind of other. Although Klein retained Freud's terminology, her understanding of the basic stuff of mind had shifted, from impulses to relationships, leading to a very different view of the underlying dramas of mental life.

Klein portrayed the infant's experience as composed of two sharply polarized states, dramatically contrasting in both conceptual organization and emotional tone. The paradigmatic images of these states involve the infant at the breast. In one state, the infant feels bathed with love. A "good breast," filled with a wondrous nutriment and transforming love, infuses him with life-sustaining milk and envelops him in loving protection. He in turn loves the "good breast" and is deeply grateful for its protective ministrations. At other times, the infant feels persecuted and in pain. His belly is empty, and his hunger is attacking him from within. The "bad breast," hateful and malevolent, has fed him bad milk, which is now poisoning him from within, then abandoned him. He hates the "bad breast" and is filled with intensely destructive retaliatory fantasies.

It is important to keep in mind that this account, written in adult language, makes assumptions about the experiences of preverbal infants; it attempts to cross a boundary that we can never fully cross. Klein and her collaborators always assumed that what they were depicting in more or less clear verbal terms referred to experiences in the child that were likely to be neither clear nor verbal, but amorphous and phantasmagoric, at some distance from what adults are able to remember or experience themselves.

The divided world Klein depicted was seen as being formed long before any capacity for reality-testing of any sort. The infant believes that his fantasies, both loving and hateful, have powerful actual impact on the objects of those fantasies: his love for the "good breast" a protective and restorative effect, his hatred for the "bad breast" an annihilating destructiveness. It is precisely because of the omnipotence with which the child experiences his impulses that this world is an extremely dangerous place and the stakes are always very high.

Emotional equanimity in this earliest organization of experience depends on the child's ability to keep these two worlds separate. For the good breast to be a safe refuge, it must be clearly distinguishable from the malevolence of the bad breast. The child's rages against the bad breast, played out in powerful fantasies of destroying it, are experienced by the child as real, doing actual damage. It is crucial that the destructive rages be contained in the relationship to the bad object. Any confusion between the bad object and the good object could result in an annihilation of the latter, which would be catastrophic, because the demise of the good breast would leave the child without protection or refuge from the malevolence of the bad breast.

Klein termed this first organization of experience the *paranoid-schizoid position*. *Paranoid* refers to the central persecutory anxiety, the fear of invasive malevolence, coming from the outside. The shit people threaten to overrun and contaminate all goodness, both in the flowers and in Rachel's love for the flowers. *Schizoid* refers to the central defense: *splitting*, the vigilant separation of the loving and loved good breast from the hating and hated bad breast. It is urgently necessary for Rachel to keep the flowers clear of the shit people and to segregate her hatred, directed toward the latter, from her love, protectively preserving the flowers.

Why *position*? Freud had delineated a progression of psychosexual "stages" centered on different libidinal aims unfolding in a maturational sequence. Klein proposed an organization of experience (of both external reality and inner reality) and a stance vis-à-vis the world. The bifurcated world of good and bad was not a developmental phase to be traversed. It was a fundamental form for patterning experience and a strategy for locating oneself, or, more accurately, different versions of oneself, in relation to various types of others.

Klein derived the paranoid-schizoid position from the urgent necessity to defend against the persecutory anxieties generated by the death instinct. All other major psychoanalytic theorists besides Klein treated Freud's notion of a death instinct as a biological, quasi-mythological speculation, but Klein built it into the center of her theorizing. Drawing on her work with disturbed children and psychotic patients, she portrayed the newborn's state of mind in terms of anxiety about imminent annihilation, deriving from a sense of the raw, self-directed destructive force of his own aggression. The most immediate and persistent problem throughout life becomes the need to escape this paranoid anxiety, this sense that one's very existence is endangered.

The beleaguered primitive ego projects a portion of the self-directed impulses outside the boundaries of the self, thereby creating the "bad breast." It is somewhat less dangerous to feel that malevolence is located outside oneself, in an object from which one can escape, than inside oneself, from which there is no escape. Some of the remaining portion of the aggressive drive is redirected toward this malevolent external object. Thus a relationship to the original bad object has been created from the destructive force of the death instinct for the purpose of containing the threats posed by that instinct. There is a malevolent breast trying to destroy me, and I am trying to escape from and also destroy that bad breast.

To live in a world filled only with malevolence would be intolerable, so the infant also quickly projects loving impulses contained in primary narcissism out into the external world, thereby creating the "good breast." Some of the remaining portion of the libidinal drive is redirected toward this loving external object. Thus a relationship to the original good object has been created from the loving force of the libidinal instinct to serve as a counterpart to and refuge from the threat of the bad object. There is a malevolent breast trying to destroy me, and I hate and try to destroy the bad breast. There is also a good breast that loves me and protects me and which I in turn love and protect.

In this account generated by Klein's original formulations, the flowers and the shit people would be understood as projective derivatives of constitutional libidinal and aggressive drives themselves. The environment, although secondary in such a perspective, is not unimportant, for good parenting can soothe persecutory anxieties, thereby diminishing paranoid fears of bad objects and strengthening the relationship to good objects. The malevolence of the paranoid-schizoid position begins with constitutional aggression; a good environment can ameliorate its terrors. In Klein's original view, the power of the shit people reflects a constitutionally strong aggressive drive; the environmental deprivations were unable to provide the necessary taming of destructiveness and the strengthening of the fragile libidinal resources represented by the flowers.[3]

THE DEPRESSIVE POSITION

There is an inherent tendency toward integration in the patterning of experience, Klein felt, that encourages in the infant a sense of a whole object, neither all good nor all bad, but sometimes good and sometimes bad. The good breast and the bad breast begin to be understood not as separate and incompatible experiences, but as different features of the mother as a more complex other, with a subjectivity of her own.

Much is gained in the movement from the experience of others as split into good and bad to the experience of others as whole objects. Paranoid anxiety diminishes; one's pain and frustration are not caused by pure malevolence and evil, but by fallibility and inconsistency. As the threat of persecution abates, the necessity for the vigilance of splitting is reduced; the infant experiences herself as more durable, less in danger of being crushed or contaminated by external or internal forces.

Yet the gains inherent in the movement out of the paranoid-schizoid position are accompanied by new and different terrors. The central problem in life, according to Klein, is the management and containment of aggression. In the paranoid-schizoid position, aggression is contained in the hateful relationship with the bad breast, safely distanced from the loving relationship to the good breast. As the infant begins to draw together the experiences of goodness and badness into an ambivalent (both loving and hating) relationship to a whole object, the equanimity that the paranoid-schizoid position provides is shattered. The whole mother who disappoints or fails the infant, generating the pain of longing, frustration, desperation, is destroyed in the infant's hateful fantasies, not just the purely evil bad breast (with the good breast remaining untouched and protected). The whole object (both the external mother and the corresponding internal whole object) now destroyed in the infant's rageful fantasies is the singular provider of goodness as well as frustration. In destroying the frustrating whole object, the infant eliminates her protector and refuge, depopulating her world and annihilating her own insides. Klein termed the intense terror and guilt generated by the damage done to the child's loved objects by her own destructiveness *depressive anxiety* and the organization of experience in which the child relates with both love and hate toward whole objects the *depressive position.*

In the paranoid-schizoid position, the problem of inherent human destructiveness is resolved through projection, resulting in an ominous sense of persecution, danger from others. In the more integrated, more developmentally advanced depressive position, the powerful force of inherent human destructiveness creates a dread of the impact of the child's own rage on those she loves. Klein portrayed the state of the infant following a fantasy of rageful destruction toward the frustrating mother as one of deep remorse. The frustrating whole object who has been destroyed is also the loved object toward whom the child feels deep gratitude and concern. Out of that love and concern, reparative fantasies (deriving from libidinal instincts) are generated, in a desperate effort to heal the damage, to make the mother whole once again.

The child's belief in her own capacity for reparation is crucial to the ability to sustain the depressive position. To be able to keep her objects whole, the child has to believe that her love is stronger than her hate, that she can undo the ravages of her destructiveness. Klein saw the constitutional balance between libidinal and aggressive drives as crucial. (Later theorists, including D. W. Winnicott, stressed the importance of an actual mother who survives the infant's destructiveness, who returns and holds the infant's experience together.) In the best of circumstances, the cycles of loving, frustration, hateful destruction, and reparation deepen the child's ability to remain related to whole objects, to feel that her reparative capacities can balance and compensate for her destructiveness.

Even in the best of circumstances, however, this is not a static and conclusive solution. In Klein's view, we are all subject, in unconscious (and sometimes conscious) fantasy, to intense rageful destructiveness toward others, whom we experience as the source of all frustration, disappointment, physical and psychic pain. That perpetual destructiveness toward loved others represents a continual source of depressive anxiety and guilt and an unending need to make reparation. At especially difficult times, the destructiveness becomes too great, threatening to wipe out the entire object world, with no survivors. At those points, a retreat to the paranoid-schizoid position provides temporary security. The frustrating other is now experienced not as a whole object, but as a bad object. There is a good object somewhere else who would not cause such pain. The child's destructiveness is now once again contained in the relationship to the evil object, and she can rest (temporarily) secure that there are good objects out there that are safe from the destructiveness of her rage.

What is so problematic about the depressive position is the irreplaceability of the whole object, which creates what the infant experiences as her abject dependence on it. An alternative solution to the pain of depressive anxiety is the *manic defense,* in which the uniqueness of the loved object and hence one's dependence on it are magically denied. Who needs this other person anyway? Mothers/fathers/lovers are easy to come by; they're all the same, with no unique features. In the blurring of the distinctiveness of the other into a general category, one regains a sense of solace, necessarily temporary and illusory, for one's intense, helpless dependency and a sense of power over one's objects.

Klein portrays the state of relative mental health not as a developmental plateau to be reached and held but as a position continually lost and regained. Because love and hate are both perpetually generated in experience, depressive anxiety is a constant and central feature of human existence. At times of great loss, rejection, frustration, there are inevitable retreats into the security provided by the splitting of the paranoid-schizoid position and the manic defense.

In less than ideal circumstances, the child experiences her rage as more powerful than her reparative love. The integration of love and hate toward a sometimes loving and sometimes hating other cannot be sustained. The shit people will overwhelm and bury the delicate flowers. Despite the persecutory horrors of the paranoid-schizoid position, the splitting provides the only possibility of sustaining any pockets of love and security. For these people, good and evil are clearly separate. They have a few friends (sometimes only in fantasy) who are all good, and enemies who are thoroughly evil. When friends disappoint, they are instantly revealed as evil and as having been evil all along. Relationships with trusted allies cannot be clouded by even the shadow of a doubt because such doubt opens the door to inevitable and inexorable contamination.

The flowers and the shit people can be integrated only if Rachel can believe that the flowers will emerge from underneath the shit. Only a belief in one's reparative capacities, the belief that one's love can survive one's destructiveness, makes possible the integration of love and hate into richer and more complex relatedness. Love in the paranoid-schizoid position is pure but brittle and thin. Love in the depressive position, tempered through cycles of destructive hatred and reparation, is deeper, more real, more resilient; but it requires the belief that the shit will fertilize new and stronger growth rather than bury all signs of life.

The following dream of a patient in psychoanalysis might be considered as representing the transition from a more or less stable paranoid-schizoid organization into the capacity to tolerate depressive anxiety. This middle-aged man had been married for over a decade to a woman he idolized and never fought with, although he had constant battles with bosses and other figures in his life he felt were malevolent and out to get him. He idealized his analyst as well; occasional flare-ups of intense rage, precipitated by some sense of betrayal by the analyst, were quickly forgotten, and the analyst was reestablished as a wholly benign and wonderful figure. The week before he reported the dream, several years into the analysis and following many months of interpretations concerning his tendency to split his love and hate, he reported with considerable excitement the first real fight he had ever had with his wife. "I completely lost my temple—I mean my temper," he said. This is the dream:

I am wandering around in an old house that has a great sense of familiarity about it. I notice a room hidden between two floors that I realize I haven't been in for a long, long time. As I enter I notice a large fish tank with beautiful and exotic tropical fish. I remember that I had set up and stocked this tank many years before, but had forgotten about it. Amazingly, the fish had survived and actually flourished. I was very excited and thought that they must be very hungry after all these years. I reached for what I took to be a box of fish food on a shelf nearby and began sprinkling it into the water. The fish suddenly started looking sick. I looked closely at the box and realized that it was a box of salt crystals. These were freshwater fish, and the salt was deadly for them. I began frantically running around trying to do something to save them. I saw another tank with water nearby. I began scooping the fish up and transferring them to the other tank. Some of them looked dead; some of them looked like they might survive. It was hard to tell how it would turn out, and I awoke in a state of great anxiety.

In the framework of Klein's concept of the depressive position, this dream expresses the depressive anxiety of someone who is terrified of his own anger and what it might do to those he loves. He tended to split his relationships into purely good and purely bad, thereby sheltering those he loved from his rage, which he greatly feared they would not survive. Only recently had he begun to draw his love and hate together, allowing himself to contain and also express frustration and rage toward those he also loved. This made him feel both very guilty and very anxious; he was confused about his own insides, about which was stronger, his love or his hate. This movement had enriched both his relationships and his sense of his own inner life, but he was terrified that if he abandoned his compulsive idealization of his wife and his analyst, his devotion to his temples, he would not be able to maintain the relationships through love and reparation.

In this reading of the dream, the fish are whole objects, buried in his unconscious experience and long forgotten. He avoids his deep confusion about his capacities to keep his objects alive by a chronic splitting of relationships into the two floors between which the fish are hidden, worshiped idols and hated enemies. He forgets about the delicate fish. Now, after months of interpretive work on this splitting strategy, he relocates a place in his experience where more complex, although fragile, life exists. But his very recognition of a different sort of object, a love for another who is not godlike but extremely vulnerable, brings him face to face with a terror about his own capacity to sustain and nurture love. Will his destructiveness (although unintended) annihilate his objects, or will he be able to repair the damage he has done? The verdict is still out at the end of the dream (and remained out for many more months of analysis).

SEXUALITY

The difference between Klein's vision and Freud's, from which she began, is nowhere as clear as in the realm of sexuality, the centerpiece of Freud's theories of development and psychopathology. In Freud's framework, sexuality concerns pleasure, power, and fear. For the woman, sexual intercourse, on the deepest unconscious levels, is seen as providing possession of the father's penis in compensation for the narcissistic wound of her own sense of castration. She longs to become pregnant as a sign of possession of the father and of her missing penis, and of triumph over the rival, the mother. For the man, sexual intercourse, on the deepest unconscious levels, is seen as being experienced as the ultimate possession of the mother, a triumph over the father, proof that he has not been castrated for his sexual ambitions. To make a woman pregnant is a demonstration of his uncastrated, potent status.

In Klein's framework, sexuality is about love, destructiveness, and reparation. Men and women are seen as deeply concerned about the balance between their own ability to love and to hate, about their capacity to keep their objects alive, both their relationships to others as real objects and their internal objects, their inner sense of goodness and vitality. Klein viewed sexual intercourse as a highly dramatic arena in which both one's impact on the other and the quality of one's own essence are exposed and on the line. The ability to arouse and satisfy the other represents one's own reparative capacities; to give enjoyment and pleasure suggests that one's love is stronger than one's hate. The ability to be aroused and satisfied by the other suggests that one is alive, that one's internal objects are flourishing.

Pregnancy is tremendously important in this framework not as a symbolic equivalent of the penis or potency, but as a reflection of the state of one's internal object world. Fertility, both for the man and for the woman, suggests inner vitality, an internal experience that has been kept alive and flourishing. Infertility, both for the man and for the woman, is seen as arousing fears not of castration but of inner deadness, the failure of love to repair and sustain important connections with others, the inability of the self to maintain vital and nourishing relationships. For Freud, artistic creativity was a sublimated form of bodily pleasures. For Klein, both artistic creativity and bodily pleasures were arenas in which the central human struggle between love, hate, and reparation is played out.

ENVY

One of Klein's most important concepts, envy was introduced relatively late in her life but became an important feature in the development of Kleinian thought after her death.

Klein's understanding of envy is best grasped by comparing envy to greed. The infant at the breast, as is typical for Klein, provides the prototype. Infants, as Klein portrayed them, are intensely needy creatures. They feel abjectly dependent on the breast for nourishment, safety, and pleasure. The infant experiences the breast itself, Klein imagined, as extraordinarily plentiful and powerful. In more suspicious moments, the infant thinks of the breast as hoarding its wonderful substance, good milk, for itself, enjoying its power over the infant, rather than allowing the infant continual and total access to its resources.[4]

Oral greed is one response to the infant's helplessness at the breast. He is filled with impulses to totally appropriate the breast for his own needs, to use it up. The intent is not to destroy but to possess and control. The farmer in the fairy tale of the goose that laid the golden eggs, a classic allegory of greed, does not want to hurt his goose; he loves his goose. Yet he cannot stand being delivered only one golden egg each morning and kills the goose in his effort to gain access and control over her resources. Similarly, the infant's greed is not destructive in its intentions toward the breast, but deeply resentful of receiving its precious bounty only in drips and drops. Greed thus becomes ruthless in its acquisitiveness.

Envy is a different response to the same situation. The envious infant no longer wants to gain access to and possess the good, but now becomes intent on spoiling it. The infant cannot tolerate the very existence of something so powerful and important, able to make such an enormous difference in his experience, yet outside his control. The infant would rather destroy the good than remain helplessly dependent on it. The very existence of goodness arouses intolerable envy, the only escape from which is the fantasied destruction of the goodness itself.

Envy is the most destructive of all primitive mental processes. All the other hatred and destructiveness that characterize life in the paranoid-schizoid position are contained in the relation to the bad breast; through splitting, the good breast is protected as a refuge and source of solace. The extraordinary and unique feature of envy is that it is a reaction not to frustration or pain, but to gratification and pleasure. Envy is an attack not on the bad breast, but on the good breast. Thus envy undoes splitting, crosses the divide separating good from bad, and contaminates the purest sources of love and refuge. Envy destroys hope.

With her tendency to derive all important psychological processes from constitutional factors, Klein attributed excessive envy to an unusually strong inborn aggressive drive. Her depiction of envious spoiling can also be set into a different causal framework and regarded as a child's response to dramatically inconsistent parenting, where hope of responsiveness and love is perpetually stimulated but most often cruelly disappointed (see Mitchell, 1988).

Klein's concept of envy became a powerful clinical tool for understanding patients with the most severe and inaccessible psychopathology, those who have great difficulty in utilizing what psychoanalysis has to offer. Freud had described the *negative therapeutic reaction,* whereby the patient not only fails to get better through psychoanalysis but gets worse. From Freud's perspective, the problem was oedipal guilt; because of incestuous and patricidal wishes, these patients did not feel they deserved a better life. It is illustrative of the difference between Freud and Klein that the latter located the roots of the negative therapeutic reaction not in guilt over sexual and aggressive impulses but in the envious destruction of the good breast, the obliteration of any sense of goodness out in the world that might be of help. Although longing for help, these patients cannot tolerate the possibility that an analyst might be able to help them. To believe that the analyst might actually possess something so important to them, so desperately sought, plunges them into a sense of envious helplessness they cannot endure. The only way not to feel at the mercy of the analyst is to destroy the value of what the analyst has to offer, most especially the value of the analyst's interpretations. This envious destruction of the interpretations operates on a continuum from direct, assaultive devaluation to apparent agreement in which the interpretations are never really considered or allowed an impact.

A dramatic and literal expression of this process is sometimes enacted by patients with eating disorders. Jane, who sought psychoanalysis for help with bulimia, among other troublesome symptoms, described her considerable anxiety after a session in which she felt important contact had been made and something useful given her by the analyst. The discomfort she felt led her to buy a giant bag of cookies, which she devoured eagerly and then induced herself to vomit. Her experience was of burying what the analyst had given her under the gooey mess of cookies and then expelling the entire contents. The interpretations were spoiled and voided. It was only with the experience of a clean and empty inside that the anxiety generated by the session was alleviated.

PROJECTIVE IDENTIFICATION

A second concept Klein introduced late in her life that became central in subsequent Kleinian theorizing is projective identification. *Projection* was a term used by Freud to designate the fantasied expulsion of unwanted impulses: that which could not be experienced as in the self was experienced as located in others, external to the self.

Klein extended this concept in a characteristic fashion. In projective identification, Klein suggested, what is projected is not simply discrete impulses, but a part of the self—not just aggressive impulses, for example, but a bad self, now located in another. Since that which is projected is a segment of the self, a connection to the expelled part is maintained, through an unconscious identification. The projected psychic content is not simply gone; the person struggles to keep some connection to and control over that content.

Consider the following common types: the person who feels modern society is rife with sexuality, and devotes her life to the detection and obliteration of obscenity and the ferreting out and control of the promiscuous; the person who feels that violence in movies is the greatest plague in contemporary life, and cannot stop talking, often in bloodthirsty terms, about those who promulgate this vice; the person who is enormously attuned to the sufferings and needfulness of others and devotes his life to the relief of others' afflictions. These are all suggestive of the kind of process Klein thought of as projective identification. A piece of experience, not simply an impulse but a generic dimension of human relatedness, does not register within the boundaries of oneself, but rather is experienced in a dramatically highlighted fashion in others, where it becomes an object of great focus, concern, and efforts at control.[5]

WILFRED BION AND CONTEMPORARY
KLEINIAN THOUGHT

Klein's ideas have had an enormous impact: on her explicit theoretical heirs; in forming the basis of various object relations theories like those of Fairbairn and Winnicott; and, generally without attribution to Klein herself, in many innovations and subtle transformations in contemporary psychoanalytic thought. In theorizing explicitly designated as "Kleinian," Klein's concepts have been extended and interpreted so fundamentally through the contributions of Wilfred Bion that contemporary Kleinian thought is more accurately designated Kleinian/Bionic.

Bion (1897–1979) was an analysand and student of Klein's whose own seminal concepts were shaped by his work with schizophrenic patients. Bion was raised in colonial India and suffered through tank combat in Northern Africa during World War II. He lived in England most of his life but resided in the United States from 1968 until shortly before his death. Bion became dissatisfied with the formulistic way many clinicians applied psychoanalytic concepts (including Kleinian concepts), and took a particular interest in trying to explore and convey the dense texture and ultimate elusiveness of experience.

Eventually Bion's writings veered off in their own somewhat mystical direction and have attracted a group of adherents. However, some of his basic concepts had more general applicability to Kleinian thinking and have had broad impact on contemporary Kleinians. Bion's writings are extremely opaque and abstruse, perhaps (along with those of Lacan, to be discussed in chapter 7) the most difficult of all the major psychoanalytic authors'. But no introduction to Klein would be complete without a consideration of several of Bion's basic contributions, particularly his extensions of Klein's late theorizing about envy and projective identification.

In Klein's formulation of envy, there is an attack on an object; in the case of the original paradigm of the infant at the breast, the infant destroys the breast and spoils its contents. Bion's early efforts to grasp the origins and nature of schizophrenic thought and language, so striking in their fragmentation and apparent meaninglessness, led him to feel that a connection existed between schizophrenic fragmentation and the kind of envious attacks described by Klein, but that what was attacked was not only the object itself but the part of the child's own mind that was connected to the object and reality in general. The envious infant experiences her whole link to the object as unbearably painful, and therefore attacks not just the breast, but her own mental capacities that connect her to the breast, Bion theorized. There is not only a fantasied attack on the object, ripping it to shreds, but an attack on the infant's own perceptual and cognitive apparatus, destroying her capacity to perceive and understand reality in general, her capacity to make meaningful connections with others. Envy, for Bion, became a kind of psychological autoimmunological disorder, an attack by the mind on itself.

The following two brief dream images suggest the kind of experiences and processes Bion was trying to get at in his formulations concerning the envious destruction of mind and meaning.

Jim, a middle-aged analytic patient, reported a dream in which someone was looking into his ear. He then somehow looked into his own ear and saw spaces in which the tissue was covered with bloody blisters, ulcerated.

The following week he reported a fairly typical phone conversation with his brother, to which he had an uncharacteristic reaction. His brother, who was continually critical of him, his family, his way of life, but was always professing great love for him in sentimental terms, informed him that he would be visiting Jim's city in a couple of days. He would be staying with and spending almost all his time with old friends of his whom he had met through Jim. He didn't invite Jim to join them, but wanted Jim to arrange a brief visit for him with his children. Jim got furious and began to voice his hurt and resentment. His brother responded curtly, "Don't be so self-centered," expressed outrage that he thought this had anything personal to do with him, and listed several practical reasons for the trip to be arranged in this way. Embedded within this list of reasons was his recurrent accusation toward Jim for being "dead" and his expression of pleasure that, even though it was totally unjustified, Jim could still be alive enough to get angry.

The brother's approach to Jim was characteristic of Jim's place in the family in general and was very much modeled on their mother's way of dealing with him. Ordinarily, he responded to such conversations by becoming confused and deadened and by feeling enormously incompetent. This time he reported "bursting with rage" at the powerful, double-binding postures of his brother.

His chronic sense of himself was of someone deeply damaged, unable to think or understand or operate effectively in the world. The dream image is suggestive of Bion's notion that this experience of himself resulted from self-directed attacks on his own mind; they functioned as a reaction to and protection from unbearable ties to significant others in which he felt painfully and hopelessly entangled.

Another patient, in analysis for three years, reported a dream in which she was walking around a garden, taking pictures with a camera that had no film, which she was trying to learn how to use. This was a woman who experienced herself as empty, valuable only through desperate connections with men to whom she would become slavishly devoted. Again following Bion, one might regard this dream image as representing her sense of herself as not retaining experience, of registering events without assigning value or meaning to them, of voiding her own mental functions. Interestingly, in the same session in which she reported the dream, which also suggested the possibility of something new and different, she asked the analyst whether a still-life of flowers on the wall of the office was a recent purchase. The painting (remember the garden in the dream) had been there all along, unnoticed, or not retained, until now.

Bion described one of the central ways the mind attacks its own processes as *attacks on linking,* in which the connections among things, thoughts, feelings, people are all broken. One patient who might well be considered the victim of such a self-attack was a singer of considerable skill whose performance career was handicapped because, although he sang each note with beauty and skill, he could not connect the notes into musical phrases.

We noted that projective identification, in Klein's original formulation, is a fantasy in which some segment of the self is experienced as located in another person, with whom the self remains identified and attempts to control. Bion became interested in the impact of projective identification, a mental event in the mind of one person, on the person who is projected onto. His theorizing grew out of experiences in clinical work with very disturbed patients, in which he found himself having intense feelings that seemed to correspond to the patients' affective life. The analyst, Bion began to suspect, actually becomes a container for mental content originally located in the patient's experience. An event inside the patient's mind, in which a segment of the self is fantasied as relocated (contained) in the analyst, becomes somehow translated into an actual experience for the analyst.

In theorizing about the origins of projective identification, Bion envisioned the infant as filled with disturbing sensations that he cannot organize or control. The infant projects this disorganized mental content onto the mother in an effort to escape its noxious effects. The receptive mother, in a loosely flowing reverie, is responsive to this mental content, and in some sense organizes the experience for the infant, who then introjects it in a form that is now bearable. The mother who is not attuned to her infant is unable to contain and process the infant's projective identifications, leaving the infant at the mercy of his fragmentary and terrifying experience. A similar process, Bion began to suspect, operates in the relationship between patient and analyst. In extending Klein's concept of projective identification, Bion interpersonalized it, changing it from a fantasy in the mind of one person to a complex relational event in the minds of two people.

Bion's understanding of projective identification has been used in a variety of ways. One usage, somewhat spooky in quality, takes for granted a form of mental telepathy in which content is simply transferred from the mind of the baby to the mind of the mother, or the mind of the patient to the mind of the analyst. One can also think about projective identification in connection with the phenomena of intuition and affective contagion. There are mothers who are very much in tune with the affective states of their infants. They seem to be able to sense what the infant is feeling, what the infant needs, and to respond in a way that is organizing and soothing. Another type of mother never seems to get it right, never adjusts to the infant's own state and rhythm, and ends up with a very frustrated and anxious baby. What happens in these situations?

Affects are contagious. (Recall Sullivan's view that there is a direct "empathic linkage" through which affects are communicated, especially between mother and infant.) One person's excitement and enthusiasm can arouse excitement and enthusiasm in others. One person's anxiety can put others on edge. One person's depression can bring other people down. Affects in babies are particularly contagious. There are few things as exhilarating as a baby's smile of pure joy; few things as distressing as a baby in pain. When people are in tune with each other, affective resonance operates like tuning forks spontaneously reverberating at the same pitch. Affective attunement seems to be an intrinsic feature of human intimacy and, perhaps, is a highly adaptive survival mechanism in the relationship between parents and infants, whose affective states need to become known without language.

Bion's account of projective identification in the relationship between infant and mother might be understood in this context. The affective state of the infant, particularly the infant in distress, is picked up by the mother, who has resources for processing it, for soothing both herself and the infant.[6] The infant experiences, absorbs, and, over time, identifies with the mother's organizational capacities. Although Bion assumed an intent to communicate on the part of the infant, a seemingly untestable assumption, one can use his perspective without making such an assumption.

THE ANALYTIC SITUATION

Klein's formulations, particularly in the ways they have been amended by Bion, created a view of the analytic situation that is quite different from Freud's. For Freud, the patient and analyst have well-defined roles and clearly separate experiences. The patient needs to remember, and free association is the activity through which links to the crucial memories are revealed. The analyst hears the associations from a well-measured distance and gives the patient interpretations linking the patient's associations to the memories to be uncovered and reconstructed. The interpretations are informational, designed to reveal the patient's resistances to her own memories, to alter the organization of experience inside the patient's head. Transference periodically emerges as last-ditch resistances to the memory work.

Kleinian analysts use all the same terms to describe the analytic situation, but the basic sense of what is going on is quite different. The patient and analyst are much more fundamentally enmeshed than in Freud's view. It is not as if the patient is simply revealing the contents of her own mind to a generally neutral (except when distracted by countertransference) observer; the patient experiences the analytic situation in terms of her primitive object relations. At times, the analyst is a good breast, magically transformative; interpretations are good milk, protective, nurturing, restorative. At times, the analyst is a bad breast, deadly and destructive; interpretations are poisonous, destroying from within if ingested. In this view, transference is not a resistance to or distraction from the baseline of the analyst's observational position; the patient inevitably and necessarily experiences the analyst and the analyst's interpretations with profoundly intense hopes and equally intense dreads, through her unconscious organizations of experience.

For Freud, the analyst's experience in the analytic situation is one of relative detachment. The analyst uses his own associations, conscious and unconscious, to understand the patient's associations. Yet unless the analyst himself is distorting the patient because of unfinished business (countertransference) from his own past, his affective experience with the patient will be one of relative calm.

Klein describes the experience of the analyst in terms similar to Freud's. But Bion, by interpersonalizing the concept of projective identification, regards the analyst's affective experience as much more centrally involved in the patient's struggles. The analyst finds himself resonating with and containing intense anxieties and disturbing states of mind. The analyst's own depressive anxiety and need to make reparations, which undoubtedly drew him into a "helping" profession in the first place, are always on the line. The patient's systematic envious destruction of the analyst's (hopefully reparative) interpretations is inevitably powerfully disturbing to the analyst. For Freud, psychoanalysis was an arena in which one person observes and interprets the affective experience of another from a measured distance. In the contemporary Kleinian perspective, psychoanalysis is an arena in which two persons struggle to organize and make meaningful the affective life of the patient into which the analyst is inevitably and usefully drawn.

Heinrich Racker and Thomas Ogden have both applied Bion's interpersonalization of projective identification to the complex interactions between analysand and analyst. Racker, an Argentinian psychoanalyst (1910–1961) who wrote a series of brilliant papers on the psychoanalytic process, focused on extending Klein's concepts in a study of transference and countertransference, strikingly anticipating many features of the most recent innovations in psychoanalytic thought, whereby the analytic relationship is understood in increasingly dyadic terms (see chapter 9). Racker stressed the importance and utility of the analyst's identifications with the patient's projections, the versions of self and object that the patient experiences as inside the analyst. Racker (1968) portrayed the analyst (like everyone else) as struggling with dynamics similar to those of the patient: persecutory and depressive anxieties and a need to make reparation. He argued against what he called "the myth of the analytic situation," the assumption that "analysis is an interaction between a sick person and a healthy one." Racker stressed the analyst's embeddedness and participation in the analytic process:

> The truth is that it is an interaction between two personalities, in both of which the ego is under pressure from the id, the superego, and the external world; each personality has its internal and external dependencies, anxieties, and pathological defences; each is also a child with his internal parents; and each of these whole personalities—that of the analysand and that of the analyst—responds to every event of the analytic situation. (p. 132)

It is precisely because the analyst has anxieties and conflicts similar to the patient's that the analyst is able to identify with the patient's projections onto her and then use those identifications to understand the patient.

The American psychoanalyst Thomas Ogden has generated an extremely rich and original series of books on the nature of mind and the analytic process, in which he struggles to integrate Kleinian thinking with the contributions of others, particularly Winnicott. Ogden, in a manner similar to Racker's, illustrates how the patient's fantasy of projecting segments of self onto the analyst leads him to actually treat the analyst in a provocative manner, compatible with the fantasy. A patient with an unconscious fantasy of placing murderous rage onto the analyst is likely to treat the analyst as if he or she were dangerous and evil, which is likely to provoke irritation and perhaps sadism in the latter. The patient's intrapsychic fantasy becomes a form of interpersonal transaction that stimulates intense experiences in the analyst, whose countertransference offers clues to the patient's unconscious fantasies.

Bion recommended that the analyst strive to maintain a discipline in which each session is approached with "neither memory nor desire," in an effort to purify the analyst as a container for the patient's projections. In this sense, his notion of the analyst's ideal demeanor is an extension of the classical principle of neutrality and anonymity. Racker and Ogden, in contrast to Bion, believe the patient's projections are likely to be received not apart from but through the analyst's own anxieties, conflicts, and longings. In this sense, their notion of the analyst's inevitable participation in the analytic process is more consistent with the interactive perspective of interpersonal psychoanalysis.

Bion's formulations concerning attacks on meaning and linking and projective identification have provided powerful clinical tools in analytic work, particularly in the treatment of very disturbed patients. Ogden has suggested that the most difficult feature of such work is the understanding and management of the countertransference, the intense feelings of despair, terror, rage, longing, and so on stimulated by deeply disturbed patients. Bion's formulations provide a framework for analysts to tolerate and, in fact, become fascinated with their reactions to such patients by establishing the following assumptions: the apparent meaninglessness of the communications is generated by an active destruction of meaning; the apparent hopelessness and disconnection are generated by an active intent to destroy hope and connection; the agonizing feelings generated by sustained contact with such persons are the product of primitive efforts on their part to communicate and share their tortured states of mind. What appears disorganized and meaningless is organized and made meaningful, at first in the analyst's experience and, through interpretations over time, in the patient's.

Betty Joseph, following Bion, has also had a great impact on technique, arguing against the earlier Kleinian tendency to make continual interpretations of "primitive experience" in the symbolic language of body parts. Klein assumed that such interpretations could make contact with the patient's stream of unconscious fantasy in a direct and immediate way. Joseph maintains that the patient is likely to be able to relate to such interpretations only in the form of intellectual submission and recommends a less active analyst, struggling for a longer time with confusion, only gradually sorting out the patient's projective identification, thereby making accurate interpretations possible, always in language that is close to the patient's experience. She further argues against a focus on the past, against efforts to create facile and speculative reconstructions of the patient's early experience. What is most central, she feels, is the form of connection and disconnection between patient and analyst in the here and now of the analytic relationship.

These contemporary Kleinian notions proved useful for an analyst's efforts to make sense of his difficult clinical experience with George, an extremely detached and isolated middle-aged man, who had been in psychoanalysis for several years following a brief earlier analysis which he felt had been completely unhelpful. George had no intimate relationships at all; he went to work, returned home, and read or watched television. He has never had sex in any form with another person. He masturbated occasionally to fantasies of himself watching other people having sex. Thus even in his fantasies he was removed from actual contact with others.

In sessions he would offer matter-of-fact descriptions of his daily routines and express an occasional tepid longing for something more or different. A few feeble efforts at getting involved with women came to nothing when the women apparently grew impatient with his passivity and seeming lack of sexual interest.

The analyst found the work with George "killing." He would spend sessions fighting an overwhelming exhaustion. He would do different things to try to remain alert and in contact: ask questions, make interpretations, and occasionally find himself subtly urging a more active approach to living. George would go along with these well-meaning efforts to help him, but the treatment never seemed to get anywhere. George's response to the analyst's interpretations often was to tap his finger against his forehead and say, "In my head what you say makes sense." The analyst felt as if he were caught "in a sea of glue," fighting for air. He repeatedly found himself, when in George's presence, thinking of the poem "Richard Cory" by Edwin Arlington Robinson, about the quiet "gentleman from sole to crown" who "one calm summer night, / Went home and put a bullet through his head."

Consider this analyst's experience from the Kleinian perspective. One might speculate that George was responding to the analyst's efforts to help him with intense, envious spoiling. By tapping his head and saying, "In my head what you say makes sense," George was expressing: I can't tolerate the possibility that you could give me anything that would really matter to me in a deep way; I treat your words as empty ideas, and I trivialize and thereby empty out and destroy both your ideas and my own mind which contains them; I blow my brains out not in a sudden explosion, but through a subtle, perpetual destruction of meaning and the possibility for hope, and, in that same process, I also destroy you, and any faith you have in your own capacity for love and reparation.

One might also speculate that George in some sense was provoking hope in the analyst, inducing the latter to keep trying, as a way of getting the analyst to contain the most feared segment of his own experience: the part of him that was still alive. He then systematically destroyed the hope he aroused in the analyst. Through the communicative dimensions of projective identification, the analyst came to learn firsthand of the patient's experience of both deadness and a desperate, flailing hope that is perpetually crushed.

As the analyst began to use his experience in the countertransference to generate hypotheses about the organization of George's experience, George brought in the following dream.

> I was living in a large living space. (The setting is New York City, where space is enormously precious.) Yet I was using only a small portion of it. The front of the apartment was like a furniture showcase, with three or four large rooms, well decorated and beautiful, but not used. I was living behind a locked door in a small room in the back.

The session in which this dream was reported and discussed in terms of the patient's empty existence and hidden flickers of life was the liveliest session in some time, but was followed by a return to the familiar monotony. The analyst inquired about George's experience between sessions. "Oh, I never retain what we talk about," George said. "When I leave, I just turn down the volume. Sometimes I turn down the volume even when I am here."

From a contemporary Kleinian perspective, the work in this case does not center on using the patient's associations to generate interpretations aimed at the lifting of repressions through reconstruction and insight. The work centers on the analyst's own experience in the countertransference as a vehicle for grasping the various segments of the patient's self and his use of others to maintain a static equilibrium.

Until recently, Kleinian psychoanalysis has been a world unto itself. The tendency to make frequent "deep interpretations," the density of the technical language, the imaginative presumptions about the infant mind, the continual emphasis on infantile aggression—these features set the Kleinian approach apart from other schools, particularly ego psychology and interpersonal psychoanalysis. Partly under Joseph's influence, there has been a marked shift in the recent Kleinian literature away from imaginative reconstructions of infancy, arcane language, and extreme interpretations of aggression toward a greater emphasis on the transferential relationship with the analyst in language accessible to the patient. This has brought the contemporary Kleinian vision of the analytic situation much closer to that of both the interpersonalists, with their emphasis on the here and now in the analytic relationship, and also to Freudian ego psychology, with its careful emphasis on a gradual, step-by-step analysis of defenses. (See Schafer, 1994, for a discussion of what he regards as the current rapprochement between the contemporary Kleinian and ego psychology traditions.)

Klein built her theories slowly from her clinical work in the trenches, with no real interest in the intellectual currents around her. Yet she generated a way of thinking about mind and self that is, in fact, consistent with and in some sense reflective of many of the themes that characterize contemporary culture, often associated with the term *postmodernism:* the decentering of the singular self, the dispersal of subjectivity, and the emphasis on the contextualization of experience. Freud's models of mind are static, layered, and structured. Klein's vision of mind is fluid, perpetually fractured and kaleidoscopic. Further, Klein little by little managed to update the reservoir of psychoanalytic symbols. Freud's approach to symbolism provided interpreters of literature, history, and anthropology with tools for gaining access to underlying Darwinian themes of sexuality and aggression. Klein extended the palette of symbols to themes of internality and externality, life and death, blossoming and depletion, thereby making it possible to paint more contemporary themes on the interpretive canvas, for both the individual in analysis and social movements in our time.

5

THE BRITISH OBJECT RELATIONS SCHOOL:
W. R. D. FAIRBAIRN AND D. W. WINNICOTT

We only become what we are by the radical and deep-seated refusal of that which others have made of us.

—*Jean-Paul Sartre*

For Freud, in short, man was the ambivalent animal; for Winnicott, he would be the dependent animal. . . . Prior to sexuality as the unacceptable, there was helplessness. Dependence was the first thing, before good and evil.

—*Adam Phillips*

Human beings, in Freud's account, are born at odds with their environment. They are wired the way Freud and his contemporaries understood animals to be, oriented toward pursuing simple pleasures with ruthless abandon. But in Freud's Hobbesian view of human society, the individual's pursuit of egoistic satisfactions endangers other individuals, necessitating a control by the group on the hedonic aims of each individual. The project of childhood is socialization, the transformation of the infant, with his or her bestial impulses, into the adult, with his or her complex psychic apparatus and its intricate and elaborate system of checks and barriers channeling those impulses and aims into socially acceptable forms of civilized living.

112

All the important contemporary psychoanalytic schools view the human infant as less alien, more suited and adapted to the world into which he or she is born, than Freud did. As we have seen in chapter 2, Heinz Hartmann's concept of adaptation provided the central conceptual vehicle for the transition from Freud to contemporary Freudian ego psychology. It was Melanie Klein who provided the crucial bridge between Freud and modern British object relations theories.

In redefining the nature of "drive" to include built-in human objects, Klein fundamentally altered the basic premises and metaphors underlying psychoanalytic theorizing. Freud envisioned a developmental passage from animal to person. Klein portrayed a distinctly human infant from the start, an infant who does not learn about the breast through "accidental" association, but who instinctively knows about the breast because she is born with that knowledge. Just as the infant's mouth is anatomically shaped to fit the mother's nipple, the infant's instinctual impulses are shaped to fit the distinctively human world into which she is born.

Yet Klein's baby is not a very happy baby. This baby is born with the capacity to organize discomfort and pain into an image of a persecutory, "bad" Other, and to organize comfort and pleasure and pain into an image of a rescuing, "good" Other. Because early experiences collect around pre-wired *objects,* constitutional patterns of danger and refuge, that infancy is inevitably fragmented and terrifying. For Klein, the project of childhood is not socialization, but amelioration of the frightening, nightmarish conditions of the infant's experience of being in the world which derive from the intensity of the infant's needs and the overwhelming force of constitutional aggression. We are born with psychotic anxieties and, under favorable conditions, sanity becomes a developmental achievement. Although pre-wired to draw her into the human environment, the infant's instincts, in Klein's account, generate inevitable and considerable psychic pain, which, under favorable circumstances, can be contained, organized and assuaged by good parenting.

In the early 1940s, after decades of acrimonious debate, the British Psychoanalytic Society split into three groups: those who fully accepted Melanie Klein's innovations in theory and technique; those who remained loyal to more traditional Freudian concepts and practice (headed by Anna Freud and extended into Freudian ego psychology); and an "independent" or middle group, who developed non-Kleinian versions of what came to be known as object relations theories. The major figures in this middle group, W. R. D. Fairbairn, D. W. Winnicott, Michael Balint, John Bowlby, and Harry Guntrip, all built on Klein's vision of an infant wired for human interaction. Yet they also all broke with Klein's premise of constitutional aggression deriving from the death instinct, proposing instead an infant wired for harmonious interaction and nontraumatic development but thwarted by inadequate parenting.

In recalling his early days in the British Psychoanalytic Society, when the Kleinian belief in the aggressive, destructive baby predominated, John Bowlby cited as a milestone in the emergence of his own independent line of thought the moment when he rose defiantly to assert, in the middle of one such discussion, "But there *is* such a thing as a bad mother." That succinct statement might serve as banner heralding in the development of post-Kleinian British object relations theories.[1]

W. R. D. FAIRBAIRN

Freud's clinical observations charted the vicissitudes of human misery, the ways people systematically make themselves unhappy over and over again: the *symptom neurosis,* in which compulsive, bizarre behavior intrudes into experience; the *character neurosis,* in which maladaptive, self-defeating patterns of behavior compromise interactions with others; the *fate neurosis,* in which the same self-destructive destiny is orchestrated repeatedly; *depression,* in which emotional pain is perpetually regenerated. Yet Freud's broad motivational theory, anchored in his concepts of instinctual drive and the pleasure principle, is a hedonic theory: People seek pleasure and avoid pain. The motivational framework of drive theory is very difficult to reconcile with Freud's clinical observations of the *repetition compulsion,* the systematic regeneration of distress: painful symptoms, painful patterns of behavior, painful fates, painful affective states. If people are meant to seek pleasure and avoid pain, why are most of us so extraordinarily competent at keeping ourselves unhappy?

According to the pleasure principle, libido is malleable, employing a variety of interchangeable objects in its pursuit of pleasure; it ought to be able to discard painful desires and frustrating objects. Yet, Freud noted in 1905, the libido also has a property he termed *adhesiveness,* which seems to operate at odds with the pleasure principle. Libido gets painfully stuck to old, inaccessible objects, frustrated longings, thwarted desires. The Oedipus complex, the heart of Freud's clinical theory, is the prime example of this. Freud returned to this knotty problem again and again, in his efforts to explain nightmares (since he understood dreams as wish fulfillments), sexual masochism (since he understood sexuality as the pursuit of pleasure, not pain), traumatic neurosis (in which terrifying experiences are impossible to leave behind).[2]

The Object-Seeking Libido

Fairbairn's primary contribution to the history of psychoanalytic ideas is a different solution to the problem of the repetition compulsion, a different explanation for the adhesiveness of the libido. William Ronald Dodds Fairbairn (1899–1964) was trained in the British Psychoanalytic Society in the 1930s, when Klein's emendations of Freudian theory were predominant. But Fairbairn returned to his home in Edinburgh and spent the rest of his life there, in virtual isolation from the battles in London between the Kleinians and the (Anna) Freudians. This life on the periphery seemed conducive to Fairbairn's developing a radical critique of the basic underpinnings of Freudian theory, in a series of papers beginning in the 1940s.

Fairbairn questioned Freud's premise that the fundamental motivation in life is pleasure and proposed a different starting point: Libido is not pleasure-seeking, but object-seeking. The fundamental motivational push in human experience is not gratification and tension reduction, using others as a means toward that end, but connections with others as an end in itself.

Freud's infant operates as an individual organism; others become important only through their function in satisfying the baby's needs. Fairbairn, in contrast, envisioned an infant wired for interaction with a human environment. The premise that libido is object-seeking provides, Fairbairn felt, a much more economical and persuasive framework for explaining Freud's observations of the ubiquity of the repetition compulsion. The libido is adhesive because adhesiveness, rather than plasticity, is its very nature. The child bonds to the parents through whatever forms of contact the parents provide, and those forms become lifelong patterns of attachment and connection to others.

Where is pleasure in Fairbairn's system? Pleasure is one form, perhaps the most wonderful form, of connection with others. If the parents engage in pleasurable exchanges with the child, the child becomes pleasure-seeking, not as an end in itself, but as a learned form of connection and interaction with others.

What if the parents provide mostly painful experiences? Does the child, as Freud's pleasure principle would suggest, avoid the parent and seek other, more pleasure-providing objects? No.

One formative clinical experience for Fairbairn was his work with abused children. He was struck by the intensity of their attachment and loyalty to abusive parents; the lack of pleasure and gratification did not at all weaken the bonds. Rather, these children came to seek pain as a form of connection, the preferred form of connection, to others. Children, and later adults, seek from others the kinds of contact they experienced early on in their development. Just as ducklings become imprinted onto and follow around whatever caretaking object shows up at the right time (Lorenz, 1966), so, in Fairbairn's view, do children become powerfully attached to and build their subsequent emotional lives around the kinds of interactions they had with their early caregivers.

Consider the centrality of "chemistry" in human romance and relationships in general. Others are not universally desirable according to their pleasure-giving potential. Others are desirable with respect to their resonance with attachments to old objects, avenues and tones of interaction laid down in early childhood as the basic paradigms of love.

Sam sought analysis complaining of a history of unhappy entanglements with very depressed women. He felt great confusion about how it was that he always managed to end up in such relationships. He came from a family in which the parents both felt resigned and crushed by life. Over the course of the analysis, Sam began to realize how much depression had served as a family ideology: Life is miserable; therefore, anyone with any moral fiber or intellectual integrity is miserable; the best we can hope for is to connect with each other through our unhappiness; anyone who is happy is shallow and morally suspect. Sam came to see that he believed any deeply meaningful connection with someone else could only be achieved through pain. Crying with someone was the deepest form of intimacy; laughing with someone was shallow and distancing. Being a good person necessitated bringing oneself down to the level of the other's unhappiness. To be happy in the presence of another's sadness was callous and cruel. It became more and more apparent that, despite his desperate wish for more pleasurable relationships with happier people, Sam selectively and systematically shaped all his important relationships around depressive ties to miserable others. For Fairbairn, libido is object-seeking, and the objects that are found early on become the prototypes for all later experience of connection with others.

The World of Internal Object Relations

Fairbairn built his own object relations theory out of conceptual materials supplied by Melanie Klein, particularly her notions of internal objects and internalized object relations. Yet his use of these terms and his vision of mind were very different from hers. For Klein, internal objects were fantasied presences that were an accompaniment to all experience. In the primitive thinking of the child and the always primitive unconscious thought of the adult, projective and introjective fantasies based on infantile experiences of nursing, defecating, and so on perpetually generated fantasies of good and bad internal objects, loving and hating, nurturing and destroying. Internal objects for Klein were a natural and inevitable feature of mental life; internalized object relations were the primary forms of thought and experience.

For Fairbairn, healthy parenting resulted in a child with an outward orientation, directed toward real people, who would provide real contact and exchange. Internal objects of the kind Klein described were understood by Fairbairn to result from inadequate parenting. If the child's dependency needs are not met, if the affirmative interactions sought by the child are not provided, a pathological turning away from external reality, from actual exchange with others, takes place and fantasied, private presences (internal objects) are established, to whom one maintains a fantasied connection (internal object relations). For Fairbairn, internal objects are not (as for Klein) essential and inevitable accompaniments of all experience, but rather compensatory substitutes for the real thing, actual people in the interpersonal world.

Fairbairn's account of the processes through which internal object relations develop was sketchy and incomplete, but some of his concepts have rich clinical applications. He envisioned the child with largely unavailable parents as differentiating between the responsive aspects of the parents (the good object) and the unresponsive aspects (the unsatisfying object). Because the child, in his object-seeking, cannot reach the unresponsive aspects of the parents in actuality, he internalizes them and fantasizes those features of the parents as now being inside of him, part of him.

This phenomenon can be seen at work in the case of Charles, a middle-aged man seeking analysis for episodic depressions and withdrawals. His father was caring but hard, remote, and extremely demanding. His mother was a very competent and available, happy-go-lucky homemaker, a committed optimist, always bright and cheery—her nickname was Sunny. Charles discovered in analysis that although he felt his mother was physically accessible, he never felt he could connect with her emotionally, that he was denied access to what she was *really* feeling about anything. He sensed an unexplained sadness about her which she never spoke of. He began to remember times when he would hear her crying behind her locked bedroom door; she would soon emerge, her sunny smile restored. He also recalled times when he would wake during the night at the sound of his father softly playing plaintive ballads on his harmonica in the dark of the living room. Charles would creep downstairs and, unobserved, listen quietly in the dark, secretly sharing these rare moments, rich in feeling, with his father.

Charles's personality was shaped along lines similar to those of his parents; he was very active, responsible, and optimistic. Through the analysis, he began to understand his episodic depressions, atypical periods of total futility and despair, as precious links to the emotional centers of his parents' lives that he did not have access to through actual, ongoing interactions with them. Surprisingly, he felt most connected to them, at one with them, when he was depressed. When Charles felt genuinely happy and successful, he felt cut off from them. A recurrent dream image emerged during the analysis: a jellyfish man, collapsed, sad, helpless and spineless. This image seemed to capture Charles's depressive tie to his parents, a sadness with no bones, no structure, because the mournful connections to their emotionality were split off and encapsulated, not spoken about, not developed. In his depressions were preserved, like fragile icons from an archaic past, unintegrated fragments of loving ties.

Repression

Fairbairn's understanding of repression was quite different in some fundamental respects from Freud's. In Freud's early theorizing, the center of the repressed was an actual experience, the memory of which, because of its traumatizing impact, could not be allowed into consciousness. As Freud shifted from the theory of infantile seduction to the theory of infantile sexuality, he began to conceive of the center of the repressed as forbidden impulses, too dangerous to be allowed access to consciousness. Memories may very well be repressed as well, but they were now understood to be repressed not because of their traumatic nature in itself, but because they are associated with conflictual, forbidden impulses.

Fairbairn saw the center of the repressed as neither memories nor impulses but relationships, ties to features of the parents that cannot be integrated into other relational configurations. Memories and impulses may also be repressed, but not primarily because they are traumatic or forbidden in their own right; rather, they are representative of, and threaten to expose, dangerous object ties.

For Freud, the repress*ed* was composed of impulses, but the repress*or* was composed essentially of an internal relationship, the alliance between the ego and the superego. The ego, concerned with reality and safety, and the superego, concerned with morality and punishment, combined to block forbidden impulses from access to consciousness. For Fairbairn, both the repress*ed* and the repress*or* were internal relationships. The repressed was part of the self tied to inaccessible, often dangerous features of the parents; the repressor was a part of the self tied to more accessible, less dangerous features of the parents.

Zachary, a young man seeking analysis because of considerable unhappiness in his romantic relationships, illustrates Fairbairn's view of conflict as taking place between conscious and unconscious relationships rather than discrete impulses and defenses. His parents were married for only a few years. His mother was the favorite daughter of a very wealthy businessman; his father was ambitious and charming, from a poor background, and had courted and won the mother despite her family's disapproval of him. When Zachary was three years old, his mother discovered what seemed to be clear evidence of her husband's multiple infidelities. She operated in conjunction with her father and his lawyers to banish her husband from the family home and access to the family finances. He quickly became an exiled, dark character, whom Zachary had only limited access to. His mother remarried, in short order, someone who was from her own social class and known for his integrity and virtue.

Zachary had extremely idealistic notions of love and marriage, which no woman ever seemed to be able to live up to or fulfill. He was serially monogamous, but tormented by fears that he would never be able to commit himself to one woman. One key dimension of his experience in analysis was a gradual acquaintance with a dreaded aspect of himself modeled on his identification with his father. He began to realize that he both feared and longed to be like him, sexual, promiscuous, irresponsible, a version of himself he had kept carefully hidden, both from others and from himself. Memories of good times with and warmth toward his father were uncovered; various sexual impulses and fantasies were revealed. But the real danger, consistent with Fairbairn's understanding of repression, was in the connection of all of this material to his libidinal attachment to his father. Given the vicissitudes of his early history, he could never allow himself to become aware of how internally bound to him he was; even now, such a realization seemed dangerous and threatening to his conscious sense of who he was (shaped in relation to his mother and stepfather) and what made it possible for him to be liked and cared for by other people.

The Splitting of the Ego

A child with depressed parents, detached parents, or narcissistically absorbed parents might begin to experience depression, detachment, narcissistic self-absorption in herself, through which she gains a sense of connection to the inaccessible sectors of the parents personalities. It is not at all uncommon for patients in the process of overcoming their own most painful affective states to feel they are losing touch with the parents as internal presences. As they begin to feel happier, they also feel somehow more alone, until they can trust in their growing capacity to make new, less painful connections with others.

Because all of us have had less than ideal parenting, Fairbairn presumes a universal splitting of the ego. The child, in Fairbairn's system, becomes *like* the unresponsive features of the parents: depressed, isolated, masochistic, bullying, and so on. It is through the absorption of these pathological character traits that he feels connected to the parent, who is unavailable in other ways. This internalization of the parents also necessarily creates a split in the ego: part of the self remains directed toward the real parents in the external world, seeking actual responses from them; part of the self is redirected toward the illusory parents as internal objects to which it is bound.

Once the experiences with the parents have been split and internalized, a further split takes place, Fairbairn felt, between the alluring, promising features of the parents (the *exciting object*) and the frustrating, disappointing features (the *rejecting object*). For Charles, for example, his parents' hidden affectivity had two dimensions: their sadness and emotionality, which he longed to reach and share with them, and their distance, the closed doors (with his mother), the darkness (with his father). In Fairbairn's system, the longed-for emotionality is shaped into the exciting object, and the inevitable distance is shaped into the "rejecting object."

The ego becomes correspondingly further split according to the split in internal objects. Part of the ego is bound to the exciting object, the part of the self that experiences perpetual longing and hope. Fairbairn terms this sector of the self the *libidinal ego*. Part of the ego is identified with the rejecting object, the part of the self that is angry and hateful, despising vulnerability and need. Fairbairn terms this sector of the self the *anti-libidinal ego*. The hostility of the anti-libidinal ego is directed toward the libidinal ego and the exciting object, both of which, from the perspective of the anti-libidinal ego, are misguided and dangerous.

Jane, an extremely isolated and tormented young woman suffering from severe anxiety, depression, and bulimia, was discussed briefly in chapter 4. She reported during a session subsequent to one in which the analyst had said some things that seemed very helpful to her that she had felt pleased but then, almost immediately on leaving the earlier session, very frightened. On her way home she had bought a huge bag of cookies, which she devoured and then made herself throw up. This purging emptied her out and calmed her down; it was as if the analyst's interpretations were buried under and then evacuated with the sugary mess.

The inquiry into this and similar experiences revealed an internal antagonism and conflict between two very different ways of experiencing her relationship with the analyst. When she felt the analyst really was able to offer her something, which didn't happen until many months into their work together, she felt a great upsurge of hope and longing. This state of mind quickly began to seem extremely dangerous to her. She began to feel that she had been duped by the analyst as seducer. How could she have been so gullible to believe the analyst would really be able to help her? Hadn't she learned over and over throughout her life that hopes are always crushed, longings always painfully disappointed? She began to hate both the analyst with his promise of help and the part of herself that was susceptible to such promises. The cookies were the means through which she was able to bury, smother, and void the connection between her hopeful, gullible self and the alluring but ultimately disappointing analyst.

As this internal drama became articulated and developed, she recognized the hateful, embittered part of herself, the avenger with the Oreos, as a familiar one—the warden, she called it. It was as if she lived in a prison, cut off from human contact. The warden knew she was much safer in the prison. She would sometimes strain against the bars, wishing for more freedom in the world of other people, more contact, but ultimately she felt the warden knew best, knew how dangerous and treacherous the world of other people really is.

To translate these experiences into Fairbairn's terminology: The prison represents Jane's internal object world, in which she remains trapped but safe. The prisoner represents her libidinal ego, longing for greater freedom and contact (in these sessions embodied in the analyst as exciting object); the warden represents her anti-libidinal ego, identified with and hardened by chronic disappointment with and rejection by her parents.

Because of his penchant for schematization and new terminology, Fairbairn's concepts of fragmented egos and internal objects are easy to misunderstand. He was not speaking of little homunculi "inside" the mind. Nor was he speaking simply of fantasies or images (what the ego psychologists term *representations*). Although most of us experience ourselves as a single, continuous self, Fairbairn envisioned people as actually structured into multiple, subtly discontinuous self-organizations, different versions of ourselves with particular characteristics and points of view.

Each of us shapes his relationships according to the patterns internalized from his earliest significant relationships. The modes of connection with early objects become the preferred modes of connection with new objects. Another way to describe the repetitiveness of patterns in human relations is to say that each of us projects his internal object relationships onto new interpersonal situations. New love objects are chosen for their similarity to bad (unsatisfying) objects in the past; new partners are interacted with in a way that provokes old, expected behaviors; new experiences are interpreted as if they fulfilled old expectations. It is because of this cyclical projection of old patterns and the reinternalization of self-fulfilling prophecies that character and disturbances in interpersonal relations are so difficult to change.

Fairbairn's Analytic Situation

In Fairbairn's understanding of the analytic situation, the patient, although searching hopefully for something new, inevitably experiences the analyst (in the transference) as an old, bad object. The basic assumptions and prototypes of human connection established in the past and preserved in internal object relations shape the experience with the analyst. If the analyst isn't experienced through old patterns, the analyst isn't important, and the analysis isn't deeply engaged. Yet if the analyst is experienced solely in terms of old, unsatisfying relationships, how can anything new happen?

For Freud, it was insight that set the analysand free. She comes to understand that the pleasure she unconsciously pursues in her infantile strivings is not possible. The reality principle gains dominance over the pleasure principle, and the doomed longings of early childhood are renounced.

For Fairbairn, it is not unconscious pleasure-seeking that imprisons the analysand in neurosis; the neurosis embodies the only forms of relation with others the analysand believes in. She feels connected to others, both in the real world and to the presences in her inner world, only through painful states of mind and self-defeating patterns of behavior. She is convinced that renouncing these painful states and old patterns would lead to total isolation, abandonment, annihilation. Insight is not enough. Insight alone doesn't allow the analysand to realize the impossibility of her neurotic strivings; she can't imagine being herself without them. According to Fairbairn, no one can give up powerful, addictive ties to old objects unless she believes that new objects are possible, that there is another way to relate to others in which she will feel seen and touched. For the analysand to renounce the old, transferential forms of connection to the analyst, she must begin to believe in new, less constrained patterns of relatedness.

Fairbairn didn't spell out the processes through which the patient begins to experience the analyst as a different sort of object. Some authors (e.g., Racker) argue that the very act of providing interpretations makes the analyst a different sort of object. Others (e.g., Winnicott) argue that it is not the interpretations but the analytic "frame," the reliable structure within which the analysis takes place, that makes the analyst a new object. Whatever the mechanism, Fairbairn located analytic change not in the dawning of insight, but in a changed capacity for relatedness, an ability to connect with the analyst in new ways.

A middle-aged woman whose family was structured around patterns of male dominance and female submission tended to use her relationships in general and her analytic sessions in particular as opportunities for ritual humiliation. Paula would recount her failings, her incompetencies, her hopelessness in a manner which, many years ago, would provoke her father to take her over, crushing and protecting her in the same gesture. She was certain the analyst regarded her with enormous contempt, and she felt ashamed of her deep inadequacies, which she believed it was necessary to expose and document.

Several years into the work, Paula spoke of the kind of experience Fairbairn regarded as central to analytic change. She had been preparing her financial records for her accountant and discovered that she had made more money the previous year than she had ever imagined possible. She reported a flickering good feeling followed by a tremendous surge of depression and hopelessness about the increased taxes she would now have to pay. The analyst encouraged her to describe her experience of the two states. When she felt more powerful in her earning capacity, she quickly experienced a sense of being "all alone out there," somehow isolated, unattached, undesirable. She couldn't imagine the analyst feeling anything warm or deep toward her as competent and productive and imagined her treatment ending abruptly. As she plummeted into her familiar depressed and abashed state, Paula felt somehow more connected, more protected. The analyst would feel sorry for her and keep her around. Ironically, the more powerful she was, the more endangered she felt. It is only in living through such moments in the analytic relationship, moments that stand outside old patterns, containing states of mind that are "out of character," that the patient gradually begins to believe in and become able to commit herself to new modes of relatedness.

Toward the end of her analysis, Paula described a sense of herself as being like a jungle cat in a cage whose door stood open. She could see how her old forms of organizing her experiences and relationships constrained her and could sense the possibility of stepping outside them into a greater freedom. Yet her cage provided her with a safety, even if illusory, that was hard to give up. She paced back and forth, back and forth, feeling powerful but self-restrained. She could not leave until she felt that her exit would not result in a precipitous plunge; until she could believe that there was firm footing (other modes of relating) beyond the door of the cage and not an abyss.

D. W. WINNICOTT

Donald Woods Winnicott (1896–1971) was a pediatrician before he became a psychoanalyst and he continued his involvement with pediatrics throughout his analytic career. Having spent a great deal of time watching babies and their mothers, he developed strikingly innovative and enormously provocative ideas about both the sort of mothering that facilitates healthy development and the sort that leads development astray.

Like Fairbairn's, Winnicott's early contributions were written in a distinctly Kleinian mode. Winnicott had impeccable credentials as a Kleinian: his first analyst was James Strachey (the translator of the standard English edition of Freud's writings), who had been instrumental in bringing Klein to England; his second analyst was Joan Riviere, one of Klein's closest collaborators. And he was supervised by Klein herself. But in the end, his spirit was too independent, his vision of psychodynamics and development too original, to be contained within the orthodoxy Klein demanded from her disciples. (See Grosskurth, 1986, for a fascinating account of the relationship between Winnicott and Klein.)

"A baby can be *fed* without love," he wrote, "but lovelessness as impersonal *management* cannot succeed in producing a new autonomous human child" (1971, p. 127). This typical statement from Winnicott's late work contains many of his major concerns and is emblematic of the fresh perspective he brought to psychoanalytic thinking about the relationship between baby and mother and, in parallel fashion, about the relationship between patient and analyst.

False Self Disorder

Winnicott's clinical focus was not on psychopathology as traditionally defined, in terms of either symptoms (e.g., obsessional neurosis) or character deformation manifested in behavior (e.g., schizoid withdrawal). Winnicott was concerned with the quality of subjective experience: the sense of inner reality, the infusion of life with a feeling of personal meaning, the image of oneself as a distinct and creative center of one's own experience. The kind of patient he found most intriguing was not the person rent by intense conflict, or tormented by disturbing, puzzling symptoms, or burdened by depression or guilt, but the person who acted and functioned like a person but who didn't *feel to himself* like a person. *False self disorder* was the term Winnicott began to use to characterize this form of psychopathology in which subjectivity itself, the quality of personhood, is somehow disordered.

How is such psychopathology generated? Winnicott argued that fundamental disorders in selfhood originate prior to the oedipal phase (to which Freud had traced neurosis), even prior to later infancy (to which Melanie Klein had traced depressive disorders). Winnicott's most profound and most productive insight was the connection he began to draw between false self disorders in adult patients and the subtle variations he observed in mother–infant interactions from the very beginning of life. What seemed most telling was not gross abusiveness or severe deprivation, but something in the quality of the mother's responsiveness to the baby, her "management" of the baby's needs. It was not just feeding that was crucial, but love, not need gratification, but the mother's responsiveness to the "personal" features of the infant's experience. The bridge Winnicott constructed between the quality and nuances of adult subjectivity and the subtleties of mother–infant interactions provided a powerful new perspective for viewing both the development of the self and the analytic process.

Winnicott portrayed the newborn as drifting in a stream of unintegrated (not disintegrated) moments; discrete wishes and needs emerge spontaneously and, as they are met, melt back into the drift, which he termed "going-on-being." Winnicott's choice of *unintegration* to characterize the child's earliest state of mind is very important, suggesting, in contrast to Klein, an experience that is comfortably disconnected without being fragmented, diffuse without being terrifying. Winnicott saw the quality of the infant's experience of the earliest months of life as crucial for the emergence of personhood. It was the environment that the mother provided (not the child's conflictual instinctual pressures) that determined the outcome. False self disorders, in Winnicott's perspective, were "environmental deficiency diseases."

Winnicott characterized the state of mind that enables the "good-enough mother" to provide the kind of environment the infant requires as "primary maternal preoccupation." The mother is prepared in the last trimester of pregnancy for this deeply biological, evolutionarily honed function by her natural absorption with the baby, whose growth inside her is crowding her own internal organs, compromising her own mobility, her own digestive and eliminative processes, her very capacity to breathe. She becomes increasingly withdrawn from her own subjectivity, from her own interests in the world, and more and more focused on the baby's movements, on the baby's vitality. The final stages of pregnancy become symbolically emblematic of, and a literal preparation for, the mother's supplying in the earliest months of life an environment that nurtures the growth of the infant's self. In providing the environment for the infant, the mother finds her own subjectivity, her own personal interests, her own rhythms and concerns fading into the background; she adapts her movements, her activities, her very existence to the baby's wishes and needs.

The biologically mandated environment created by the mother makes possible for the infant an immersion in the kind of experience Winnicott regarded as crucial for the quickening of subjectivity, the emergence of a distinctly "human" person with a sense of life as real and meaningful. As the infant's needs and wishes emerge from the unintegrated drift of consciousness, the good-enough mother intuits the child's desire relatively quickly and shapes the world around the child so as to fulfill that desire. The physical responsiveness of the nursing mother's body (the "letting down" of breast milk) is the prototype for a more general responsiveness to the baby's "spontaneous gestures," the mother's own deeply felt need to offer herself as a vehicle for the baby's wants and expressions.

The baby's experience in this extraordinary time is one in which he is the all-powerful center of all being—*subjective omnipotence* is the term Winnicott used. His wish makes things happen. If he is hungry and desires the breast, it appears; he makes it appear; he creates the breast. If he is cold and starting to feel uncomfortable, it becomes warmer. He controls the temperature of the world around him; he creates his surroundings. The mother "brings the world" to the infant without delay, without skipping a beat, and, Winnicott suggested, her responsiveness is what gives the infant that *moment of illusion,* the belief that his own wish creates the object of his desire.

It is crucial that the mother be there when needed, but it is equally crucial that she recede when she is not needed. She creates what Winnicott termed a *holding environment,* a physical and psychical space within which the infant is protected without knowing he is protected, so that very obliviousness can set the stage for the next spontaneously arising experience.

It will probably have occurred to the reader that nobody in her right mind would be willing or able to provide such an experience for another person, no matter how adorable, for very long. But this is just the point. In Winnicott's view, the mother is not in her right mind. The state of primary maternal preoccupation is a constructive kind of temporary madness that enables the mother to suspend her own subjectivity to become the medium for the development of the subjectivity of the infant. Under optimal circumstances, the mother gradually emerges from this state of vicarious selfhood. She becomes increasingly interested in her own comforts, her own concerns, her own sense of personhood, and therefore her response to her baby's wishes and gestures begins to be more sluggish. She begins to miss a beat, then two beats, then three.

This slow, incremental failure of the mother to "bring the world" to the baby has a powerful, somewhat painful, but constructive impact on his experience. He slowly begins to realize, in the gradually widening gap between desire and satisfaction, that contrary to his plausible and compelling earlier beliefs, his desires are not omnipotent. It was not his wants and gestures that themselves created their own satisfaction, but his mother's responsive facilitation. This slowly dawning realization has enormous implications, among which is that the infant who, to the outside observer, has of course been quite helpless and dependent all along, begins to *feel* dependent for the first time. There is a gradual awareness that the world consists not of one subjectivity, but of many; that satisfaction of one's desires requires not merely their expression but negotiations with other persons, who have their own desires and agendas.

Transitional Experience

To the child's experience of subjective omnipotence is eventually added an experience of *objective reality*. The latter does not replace the former, but rather exists alongside or in dialectical relation to it. Winnicott did not regard development as a linear sequence in which each stage replaces the preceding one, and this is crucial in his innovative vision of mental health. The person who lives completely in objective reality is a false self without a subjective center, completely oriented toward the expectations of others, toward external stimuli. Being a distinctly human person with a continually regenerating sense of self and personal meaning requires the preservation of the experience of subjective omnipotence as a deeply private, never fully revealed core of experience. The temporary experience of subjective omnipotence provided for the infant by the mother's holding and facilitating remains as a precious legacy and resource. This crucial early experience enables the growing child to continue to experience his own spontaneously emerging desires and gestures as real, as important, as deeply meaningful, even though they must be integrated in adaptive negotiation with other persons.

Between the two forms of experience that Winnicott called subjective omnipotence and objective reality lies a third form: transitional experience. In subjective omnipotence, the child feels she has *created* the desired object, such as the breast, and believes she has total control over it. In experience organized according to objective reality, the child feels she has to *find* the desired object out in the world; she is acutely aware of the separateness and distinctness of the object and her lack of control over it. The "transitional object" is experienced as neither subjectively created and controlled nor as discovered and separate, but as somewhere in between. The status of the transitional object is, by definition, ambiguous and paradoxical. What is crucial in good-enough parenting with respect to transitional experience is that the parent does not challenge its ambiguity. The specialness of the teddy bear is accepted.

The term *transitional object,* like many psychoanalytic terms, has been taken up and expanded in popular usage. One of its most popular applications has been in reference to the transition between a symbiotic merger with and dependence on the mother and separation–individuation as envisioned by Freudian ego psychologists, particularly Mahler. The child's transitional object, such as the teddy bear, represents the mother to the child and enables the child to maintain a fantasied tie to the mother as she gradually separates for increasingly longer periods of time.

But Winnicott had something else in mind: not the transition from dependence to independence, but the transition between two different modes of organizing experience, two different patterns of positioning the self in relation to others. What makes the teddy bear so important is not just that it stands for the mother, but that it constitutes a special extension of the child's self, halfway between the mother that the child creates in subjective omnipotence and the mother that the child finds operating on her own behalf in the objective world. The transitional object, with its paradoxical ambiguity, cushions the fall from a world where the child's desires omnipotently actualize their objects to one where desires require accommodation to and collaboration of others to be fulfilled.

Winnicott introduced the concepts of transitional object and transitional experience in reference to a particular developmental sequence; in his later writings, however, he greatly expanded them into a vision of mental health and creativity. Transitional experience became the protected realm within which the creative self could operate and play; it was the area of experience from which art and culture were generated. A person who lived essentially in subjective omnipotence, with no bridge to objective reality, was autistic and self-absorbed. A person who lived essentially in objective reality, with no roots in subjective omnipotence, was superficially adjusted, but lacking in passion and originality. It was precisely the ambiguity of the transitional realm that rooted experience in deep and spontaneous sources within the self and, at the same time, connected self-expression with a world of other subjectivities.

Object usage is another concept Winnicott introduced in his later papers, in exploring the place of aggression in the transition between subjective omnipotence and objective reality. In subjective omnipotence, the child uses the object "ruthlessly." He creates it, exploits it thoroughly for his own pleasure, and destroys it in his total appropriation of it. From a perspective outside the child's subjectivity, this experience requires a mother who surrenders herself to and can survive being used this way. Gradually, the child begins to become aware of the other who survives his destruction of her. It is the cyclical process of omnipotent creation, destruction, and survival that begins to establish for the child some sense of externality, a real other who exists in her own right, outside his omnipotent control.

If the mother has trouble surviving the baby's usage of her, if she withdraws or collapses or retaliates, the baby must prematurely attend to externality at the price of a full experience of his own desire, which feels omnipotent and dangerous. The result is a child afraid to fully need and use his objects and, subsequently, an adult with neurotic inhibitions of desire. Adult love, in Winnicott's vision, entails periodic mutual object usage, in which each partner can surrender to the rhythms and intensity of his or her own desire without having to worry about the survivability of the other. It is a firm and solid sense of the durability of the other that makes a full and intense connection with one's own passions possible.

The Psychopathology of Not-Good-Enough Mothering

When the mother is unable to provide the kind of good-enough environment necessary for the consolidation of a healthy sense of self, Winnicott felt, the child's psychological development essentially ceases. He remains stuck in psychological time, with the rest of his personality growing past and around a missing core. The kernel of genuine personhood is suspended, buffered by an adaptive compliance with the deficient environment, until a holding environment can be found that allows the emergence of a more spontaneous, authentic subjective experience.

When things go wrong, Winnicott believed, rather than feeling held, the child experiences *impingement,* which comes in several forms. If the child expresses spontaneous desire and the desire is not fulfilled, he feels ignored or misread and impingement occurs. If the child drifts into going-on-being and is not sustained in a supportive unintegration, he feels forced to focus on and deal with some demand in the outside world and impingement occurs. Rather than providing a protected psychic space within which the self can playfully expand and consolidate, the not-good-enough mother presents the child with a world he has to immediately come to terms with, to adapt to, and the premature concern with the external world cramps and impedes the development and consolidation of the child's own subjectivity.

Peter, a mechanical engineer in his forties who specialized in repairing complex electronic machinery, sought psychoanalytic treatment because he realized that he felt a vague but painful sense of being removed from life. He held back from pursuing both activities and relationships with people. There was a "noise" level in his head that somehow distracted him from living, coming between him and the outside world. Sometimes the "noise" was in the background; sometimes it was more prominent. He had come to realize recently that it was always there.

A particular inhibition, inexplicable to Peter, precipitated his entering analysis. For a long time he had wanted to learn gliding, flying engineless planes, which had fascinated him since he was a small boy. He used to spend hours, transfixed, watching clouds and birds, buoyed up, moved by and moving through currents of air. There was something that drew him powerfully to gliding, but he had avoided starting lessons, telling himself he was too busy. He had recently gotten as far as the airfield, where he had an anxiety attack that he found totally perplexing and that led him to seek help.

As he spoke about gliding, Peter realized that it was as if he were seeking in the gliding a certain kind of experience, a suspension in air, that would hold him up, and through which he could gradually descend in a controlled and effortless way. He had always enjoyed swimming, partially because it provided similar sensations. Scuba diving, he explained, was very much like gliding. One was suspended, invisibly supported. He loved to rotate his body under the water in a fashion similar to the dips and rolls of a glider. The anxiety he felt in anticipating his first gliding lesson was like the strange dread he had felt at times in scuba diving, when he would reach the edge of a coral reef, at the point where the floor of the ocean drops off precipitously to great depths. Besides the visual shift, floating along over an ocean floor hundreds of feet below was, of course, really no different from floating along over a reef twenty or thirty feet below. But it felt very different to Peter. As the ocean floor disappeared from view, he would feel a sharp sense of dread; he no longer felt supported and buoyed, but helpless and endangered.

There was little anxiety in his anticipations of piloting the glider once he had learned to fly. All the anxiety was focused on the first lesson itself, when he would fly with an instructor behind him who would be in control. The problem wasn't in the gliding itself, but in the reliance on the instructor. Peter pictured being towed by the plane that would pull the glider up into the sky and the moment at which the tow rope between the plane and the glider would be disconnected. He began to realize that was the moment he dreaded, when he would be released into the care of the instructor behind him, on whom he would have to depend for his very survival.

Over the course of his analysis, he came to understand that in scuba diving and gliding, he was searching for a kind of experience in this physical environment which he had missed in his human environment. He had never felt he could count on his parents to take care of him in a way that would let him become absorbed in his own thoughts and wishes. His parents were involved in chronic arguments, in which he became a mediator at a very young age. He became purely logical, using his considerable intelligence prematurely to stabilize an environment that always seemed explosive.

His parents were both deeply and profoundly depressed people, defeated by life. "Why bother?" was the family motto. Peter's creative excitement and enthusiasm about things were greeted by responses like: "Don't get your hopes up"; "Be realistic"; "Don't get yourself all in a tizzy." His intelligence began to develop in an uneven way. He had great difficulty with abstract concepts that were complex and ambiguous but became extremely adept at building and fixing machinery: "If I can see it, I can understand it"; "I am what I fix." He began to understand that he used his considerable intelligence to "fix" a place for himself a world he experienced as shifting and undependable. Intellectual and emotional problems that were not immediately graspable and fixable, that required tolerating some ambiguity, some suspension in not-knowing, were very confusing and anxiety-provoking to him.

At one point, Peter recovered a memory that seemed strikingly emblematic of his childhood. His family had moved from one city to another two days before his fourth birthday. On the day of his birthday, his mother belatedly thought it would be a good idea to have a party, but of course they didn't know anyone to invite. She sent his older brother out to round up some kids from the new neighborhood for the party. Peter was horrified, both then and now. "Why not cardboard kids?" he asked with the outrage he had felt unable to express at the time.

Peter's adult life might be understood as a search for crucial, missed experiences. Spontaneous excitement was met with fear and cautiousness rather than responsive adaptation and actualization. He could never take his human environment for granted, in a way which would allow for the playful exploration of his own subjectivity, but was compelled to develop a premature, intellectual vigilance and control over his world. He longed to surrender the vigilance and control he had learned to maintain and to simply drift and float in his own experience; yet he was terrified of doing just that, particularly when it depended on the participation of another human being.

In Winnicott's view, it is chronic maternal failure that causes this kind of radical split within the self between the genuine wellsprings of desire and meaning (the true self) and a compliant self (the false self), which is fashioned out of the premature, forced necessity for dealing with the external world. In an autobiographical fragment, Sullivan vividly captured the kind of splitting Winnicott had in mind: "There was such a difference between me and my mother's son, that I often felt myself to be no more than a clothes horse upon which she hung her illusions." To become "me," with a consolidated sense of a self, experienced as real, generating one's own personal meaning, requires a maternal environment that adapts itself to the child's emerging subjectivity. The infant begins to have a sense of his "mother's son," a set of images and expectations he must come to terms with, only after "me" is firmly established, believed in, enjoyed. Having to deal with being "mother's son" too early, at the expense of coming to know and express "me," results in a jarring discontinuity at the center of experience.

Doris, a young woman in analysis for the first time, talked during the initial consultations in a nonstop, rapid, pressured fashion. Among her presenting problems were a clinging dependency on friends and a great difficulty in being alone. She lived by herself and would play the radio or television constantly to create a sense of the presence of others. In the analysis, she was very worried about having nothing to say—she was sure silences would lead to her expulsion from analysis—and prepared extensively ahead of time for each session. She seemed acutely attentive to the analyst's reactions.

It was discovered that Doris's dread of silences concerned a preoccupation with what she imagined the analyst's experience during her silence would be: an intense boredom likely to be increasingly unpleasant and, eventually, unendurable. She began to realize that she pictured the analyst's mind as a frightening place, and assumed that the analyst focused on his patients in order to keep his mind off his own internal horrors. Doris's attention on to the analyst and his expectations and needs saved the analyst from his own demons, she felt, and if she allowed herself to become absorbed in her own experience, her own going-on-being, the analyst would become intolerably anxious.

Subsequent exploration revealed that Doris's parents had demonstrated many indications of a precarious mental balance. Their often stunningly inappropriate, intrusive behavior in the present, which revealed a reluctance to allow their daughter her own life, suggested similar intrusiveness and impingement in the early years, when the delicate balance between internality and externality is established. Because of the parents' inability to be comfortable with themselves, the daughter never had an environment in which she could become acquainted with and explore her own subjectivity. Doris had learned to compulsively generate false-self experience to meet the parents' needs and to mediate the terrifying gaps in her own experience which she never discovered how to survive and enjoy.

Later in the analysis, Doris reported trying to achieve a state of "removing myself," in preparation for a trip to visit her parents. She remembered spending hours staring into a mirror when she was around ten and eleven, forcing herself not to blink, trying to dispel, quite successfully, her sense of "I." She reported a repetitive dream: "There was a baby, but there really wasn't. I'm not sure whose baby it was. It was just a head. It was a wax thing. It was supposed to be a baby, but it was going to melt."

In Winnicott's view, the baby faced with an inadequate holding environment has no choice but to disconnect her mind (the baby's head) from its sources in the body and more spontaneous experience, and to mold her experience around what is provided from the external world. The baby is no longer really a baby, in the sense of the beginnings of authentic personal subjectivity. The child shapes a false self that both deals with an external world that must be watched and negotiated and also shelters the seeds of more deeply genuine experience until a more suitable environment is found.

Winnicott's Analytic Situation

The psychoanalytic situation, as Winnicott understood it, is perfectly designed for exploring and regenerating personal subjectivity. The analyst, like the good-enough mother, provides an environment in which her own subjectivity is on hold. The analyst, like the good-enough mother, tries to grasp the deeply personal dimensions of the patient's experience, the patient's spontaneously arising desires. The patient is offered refuge from the demands of the outside world; nothing is expected except to "be" in the analytic situation, to connect with and express what one is experiencing. No continuity or order is demanded; unintegration and discontinuity are expected and accepted. The analyst and the analytic situation provide a holding environment in which aborted self-development can be reanimated, safe enough for the true self to begin to emerge.

Winnicott introduced ways of thinking about the analytic situation that were very different from those of previous authors. For Freud, the patient's difficulties stemmed from secrets, gaps in memory. The patient's free associations provided the analyst with tools to uncover those secrets, to reconstruct those memories, and to reveal and modify the patient's own internal resistances to knowing and remembering. Cure entailed an eventual renunciation of conflictual infantile longings thus revealed.

For Winnicott, the patient's difficulties stemmed from an internal division that removed and split off the sources of her own personal experience. The problem was not in specific desires, conflicts, or memories, but in the way experience in general was generated. The regressive pull of the analytic situation facilitated the emergence not so much of old desires, but old "ego needs," developmental requirements for the growth of the self. Winnicott saw the patient as powerfully self-restorative, shaping and molding the analytic situation to provide the environmental features missed in childhood. Content and interpretations, were nearly irrelevant in Winnicott's account; what was crucial was experience of the self in relation to the other.

In his work with more disturbed patients, Winnicott made every effort to shape the treatment around their spontaneously arising needs. Even setting regular times for sessions creates an artificial, external structure to which the patient needs to adapt, like an infant being fed according to a schedule rather than on demand. So Winnicott would try to provide sessions on demand. He told of one young woman he would watch for from behind his curtains. Timing was crucial. As she approached his front door and raised her hand to knock, he would open the door, as if her wish for him in fact had created him.

> [T]he infant comes to the breast when excited, and ready to hallucinate something fit to be attacked. At that moment the actual nipple appears and he is able to feel it was that nipple that he hallucinated. So his ideas are enriched by actual details of sight, feel, smell, and next time this material is used in the hallucination. In this way he starts to build up a capacity to conjure up what is actually available. The mother has to go on giving the infant this type of experience. (1958, pp. 152–153)

Similarly, the patient comes to the analytic situation looking for experiences necessary to revitalize the self. The analyst offers himself to be used freely in providing the patient with missed experiences. The analyst allows the patient to feel she has created him and, by not challenging that use of him, enables the patient to rediscover her own capacity to imagine and fantasize, to generate experience that feels deeply real, personal, and meaningful.

OTHER INDEPENDENT GROUP INNOVATORS

The other major innovative figures in the "independent" group of the British Psychoanalytic Society were Michael Balint, John Bowlby, and Harry Guntrip. The authors of this group were independent not only in relation to the Kleinians and (Anna) Freudians, but also from each other. They all drew heavily on the work of Melanie Klein, and they all shifted their emphasis from conflicts between drives and defenses to the establishment and maintenance of relations with others. However, they each did this in their own distinctive fashion.[3]

From Ferenczi to Balint

Michael Balint (1896–1970) was analyzed by Sandor Ferenczi and, in many respects, Balint's contribution was an extension of Ferenczi's. Ferenczi (1873–1933) had been one of the most innovative of Freud's early disciples, both in theory and in clinical practice. In the last several years before his death, Ferenczi had become more and more preoccupied with the impact of early deprivation on personality development, placing a central emphasis on early, chronic trauma, including sexual experiences. This was a return to the perspective Freud had rejected in abandoning the theory of infantile seduction in 1897 in favor of his theory of instinctual drive and the centrality of fantasy.

Ferenczi was also an innovator with respect to clinical technique. Consistent with his theoretical emphasis on trauma and deprivation, he became more and more convinced of the importance of the analyst providing a measured love and affection, rather than abstinent nongratification of the patient's needs and wishes. He also objected to what he felt was the hierarchical, authoritarian arrangement of the traditional analytic relationship between an analyst who dispenses interpretations and a patient who receives them. This led to brief, quickly abandoned experiments with "mutual analysis" between patient and analyst in which they took turns lying on the couch and free-associating.[4]

As the analyst of Balint, as well as of Melanie Klein and Clara Thompson, Ferenczi was a key figure in the transitions from Freud's work to several of the most important currents of contemporary psychoanalytic thought. Balint's extension of Ferenczi's innovations led him to the conviction that what patients, particularly more disturbed patients, are seeking in the analytic situation is not gratification of infantile sexual and aggressive wishes, but an unconditional love, a "primary object love," they were deprived of in childhood. Unlike Fairbairn, Balint never rejected Freud's drive theory; yet, like Fairbairn, Balint argued that object relations are not derivatives of drives but are present at the beginning of life. "This form of object relation [primary object love] is not linked to any of the erotogenic zones; it is not oral, oral-sucking, anal, genital, etc., love, but is something on its own" (1937, pp. 84–85).

In Balint's view, the earliest relationship with the mother is a passive state experienced as a "harmonious, interpenetrating mix-up" of "primary substances" (1968, p. 66). It is out of this passive state that more active forms of relating and pleasure-seeking arise. A rupture in this early relationship creates what Balint terms "the basic fault," a fragmentation and disjunction at the core of the self which, in some fundamental sense, the patient comes to the analytic situation longing to heal. Balint's contribution provides innovative approaches for reframing often difficult clinical situations to highlight the patient's effort, often only dimly understood, to recapture missed developmental opportunities through what he called "benign regression" and reown dissociated aspects of the self.

John Bowlby

Of all the major contributors to psychoanalytic thought over the past several decades, nobody has had more impact than John Bowlby (1907–1990) on the conceptualization of the relationship between psychoanalysis and other disciplines, including biology, anthropology, ethology, information processing, and research on children and families.

Bowlby's approach to psychoanalysis, like Freud's, was firmly rooted in Darwin, but Bowlby's Darwinism was distinctly twentieth-century, as opposed to Freud's nineteenth-century version. For Freud, the central and most startling message of the Darwinian revolution was humankind's ascent from "lower species," leading Freud to hypothesize a seething cauldron of underlying motives derived from what he and his contemporaries understood to be animal nature. For Bowlby, as for Hartmann (see chapter 2), the central message of the Darwinian revolution was the role of adaptation in shaping animal and human nature. For Freud, the instincts were unruly and asocial, wrestled into adaptation only through the long and arduous struggles of the ego. For Bowlby, the instincts were more usefully regarded as preadapted to the human environment, honed over millions of years by natural selection for purposes of survival.

The dimension of adaptation that Hartmann explored was cognitive and perceptual functions. The adaptive, instinctual motivation of central concern to Bowlby involved the child's tie to the mother, which Bowlby termed *attachment*. He argued that the establishment of a deep and tenacious bond to the mother is an instinctual system that enhances the infant's chances for survival. Greater proximity to the mother ensures better caretaking and protection from predators, and Bowlby delineated five component instinctive responses that lead to greater proximity, mediating attachment: sucking, smiling, clinging, crying, and following.

Within the traditional drive theory framework, the mother as a person becomes known and important to the child only because of her function as a need-gratifying object. It follows that early competent caretakers are interchangeable, and that early loss of the mother, when she is still a need-gratifying (rather than libidinal) object, produces no great psychic trauma and no mourning. But Bowlby argued that the child's attachment to the mother is instinctual, not acquired, and primary, not derivative of the mother's need-gratifying activities. He used an extensive survey of empirical studies of separation and loss in both animals and humans to substantiate his claim that early loss results in true mourning, pointing to the primacy of the child's tie to the mother.

Bowlby's concept of attachment, closely related to Fairbairn's notion of libido as object-seeking, became the centerpiece of his broad reformulation of all the central features of personality development and psychopathology. Emotional security is a reflection of confidence in the availability of attachment figures, which is built up gradually through early childhood experiences, Bowlby believed. Different kinds of anxiety are all rooted in a basic anxiety concerning separation from the object of attachment; anger is, most fundamentally, a response to and protest against separation. At the root of all defenses, Bowlby suggested, is detachment, a deactivation of the fundamental and central need for attachment, around which emotional experience is organized.

Harry Guntrip

Harry Guntrip, an analysand of both Fairbairn and Winnicott, has played an important role in explicating, codifying, and integrating (in his own fashion) the contributions of all the authors of the British middle group. Guntrip went further than anyone else in characterizing psychoanalysis as a "replacement therapy," in which the analyst operates "in loco parentis" to provide the missing interpersonal medium necessary for the growth and development of a healthy self. It is a nurturing analytic relationship, Guntrip suggested, highly personal and interpersonal, that becomes the vehicle for cure.

Fairbairn and Guntrip both regarded the schizoid phenomena of withdrawal and detachment as underlying all other forms of psychopathology. Fairbairn had suggested that schizoid withdrawal is only a withdrawal from real people in the external world, that schizoid people are powerfully involved with and devoted to fantasied presences of people as internal objects. Thus the libidinal ego (hope and longing) is very much involved with the exciting object; the anti-libidinal ego (hate and hopelessness) is very much identified with the rejecting object.

Guntrip suggested that in the face of severe deprivation, the libidinal ego itself becomes split. Part of the ego renounces object-seeking altogether, giving up both external *and* internal objects, withdrawing into a deep, hidden isolation. There is a great longing for a return to the womb and a new beginning in a more hospitable maternal environment. This part of the self, the *regressed ego,* manifests itself in a pervasive feeling of *ego weakness* and a profound sense of helplessness and hopelessness. In his effort to integrate the contributions of Fairbairn and Winnicott, Guntrip presented his concept of the regressed ego, frozen in isolation, as encompassing both the self in flight from frustrating objects (a split-off portion of Fairbairn's libidinal ego) as well as aspects of the self never actualized because of the lack of an appropriately facilitating maternal environment (Winnicott's true self).

Guntrip's concept of the regressed ego has a broad applicability to those analysands who experience and portray themselves (both in dreams and in waking fantasies) as small infants, often neglected or abandoned, particularly at points in their analysis where previously unintegrated and inaccessible feeling states and longings are reached. This kind of approach has also been disseminated by popular psychology through such concepts as "the inner child." Guntrip's approach, however, always remained deeply psychoanalytic, in his conviction that the repressed ego cannot be reached in any authentic, therapeutically useful fashion until the slow, painstaking analysis of more surface, defensive layers of the personality are worked through.

The independent group within the British Psychoanalytic Society has had an enormous impact on the theory and practice of psychoanalysis in recent decades. In their clear, explicit break with Freud's drive theory, Fairbairn and Bowlby radically realigned thinking on the nature of mind, development, and the analytic situation. Bowlby's work attained only a minor status within psychoanalysis proper, but spawned a productive and influential line of research and theorizing on attachment that has filtered into popular attitudes toward the importance of bonding between parents and infants, influencing both private lives and public policy. Fairbairn's work has had an increasing effect on the movement toward a "two-person psychology" within psychoanalysis, particularly in the more recent integration of object relations theory and interpersonal theory in current relational psychoanalysis (see chapter 9). Winnicott, although he never explicitly broke with Freudian tradition, introduced an evocative vision of early development that has had broad impact both within and outside psychoanalysis proper. And Winnicott's depictions of parental functions such as the holding environment provided powerful new developmental metaphors for thinking about the analytic relationship and the analytic process.

6

PSYCHOLOGIES OF IDENTITY AND SELF: ERIK ERIKSON AND HEINZ KOHUT

There are situations in which hope and fear run together, in which they mutually destroy one another, and lose themselves in a dull indifference.

—*Johann Goethe*

One must learn to love oneself . . . with a wholesome and healthy love, so that one can bear to be with oneself and need not roam.

—*Friedrich Nietzsche*

How does a being become a *human* being? Are the qualities we define as human superimposed on a basically animal nature? Or are the essential features of humanness intrinsic, innate potentials awaiting necessary conditions to emerge? Or is the infant's nature essentially receptive and formless, requiring cultural education and socialization to create and shape unformed potentials into a *human* being? Finally, does arriving at meaningful answers to these questions require one to make a distinction between "being" human in the sense of acting and looking as though one fits in, and "feeling" human in terms of the quality of one's subjective experience? Crucial differences among contemporary psychoanalytic schools of thought, which extend into very different understandings of mind, difficulties in living, and treatment, are defined by the answers to these questions.

Freud was born into a world where the ways of thinking about these kinds of questions were in transition. Generations prior to Freud's time viewed humans as the maverick children of the divine, designed in God's image in a unique and special fashion. But the scientific speculation of Freud's era no longer allowed humans this unquestioned privilege. Darwin's influence cast a long, gray shadow over what had been a black-and-white divide between humans and other creatures; Freud was fascinated not with humankind's godlike visage but with the beast in men and women. The rich illumination Freud brought to our contemporary understanding of human experience often entailed pointing out the call of the wild, primitive impulses and fantasies beneath the thin veneer of civilized conduct and demeanor.

For Freud, the process of socialization involved the taming of the beast. He saw infantile experience as dominated by raw sexual and aggressive impulses, culminating in the oedipal crisis. As that crisis was resolved under the threat of castration, it was essential that the sexual and aggressive energies be rerouted into less dangerous pathways, and it was this energy, now expressed in socially acceptable and sublimated forms, that was employed in the service of enculturation. For Freud, the distinctly human form of being was generated in the very process through which the primitive, bestial sexual and aggressive impulses were brought under control.

In chapter 2 we traced the gradual shift in Freud's later work to an emphasis on the ego in addition to the drives (originating in the id) and the complex elaboration of that shift in subsequent Freudian ego psychology. The domain of the ego includes all those processes that were taken for granted in Freud's earlier focus on the channeling and rerouting of infantile sexual and aggressive energies. Anna Freud's study of the complexities of defenses, Hartmann's introduction of the importance of adaptation and autonomous ego functions, and the explorations of the developmentalists into early relations with caregivers all established the ego, its development, and developmental processes in general as crucial areas of psychoanalytic concern, both in theory and in clinical practice.

"Id" and "ego" are neither places nor things; they are words that embody an approach to organizing and thinking about the enormous complexities of human experience. The shift from id psychology to ego psychology signaled a shift in the way the fundamental project of psychoanalysis was conceived. In broad strokes, id psychology was the exploration of the implications of the Darwinian revolution for the study of the human psyche; ego psychology became an avenue for the study of the ways individuals develop a distinct and secure sense of themselves. But ego psychology itself never abandoned drive theory. The energy that fuels the ego's functions was still thought to be libido and aggression (even if, as we discussed in chapter 2, this energy is "neutralized" or "fused"). The key processes of early ego development were thought to rely on the vicissitudes of drive processes: Mahler detailed the growth-enhancing impact of libidinal gratification; Jacobson spelled out the complementary growth-stimulating jolt of aggression-promoting frustration.

Erik Erikson's elaboration of the concept of identity and Heinz Kohut's development of self psychology have been two of the most important and influential offshoots of ego psychology. Both Erikson and Kohut were steeped in Freudian ego psychology and drew heavily on its concepts. Yet each, in his own way, created a psychoanalytic vision that broke with ego psychology in fundamental respects. Whereas ego psychologists traced the development of the individual *within* the framework of instinctual conflict, both Erikson and Kohut established fresh frameworks, fully centered on the emergence of a deep and complex personal subjectivity within an inter-personal and cultural context.[1]

Erikson and Kohut are not often linked, but their contributions grew out of a common source in Freudian ego psychology and their innovations were complementary. Erikson placed the individual in his historical time and cultural context. Kohut explored the phenomenology of selfhood. Taken together, they (along with Winnicott) opened up the problem of personal subjectivity and meaning for contemporary psychoanalytic exploration.

Erikson's legacy offers one of the most interesting ironies of contemporary psychoanalytic thought. In terms of both the popular culture and related disciplines like history and anthropology, Erikson has been among the most widely read and influential of psychoanalytic authors, yet within the psychoanalytic literature itself he is rarely acknowledged. Erikson always saw his own contributions as simply adding dimensions to existing Freudian thought. Yet Freudian analytic authors had a hard time bridging their traditional emphasis on intrapsychic instinctual conflict with Erikson's rich sense of the complex relationships between the individual and the surrounding culture. In this sense, Erikson was ahead of his time.

Kohut similarly introduced his innovations, twenty years later in the early 1970s, as elaborations of the ego psychology system. But he gradually came to regard his explorations of the self as constituting a distinct psychology in its own right. Even though he broke explicitly with traditional drive theory, he has been an important presence in contemporary psychoanalytic discourse; he has been argued about, dismissed, built on by some, assimilated by others, but certainly, unlike Erikson, not ignored.

ERIK ERIKSON

The life of Erik Erikson (1902–1994) spanned the twentieth century and, therefore, he witnessed most of the important shifts and developments in the history of psychoanalytic ideas. (See Coles, 1970, for an appreciative and insightful biography of Erickson.) Erikson was born to Danish parents who had separated before his birth; he was raised in the home of his German stepfather. Although brilliant and profoundly intellectual, Erikson could never commit himself to formal education past his rich secondary school education; he became an artist and a wanderer. Peter Blos, a friend from his school days, had been hired as a teacher for her children by Dorothy Burlingham, an American who had come to Vienna to be psychoanalyzed and who had developed a close association with Anna Freud. In 1929, Burlingham and Anna Freud encouraged Blos to establish a small progressive school based on psychoanalytic principles, and Blos invited Erikson to Vienna to teach at that school. Erikson and Blos thereby joined the "chosen," the small group of students taken into the inner circle of the Freud family and trained directly by them. Thus Erikson became a stepson once again. As part of his training, he began an analysis with Anna Freud herself. These tentative beginnings proved fateful to the subsequent history of psychoanalysis. Burlingham and Anna Freud became collaborators and pioneers in the application of psychoanalytic ideas to child development and education. Blos became a key contributor to the Freudian understanding of adolescence. And Erikson became one of the most widely read and influential psychoanalytic authors since Freud himself.

Consider the historical (psychoanalytic) setting in which Erikson began to acquaint himself with what was to become his life's work. Freud had published *The Ego and the Id* in 1923, heralding a shift in focus from an exclusive emphasis on the instincts to the study of the ego and its relations with the external world. In the first decade of Erikson's immersion in psychoanalysis, the classic monuments of Freudian ego psychology were to appear: in 1936, Anna Freud's *The Ego and the Mechanisms of Defense,* and in 1937, Hartmann's *The Ego and the Problem of Adaptation.*

Although Sigmund Freud had been psychoanalyzing adults for more than twenty years and had developed startling and innovative theories of child development, very little direct observation of and clinical work with children had taken place. Erikson loved working with children, and combined his psychoanalytic education with Montessori training as a teacher. Thus Erikson arrived on the psychoanalytic scene at the brink of a dramatic expansion of analytic concerns: from the inner world of the drives to the relations of the individual with the environment; from psychopathology to normality; from the adult patient to child development.

Erikson became a wanderer once again when he moved to the United States in 1933. His direct personal experience of cross-cultural differences was complemented by his exposure to the American cultural anthropology of Ruth Benedict, Margaret Mead, and Gregory Bateson. He took every opportunity to augment his analytic work with children with the study of normal children and child development in different cultural and subcultural settings. It was this mix of new psychoanalytic ideas and interests, the blossoming of the comparative study of culture, and the personal experience of translocation and forced transitions that created the medium from which Erikson created a rich, highly textured psychoanalytic account of the development of the individual within the social world.

The Psyche and Culture

The title of Erikson's classic work, *Childhood and Society,* succinctly summarizes his fundamental concern. Freud had created a complex account of child development, centered on the sequential, maturational unfolding of body-based, instinctual drives. Freud's understanding was fundamentally psychobiological: the psyche is an extension and derivative of the body; the mind develops to channel and control instinctual energies that emerge as peremptory physical tensions demanding action and discharge. The social world, in Freud's scheme, is where the drives come up against a reality that necessitates their control, repression, or largely disguised gratification. From a traditional psychoanalytic viewpoint, society is simply an extension of the ego in its campaign to regulate the drives: cultural leaders are quasi-parents; social forces are camouflaged defenses; group processes are psychodynamics writ large.

Erikson found this to be a lopsided approach to the world as he understood it, a world where culture and cultural differences mold the development of the individual. The central theme throughout his theorizing is the interpenetrability of individual and culture: the individual psyche is generated and shaped within the requirements, values, and sensibilities of a particular cultural context; cultural and historical change are effected by individuals struggling to find meaning and continuity in their lives.

For example, in his study of various Native American cultures Erikson found that geography and economics, mediated through child-rearing practices, shape personality to create the sort of individuals the culture requires. The Sioux, hunters of the plains, were wanderers, with a centrifugally organized world; the Yurok were fishermen who harvested the salmon that annually swim up the Klamath River; they had a centripitally organized world. Whereas the Sioux valued strength, the Yurok emphasized control and cleanliness. Anxiety for the Sioux centered on emasculation and immobilization; anxiety for the Yurok centered on being left without provisions. Child-rearing practices of the Yurok, in contrast to those of the Sioux, stressed the importance of restraint and prohibitions against greed. The commencement of nursing was delayed, and weaning was imposed suddenly and relatively early, with a forceful disengagement from the mother. These practices, Erikson suggests, create an infantile nostalgia for a time of abundance and a supplicant attitude toward supernatural powers—all adaptive for the life of the salmon fisherman.

Thus Erikson added an equally weighted psychosocial dimension to Freud's psychobiology. Freud viewed childhood as a time when psychobiological drives unfolded, expressed themselves, and then were brought under social control; Erikson viewed childhood as, additionally, a way that culture preserves itself, by giving meaning to infantile anxieties and bodily experiences. Traditional psychoanalytic understanding established instinctual drives as the stuff of mind, to be shaped and honed by external, social forces. Erikson regarded culture and history as giving life to mind, as the medium within which shapeless biological potentials can be transformed into a distinctly human life.

> Instead of emphasizing what the pressures of social organization are apt to deny the child, we wish to clarify what the social order may first grant to the infant as it keeps him alive and as, in administering to his needs in specific ways, it introduces him to a particular cultural style. Instead of accepting such instinctual "givens" as the Oedipus trinity as an irreducible schema for man's irrational conduct, we are exploring the way in which social forms codetermine the structure of the family. (Erikson, 1968, p. 47)

The importance of this shift is profound. Erikson was not merely suggesting a change in emphasis. He was relocating the basic constituents of mind and thereby introducing a fundamentally different psychoanalytic framework, with enormous implications for both clinical practice and the ways psychoanalytic ideas affect contemporary culture and experience.

The metaphor of depth was always a central feature of Freud's vision: Beneath the surface of mind operate hidden psychodynamic forces; beneath the present lie the residues of the past, of both the individual and the species; beneath the manifest level of social interaction, instinctual forces push for expression. The former element in each of these pairs can be understood only reductively in terms of the latter. For Freud, this was what made psychoanalysis a "depth" psychology.

Erikson, although continually drawing on traditional psychodynamic understanding, was struggling to make these relationships dialectical rather than reductive. Culture and the individual, present and past, the social and the biological interpenetrate and create each other. Thus Erikson bridled at the ways psychoanalysis

developed a kind of *originology* . . . a habit of thinking which reduces every human situation to an analogy with an earlier one, and most of all to that earliest, simplest and most infantile precursor which is assumed to be its "origin." (1958, p. 18)

Consider the subtly graded differences between traditional ego psychologists and Erikson in the way they rank the constituents of experience. We noted in chapter 2 that Hartmann and Kris expanded psychoanalytic concern from the depth to the surfaces, the interface between the individual and the environment, between infantile conflicts and daily adult functioning. But for Hartmann, Kris, and their collaborator, Loewenstein, the deeper meanings of these surfaces are shaped from below.

There is little doubt that the way in which the initial contact between the Frenchman, the Englishman, the New Yorker, the Bostonian and the psychoanalyst is established covers wide ranges, e.g. from curiosity to restraint, familiarity to suspicion; certain of these attitudes are more frequent in one group than in another. However, as soon as this superficial and initial contact develops into transference, the differences appear to be much more limited. . . . No significant difference exists in the formation of transference—positive or negative—or in its intensity, structure or essential manifestations. . . . Impact (of differences in national character) on the analytic observer tends to decrease as work progresses and as available data move from the periphery to the center, that is from manifest behavior to data, part of which is accessible only to an analytic investigation. (Hartmann, Kris, & Loewenstein, 1951, pp. 19–20)

For Erikson, in contrast to more traditional Freudian ego psychologists, cultural processes constituted an independent, causative dimension that generated meanings of their own. Erikson presented a framework with two centers that have a complex dialectical relationship between them rather than a single center.

For we deal with a process "located" *in the core of the individual* and yet also *in the core of his communal culture,* a process which established, in fact, the identity of those two identities. . . . The whole interplay between the psychological and the social, the developmental and the historical, for which identity formation is of prototypical significance, could be conceptualized only as a kind of *psychosocial relativity.* (Erikson, 1968, pp. 22–23)

Epigenesis and Development

At the center of Erikson's contribution is his theory of ego development, which envisions the ego, like the drives, as unfolding across a sequence of stages or crises:

Basic trust vs. basic mistrust

Autonomy vs. shame and doubt

Initiative vs. guilt

Industry vs. inferiority

Identity vs. role confusion

Intimacy vs. isolation

Generativity vs. stagnation

Ego integrity vs. despair

Each ego stage corresponds to, and is in a dialectical relationship with, a libidinal phase of drive maturation. Thus, for example, the conflict between basic trust and basic mistrust is coterminous with the oral phase. The libidinal pleasures of nursing and playing at the breast in some sense precipitate a crisis of attitude toward the outside world: Can external supplies be comfortably taken in? Are they dangerous? Is the world of the infant sustained in a way that allows her to relax and feel comfortable? Thus Erikson takes Freud's concept of oral libido, a component of psychosexuality as it unfolds across infancy, and builds a complex subjectivity around it. He envisions the infant as struggling in her orientation to the world, as attempting to master a problem at the core of her sense of self in relation to others, as striving for a way to position herself in her world that will allow for future ego growth.

It is instructive to compare Erikson's approach to these developmental passages to other psychoanalytic developmental models. For example, Klein's concept of the paranoid-schizoid position organized around the polarity between the good breast and the bad breast addresses the same struggle as Erikson's first stage of ego development does. For Klein, good and bad derive from the infant's instinctual conflicts between libido and aggression, while for Erikson, trust and mistrust are *experiences* derived from the child's interactions, successful and unsuccessful, with caregivers. For Winnicott, the quality of the holding environment that provides opportunities for either true-self or false-self experiences is determined by the mother, her own psychodynamics and character. Similarly, Sullivan saw points of anxiety in the mother as the origin of the child's early splitting of good and bad. For Erikson, the mother is the representative of and vehicle for a cultural approach to living that organizes and ranks safety and danger, pleasure and restraint, gratification and frustration. Thus, for Erikson, the baby's experience and subsequent identity are shaped through child-rearing practices that reflect the values and needs of the culture into which the child is born.

Erikson's transformation of Freudian theory resonates with that of other major contributors to postclassical psychoanalytic thought in many ways. However, by bridging Freud's biologically based drive theory and the realm of culture drawn from anthropology, Erikson's vision mostly skipped over and left undeveloped the major dimension along which the other principle post-Freudian schools of psychoanalytic theorizing developed: the relationships between the child and particular caregivers (see Seligman & Shanok, in press).

Erikson approached other stages of ego development in a similar fashion, elaborating Freud's psychosexual state into a struggle to find a place and posture in a cultural, historical context: autonomy vs. shame and doubt is linked with the anal phase; initiative vs. guilt with the phallic and oedipal phases; industry vs. inferiority with the latency phase. But at this point, Erikson ran out of Freudian psychosexual phases to use as the skeleton for his sequence of ego development. In Freud's theory of development, all the significant processes are complete in the resolution of the Oedipus complex at the beginning of latency. The rest of life is largely a playing out of the structures established by that time. Erikson viewed the ego's growth as extending significantly beyond the oedipal period, so he added to Freud's phases additional somatic crises, psychobiological events, to anchor his own psychosocial contributions. He linked identity vs. role confusion and intimacy vs. isolation with puberty and adolescence; generativity vs. stagnation with childbearing; ego integrity vs. despair with the physical senescence of aging.

Erikson borrowed the term *epigenesis* from biology to describe this vision of ego growth and development. The fetus develops in the womb through the emergence and predominance of one organ system after the next, each taking its place in the final, complex integration of physical processes in the functioning baby. Similarly, Erikson suggested, the ego develops by an organic process of different capacities and qualities unfolding through this series of crises, leading to the eventual psychosocial integration of the individual in the world.

Erikson's developmental vision is enormously complex and highly textured, but there are several features of his way of presenting it that lend themselves to oversimplification and misreading.

First, Erikson framed the crises of the ego in terms of a battle, one thing vs. another, as if healthy development at each stage would result in a victory and a banishment. But Erikson actually regarded these crises less as battles and more as dialectical tensions. Trust is always complemented by and in a creative tension with mistrust, autonomy with shame and doubt, and so on. Further, even though one or another crisis is in the forefront at any particular time, all these issues and tensions are active throughout the life cycle. Each stage is reworked anew by the struggle with subsequent ego qualities, and Erikson envisioned ego development across the life cycle less in terms of a stepladder and more in terms of a complex set of vital tensions, progressively unfolding and in constant resonance with each other.

Second, Erikson presented his psychosocial stages as extensions of Freud's psychosexual stages. But they are much more than extensions. Erikson changed the very concept of the drives, not simply added on to them.[2] In his integration of Freud's maturational timetable of biological instincts with the structure of social institutions, Erikson transformed the psychoanalytic understanding of both drives and the social world. For Freud, social reality is the realm in which the drives are gratified or frustrated; for Erikson, social reality is a realm that shapes the drives in a culturally distinct fashion. In Freud's framework, the individual is pushed by the drives; in Erikson's framework, the individual is pushed by the drives and pulled by social institutions. "Something in the ego process, then, and something in the social process is—well, identical" (1968, p. 224).

Erikson's most widely known concept was his formulation of ego identity, associated with adolescence, the transition between childhood and adulthood, the point of intersection between the individual and the social world. Erikson deliberately used the term *identity* in a variety of ways, and it is that very elasticity which facilitated his exploration of the interface between the psychoanalytic understanding of the individual and other disciplines such as history, biography, and cultural anthropology.

By letting the term identity speak for itself in a number of connotations, at one time . . . it will appear to refer to a conscious *sense of individual identity;* at another to an unconscious striving for a *continuity of personal character;* at a third, as a criterion for the silent doings of *ego synthesis;* and finally, as maintenance of an inner *solidarity* with a group's ideals and identity. (Erikson, 1959, p. 102)

HEINZ KOHUT

Freud, as we have seen, envisioned the establishment of "human" nature as consequent to a long-standing battle between animal appetites and civilized standards of behavior. In his view, a painfully guilty conscience was a triumph of sorts, heralding a civilized code of ethics in an otherwise lower nature. Psychopathology, for Freud, reflected an imbalance in these necessarily conflictual internal forces.

Heinz Kohut (1923–1981) offered a very different vision of human experience, consistent with the major themes in late-twentieth-century literature and social analysis. He spoke not of battles but of isolation—of painful feelings of personal alienation, the existential experience anticipated and so hauntingly captured in Kafka's *Metamorphosis,* where a person is terrifyingly separated from a sense of his humanness and feels himself to be a "nonhuman monstrosity" (1977, p. 287). Kohut's man in trouble was not riddled with guilt over forbidden wishes; he was moving through a life without meaning. Devoid of that zest for life that infuses the mundane with interest, he looked and acted like a human being but experienced life as drudgery, accomplishments as empty. Or he was held captive on an emotional roller-coaster, where exuberant bursts of creative energy alternated with painful feelings of inadequacy in response to disrupting perceptions of failure. The creative process was short-circuited; creative strivings defied realization. Relationships, eagerly, even desperately, pursued, were repeatedly abandoned with an increasing feeling of pessimism at ever getting what one really "needs" from another. Freud's man was appropriately guilty; Kohut's man was decidedly "tragic" (1977, pp. 132, 133).

Like Hartmann, Kohut envisioned development less as "culture shock," whereby civilized society impinges on and eventually tames bestial humans, and more in terms of intrinsic "fit." Human beings, Kohut came to feel, must be designed to flourish in a certain kind of human environment. That environment must in some way provide necessary experiences that allow a child to grow up not only *being* human but *feeling* human, an energized, connected member of the human community. Kohut attempted to identify these crucial environmental conditions in a child's early life.

But Kohut's writings were not simply extensions and elaborations of his predecessors' ideas. As has been true for many psychoanalytic innovators, the transformation in Kohut's thinking came about primarily in response to his encounter with clinical problems that seemed opaque and intractable within the framework of existing theory.

Narcissistic Character Disorders

Kohut's initial contributions were introduced in terms of a radical reformulation of Freud's concept of narcissism. Freud believed that all the infant's libidinal energy was initially self-directed, a state that he termed *primary narcissism*. The infant's early experience was magical and fantastical. Caught up in what Freud called the *omnipotence of thought*, the infant feels herself to be perfect and all powerful. Early instances of frustration in gratifying herself through these fantasies of omnipotence and grandeur interrupt the infant's narcissistic self-absorption. Unable to secure gratification via this route, the infant turns her libidinal energy outward toward others in her search for palpable, albeit imperfect, satisfaction. In this process, narcissistic libido normally becomes transformed into object libido, and the child takes her parents as the crucial love objects of her infancy. This attachment to the parents, and the oedipal fantasies that develop within it, pose the next psychic hurdle; if the child is unable to relinquish these oedipal fantasies, her libido becomes fixated on her infantile love objects and she becomes neurotic. Later, when she enters psychoanalytic treatment as an adult, the transference of those enduring infantile attachments onto the person of the analyst allows them to be both intensely experienced as well as available to curative analytic interpretation.

Object libido and narcissistic libido were conceptualized as inversely proportional. Freud compared the pool of libido to the protoplasm of the amoeba: the more protoplasm in the central body of the amoeba, the less in the outreaching pseudopodia, and vice versa; the greater one's self-involvement, the less energy is available for attachments to others, and vice versa. Freud understood schizophrenic states to be the product of a massive withdrawal of the libido from its objects into a state of *secondary narcissism,* which propels the individual past even her infantile attachments to parents, back into the state of magical self-absorption that characterizes the early months of life. Here she cannot transfer her libidinal attachments to her parents onto the person of the analyst because there are no attachments left to transfer. Contemporary analysts continued to draw upon this theory of narcissism to explain certain clinical difficulties they encountered.

Eduardo, a homosexual man in his early twenties, sought treatment for a vague, pervasive feeling of depression and a sense of "being at loose ends. . . . I can't seem to find myself." A recent college graduate with a sophisticated, gentlemanly manner, he began the analysis with great energy, describing his ambitions to be a millionaire. Although he was then unemployed and lacked a promising work history, he gave little consideration to developing his areas of interest or devising strategies and long-range plans for achieving this goal. Eduardo seemed to have no concept of the difficulties of the task he had set for himself. Job interviews were anticipated with a pressured optimism; he discussed plans for reaching the top of the company in question, with no awareness of the possibility that he might not be hired, or that, once hired, a rise to the top was not automatic but would require great effort.

Eduardo's social life was a frequent topic in the early sessions. Although attractive himself, he was continuously searching for a more perfect other, a handsome, muscular man with a "big cock," who, he said, would "fill me up" and "make me powerful." His depressions were closely related with this yearning. The dysphoria would abate when he was "on the hunt," when he felt actively in pursuit and the goal seemed reachable; it would return as a dulling sense of emptiness and fragility when the hunt failed to secure the prize. Such disappointments led to withdrawal. He would lose all interest in being with other people and spend long evenings in his apartment, often masturbating.

Eduardo, who was handsome, bright, and articulate, his Latin background contributing a certain exotic quality to his self-presentation, attracted the interest of many men. He was, however, scornfully disdainful of their attention; it did not register as particularly meaningful, as a connection to be developed or common interest to be shared. These were but minor trophies to be collected en route to his ever elusive goal. Eduardo's approach to relationships seemed like a game of checkers; people who showed interest were jumped over and unsympathetically removed from the board in his pursuit of coronation.

As the analyst attempted to articulate and explore these patterns, she repeatedly encountered the same response: Eduardo would pause, always politely, until she had finished offering him her observations and then resume as though the content of her words had no meaning whatsoever. The intervention had registered only as a disruption of Eduardo's presentation of *his* experience, a disruption that he patiently endured until she finally stopped speaking and resumed her position as his attentive audience.

This pattern was broken only once in the initial sessions, when Eduardo paused in the middle of his comments. Looking as though something had caught his attention, he silently studied the analyst for a moment. Then his puzzled look resolved and he commented, "Gray is not a good color for you, you know—blue would be much more attractive." When the analyst expressed interest in this comment, Eduardo waved her question aside, noting that she had "read too many books" and was making too much of a casual remark. He then resumed where he had left off before the interruption.

Feeling unable, in these early sessions, to offer him anything that seemed remotely helpful, over time the analyst became generally silent. She became aware of fleeting fantasies while with him. She envisioned herself getting up and quietly leaving the room; as long as she reappeared to end the session and bid him farewell, she imagined, he would never notice she was gone. More disturbing, however, was a sense that she had become invisible, a feeling that she didn't exist. Clearly, transference in the classical sense was not taking place. Consequently, she was genuinely surprised that, when she needed to cancel one of his sessions, Eduardo became angry and depressed.

Narcissistic Transference: The Classical Perspective

For Freud, the transference became the emotional heart of analytic treatment. The discovery of conflicted unconscious strivings must occur, Freud decided, within an emotionally engaged context, in which the patient experiences intense, conflictual emotions from childhood toward the person of the analyst. Thus Freud designated the capacity to develop a transference as the sine qua non of the analytic patient: "It is on that field that the victory must be won—the victory whose expression is the permanent cure of the neurosis. For when all is said and done, it is impossible to destroy anyone *in absentia* or *in effigie*" (Freud, 1912, p. 108).

Transference became such a crucial feature of analyzability to Freud that he based upon it his most fundamental diagnostic distinction among different types of psychopathology. What makes the psychotic patient untreatable, Freud believed, is a massive self-absorption, which precludes the development of transference.[3] Thus Freud distinguished between the "transference neuroses," which included various analyzable neurotic conditions like obsessionalism and hysteria, and the "narcissistic neuroses," which included various psychotic conditions like schizophrenia and severe depression that were not amenable to the analytic process.

Patients like Eduardo pose a problem for the traditional analytic frame of reference. Eduardo was clearly not psychotic; he was oriented toward reality, functional, socially appropriate, and highly verbal. He ought to have been analyzable. Yet as Eduardo's analyst quickly discovered, engaging him in a meaningful analytic process seemed impossible. While no break with reality-testing had occurred, Eduardo seemed so caught up in his sense of his own grandeur and perfection that the analyst (and most everyone else) seemed unimportant to him. Unlike a psychotic, Eduardo can certainly cooperate with the practical requirements of psychoanalytic treatment; yet he seems emotionally impenetrable.

Eduardo had all the signs of a narcissistic character disorder, a diagnosis that was virtually equivalent to a verdict of unanalyzability in the classical tradition: self-absorption, superficial smooth presentation, grandiosity, sensitivity to slights, impersonal use of the analyst instead of a genuine involvement in collaborative analytic inquiry. According to classical drive theory, such a patient's libido had once been more outwardly oriented but had retreated to a defensive narcissistic orientation to avoid being confronted with the oedipal disappointments inherent in a more mature involvement in the real world. The only hope for curative impact with such patients, it was believed, depended on the analyst's ability to somehow pry the self-directed libido out of its defensive, narcissistic orientation and back into a more mature, outwardly directed channel. Because, by definition, this very self-involvement precluded the development of the powerful therapeutic vehicle of the transference, the analyst was understood as beginning with a massive handicap. The traditional clinical approach in such cases relied heavily on analyzing resistance and defenses to expose, and hopefully undo, manifestations of the defensive process that made a true transference impossible to establish. Using persistent, repetitive confrontations, the analyst would, for example, point out the patient's infantile self-centeredness or arrogant feelings of entitlement. Sometimes, attempting to break through a narcissistic patient's grandiosity, analysts would "adopt a joking, ironic stance that was supposed to kindle the patient's humor, but often slid into sarcasm, ridicule, even mockery" (Kligerman, 1985, p. 12).

Kohut and the Classical Tradition

Until the last ten years of his life, when his writings became too divergent from the mainstream, Kohut was an eminent spokesman for and teacher of classical psychoanalysis. Although he lived in Chicago from age twenty-seven until his death at age sixty-eight, his Viennese roots, which he shared with Freud, were very deep. He enjoyed personal ties with Anna Freud and Heinz Hartmann and found a deep satisfaction in locating himself within the powerful lineage of Freud's descendants.

Despite this deep connection with the classical line of thinking, Kohut grew increasingly dissatisfied with the limitations of a classical approach in understanding and engaging the most fundamental issues with patients like Eduardo. A 1979 paper, "The Two Analyses of Mr. Z," illustrated both Kohut's original classical approach to the treatment of narcissistic character pathology as well as the kinds of compelling clinical experiences that caused him to abandon it in favor of an alternative orientation, which he called *self psychology*.[4]

Mr. Z, a handsome young man who lived with his mother, was in his early twenties when he initially sought treatment, complaining of vague somatic problems and difficulties establishing a relationship with a woman. Like Eduardo's, Mr. Z's father had been absent during crucial years of his life and Mr. Z's mother was intensely involved with the son. Like Eduardo, Mr. Z was described as very sensitive about his analyst's attentiveness to him, becoming upset and angry when frustrated with interruptions in their working schedule, and was unreceptive, often openly rejecting of his analyst's interventions.

From his original classical perspective, Kohut observed that this analysand had been "spoiled" by his mother's excessive attention and involvement with him, which inappropriately encouraged his childish grandiosity. Coupled with the father's untimely absence during the oedipal phase, this maternal overindulgence, Kohut speculated, had nurtured Mr. Z's most gratifying and unrealistic fantasy: that he was the sole possessor of his mother. When, at age five, his fantasy was directly challenged by his father's return, Mr. Z was disinclined to take on the next developmental challenge: confronting the reality of the father as the clear oedipal winner. He was unable to mobilize normal competitiveness and aggression, to endure the terrifying fantasies of his father's castrating retaliation and the loss of his mother. Because his preoedipal fantasies of power and specialness had been overly gratified, he now regressed, his libido returning to an infantile, narcissistic organization in which he experienced himself as the object of his mother's preoedipal devotion, despite his father's return. From this classical perspective, Mr. Z was understood to be duplicating this defensive, immature psychic posture in the treatment, by demanding that "the psychoanalytic situation should reinstate (him to) the position of exclusive control, of being admired and catered to by a doting mother" (1979, p. 5). Using classical technique to try to pry Mr. Z's psyche out of this regressive channel, Kohut repeatedly confronted Mr. Z's defenses: his narcissism, his unrealistic, delusional grandiosity, his use of denial to internally edit out the reality of his father's return. Mr. Z would respond to these confrontations with rage, a response that was interpreted as his attempt to dispel reality by acting as though issues of competition and aggressive strivings had no place in his life; all attentions should be centered on him as a pampered little boy who should not have to endure any frustration.

Many features of Eduardo's history could also easily fit into the classical framework Kohut described in this paper. As a boy, Eduardo had been enthusiastically praised as perfect by his mother; she stressed what a great improvement he was over his father, who had abandoned the family when Eduardo was four, after suffering years of verbal abuse from his dissatisfied wife. Eduardo's mother, referring to her handsome son as her "little prince," subsequently attended social events with him at her side. She systematically indulged his infantile self-image as her perfect and preferred male, rather than allowing him to feel the tempering impact of an adult male's position and value in her life. From this classical perspective, his presentation in the analysis could be seen as a playing out of this defensive infantile organization: he alone was important, he alone should be admired and attended to, he should have anything he wanted, be unlimited in his aspirations for advancement on any front.

While the facts of Eduardo's history, like Mr. Z's, seemed to fall neatly into the categories provided by the classical approach to narcissistic character disorders, Kohut grew increasingly aware of crucial dimensions of experience with narcissistic patients that remained unaddressed. He found, for example, that convincing a patient like Eduardo to give up his protective narcissistic organization inevitably exposed him to deep feelings of inadequacy and painful humiliation. Confronting him with his shortcomings tended to produce a profound sense of utter despair. Despite being, by definition, too full of themselves, narcissistic patients like Eduardo seemed quite fragile, tending to plummet precipitously from a sense of soaring superiority to a clumsy crash-landing on earth.

Even more disturbing was Kohut's observation that a well-conducted, "successful" psychoanalytic treatment did not seem to get at certain particularly troubling qualities of such a person's experience. After Mr. Z completed his initial four-year classical analysis with Kohut, he dropped his insistence on special treatment, moved out of his mother's house, began to date women, and showed more assertiveness in his career (Kohut, 1979). But when this patient sought additional therapy five years later, he reported that the love relationships he had developed seemed emotionally shallow and that he felt no real sexual satisfaction, and he described his work not as a joy or as an exciting challenge, but as a chore and a burden.

From Freud to Kohut

Freud once proposed that normality is defined by an ability to love and to work (Erikson, 1950, p. 264). By this criterion, Mr. Z's initial analysis might be claimed a success. In listening to Mr. Z five years later, however, Kohut was struck by a crucial missing element in Freud's formula: the ability to feel joyful and proud of these capacities. Without this inner vitality, the victory seemed a hollow one. Psychoanalysis had offered Mr. Z a more "realistic" orientation, a recognition that his fantasies of specialness were unrealistic, but gave him nothing to replace the spark and the excitement the now-abandoned fantasies of narcissistic grandeur had provided. And, from Kohut's perspective, the existing theory of psychoanalysis seemed to offer no real way to conceptualize this particular problem.

Freud's theory of libidinal development—the inverse relationship between self-love and love of others—seemed to Kohut to be in need of reformulation. Is love of self really fundamentally inimical to love of others? Is it in the interest of mental health to abandon as immature a high regard for one-self and a desire for attention and praise from others? And are relationships with others worthwhile if pursued at the expense of loving oneself? Might not good feelings about oneself in fact often contribute a vitality and rich-ness to one's encounters with others?

These kinds of concerns motivated Kohut to challenge Freud's theory of narcissism, an act regarded by many as bordering on the heretical. Inter-estingly, Kohut did not initially share this perspective; he did not see his for-mulations as constituting a break with the classical tradition. Kohut's per-ception of Freud's genius and hence his deepest intellectual and professional loyalty to him centered not on Freud's specific theories but rather on the psychoanalytic method, a method he felt was established in the earliest of recorded accounts of a psychoanalytic treatment. As Kohut saw it, the defining moment for psychoanalysis was when Anna O. told Breuer,

I want to say something that occurs to me; and a scientist was scientific enough to say "go ahead," and he sat down and wrote down what she said in order to bring order to the data. That is the great step that created analysis. The particular theories that Freud's ordering mind instituted are particular theories. He may be the Newton of psychoanalysis. He undoubtedly is. But this doesn't mean there are not other ways of order-ing data. (Kohut, in Kirsner, 1982, p. 492)

The *theory* of psychoanalysis, Kohut would eventually conclude, had been elevated to such a sacrosanct position in the field that it had come to have a destructive impact on the *process* of psychoanalysis, Freud's true gift to posterity. An overly rigid adherence to the content of Freud's particular theories, such as his theory of narcissism, encouraged the analyst to impose a preformed belief system on the process that fit the patient's communica-tions into predetermined categories of meanings, rather than formulating tentative hypotheses that would allow continual, open receptivity to the *patient's* unique experience of his plight.

Vicarious Introspection and the Narcissistic Character

In his work with narcissistic patients, Kohut tried to suspend his own classical organizing frame of reference, as well as all preconceived ideas about the meaning of the patient's communications. He tried to put himself in his patient's shoes, to understand the experience from the patient's point of view. This approach, which he described as *empathic immersion* and *vicarious introspection* (1959), became, for him, the defining feature of psychoanalytic methodology. "We designate phenomena as mental, psychic or psychological if our mode of observation includes introspection and empathy *as an essential constituent*" (p. 462). This methodology, Kohut recalled, "allowed me to perceive meanings, or the significance of meanings, I had formerly not consciously perceived" (1979, p. 3).

What kinds of new meanings became available by using vicarious introspection? What might Eduardo's analyst learn about him by hearing his communications in terms of their meaning *to him* rather than trying to fit him into an established grid of psychic functioning and meaning?

Despite his apparent self-absorption, Eduardo experienced people as very important to him; he worked hard to get people involved with him, expending great energy in finding his ideal partner and clearly signaling the analyst that he wanted her to be there with him. What was striking about his implied requests, and what made them hard to perceive, was that although his need of another was very intense, it was also highly specific, excluding by design a range of experiences that are usually an important part of relationships. Specifically, his analyst discerned that Eduardo seemed to be seeking two particular kinds of experiences with others. The first, most visible in the relationship with the analyst, was that of an attentive, interested other who would allow him to show himself without disruption, remaining steadfast and soothing when he was upset or overly excited. The second, initially more apparent in his life outside the treatment, was the experience of a connection with an idealized, powerful other through which he hoped he would come to feel himself to be strong and powerful as well. Both relationships had a profound effect on his self-esteem. When they seemed possible, when the analytic connection was in place for him and when he felt hopeful in his pursuit of the ideal man, Eduardo seemed confident, poised, and alive. When they were disrupted or unattainable, he collapsed emotionally.

When viewed within established psychoanalytic understandings, Eduardo's history had strongly suggested his being "spoiled," his grandiosity being indulged. How might this same history be understood if investigated with a focus on the experience of the person who lived through it? As Eduardo felt increasingly understood by the analyst, the images of being mother's special and perfect boy receded. In their place, he began to articulate a very different perspective on his relationship with his mother. A dream vividly captured the state of his self-experience. Eduardo dreamed that he was a spindly wooden puppet hanging from strings that were manipulated by his mother. Far from the crowned prince in his mother's court, Eduardo anxiously remembered recurring feelings that he had no self; he was an inhuman, fragile performer with no sense of personal volition. He had intense bursts of energy, but he could not organize or harness this energy to his long-range benefit.[5] His mother had been happy to show off her handsome, talented son, but Eduardo felt that she used him for her own needs. She had little sense of what he was actually like, what he wanted, where he was going, and how she could help him develop but possessively criticized him if he turned to anyone else.

To employ the methodology described by Kohut is to come to see Eduardo in an entirely different way, not in terms of having gotten too much attention, but rather in terms of the kind of attention he got. His mother offered him a deadly combination: stimulating his childish grandiosity and omnipotence, leaving him feeling he *should* be able to do anything, but remaining oblivious to him as a person in his own right, thus seriously compromising his ability to develop. Increasingly aware that his connection to his mother relied on his looking good and not needing help, Eduardo established a smooth, apparently capable persona that hid his true experience of himself. This he characterized as "a raw egg inside a thin and perfect shell."

Using his background in Freudian ego psychology as a springboard in conceptualizing the difficulties of patients like Eduardo, Kohut emphasized problems in early development rather than issues of conflict. Something was awry in the basic way these patients (and, Kohut eventually came to feel, all patients) experienced themselves *as selves*. Underlying whatever conflicts they may have had regarding sexual and aggressive impulses was a fundamental problem in self-organization, self-feeling, self-regard (captured in Eduardo's poignant sense of being unable to find himself). Kohut came to believe the problem was only superficially grasped if it was thought of as "too much" narcissism. The normal development of healthy narcissism, Kohut concluded, would be reflected in a feeling of internal solidarity and vitality, the ability to harness talents and reach steadily for goals, self-esteem that is reliable and durable in the face of disappointments and that allows for expansive pride and pleasure in success. A clinical picture like Eduardo's documents the disruption of this normal developmental process. Intense grandiosity is coupled with an absence of capacity for sustained effort. Self-esteem vacillates between dizzying highs and horrifying lows; there is no steadying counterbalance to temper unrealistic plans or absorb frustration and defeat.

The Development of Normal Narcissism

Children live in a world of superheroes and superforces. At times they imagine themselves totally perfect and capable of anything. At times they imagine their caregivers, to whom they are attached, as larger than life and all-powerful. Consider the terms that traditional psychoanalytic theorists applied to this early phase of development: *omnipotence, grandiosity, exhibitionism, archaic idealism*. Traditional theory regarded the inflated overestimation of self and caregivers that characterizes the early years of life as shot through with infantile fantasy, as an immature irrationality to be overcome, thereby allowing the development of realistic connections with others and the outside world in general.

Kohut took a fresh look at these early experiences in light of his patients' narcissistic disorders. What he saw in the world of early childhood was a vitality, an exuberance, an expansiveness, a personal creativity that were often missing in adults who led lives devoid of excitement and meaning, or else, like Eduardo, defensively guarded a brittle, exaggerated self-image that isolated and undermined them. Kohut became interested in the fate of infantile vitality and robust self-regard, the developmental process through which it can be preserved in healthy adulthood or become derailed into pathological narcissism.

According to the theory Kohut eventually arrived at, a healthy self evolves within the developmental milieu of three specific kinds of selfobject experiences. The first experience requires selfobjects "who respond to and confirm the child's innate sense of vigor, greatness and perfection," who, looking upon him with joy and approval, support the child's expansive states of mind. The second type of developmentally necessary experience requires the child's involvement with powerful others "to whom the child can look up and with whom he can merge as an image of calmness, infallibility, and omnipotence" (Kohut & Wolf, 1978, p. 414). And, finally, Kohut felt healthy development required experiences with selfobjects who, in their openness and similarity to the child, evoke a sense of essential likeness between the child and themselves.

How does the child emerge from these childhood narcissistic states? Not, Kohut came to believe, by confronting their unrealistic features. The child who is swooping around the living room in his Superman cape needs to have his exuberance enjoyed, not have his fantasies interpreted as grandiose. The child who believes his mother makes the sun rise in the morning needs to be allowed to enjoy his participation in the divine, not to be informed of his mother's diminutive status in the universe. These early narcissistic states of mind contain the kernels of healthy narcissism; they must be allowed slow transformation on their own, Kohut suggested, simply by virtue of exposure to reality. The child comes to appreciate the unrealistic nature of his views of himself and his parents as he suffers the ordinary disappointments and disillusionments of everyday life: he can't walk through walls, her father cannot decree that her soccer team will always win, and so on. In healthy development, the inflated images of self and other are whittled down, little by little, to more or less realistic proportions. Inevitable yet manageable, optimal frustrations will take place within a generally supportive environment. Against this secure backdrop, the child rises to the occasion, survives the frustration or disappointment, and in the process internalizes functional features of the selfobject. For example, he learns to soothe himself, rather than collapsing in despair; he comes to experience internal strength despite defeat. Kohut felt that this process, which he termed *transmuting internalization,* is repeated in countless little ways and builds internal structure, eventuating in a secure, resilient self that retains a kernel of the excitement and vitality of the original, immature narcissistic states.

Selfobject Transferences

Kohut found clues about the workings of infantile narcissism in the narcissistic transferences of his patients, regarding the transferences as defining the kinds of normal and needed experiences that had been compromised in their early lives. Kohut felt that earlier analysts had misunderstood these "selfobject transferences" because they were primed for a traditional neurotic transference, in which the patient approaches the analyst as a separate person from whom he wants intense gratification in some form. Narcissistic patients like Eduardo treat their analyst and envision their ideal partner as extensions of themselves, as intensely needed, functional aspects of their own subjective experience. Eduardo's ever elusive partner would be strong and phallic and would fill him up. Eduardo envisioned a hand-in-glove union, not a relationship between two separate people. Similarly, the analyst, when properly in place for Eduardo, fit into his experience so seamlessly that she no longer experienced herself as a distinct other person. The analyst had, Kohut would feel, experientially grasped in the countertransference what he defined as the selfobject transference.

Kohut identified three basic types of selfobject transference (which reflected the three kinds of selfobject experiences needed in childhood). Some patients, like Eduardo, establish a powerful attachment to the analyst based on a need for the analyst to grasp and reflect back their experience of themselves, their excitements, their perceptions, as well as their disappointments. Although the analyst may seem to be insignificant to the patient in a traditional way, she is actually essential as a kind of nurturing context (much like Winnicott's "holding environment") within which the patient can begin to feel more seen, more real, and more internally substantial. Kohut called this the *mirroring transference*. A second type of narcissistic transference develops when the patient regards the analyst as perfect and wonderful and feels himself to be increasingly strong and important by virtue of his connection to this powerful and important other. Kohut called this the *idealizing transference*. Eventually Kohut identified an *alter ego* or *twinship* transference, wherein the patient yearns to feel an essential likeness with the analyst, not in terms of external resemblance but in significance or function (i.e., feeling a like-gendered analyst shares a sensibility about being male or female).

Since the analyst in these forms of transference is experienced not as a separate being but as a needed extension of the patient's weakened self, the patient's expected control over the analyst/selfobject will feel closer to the control an adult expects to have over his own body and mind (Kohut & Wolf, 1978, p. 414). Consider, for example, Eduardo's comfortably instructing the analyst on his choice for the color of her clothing. (Perhaps in the choice of blue, he was expressing a longing for same gender resonance.)

None of these transferences are much like the oedipal transferences that are the hallmark of classical psychoanalysis. Most striking is that interpretation of narcissistic transferences in accordance with traditional technique is, Kohut found, disastrous. If the analyst interprets (in the mirroring transference) that the patient's self-perceptions are inflated and need to be renounced or (in the idealizing transference) that the patient's view of the analyst is inflated and needs to be abandoned or (in the alter ego transference) that the presumed likeness between patient and analyst is defensive or illusory, self-esteem collapses and either a demoralizing sense of emptiness and futility or a rageful outpouring ensues.

What happens if these transferences are not interpretively disrupted but allowed to flourish? Classical theory would predict a deepening fixation, or regression, as the analyst colludes in and gratifies the patient's infantile, self-absorbed fantasies. Kohut found, however, that his patients needed an extended immersion in these transferential states to gradually develop a more reliable sense of vitality or well-being. After some period of time, these patients, rather than regressing, began to flourish, developing a much more cohesive, resilient, robust sense of self, capable of enduring disappointments, adjusting to the realities of life, and finding vitalizing pleasure in personal experience. Thus, for a patient like Eduardo, this way of involving himself in treatment was his spontaneous attempt to grow: to establish a relationship with the analyst that would help him hatch a more substantial self from the once raw "egg."

The Psychoanalytic Situation

Kohut advocated technical innovations that directly challenged long-standing tenets of classical technique. As we have seen, he argued for a radically different approach to working with the transference. In the analytic situation, he saw the patient as attempting to reanimate a disrupted developmental process. The analyst must not ignore or resist these transferences, despite the countertransferential anxiety they may engender, but allow the patient to experience her in the needed developmental role, thus allowing the patient's stalled developmental process to be once again resumed. (Kohut's clinical approach has much in common with that of Winnicott and Balint; see chapter 5.)

Before Kohut's arrival on the scene, empathic responsiveness, reflected in both attitude and intervention, was undoubtedly already part of any good analytic technique, but because nongratification was an essential principle of cure within a classical model, this aspect of the experience between patient and analyst was rarely discussed openly and consequently was never really refined. Similarly, the patient's idealization of the analyst had not been held in focus and considered for its therapeutic potential. In its extreme presentation, it was interpreted as a projection onto the analyst of the patient's narcissistic overestimation of self. In milder forms, it could disappear into Freud's larger category of the *unobjectionable positive transference,* composed of the patient's generally benign feelings toward the analyst, which Freud felt provided the rails on which the analysis rides and therefore should not be subject to interpretation until the final phases of the treatment. Kohut pulled these two dimensions of experience between patient and analyst out of the shadows, allowing their developmental potential for the patient to be explored as well as greater sophistication in their technical implementation to be considered.

Kohut discovered that in the early stages of selfobject transferences (in some cases for long periods of time), interpretation is not only unnecessary, but destructive; interpretation may call attention to the analyst's separateness and thus interfere with the patient's immersion in the developmentally necessary selfobject experience. Rather than interpretation, analytic interventions are aimed more at articulating how the patient is needing to regard the analyst's function in the transference, openly accepting this need and empathizing when the patient experiences the analyst's shortcomings in this role. Like the parent, the analyst cannot (indeed, should not) always be perfectly attuned to the patient's needs. Like the parent, the analyst cannot make the sun come up or protect the patient from the harsh realities of life. So the analyst, like the adequate parent, fails the patient slowly and incrementally, allowing the narcissistic transferences to become transformed (through transmuting internalization) into a more realistic, but still vital and robust, sense of self and other.

New Wine in Old Bottles

The theory of self psychology has developed in breadth and complexity since its introduction in 1971 in Kohut's *Analysis of Self*. Kohut had introduced his work in the modest frame of a scientific observation. He had noticed, he said, an emerging, heretofore unidentified transference that seemed reflective of the pressure of a third instinctual drive: narcissistic libido. He very much wanted to remain within the classical tradition.

This effort could not, however, contain the expansive creativity of his thinking for long. Increasingly, from his earliest writings on, one senses in Kohut a voice fundamentally different from Freud's, a different feel for human experience and its meaning.

Kohut emphasized the chronic traumatizing milieu of the patient's early human environment, not the primitive urges arising from within; he described the patient's anxious efforts at self-protection, not his clever routes for obtaining forbidden gratification. In particular, Kohut's words repeatedly reveal his deep respect for and appreciation of the patient's often ill-fated but ever hopeful attempts to keep growing despite adversity, a theme that rarely emerges in the classical literature.

> Just as a tree will, within certain limits, be able to grow around an obsta-
> cle so that it can ultimately expose its leaves to the life-sustaining rays of
> the sun, so will the self in its developmental search abandon the effort to
> continue in one particular direction and try to move forward in another.
> (1984, p. 205)

He saw the intense sexual and aggressive pressures that Freud had defined as basic to human motivation as secondary, "disintegrative by-products," consequences of disruptions in the formation of the self that may now express attempts to rescue some feeling of vitality in an otherwise depleted inner world. He explored this idea particularly creatively in connection with sexuality, as, for example, in his discussion of the function of masturbation in sustaining a person's internal experience.

> Since he could not joyfully experience, even in fantasy, the exhilarating
> bliss of growing self-delimitation and independence, he tried to obtain a
> minimum of pleasure—the joyless pleasure of a defeated self—via self-
> stimulation. The masturbation, in other words, was not drive-motivated:
> was not the vigorous action of the pleasure-seeking firm self of a healthy

child. It was his attempt, through the stimulation of the most sensitive zones of his body, to obtain temporarily the assurance of being alive, of existing. (1979, p. 17)

Similarly, he understood the patient's aggression and rage in the treatment not as expressing an intrinsic force but as evidence of a legacy of vulnerability. Aggressive denigration could be the patient's way of protecting himself from the risk of retraumatization inherent in embracing the analyst as selfobject.[6] Bitter fury could be understandably precipitated by the patient's perception of the analyst's unreliability, weakness, lack of attunement, when, having entered into a reanimation of this needed selfobject tie, he has become deeply and desperately dependent on its effective functioning. Aggression, for Kohut, was reactive, not fundamental.

Gradually, the range of issues in Kohut's writings broadened beyond self-esteem per se. He fundamentally reconceptualized the basic human project. An investigation of issues like creativity, feelings of internal coherence and viability, and functional harmony replaced traditional analytic attention to the vicissitudes of sexual and aggressive drive gratification. The patient's subjective sense of self-realization and the underlying experience of himself as well-put-together, of a piece, holding a sameness over time, containing and balancing varied emotional states, became the crucial focus. Kohut tried to cull out what might be the operational building blocks of this self-realization, settling on two basic components: a vitalizing, expansive ambition and basic idealized goals. Kohut envisioned a healthy self as launching, via talents and skills, from this energizing platform of ambition toward goals that were idealized—infused with personal meaning. His emphasis, again, was not on "doing" it right but on the capacity to feel one's life experience as energized, creative, and personally meaningful.

As if in illustration of what he would come to describe as the process of healthy self-development, Kohut finally extracted his new wine from the old bottles he had originally poured it into. His vision became more explicit, filled out and internally coherent. It was as though, despite his efforts to remain within the classical tradition, he was himself propelled by some inner force, urging him to grow and to realize his own "intrinsic design."

Freud had used the concept of self only casually and unsystematically; Hartmann had carefully, but abstractly, defined the self as a "representation within the ego"; the concept became more vivid in Jacobson's writings as she built it up developmentally in a step-by-step vision of the interpenetration of constitution, drives, ego development, and relations with others. But for Kohut, the self became "the core of the personality," the center of human initiative with its own motivational force aiming toward "the realization of its own specific programme of action" (Kohut & Wolf, 1978, p. 414).

By 1977 (in *The Restoration of the Self*), Kohut had come to regard his theories not just as applicable to a narrow range of more disturbed patients but also as providing a perspective, complementary to Freud's, for viewing all patients, all people. All of us might be regarded as struggling most fundamentally with problems of self-regulation, self-esteem, and personal vitality. Finally, in the years prior to his death in 1981, it had become clear that Kohut regarded self psychology not simply as a complement to Freud's drive theory, but as a preferable, comprehensive alternative.

Controversies Within Self Psychology

Many points of controversy have arisen within the self psychology tradition. One issue concerns the fate of the kind of transferences that Freud had initially described, in which the patient clearly experiences (and represents) the analyst as a person separate from himself (for example, the patient wants to seduce the analyst, or thinks he is controlled by her "just like" the patient's mother controlled him). In initially factoring out a separate developmental course for narcissistic libido and taking that process, and its manifestation in selfobject transferences, as his clinical focus, Kohut had left relationships with differentiated others more or less out of the clinical picture. As Kohut's vision broadened, drives (such as narcissistic libido and object libido) were eliminated as basic motivational forces; self psychology was seen as having generalizable applicability rather than offering a specific kind of treatment designed for those, like Eduardo, who presented with traditionally defined narcissistic disturbances. The role of differentiated object relations in development and in the clinical situation now needed rethinking.

Mahler's portrayal of development as proceeding from symbiosis to separation–individuation (described in chapter 2) had the potential to cast some light on this problem. If her theory held, it made sense to think of two types of transferences: developmentally earlier selfobject transferences (based on merger with the object) and transferences (based on a differentiation from the object) that originated in later development. Daniel Stern, however, synthesized a wide range of experimental research on infancy and found considerable evidence that the infant can differentiate herself from significant others in the first several months. Stern suggested that the child (and later the adult), through whatever physical capacities she has available to her, moves back and forth between points of connection and points of disconnection throughout life. This model contrasts with Mahler's depiction of the infant's state of symbiotic merger as initially total, evolving only over many months of crucial maternal involvement into separation and differentiation, a process whereby she leaves mergerlike states behind.

Stern's vision of human experience as oscillating, from the beginning of life, between intense connectedness and differentiation was resonant with Kohut's eventual conceptualization of selfobject experiences as an ongoing, sometimes background, sometimes foreground feature of psychological life. Kohut came to regard selfobject needs for affirmation, for admiration, for connections with others who can buoy us up and whom we can respect, as undergoing maturation and change of form but operating continually from birth till death, and as fundamental to human experience as are the needs for companionship or solitude. We do not outgrow them. Stern's depiction of the infant as not only deeply connected with his mother but as "outward looking" from birth, exhibiting rudimentary self-definition, a condition fundamental to the establishment of object relations, was consistent with newer views of the transference that were evolving within self psychology. Just like the infant, the adult patient may also be shifting back and forth between two ever-present dimensions of experience with others: one that is deeply fundamental to self needs for development and continuity of vitality (the selfobject dimension), and another that relies on an experience with other people viewed as both separate from the self and needed in quite different ways—for loving, for exchange of ideas, for competition, and so on. An important part of the analyst's craft is determining which dimension is foreground and which is background in the patient's transference experience at any given time (see Fosshage, 1994; Lachmann & Beebe, 1992; Stolorow & Lachmann, 1984/85).

An interesting effort has been made in the recent self psychology literature to reconceptualize the nature of transference itself. Originally within classical theory, transference was viewed as representing a displacement from the past, with the patient distorting the present in order to make room for the expression of some encapsulated earlier fantasy or experience. An alternative formulation sees transference as reflecting "a universal psychological striving to organize experience and construct meanings" that operates in an *ongoing* way, "an expression of the *continuing influence* of organizing principles and imagery that crystallized out of the patient's early formative experiences." Rather than using distortion to smuggle into the analytic relationship something from the distant past, the transference is the patient's here-and-now experience of the analyst.[7] Implicit in this formulation is an acknowledgment of the subjective validity of the patient's experience of the analyst, whose person and actions the patient "assimilates" into the structures of meaning that shape his or her subjective experience (Stolorow & Lachmann, 1984/85, pp. 35, 26).

Since Kohut's death in 1981, a single voice dominating the field of self psychology has been replaced by a multiplicity of voices in complex relationships to one another.[8] Some regard the various developments and spinoffs from Kohut's contributions as all encompassed within self psychology. Others regard one or another of the major developments in post-Kohut self psychology as the true path. Only time will tell whether the various descendants of Kohut's self psychology will hold together under one roof or diverge into wholly independent theories and clinical sensibilities.

All post-Kohut self psychologists tend to regard as the most central and creative features of Kohut's contributions the methodological innovation of sustained empathic immersion in the patient's subjective reality and the theoretical concepts of the selfobject and selfobject transferences. Perhaps the most productive area of cross-fertilization has been in the exploration of the interface between Kohut's developmental concepts and the burgeoning field of infant research. Joseph Lichtenberg has done extensive work in this area, culling and integrating many areas of empirical research, focusing particularly on the theory of motivational systems; Frank Lachmann and Beatrice Beebe (1994) have extended the close empirical study of mother–infant interactions to a view of the developmental process as generated in an interactive field entailing mutual, reciprocal regulation. This branch of theorizing tends to take Kohut's seminal concepts as a starting point, broadening and enriching them. Thus, for Beebe and Lachmann, Kohut's notion of internalization resulting from graded frustration (transmuting internalization) needs to be expanded into a view of internalization as resulting from a multiplicity of routes including mutual and self regulation, disruption and repair, and heightened affective moments.

Other contemporary authors have been more ambitious, positioning Kohut's oeuvre as a transitional development on the way to a more encompassing, more comprehensively revolutionary paradigm. Robert Stolorow and his collaborators, for example, have developed "intersubjectivity theory," which they regard as a more complete field or systems model. (They point to similarities between their approach and "relational" theories drawn from British school object relations theories and interpersonal psychoanalysis, as integrated, for example in Mitchell [1988].) Rather than the individual, isolated self, Stolorow's emphasis is on the fully contextual interaction of subjectivities with reciprocal, mutual influence.

In a different but closely related fashion, Howard Bacal also regards Kohut's self psychology as incomplete and transitional (Bacal, 1995; Bacal

& Newman, 1990). Bacal positions self psychology as half a relational revolution, with object relations theories constituting the missing half. Self
psychology leaves the other only implicit in its relation to the self; object
relations theories leave the self only implicit in its relation to objects.
According to Bacal, people suffer not just from self-depletion but from self-
distortion; he highlights (as do object relations theorists) the embeddedness
within the self of the history of unsatisfying relationships with others.

One of the deepest fears stirred up by psychoanalysis throughout its history
has been the dread that analysis might destroy both creativity and passion.
Many artists have regarded psychoanalysis as a threat to their creativity;
they feared that analytic understanding, while relieving their neurotic misery, might also deplete the source of their artistic inspiration. As Rilke put
it, "If my devils are to leave me, I am afraid my angels will take flight as
well" (quoted in May 1969). Peter Shaffer's play *Equus* (1973) explored
the concern that analytic understanding of perversion is likely to disperse
the wellsprings of passion.

These fears may be unfounded. Many artists have been helped by psychoanalysis, both in their work and in their life. And there is no empirical
evidence that we know of concerning the impact of psychoanalysis on
artists in general. Yet it is true that classical psychoanalysis was pervaded
by a rationalism, objectivism, rigid patriarchalism, and an idealization of
conventional maturity (a developmental morality) that run counter to the
irrationality or nonrationality that is often intrinsic to both creativity and
passion. The very term *analysis* was employed by Freud and his contemporaries to suggest a breaking up of things into their underlying component
parts. Adult passions and compulsions were seen as driven by infantile
wishes and antisocial impulses. Classical analytic interpretation had a
reductive quality to it, revealing the underlying, conflictual, infantile meanings of adult activities and experience. Further, the classical analytic process
was marked by a renunciatory spirit: once exposed, infantile wishes were necessarily renounced, so that sexual and aggressive energies could find more
mature modes of gratification. In this framework, narcissism—including
the self-absorption and grandiose flights of fancy that accompany so much
creative production—could only be regarded as self-indulgent and infantile.

A fundamental feature that distinguishes postclassical psychoanalysis is
the shift in emphasis and basic values from rationalism and objectivism to
subjectivism and personal meaning (see Mitchell, 1993). Winnicott and
Kohut were among the most important figures in this movement. In chapter 5 we noted Winnicott's emphasis on play and the anchoring of authentic self experience in the omnipotence of subjective experience. Similarly,

one of the central features of Kohut's revolution, both in theory and in clinical practice, was the reconceptualization of narcissism from a form of infantilism to a source of vitality, meaning, and creativity. For many contemporary psychoanalytic authors, the analyst's interpretive understanding is much less important than the reality and personal meaning of the patient's productions *to the patient*. In this sense, the basic features of contemporary psychoanalytic thought are consistent with, are reflective of, and have played a role in shaping what many have termed postmodernism. Meaning is to be found not in an objective, rational perspective, but in local, personal perspectives; the value of life is not measured by its conformity with a mature and transcendent vision, but by its vitality and the authenticity of its passion.

Erikson's transformation of the nature of psychoanalytic understanding was a further extension of this reorientation. Childhood conflicts are seen not simply as battles for drive gratification but as existential crises in the life-long search for meaning. In his approach to historical figures such as Luther and Gandhi, Erikson understood their adult achievements and triumphs not as reductive derivatives of their infantile conflicts; rather, he demonstrated a continuity that transcended age, between childhood struggles in a world of problems relevant to children and adult struggles for meaning, devotion, and commitment in a world of problems relevant to adults. (In the chapter 7, we shall see that the Freudian revisionist authors Schafer, Loewald, and Lacan were centrally involved, each in his own fashion, with this fundamental reorientation of the values and epistemology of psychoanalysis.)

It should also be noted that Kohut's work (along with Winnicott's) has greatly contributed to the repositioning of the role of the analyst with regard to conventional gender roles. The voice of the classical analyst, alternating between silence and the delivering of definitive interpretations, is the epitome of the conventional patriarch. (Lacan was to institutionalize this in his view of the analyst as symbolizing the law and the "name of the father.") Kohut's advocacy of a less objectively positioned, less interpretive involvement, his encouragement of empathic resonance with the patient's experience, and his legitimization of the therapeutic impact of what had previously been labeled "gratification"—these are all departures from standard technique that introduce an analytic presence organized around qualities that are regarded as much more conventionally female. Thus, in this sense as well, contemporary psychoanalytic thought both reflects and has contributed to the redefinition of the nature of authority and the reworking of traditional gender roles that has been such a central feature of postmodern currents.

7

CONTEMPORARY FREUDIAN REVISIONISTS: OTTO KERNBERG, ROY SCHAFER, HANS LOEWALD, AND JACQUES LACAN

There is no absolutely specific and static Freudian essence. Nothing lies beyond any one writer's rhetoric and thus beyond the realm of implicit and explicit dialogue.

—*Roy Schafer*

Freud regarded his own genius as having a wayward potential. He loved to develop grand, speculative theories about the broadest and most universal questions that occupied philosophers, historians, and anthropologists. Because it was so much fun and so easy, Freud feared that these speculative flights might draw him away from the hard, tedious work of clinical research and scientific theorizing. He therefore allowed himself only brief intellectual vacations from his major project of mapping the unconscious and building models of mental processes.

On one of these vacations, eventuating in the book *Totem and Taboo* (1913), Freud developed an anthropological fantasy, a kind of myth of origin for the human race. His clinical research and theory-building had been proceeding at fever pitch. His shift in 1897 from the theory of infantile seduction to the theory of infantile sexuality had opened up a dazzling array of conceptual and technical avenues, and he had been pursuing many of them: drive theory, infantile sexuality, transference and resistance, neu-

170

rotic conflict and symptom formation. The Oedipus complex was the hub of them all. So when Freud took time out to allow himself some unrestrained intellectual wandering, he found himself speculating about how the Oedipus complex, which he had come to regard as the centerpiece of mental life, might have come into being.

In *Totem and Taboo* Freud envisioned the original human social group as a "primal horde," with one powerful male dominating and possessing all the females and their offspring. This primal father was a major stumbling block for the young males as they came to maturity, because he denied them access to both power and sexuality. In examining totem mythologies of non-Western cultures that anthropologists of his day were collecting, Freud found evidence that the primal fathers were murdered by collective groups of sons. Afterward the sons were overcome by guilt and fear, and, Freud argued, many of the rituals of "primitive religions"—the prohibitions, the worship of powerful animals that are killed and ceremoniously eaten—are symbolic reenactments of and expiations for this prototypic crime of patricide. Thus the Oedipus complex that Freud envisioned residing in the unconscious mind of each of us, that dominates everyone's childhood, is a recapitulation of the actual oedipal murder of the fathers of the human race.

Although not very sound as anthropology, Freud's speculations about the primal horde have provided a rich framework for thinking about generational strife as a universal human experience.[1] How does the increasingly vital younger generation appropriate the power of the decreasingly vital older generation? The generational transfer of power and authority has been one of the greatest challenges for all human cultures and subcultures.

Generational succession within the psychoanalytic subculture has been complex and varied. The many sons and daughters of the primal father have dealt with Freud's legacy and their accession to their own maturity through many different strategies. On one end of the psychoanalytic continuum have been those descendants who have remained devoted to Freud's texts in their pristine form. Orthodox (or "strict") Freudians try to preserve Freud's own concepts as a sufficient and exclusive basis for current clinical practice. On the other end of the continuum are those who have found it most compelling to assimilate many of Freud's clinical insights and discoveries into their own emerging body of thought, often replacing Freud's basic theoretical concepts with fundamentally different alternatives (as did Sullivan, Fairbairn, and Kohut, for example). To update our image of the primal father, we might picture the father of psychoanalysis, after his death, as having left to his heirs a Victorian mansion on a hill. On one end of the continuum of legatees are those who want to preserve the mansion in its original, landmark condition; on the other end are those who want to raze it and erect a more modern structure on the same lofty site, integrating some of its salvaged components (a stained-glass window here, a chaise longue there) into a wholly contemporary look.

Between these two extremes are the Freudian revisionists, who want to preserve Freud's concepts yet, at the same time, alter them in fundamental ways—to keep the old building, but find a way to modernize it and make it functional as a contemporary abode. There are many ways one might go about such a project; we will consider the four very distinctive approaches of the most creative and influential of the Freudian revisionists: Otto Kernberg, Roy Schafer, Hans Loewald, and Jacques Lacan. We will consider them in this order because, from Kernberg to Schafer to Loewald to Lacan, Freud's texts become increasingly stretched beyond the ways his contemporaries (and Freud himself) seem to have understood them.

From Freud's day on, a rich cross-fertilization has taken place between psychoanalysis and other intellectual disciplines: literature, anthropology, comparative mythology, the visual arts, history, philosophy, and sociology. These relationships were based on the classical Freudian system and shaped by devotees of that system. Thus, until recently, the version of psychoanalysis cited in most interdisciplinary efforts was Freud's biologically grounded drive theory. Over the past two decades, the relationships between psychoanalysis and other disciplines have been largely reshaped; the most productive and stimulating ideas are now drawn not from the classical Freudian system but from contemporary psychoanalytic authors, many of them taking revisionist approaches to basic Freudian concepts. It is for this reason that any honest attempt to address the place of psychoanalysis in modern thought, either appreciatively or critically, must look beyond Freud to the ways Freud's ideas have become revised and transformed in the hands of current analytic authors and clinicians.

OTTO KERNBERG

Kernberg has been the systematizer extraordinaire of contemporary psychoanalysis. His fundamental project (1975, 1976, 1980, 1984) has been to bring together, in a genuinely integrated and comprehensive fashion, major features of traditional instinct theory and Freud's structural model, the object relations theories of both Klein and Fairbairn, and the developmental perspective of Freudian ego psychology, particularly Jacobson's work on pathological forms of early identifications. At the same time, Kernberg's concerns have ranged from the most detailed and concrete clinical problems of severely disturbed patients to the most abstract dimensions of metapsychology. He has maintained a steadfast commitment to the classical clinical principle of the centrality of interpretations in generating meaningful change; yet he has also been a key figure in the exploration of the analyst's personality and the relevance of the analyst's passionate experiences in the analytic process.

Although the technical density of Kernberg's language makes him one of the least accessible of contemporary analytic authors, his basic frame of reference has been consistent throughout, and once grasped, it provides the necessary conceptual map on which his forays into various areas of human experience can be charted. In the broadest terms, Kernberg's contributions are all locatable, and only correctly understood, in the context of his hierarchical integration of three quite different visions of the development of human experience, those of Freud, Jacobson/Mahler, and Klein.

Recall the general features of Freud's developmental perspective: We are born with an array of bodily based impulses, sexual and aggressive, that unfold sequentially over the course of early childhood. These impulses reach their crescendo in the genitality of the oedipal phase, where their incestuous and patricidal goals are experienced as highly dangerous. The mind becomes organized and structured for the sole purpose of channeling these dangerous drives so as to maximize the satisfactions they provide while keeping hidden and/or diverted their antisocial intents.

Edith Jacobson, consolidating the contributions of many in the field of ego psychology, including Margaret Mahler, proposed that our psychological birth is not coincident with our physical birth. A distinct and reliable sense of individual selfhood emerges only gradually over the first eighteen months of life, from an earlier mode of being in which there is no independent sense of self, but rather a diffuse, symbiotic merger with the mother, as conceptualized by Mahler. The mother's cognitive capacities and physical resources are, for an extended period of time, experienced as *inside* the boundaries of the child's self, Jacobson believed. Only gradually is a separate self articulated, during the process of separation–individuation, as the child's own ego capacities mature and develop, making possible a psychological differentiation from the mother.

In Melanie Klein's vision of the essence of human experience, we are born with two powerful, primitive, passionate modes of relating to the world: an adoring, profoundly caring, deeply grateful love and a horrifyingly destructive, spoiling, intensely envious and spiteful hate. Our love creates the possibility for caring, reparative relationships with others experienced as good and nurturant; our hate creates aggressive, mutually destructive relationships with others experienced as evil and dangerous. All humans struggle throughout life, from the first few months until their death, to reconcile these two modes of experience, to protect good, loving experiences from hateful, destructive feelings, to knit together the affective polarities within which they operate.

Although sharing some common ground, Freud, Jacobson, and Klein each propose a quite distinctive vision of the psyche, its origins, its fundamental nature, its tensions. Disregarding theoretical boundaries, Kernberg sensed the potential complementarity among these different visions, drawing together their contributions concerning the pathology of internalized object relations, an issue he felt was of particular relevance to an understanding of severe personality disorders. To some extent, Kernberg stacked these three models hierarchically on top of each other, thereby creating an elaborate and complex framework for understanding emotional development and psychological conflict and for locating psychopathology according to level of severity.

A Developmental Model

In concert with Jacobson and Mahler, Kernberg envisioned the infant during the first few months of life as sorting out experience on the basis of its affective valence, and thus as moving back and forth between two strikingly different affective states with very different qualities: pleasurable, gratified states and unpleasurable, painful, frustrated states. In both states, there is no distinction between self and other, between the infant and the mother. In one situation, the satisfied infant feels merged with a gratifying, pleasure-giving surround; in the other, the frustrated, tension-filled infant feels trapped in an ungratifying, painful surround.

The first major developmental task, in Kernberg's scheme, entails psychic clarification of what is self and what is other (a separation of self images from object images). If this is not accomplished, no dependable sense of self as separate and distinct emerges, no reliable boundary can develop between internal and external, no clear distinction between one's own experience, one's own mind, and the experience and mind of others. A failure to accomplish this first major developmental task is the central, defining precursor of psychotic states. All schizophrenic symptoms—hallucinations, delusions, psychic fragmentation—derive from a fundamental failure in differentiation between self and object images.

The second major developmental task is the overcoming of splitting. After self and object images are differentiated from each other, they still remain affectively segregated: the good, loving self images and the good, gratifying object images are held together by positive (libidinal) affects and are separated from the bad, hateful self images and the bad, frustrating object images, which are themselves joined by negative (aggressive) affects.

This developmentally normal splitting is overcome as the infant develops the capacity to experience "whole objects" that are both good *and* bad, gratifying *and* frustrating. Simultaneous with the integration of the object images is the integration of the self images; now the self is felt to be of a piece, experienced as both good *and* bad, loving *and* hating. This integration allows a concomitant integration of basic drive dispositions. Because good and bad feelings are combined, the singular intensity of loving or hating is tempered. A failure to accomplish this second developmental task results in "borderline" pathology. In contrast to the psychotic, the borderline personality is developmentally able to distinguish between images of self and others, but defensively retreats from the capacity to knit together good and bad affects and object relationships.

Thus Kernberg established developmental tiers that correspond to levels of psychopathology. In the first tier are varieties of psychosis, people who have been unable to accomplish the first major developmental task (as envisioned by Jacobson), the establishment of clear boundaries between self and others. In the second tier are varieties of borderline personalities, people who experience clear boundaries between self and others but who have been unable to accomplish the second major developmental task (as envisioned by Klein), the integration of loving and hateful feelings into a fuller, ambivalent relationship with complex others. Freud's classical theory of neurosis as structural conflict is Kernberg's third tier, reflecting psychopathology with higher-level personality development, where self–object boundaries are intact and self images and object images are integrated.

In the beginning, in Kernberg's system, there are no drives. Over the course of early development, the infant's diffuse good and bad affect states become consolidated and shaped into libidinal and aggressive drives. Subjectively registered good, pleasurable, satisfying interactions with gratifying others consolidate, over time, into a pleasure-seeking (libidinal) drive. Similarly, subjectively registered bad, unpleasurable, unsatisfying experiences with ungratifying others consolidate, over time, into a destructive (aggressive) drive. The child wants to maximize pleasurable experiences with good objects and to destroy bad objects who provoke unpleasurable experiences.

The libidinal and aggressive forces that emerge from the powerful affective states that dominate early object relations are themselves conflictual in Kernberg's account, just as in Freud's. Libidinal impulses, because they are infused with childhood sexual aims, are experienced as potentially antisocial and dangerous. Aggressive impulses are dangerous (once splitting is overcome) because they are directed toward the very objects that are also loved. Thus, the third tier of Kernberg's developmental hierarchy of psychopathology is neurosis. Individuals who have achieved the separation between self and others and overcome splitting qualify for the kind of neurotic conflict between impulses and defenses that constituted classical Freudian theory of psychopathology.

What Kernberg did, in concert with Jacobson, was to broaden and deepen Freud's drive theory by deriving drives from a complex developmental sequence centered around early object relations. Drives for Freud were given, inborn; drives for Kernberg are still dependent on constitutional predispositions, but are ultimately forged in interaction with others and are thus developmentally constructed. Kernberg stacks theories.

By excavating and erecting new scaffolding beneath classical drive theory, Kernberg was able to preserve Freud's basic understanding of neurosis as generated by instinctual conflict, and, at the same time, employ Kleinian theory, object relations theories, and ego psychology in understanding more severe psychological disturbances.

Character and the Pathology of Love Relations

Kernberg's revisions of Freudian theory seem quite abstract, but they make an enormous difference in the understandings they generate of what people are most fundamentally about. In classical Freudian theory, the centerpiece of personality is the predominant mode of instinctual gratification. For Kernberg, the centerpiece of personality is the developmental level of internal object relations the patient has reached. A comparison between the ways Freud and Kernberg categorized different types of personalities reveals just how far Kernberg's revisions moved Freudian theory.

By 1920 Freud (in collaboration with Karl Abraham) had classified types of people according to their level of instinctual organization. As the libido moves through its phases of development—oral, anal, phallic, genital—it is always varied and diverse in its aims and objects (polymorphously perverse), but at each phase one libidinal aim becomes predominant and assumes a kind of hegemony over the others, Freud speculated. The kind of psychopathology that emerges later in adulthood is determined by the libidinal fixation point, the particular phase of childhood sexuality that had the strongest valence. Thus, for example, Freud and Abraham believed that depression results from an oral fixation (from a longing for nurturance and a sense of abandonment) and obsessional neurosis from an anal fixation (see chapter 1). People within the normal range can also be classified by their predominant libidinal organization: oral characters, anal characters, phallic characters, and, the paragon of mental health, the genital character.

What does it mean to be an oral, an anal, a phallic character? Experience can be organized and processed in an infinite number of ways; according to classical theory, the predominant libidinal fixation provides any given individual with a central set of bodily based metaphors around which all experience comes to be organized.

Consider an excerpt from Abraham's description of the obsessional (anal) character:

> The anal character sometimes seems to stamp itself on the physiognomy of its possessor. It seems particularly to show itself in a morose expression . . . and surliness. . . . A constant tension of the line of the nostril together with a slight lifting of the upper lip seem to me significant facial characteristics of such people. In some cases this gives the impression that they are constantly sniffing at something. Probably this feature is traceable to their coprophilic pleasure in smell. (1921, p. 391)

In the Freud/Abraham system, even the most mature character type is no less grounded in body parts and processes; the central organ and activity have merely shifted to a different libidinal component. Wilhelm Reich (1929) offered this description of the genital character:

> Since he is capable of gratification, he is capable of monogamy without compulsion or repression; but he is also capable, if a reasonable motive is given, of changing the object without suffering any injury. He does not adhere to his sexual object out of guilt feelings or out of moral considerations, but is faithful out of a healthy desire for pleasure: because it gratifies him. He can master polygamous desires if they are in conflict with his relations to the loved object without repression; but he is able also to yield to them if they overly disturb him. The resulting actual conflict he will solve in a realistic manner. There are hardly any neurotic feelings of guilt. (p. 161)

Kernberg's contributions on the nature of and capacity for love are among his most important, and it is here we can see most clearly the radical renovations he has made in the classical mansion.

The most severely disturbed individuals in Kernberg's schema of love relations experience love and sexuality in the context of their inability to establish and maintain stable boundaries between self and other. For them, relationships with others do not occur on a continuum from privacy to intimacy; either there is no relationship, or there is total, confusing, often terrifying merger.

Robert, for example, had given up sexual experiences with actual others in midlife. He described his earlier sexual contacts as cataclysmic encounters; he experienced sexual arousal as a terrifying state of dangerous excitement. His mother was clinically depressed; his father had died when he was three, and he spent long stretches of time in isolation as a child. When on a date with a woman he was attracted to, he felt compelled to push for sexual intimacy almost immediately. The excitement itself felt unbearable; it made him totally vulnerable to the woman, whom he desperately needed to possess to regain a sense of control and integrity. If he did not succeed in bedding the woman, he felt shaken for days afterward. If he did succeed, he felt a strong need to be rid of her, spending days afterward in a well-protected isolation in which he felt he did his best, most creative work. Robert's lust had an undifferentiated quality; the women rarely seemed distinguishable to him as people. Their most important feature was the dangerous arousal they generated in him. By early middle age he had given up sex with all women except prostitutes, because the control he could maintain in those encounters made them less disturbing and dangerous. Finally, only the total control of masturbatory fantasies provided Robert the protection he needed from the precarious fissures in his self-integrity that sexual desire opened up.

In Kernberg's account, individuals in the borderline range experience love and sexuality in the context of their inability to integrate good and bad object relations into a single, complex relationship. For them, sexual desire is often keyed to a highly particular scenario whose perverse, often violent qualities are too disturbing to integrate into the tender, intimate side of their relationships.

Joyce, a writer in her twenties, could experience sexual arousal in a wide set of circumstances in relation to different types of men, but she could achieve orgasm, either with a man or in masturbation, only if she conjured up a fantasy of being brutally treated and punished. Both her parents were remarkably self-absorbed, narcissistic people who had tended to ignore and abandon her for long stretches of her childhood; when they were involved with her, they often teased her cruelly. Analytic inquiry suggested that she felt really connected to a man only when he was focused enough on her to punish or abuse her, which also enabled her to feel her own destructiveness was safely contained through identification with the man's sadism. Although she sought relationships with men she felt were loving and kind, she secretly believed all men were abusive; if they were not abusing her now, then they would shortly. To allow herself to surrender to orgasm in the context of love and tenderness was unconsciously felt to be impossibly dangerous; the love would inevitably be destroyed by either her own aggression or the man's turn toward destructiveness. Only by evoking images of mistreatment she knew, understood, and would not be surprised by could she feel safe enough to let herself go sexually. Ironically, Joyce's relationships with men lasted only a short time. When she decided they were not kind or interested in intimacy (i.e., when she felt they actually corresponded to her required sexual fantasy), she broke off the relationship to search for a man she could be close to.

A similar kind of radical splitting characterized the sexuality of Harold, whose actual relationships with women tended to be largely asexual. Although he had a rich fantasy life, he became involved in essentially platonic relationships and felt retrospectively worried that he had been too aggressive and coercive when he had had sex with women in the past. One of these largely platonic relationships was with a woman who had chronic vaginal pain and wide-ranging sexual inhibitions and phobias. She would allow Harold to have sex with her once or twice a year, but only if he applied antibiotic ointment to his penis, inserted it very gradually, and withdrew quickly.

In Kernberg's framework, the experience of sexuality for Joyce was organized into her borderline world rent by the polarization of good and evil, love and hate. The passions of sexuality were infused with meanings having to do with aggression and violence; love and tenderness were unintegratable with sexual desire. Thus, Joyce could allow herself sexual release only through a compromise arrangement in which sadomasochism was played out in fantasy, and Harold could allow himself sexual intercourse only if he offered himself to serve as a human medicine applicator, therein relying on an external ritual to contain and control his expected aggression.

Neurotic-level issues involving love and sexuality are understood, in Kernberg's system, in terms of classical impulse–defense conflicts. Neurotic patients have established self–object differentiation and have overcome splitting. They relate to whole objects with an integrated self, and their difficulties concern conflicts over impulses (in contrast to irreconcilable rifts between mutually dissociated versions of the self). Kernberg would understand Gloria (discussed in chapter 1 in terms of Freudian theory) in much the same way as did Freud. Her relationships were whole object relationships compromised by oedipal conflicts and subsequent inhibitions.

Thus, Kernberg's synthesis has preserved much of Freud's system by recontextualizing it within a broader frame of reference and by deriving Freud's drive psychology from a prior developmental progression of ego differentiation and object relations. In this revised Freudian theory, sexuality still plays a central but no longer a causative role. The meanings of sexuality itself are derived from earlier and deeper structures composed of self–object relationships. As Kernberg stresses, "It is the world of internalized and external object relations that keeps sexuality alive and provides the potential for 'eternal' sexual gratification" (1980, pp. 294–295).

One of the most interesting ideological battles in the psychoanalytic literature of recent years has been between Kernberg and the self psychologists. It is worth noting some of the issues that divide the two camps, because they reflect the difference between a revisionist position, like Kernberg's, that nevertheless remains loyal to certain basic features of Freudian thought and a more radical position, like Kohut's, that left Freud's drive theory more completely behind. Kernberg views Kohut's self psychology as deemphasizing the body, sexuality, and, especially, aggression. For Kernberg, the central dynamic struggle is between love and hate, and these manifest themselves necessarily in the transference to the analyst. As we noted in chapter 6, Kohut regarded aggression as well as impulsive sexuality as byproducts of narcissistic injury. In Kohut's model, people strive for self-organization and self-expression. In Kernberg's model, people are torn by powerful passions of love and hate. Kohut saw the narcissist as attempting to protect a brittle self-esteem. Kernberg sees the narcissist as contemptuous and devaluing. Kohut thought the analyst should empathically reflect the narcissist's self-experience so that a more consolidated, more robust self could develop. Kernberg believes the analyst should interpret the narcissist's underlying hostility so that more integrated object relations could develop. The tension between these two approaches, often mirror images of each other, has had an invigorating effect on psychoanalytic theorizing and broadened the range of clinical options for practitioners.[2]

ROY SCHAFER

Roy Schafer has explored many areas of psychoanalytic theory and clinical practice and has had an enormous impact on the shaping and development of contemporary psychoanalytic thought. Because of their range and variety, Schafer's contributions can be approached from many different perspectives. Among his innovations are an analysis and redefining of classical Freudian terminology (1968); a philosophical critique of psychoanalytic language, grounded in the analytic philosophy of Wittgenstein and Ryle and having important clinical implications (1976); and, along with Donald Spence, the introduction of hermeneutics and the concept of "narratives" into psychoanalytic discourse (1983, 1992). Simply establishing Schafer's place in the field of current analytic theorizing is difficult to do. In some respects, he is one of the most persuasive spokespersons for the Freudian sensibility; in other respects, he has been one of its most trenchant and devastating critics.

Agency

The relationships among Schafer's varied and far-ranging contributions can be grasped most easily through an appreciation of his struggle with one basic, recurrent issue: the problem of agency. To understand why agency became such a nettlesome and also highly productive struggle for Schafer, we have to return to Freud once again, from yet another vantage point.

Freud demonstrated convincingly that his contemporaries had a vastly oversimplified understanding of the nature of mind, which they took to be transparent to itself and of a single, integral piece: "I am what I know about myself, and I am in control of what I am." Freud demonstrated that mind was not integral but composed of many different motives and intentions in conflict with one another: mind is not transparent to the knower but contains a great deal that is opaque and inaccessible—an immense array of unconscious processes.

In developing this much more complex vision of mind, Freud drew on the scientific understanding of his day, borrowing from Newtonian physics the idea of the universe as an intricate system of mechanisms composed of matter and forces and applying it to the mind, envisioning it as a psychic apparatus composed of structures and psychodynamic forces. Freud demonstrated that the subjective sense of self as an omnipotent agent over one's experience and actions is an illusion. Consciousness is merely the tip of an iceberg; thoughts and feelings are actually (psychically) determined by unconscious forces not accessible to self-reflection. One often does not, in fact, know what one is *really* doing. Consequently, in Freud's system the person as agent is dispersed. A conscious sense of agency is illusory; the conscious self is more correctly depicted as a puppet. The strings are being controlled elsewhere, in the unconscious, by psychic agencies (id, ego, and superego) and by dynamic forces (instinctual impulses and defenses).

Kleinian theory and various British object relations theories inspired by the work of Fairbairn and Winnicott brought about in the 1950s and 1960s a population explosion in the psychoanalytic world of unconscious quasi-agents. Not only were the strings of mind seen as being controlled by Freud's puppeteers (impulses, defenses, id, ego, superego), but to these were added all sorts of personifications: internal objects, introjects, identifications, incorporations, part objects, and many more. Analysts had begun to write and speak in a fashion that assigned both intentionality and power to these internal agents (e.g., "His maternal introject attacked him mercilessly").

Schafer's first extended psychoanalytic work (1968) can be understood as a response to this proliferation of quasi-agents in psychoanalytic discourse. In the style of his mentor, David Rapaport (who had attempted to systematize, codify, and empiricize psychoanalytic theories), Schafer undertook the task of more precisely and clearly defining basic psychoanalytic concepts and terminology. The thread running through these redefinitions was the struggle to reestablish the *person* as the agent of his experience— to reassemble the *subject* that had been dispersed in the creation of psychoanalytic understandings. Schafer felt that it had become crucial to clarify just who was doing what to whom.

By the early 1970s, Schafer had abandoned what might be considered Rapaport's project, his attempt to rescue traditional psychoanalytic language. The problem was deeper and more pervasive, Schafer decided; what was necessary was a whole new way of talking. There was something fundamentally misguided about the way psychoanalytic ideas are understood and communicated; it is at odds with the basic nature of the analytic process, he believed.

What actually happens, in broad strokes, over the course of an analysis? The patient comes into treatment with a set of convictions about herself and the world she lives in: I am damaged because my father crushed me; the world is a dangerous place in which people are after me. Over the course of the analysis, these convictions change—they come to be experienced and understood in a very different way. What is the nature of that change?

In Schafer's account, the basic transformation that takes place in the analytic process is the patient's gradual assumption of agency with respect to previously disclaimed actions. The patient initially considers her beliefs about herself and her world to simply be true. She *has* been crushed; the world *is* dangerous. These are taken as givens, objective facts. In analysis, the patient comes to see that these "facts" have actually been created by her; even though she suffers greatly because of them, she both needs and wants to see herself and the world in just this way. She comes to understand that she derives secret satisfactions from these beliefs; they generate unconscious pleasures, and they provide her with a sense of safety and control. She comes to see that even though she hates thinking about herself and the world in these ways, she systematically refuses to have it any other way. She is committed to these beliefs and experiences. Her objectionable experience of herself and her world is not simply given or discovered; she is dedicated to keeping both herself and her world just this way. She is the agent of her world, the designer, the builder, the interpreter, yet she disclaims her agency and thereby feels herself to be at the mercy of her situation and her fate. As the analysand comes to understand and experience herself as the agent of her (internal and external) world, it becomes possible for her to imagine herself making other choices, acting in the world and organizing her experience in a more open, more constructive fashion.

From Schafer's point of view, the problem of agency, at first disclaimed and then gradually reclaimed, has been at the center of clinical psychoanalysis from its inception and is at the heart of each truly analytic process. Yet because of Freud's disagreement with Victorian notions of an omnipotent will and because of the scientism of his age, Freud constructed a language to speak about psychoanalysis using terms of impersonal forces, a language that, like the neurotic, systematically leaves out the agent herself.

Schafer then asks us to consider more closely the language Freud chose to describe psychodynamic processes. Drives build up autonomously "inside" the mind, pressing for discharge. If they are not discharged, they become dammed up and grow toxic. This language, Schafer points out, is the language of primitive bodily processes, of urination and defecation. Freud was describing the mind as if it were a body, with clear boundaries, interior spaces and substances. Not only is this not an adequate language for depicting the way the mind works, it is riddled with the same misunderstandings and fantasies that neurotic patients need analysis to clarify, Schafer argues. Freud bequeathed us a language for understanding neurosis that is saturated with neurotic fantasies and infantile misunderstandings. And, ironically, the most widespread omission in traditional psychoanalytic language is, precisely, the person as agent, the central focus of clinical psychoanalysis as it is actually practiced.[3] So in *A New Language for Psychoanalysis* (1976) Schafer attempted no less than a broad translation of the basic principles and concepts of psychoanalysis from the language of forces and structures to an action language of agents and intentions.

Narrative

The Wittgensteinian action language proposed by Schafer in 1976 proved awkward both in clinical process and in theoretical discourse and has not found wide acceptance. But Schafer's critique of the underlying ideas about the mind that pervaded classical concepts had an important impact, and by the 1980s he had found a much more compelling device for conveying his innovative understandings: the concept of narrative.

Mind is not the end result of impersonal forces, as Freud had described—mind is generated by actions, particular kinds of actions; mind is generated by and organized according to narratives, Schafer proposed. Drawing on the burgeoning interest in hermeneutics in the humanities and the social sciences, Schafer began to present traditional psychoanalytic concepts not as scientific principles but as interpretive storylines. (The broader implications of hermeneutics for psychoanalysis will be taken up in chapter 8.) Schafer's original alternative to Freud's field of dynamic forces, the agent of actions, was now depicted as the narrator of stories. And this narrative approach has served as a robust context in which Schafer has assimilated into a basically Freudian clinical framework many of the innovative features of self psychology (in *The Analytic Attitude,* 1983) and Kleinian theory (in *Retelling a Life,* 1992).

Schafer's revision of psychoanalytic concepts and language is anchored in broad, abstract philosophical concerns but has enormous practical implications for the way clinical material is thought about and worked with.

Consider the dream of a patient, Ronald, who had been in psychoanalysis for three years. At the point when the dream appeared, Ronald was feeling he had gotten a great deal out of the analysis, although he was periodically gripped by profound doubts that anything would ever really help him.

Ronald initially sought treatment because of a long-standing depression and sense of paralysis. He had been quite successful in many ways, but always had a feeling of unreality about his activities and achievements. Even though he generally seemed to be passionately involved in whatever occupied him at any time, he would suffer waves of doubt and confusion about the meaning of everything. He had an image of himself as an outsider, as not really alive, as going through the motions. Whatever activity he had chosen was not really the *right* activity for him; whatever woman he was with was not really the *right* woman. Ronald often felt as if the depression and deadness he had felt as a child were the only real things about him, as if everything else was simply playacting.

Analytic inquiry had shed considerable light on Ronald's depression, which had originated and seemed closely bound up with his relationship with his chronically ill mother. She had suffered with cancer throughout his early childhood and had been hospitalized many times. She finally died when he was twelve. Ronald's father, a prominent politician, dealt with his wife's illness by withdrawing from her and hiding the family's difficulties from the community. Outside the home he was charming and outgoing. Inside the home he was either remote or enraged. Ronald, an only child, felt abandoned by both parents; he felt that his father had left his mother to him. He felt very much chosen by her, but the responsibility for being her companion and her nurse was overwhelming.

Ronald had come to understand a great deal about the relationship between his early childhood experience and his current struggles. He had felt his father's public personality was a fake and a lie, that the shameful, secret reality of his mother's illness and the family's problems was the ultimate truth about his parents and about himself. He felt he had been damaged severely by the emotional deprivation of his childhood, which he, by imitating his father, had learned to cover over in public.

Ronald felt deeply emotionally involved with the analyst and the analysis. As he and his analyst explored his childhood despair and dread and his current conflicts and doubts, he felt cared about and connected to in a way he had never felt before. In the course of treatment Ronald had begun to feel more able to commit himself to whatever it was he was involved in. He had begun to have a sense of himself as living in a community of other people, as inside the circle of human activities, rather than as the desolate outsider he had always felt himself to be. It was at this point that he had the following dream:

I am looking out the back window of (the graduate school he attends). I notice this blob that is moving toward the building. It progresses slowly, devouring everything in its path. When it gets near something, like a chair or a bush, it at first becomes like that thing, only a giant version of it. After a few seconds, the thing itself is gone and the blob loses its shape and becomes a blob again. It is moving closer and closer. Your chair is out there, and the blob is starting to become a big version of that, but then I woke up.

Although the dream at first seemed odd, Ronald soon began to feel that the dream graphically caught something of his typical inner sense of himself. The blob was his depression, shapeless, formless, menacing. Whatever he tried to do, whatever he became involved with, seemed real and vivid for a while, but then it would dissolve; the meaning would be lost, and he would be only a blob once again. Now the analysis had become important, larger than life. But it too, Ronald feared, would dissolve into meaninglessness. No matter how hard he tried, the blob was inescapable. The dream seemed to vividly capture his tortured experience of what it was like to be him.

Consider some of the possible ways of understanding the blob: The blob is an expression of anal sadism, the instinctually driven wish to bury and destroy everything he is connected to (Freud); the blob is his true self, inchoate and unformed, seeking conditions for possible growth (Winnicott); the blob is a representation of his malformed, structureless interior, lacking in stable identifications and regulatory mechanisms (ego psychology); the blob represents the state of his self, portraying the aborted development of his sense of subjectivity or personhood (self psychology).

The problem with all such interpretations of the dream, from Schafer's point of view, is that they leave out the dreamer's activity. For Schafer, the dream is a creation, a narrative construction in which Ronald has organized his experience along selected lines for specific purposes. There is no singular correct interpretation; rather, the dream, like other narrative constructions, such as poems or novels, lends itself to various understandings. When the meaning of the dream is approached from this angle, the emphasis shifts to the functional utility of different narrative approaches, both for Ronald, in dreaming the dream, and for Ronald and the analyst in their efforts to use it.

What purpose does it serve for Ronald to represent himself to himself as a blob? From Schafer's point of view, the blob is not Ronald's anal sadism; Ronald has borrowed anal imagery and bodily metaphors to represent his destruction of the value of his experiences. The blob is not Ronald's true self, his ego structures, or his subjectivity; Ronald has portrayed himself to himself along these story lines for a variety of purposes. They might include such dynamics as: maintaining a powerful unconscious tie to his mother in her sickness and withdrawal, defeating the father and his model of living in the outside world, preserving a fantasy of oneness and infinite potential that transcends public and private, and so on.

What purpose does it serve Ronald and the analyst to understand the dream in one way or another? For Schafer, the value of an interpretation of a dream lies not in its objectivity or correctness, but in its potential for opening up new forms of experience and allowing the dreamer to claim a deeper and broader sense of his own activity.

Thus Schafer's most important contribution has been to recontextualize the traditional content of Freudian analysis. Schafer has asked us to consider the anachronistic features of Freud's very understanding of what he was doing when he developed a psychodynamic approach to mind. The scientistic underpinnings of that understanding are no longer persuasive. But if Freud's work is reset into a contemporary hermeneutic framework, Schafer suggests, not only does it work better, its interpretive power to elucidate clinical process is more fully revealed.

HANS LOEWALD

Of all the major figures in the contemporary psychoanalytic world, Hans Loewald (1906–1993) is perhaps the most difficult to position. Loewald came to the United States in the early 1940s after studying philosophy with Martin Heidegger. He worked with Harry Stack Sullivan and Frieda Fromm-Reichmann during his analytic training in the Baltimore area. But his abiding passion was Freud. He has carefully and lovingly found places in Freud's theory to root all the features of his own; yet his own thinking has blossomed into approaches to mind and the psychoanalytic process that are powerfully unique and visionary. His prose is scholarly, extremely dense and closely reasoned, yet he describes and evokes experiences that are extraordinarily rich and deeply sensual, seeming to call for a mystical transformation. His reading of Freud appears offbeat, at some points stunningly fresh and at other points strained; it is always at odds with the way Freud has been understood in the American ego psychology mainstream. Yet Loewald's revisionary and revitalizing approach to Freud has had extraordinary impact on how Freud is being read today by those who draw their inspiration from classical theory.

Loewald's contributions span nearly forty years in which he has struggled over and over with the same central problems, now one facet, now another, now from one angle, now from another. This concern has been with the most fundamental assumptions of psychoanalytic theory-building, our most basic preconceptions about the nature of mind, reality, and the analytic process.

Loewald on Language

Language has always been a central feature of psychoanalytic theorizing, from Freud's early contributions on dreams and slips of the tongue. Leowald approached language from a perspective that is unique among analytic theorists. Consider a one-year-old child who sits at the breakfast table, singing, babbling, playing with sounds and with her food. She has recently been uttering words that are recognizable and even, on occasion, stringing two or three together. Orange juice is a big favorite of hers, and today she asks for more by saying something like "Numa numa numa numa joooooose." Her parents are delighted. They meet her request, saying as they do: "More juice?"

Experiences like this one constitute a crucial developmental bridge. On the near side of the bridge, the child is embedded in an idiosyncratic world of distinctly personal experience, accidental connections, autistic reveries. She has powerful connections with others in her preverbal world, but they are unique and exclusive connections, based on shared private meanings, dependent on intently attuned caretakers. On the far side of the bridge, the child is entering a social world of consensual experience, agreed-upon meanings, abstract and general understandings. Communications and connections with others will become generalizable; experience will become much more easily and reliably shared.

Different authors have broadly varying attitudes toward this crucial developmental transition. At one extreme, Sullivan regarded preverbal (parataxic) experience as idiosyncratic and distorted; language creates the possibility for shared (syntaxic) experience, established with others through consensual validation, and becomes progressively stripped of its idiosyncrasies, thereby providing for the child a wonderful vehicle for escaping iso-lation and self-absorption into a world of clarity, shared experience, and meaningful connection. The consensual, shared use of language is an unmitigated blessing, Sullivan believed.

Daniel Stern, a contemporary researcher who has written both technical and popular books integrating empirical infant research into a vision of infancy and childhood, feels that a sensual, sensory richness of preverbal experience is sacrificed in the packaging of experience into language. The gain in clarity is accompanied by a loss in variety. Language for Stern is a mixed blessing.

What Sullivan and Stern have in common is that they both see a gulf between preverbal and verbal experience. (Although for Stern, earlier forms of experience are maintained in the perpetuation throughout life of "pre-verbal senses of self" alongside a verbal sense of self.)

Loewald takes a very different approach. The use of language that both Sullivan (happily) and Stern (regretfully) take for granted is, for Loewald, a debased, shallow, disembodied form of communication. He envisions the beginnings of language not as a translation *from* sensory experience, but as a form *of* sensory experience. "One might say that while the mother utters words, the infant does not perceive words but is bathed in sound, rhythm, etc., as accentuating ingredients of a uniform experience" (1980, p. 187). As development proceeds, the words *also* take on meaning as signifiers, referring to things beyond themselves.

Loewald terms language in the first, embedded, embodied mode "primary process," in the second, generalizable, differentiated mode "secondary process." (Here Loewald is retooling Freud's distinction of channels of energy flow to refer instead to forms of experience.) What is crucial for Loewald is the connection or lack of connection between these two modes of expe-rience. This issue of rupture and/or reconciliation between levels of organi-zation is *the* central problem Loewald returns to again and again through-out his writings. Language and other forms of secondary-process experience that have been ruptured from their original primary-process density, from the global, sensual experience out of which they emerged, are pathological, he believes. Mental health is contingent on the richness of experience that is generated by open channels between primary process and secondary process, primitive and sophisticated thinking, lower and higher forms of intellectual organization.

The child's request for more juice embodies in itself a tension between the abstract meaning of the request and the sensuality and playfulness of gen-erating the sounds "numa numa numa numa joooooose." From Loewald's perspective, what is crucial to the richness of her subsequent experience is that the increasing clarity and generalizability of her verbalizations are not accompanied by a loss of the sensory and sensual pleasures of her experience of playing with food, gestures, and sounds at the breakfast table with her parents. For Loewald, pathological development entails a split between primary and secondary process, between the sensual and the abstract, between fantasy and reality, between past and present. Healthy development is characterized by a perpetual reconciliation and interpenetration between these different dimensions of experience.

The Unitary Whole

The traditional reading of Freud assumes a material reality "out there." The baby, containing various biological resources and propensities, is born into that material reality. Among the baby's constitutional givens are a set of instinctual drives, urgently pressing for discharge, which inevitably clash with the social environment. Mind is the apparatus built up to channel and regulate the drives, necessarily negotiated between the baby and the environment. Other people, "objects" of the drives, serve as both vehicles for drive discharge and an aid (through internalization into the superego) for drive regulation and control.

Loewald challenges all these traditional premises, positing instead an original, unitary whole composed of both the baby and the caregivers as a starting point for psychological development. In the beginning, there is no distinction between self and other, between ego and external reality, between instincts and objects. Everything that traditional psychoanalytic theory takes for granted as basic and irreducible, Loewald regards as secondary and derivative of dichotomies that emerge from this original unity. One of the central implications of this perspective is that there is nothing in the developing child which was in the baby from the start (neither instincts nor a "true self" in Winnicott's sense). Everything in the developing child, and later the adult, is a product of interaction.

Loewald's radical interactionalism is a far cry from Freud's drive theory perspective. Yet Loewald is adept at wresting new meanings from Freud's language and images. One key strategy in Loewald's reinterpretation of Freud is his claim that Freud himself underwent an abrupt shift in his thinking about the drives.

In Loewald's view, Freud really had two different understandings of the nature of the drives, before and after 1920. The earlier theory, drive as discharge-seeking, is generally taken to represent Freud's thinking in general. This earlier theory, Loewald argues, was wedded to nineteenth-century scientific materialism, and based on hydraulic and machine metaphors of Freud's day. In introducing the concept of Eros in 1920 (in *Beyond the Plea-*

sure Principle), Freud was radically altering his view of libido as a drive, Loewald believes, no longer discharge-seeking but connection-seeking, not using objects for gratification but for building more complex mental experience and for reestablishing the lost original unity between self and others.

Loewald's revision of Freud's drive theory demands a radical reformulation of virtually all traditional psychoanalytic concepts. Consider, for example, Loewald's reworking of Freud's "archaeological simile." In Freud's theorizing, the id is understood as never in contact with external reality. Its discharges in the real world are mediated through the ego. The id operates beneath external reality, expressing the archaic heritage that is present at birth. The digging of the archaeologist takes him deeper into the past; the interpretations of the psychoanalyst enables him to sift through the surface, daily interactions to uncover the deeper, inherited primal fantasies.

Loewald asks us to consider this simile more closely. The ruins of the ancient cities may bear no relationship to current political and economic processes in the modern countries they are buried under. But the ancient cities were surely built in close connection and interaction with the political and economic processes of *their* time. It is only in relation to the current, surface culture that the relics seem remote and disconnected.

Similarly, it is a serious mistake to assume that the ancient remains uncovered by the psychoanalytic archaeologist, just because they may be unrelated to present-day activities, were unrelated to the external environment, the interactional context, of their day. The id deals with and is "a creature of 'adaptation' just as much as the ego—but on a very different level of organization" (1980, p. 232).

What Freud finds in the past are, ultimately, primeval forces, which rule current experience from their remote depths. Loewald finds discarded relics that were generated by ancient civilizations which once dominated the scene. Freud's id is an unchanging biological force clashing with social reality. Loewald's id is an interactional product of adaptation rather than a constant biological force. Mind does not become interactive secondarily, but is interactive in its very nature. Loewald sees life as beginning in a union between the baby and the mother; the mother's handling of the baby, the mother's image of the baby, the mother's sensual experience of the baby all become essential dimensions of the baby's own experience of himself. Whatever "drives" come to motivate the developing child are shaped through interaction with the mother; they do not preexist and find the mother as their object.

Loewald portrays the mind as extremely rich in internal connections between past and present, inside and outside, infantile and mature, self and other, fantasy and actuality. He understands these distinctions as richly interpenetrating dialectics, not sharp dichotomies. Thus Loewald suggests that infantile, oedipal love detracts from and interferes with adult love when childhood experience is repressed, too strictly separated from adult experience. Then the loves of childhood operate like ghosts who, according to legend, have been improperly buried and haunt the living in their effort to find peace.

When the experiences of childhood are released from repression, accepted and worked through, they have a very different relationship to current experience. One doesn't have to choose, Loewald suggests, between childhood love and adult love, past and present. Experiences with early love objects are not best thought of as relinquished, but as refound and re-created with adult love objects. The new love is neither wholly different from nor merely a stand-in for the old love. The new love is both new and old, providing new experiences within which are found resonances of old experiences. Early love objects, like ancestors, provide guidelines to new experiences; when they have been properly buried and revered, they have continual access to the present and no longer have to dominate it from their anguished seclusion, seeking the "blood of recognition" (1980, p. 249).

Sublimation and Symbolism

Freud's early contributions on symbolism and its function in the formation of dreams and neurotic symptoms has had a profound impact not only on psychoanalysis but on many other intellectual disciplines. Body parts and bodily processes, as well as various disturbing facets of personal experience, become represented in dreams and symptoms in disguised forms. A snake in a dream or a phobia, for example, is a stand-in for the penis. The snake symbolizes the penis and performs a delicate double function, both revealing and concealing, representing the repressed image, but in a camouflaged form.

It was a short step for Freud and others to perceive similar symbolic processes as working in culture at large: in anthropology and sociology, in art and literature, and, eventually, in politics and history as well. The application of Freud's understanding of symbolism was greatly broadened through his use of the concept of *sublimation*. Symbolic representation makes it possible for instinctual impulses to find disguised, socially acceptable forms of gratification, not as satisfying as direct physical pleasure, but a reasonable compromise with necessary social constraints. Thus the snake charmer, and the architect of skyscrapers and the violinist, have found symbolic masturbatory equivalents. In fact, Freud became convinced, all of culture is built on sublimation, the disguised gratification of infantile sexual and aggressive impulses.

In the conventional application of psychoanalytic interpretation, both to clinical data and to cultural phenomena, the symbol is a substitute for the symbolized (the snake for the penis). In the act of interpretation, the snake is revealed as a camouflaged equivalent of the penis; its disguise is exposed; its real meaning unmasked. Traditional psychoanalytic interpretation is reductive: the symbol, once revealed, collapses into the symbolized. The snake is nothing but the penis, deceptively packaged.

The traditional psychoanalytic understanding of sublimation and symbolism opened up a whole new world of interpretive possibilities; it also created some serious problems for many psychoanalysts, including Loewald. Is all culture—the arts, the creative achievements of human civilization—best understood as disguised versions of infantile sexual and aggressive conflicts?

In the preceding chapters we have noted various solutions to this and other closely related problems. The neo-Freudians (Sullivan, Fromm, Horney) and the more radical of the object relations theorists (Fairbairn, Bowlby, Guntrip) abandoned Freud's drive theory altogether. Thus they didn't regard the higher pursuits of culture as being derived from Freud's dual-instinct theory. Hartmann and other ego psychologists took a different route, maintaining drive theory but using the concept of drive neutralization to legitimate motives other than sex and aggression. Culture could be seen as being derived from the ego's autonomous motives for mastery, functional expression, and so on.

Loewald wasn't happy with either of these solutions. For Loewald, Freud's discovery of the pervasive power and significance of infantile bodily experiences was one of the great discoveries of Western intellectual history. Loewald wanted to maintain Freud's emphasis on sexuality and aggression, and he didn't want to separate the ego's motives from the id's (like Hartmann did). For Loewald, the concept of neutralization watered down and threatened to negate what was most precious and powerful in Freud's vision.

Loewald's characteristic approach was to try to find a way to reconcile rather than choose between modes of experience, levels of organization. He saw higher-level mental processes, creative cultural pursuits as always connected with, yet never simply reducible to, lower mental processes, primitive infantile experience. The snake or the skyscraper is always a penis, but never *just* a penis. Further, the penis, once represented by the snake or skyscraper, is no longer simply a penis, but has become transformed and enriched through the symbolic process. Symbolism is not a process of camouflage, but of mutual transformation.

Thus the symbol for Loewald is not a disguised version of something that already exists; the symbol creates a novel experience. As in the relation between fantasy and reality, past and present, childhood and adult love, the symbol gives new and enriched life to the symbolized. Culture is a representation of infantile experience, but not only a camouflaged equivalent. Culture is a re-presentation and reconciliation of childhood experience on a new, expanded, and enriched level of organization.

Because he understood drives as prehuman residues, essentially antipathetic to human culture and civilization, Freud's most optimistic vision was of infantile sexuality and aggression drained of their intensity and harnessed, through sublimation, for other purposes. Freud (1933, p. 80) invoked the image of the Zuider Zee to portray the appropriation by civilization of the power of natural forces. "Where id was, there ego shall be."

Loewald understands "drives" as fully human residues of previous interactions and interpersonal integrations. For Loewald, the draining of the sea for purposes of civilization would be a disaster. Reclaimed, unrepressed infantile experience enriches rather than detracts from adult experience. The sea is always there, powering, enhancing, resonating through more complex, higher-level experience, in which it finds new life.

JACQUES LACAN

The place of Jacques Lacan (1901–1981) in contemporary psychoanalytic thought is unlike that of any other author. He reigned over French psychoanalysis for decades, and his work is a dominant presence in psychoanalysis both in Europe and in South America. Although his influence on English-speaking psychoanalysts has been minimal, his impact on academia, particularly literary criticism, has been considerable. An enormous industry of explications and commentary has grown up around him; yet there is a complete lack of consensus about what his dense and difficult contributions really mean. His more enthusiastic followers consider him the most important French thinker since René Descartes (Lacan was continually grappling with traditional philosophical and epistemological problems) and compare him favorably to Nietzsche and Freud; his critics consider him deliberately obscurantist, an outrageous showman and stylist with little substance. (It is not uncommon to hear detractors quip about the way in which the psychoanalytic world has been la-conned.)

Lacan entered psychoanalysis through the unusual double route of medicine and surrealism. He lived in Paris, where his friends included many prominent surrealist painters and writers (he was closely associated with André Breton), and he contributed influential essays to early surrealist journals. French psychoanalysis, like so much in French cultural life, was decimated by World War II, and Lacan was at the center of the intense power struggle among the small group of French analysts that reconstituted the Paris Psychoanalytic Society after the war. Lacan had been experimenting with short, variable sessions (as opposed to the dependable routine of scheduled analytic hours), which became the focus of great opposition to him in both French and international psychoanalytic circles. He eventually left the Paris Psychoanalytic Society in 1953. At several different points, the groups he was associated with were denied admission to the International Psychoanalytic Association, consolidating Lacan's reputation as renegade. Further splits and splintering ensued, and in 1964 Lacan founded the Ecole Freudienne de Paris. By then he had become a major figure in French intellectual life; until his death, his public seminars were major cultural events, drawing spellbound and enthusiastic students of all intellectual disciplines from around the world.

Any discussion of Lacan's ideas necessarily begins with a consideration of why they are so difficult to understand.[4] Several factors are important. First, for the non-French reader, there is the problem of translation. Lacan approaches psychoanalysis through linguistics and literature, and his highly idiosyncratic style of writing and speaking is much more poetic than expository. (Commentators such as Mehlman, 1972, and Turkle, 1978, have suggested that his style was modeled on Mallarmé's.) According to some commentators, Lacan's central concepts, like good poetry, are simply untranslatable (Schneiderman, 1983, p. 92).

Second, Lacan was a creature less of psychoanalysis as a clinical discipline and international movement than of French intellectual life. There is no better example than Lacan's work of the way psychoanalysis in different countries takes on a distinctly national character. Lacan's presentations were spectacles, filled with the conceptual and verbal gamesmanship characteristic of the French intelligentsia: sweeping philosophical, political, and literary references and allusions, a contemptuous, combative posturing (the title of Julia Kristeva's novel depicting the intellectual world in which Lacan lived is, tellingly, *The Samurai*), and a complex blend of authoritarian fiat and antiauthoritarian defiance. These translation problems, both of language and of milieu, have left many readers interested in psychoanalysis content to remain, with respect to Lacan's contributions, among the uninitiated.

But there is more to it than that. Lacan's mode of presentation was intimately connected to what he was trying to teach about psychoanalysis. He was deliberately obscure, elusive, provocatively difficult. He did not want to be easily understood, at least not in the usual way we understand one another's communications.

The surrealists adapted from Freud the vision of an unconscious that is directly accessible and expressible through startling imagery and unguided language (such as automatic writing). Lacan's manner of presentation, some commentators (e.g., Oliner, 1988; Plottel, 1985) argue, was designed to embody the surrealist/Freudian unconscious. He repeated conundrums (the unconscious is the discourse of the Other; man's desire is the desire of the other; the unconscious is structured like a language) not to convey understanding but, like the Zen master's use of koans, to break up conventional thought patterns, provoking a grappling with deeper meanings. His words slide around, their meanings tumbling and reversing themselves, to demonstrate the way the mind plays with language, linking and unlinking words through puns, jokes, associations of sounds, meanings, and proximity. According to the most accessible of his interpreters, reading Lacan conveys "less clearly an impression of *what* Lacan thinks than *how*" (Muller & Richardson, 1982, p. 415).[5] In this sense, the purpose of Lacan's presentations is not the lucid communication of ideas but a Socratic sabotage, designed to push the reader into a novel, disconcerting kind of experience. (Both Sullivan and Bion, each in his own fashion, were similarly concerned with being easily understood or misunderstood; both, like Lacan, are very difficult to read.)

Lacan and Language

Lacan anchored his contributions in a reading of Freud (advertised under the banner of a "return to Freud"). Lacan shared a common starting point with some other contemporary interpreters of Freud but ended up moving in a unique direction. What Lacan has in common with many other important interpreters of Freud is the claim that Freud's most original and important innovations were obscured and compromised by his efforts to embed psychoanalysis in biology and thereby to scientize his vision of the psyche. (Habermas, Loewald, Schafer, and Guntrip all make similar arguments.) The differences, however, concern what Freud's central, innovative contribution is understood to be. For Lacan, the essential Freud was the pre-1905 Freud, whose concerns were the interpretation of dreams, neurotic symptoms, and (Freudian) slips. Lacan argued that Freud's understanding of all these phenomena derived from a revolutionary way of understanding language and its relation to experience and subjectivity. According to Lacan, an appreciation of Freud's real meaning is impossible unless one is grounded in the turn-of-the-century linguistics of Ferdinand de Saussure as well as the contemporaneous (to Lacan) linguistics of Roman Jakobson and the structural anthropology of Claude Lévi-Strauss, all icons in Lacan's French intellectual milieu. Both ego psychology and object relations theories are based on fundamental (and complementary) misreadings of Freud in which the ego and object relations are given priority, Lacan believed; the determinative dimension in human experience is neither self (i.e., ego) nor relations with others, but language.

The "Imaginary"

Lacan's concept of the "imaginary," which is essential to his continual, scathing critique of other analytic schools, was developed along two recurrent lines. The first was his portrayal of the prototypical experience of the imaginary, the mirror stage. In Lacan's account, the child between the ages of six and eighteen months undergoes a powerful, transformative experience when she notices and then becomes captivated by her own image in a mirror. The child's experience up to that point is discontinuous, fragmented, disjointed. She has incomplete control over her limbs and movements and no superordinate organization for integrating her various mental states. But reflected back in the mirror is a quite different creature: a whole, integrated, coordinated image. This image, which the child can control through her own movements and gestures, is an idealized version of herself. The mirrored image becomes the central node of an increasingly complex nexus of thoughts and feelings about what she is like, the core, the "Urbild" of the ego. Lacan wanted us to understand the mirror stage not in specific, concrete terms, but as an "exemplary function" (1988a, p. 74), representative of the way the ego is built around illusions, images, which then become the basis for the imaginary (*image*-inary).

The second grounding for the development of the imaginary was Lacan's analysis of the nature of human desire, which he saw as different from needs. The child has many needs in relation to the mother, who is able to satisfy those needs, but desire, the wellspring of passion, is more encompassing than the pursuit of satisfaction and the quelling of need—it is ultimately necessarily ungratifiable, Lacan believed. In desire, the child wishes to be totally captivating, to be everything for the (m)other. To truly be everything for the other would be to embody everything the other desires. Thus, for Lacan, the child comes to desire above all else to be the completing object of the (m)other's desire.

The following example strikingly illustrates Lacan's notion of desire as desire of the other.

Michael, a young man in his late twenties, entered psychoanalytic treatment because he could not reconcile his life with his goals for himself. He had grown up poor in the inner city and with effort had attained a considerable degree of professional and personal success. He wanted a committed relationship and a family. He frequently made progress in this direction by becoming involved with women with whom he was able to attain substantial intimacy. The problem was his passionate addiction to a different sort of woman, with whom he spent time dancing in nightclubs, a world that seemed incompatible with the domesticity he was seeking.

Michael frequented clubs that catered to dancers so elaborately and provocatively dressed that they were almost in costume. Michael was so well known and so accomplished as a dancer that he was a recognized "character" at these clubs. His style of dancing was highly erotic and romantic. He loved to dance with at least several different partners each night and was in great demand. This experience gave him a powerful charge that he could not do without.

What did Michael want? What was his desire? In analysis he came to understand that what he sought was neither to satisfy any needs of his own nor to develop an intimacy with any particular woman or dancer, but to occupy a central place in the minds of these women, to be wholly captivating to them, to be the total object of their desire. Of course it was not his real self occupying that place, but rather the character he had fashioned himself into, designed precisely for the purpose of sweeping women off their feet. In Lacan's sense, Michael lived in a world of the imaginary, organized around images of himself (the character he transformed himself into) and images of others (transformed into pure desire for his character).

Life in the realm of the imaginary (which, in Lacan's view, is where most ordinary, conventional living takes place) is experienced in a hall of mirrors, organized around mirages. The self each of us generally takes himself or herself to be is as much a social creation as Michael's character, constructed out of reflections of the perspectives of others.[6] We strive to be characters we are not, with various intense needs in relation to other characters who, because they are also social creations, also are not.

> If the object is only ever graspable as a mirage, the mirage of a unity . . . every object relation can only be infected with a fundamental uncertainty by it. . . . The object, at one instant constituted as a semblance of the human subject, a double of himself, nonetheless has a certain permanence of appearance over time. (1988a, p. 169)

The patient who enters the consulting room is fully embedded, in an unself-conscious fashion, in this alienated world of images and illusions, reflections of reflections. "The ego is the sum of the identifications of the subject . . . like the superimposition of various coats borrowed from what I would call the bric-a-brac of its props department" (1988b, p. 155).

From Lacan's point of view, the big mistake (and it is a very big mistake) of all other schools of contemporary psychoanalytic thought is that they take the imaginary to be real: Ego psychology, by focusing on the ego, its defects and its development, is the psychology of a social construction, a mirage mistaken for a reality (1977, p. 238); object relations theories, in their focus on the real and the fantastic relationships between the self and others, is a psychology of interpersonal fictions. Lacan believed that these trends degraded psychoanalysis and buried what he took to be Freud's fundamental contribution: the discovery of the (linguistic) unconscious beneath the petty, everyday concerns of the patient and his social relations with others. The ordinary subjectivity of the patient, the character he takes himself to be and acts like, is precisely what needs to be subverted and dispersed in analysis to a deeper connection with the transpersonal, "transindividual" (1977, p. 49) unconscious and a more creative, revitalized life.

In chapter 1 we suggested that Freud regarded the secret of dream interpretation as his greatest discovery because the dream is a metaphor for subjectivity in general. The real, latent meaning of the dream is disguised in the manifest content, which, through the process of secondary elaboration, has been shaped into a distracting little story. In Lacan's view, it is not just dreams but conscious subjective experience in general that is organized into distracting little stories, and it is the folly of ego psychology and object relations theories to have bought into the disguises offered by secondary elaboration, to have taken the illusory stories as real, rather than covers for an underlying sense of loss, absence, castration. "The subject," Lacan suggested, "doesn't know what he is saying," and the task is "to get the subject to shift from a psychic reality to a true reality" (1988b, pp. 244–245).

The idea that the analytic process is concerned with the dispersal of ordinary subjectivity is shared by other important contemporary psychoanalytic authors. For example, Thomas Ogden, in *Subjects of Analysis* (1994), decenters subjectivity and relocates it within a complex matrix of dialectical tensions among various modes of experience. And Bromberg (1991, 1993) has explored the emergence in analysis of discontinuous, dissociated states of mind. What distinguishes Lacan's approach from these closely related projects is his claim that the ordinary subject of experience is wholly illusory, not in a dialectical relationship with other modes of experience. This "ever more radical depersonalization of the subject" (Muller & Richardson, 1982, p. 416) is grounded in Lacan's understanding of language and its relationship to experience.[7]

Lacan's approach to language (which paralleled other recent French intellectual trends, such as structuralism, deconstructionism, and postmodernism in general) assumed that language predates and largely shapes individual experience. "The child," Lacan stressed, "is born into language" (1977, p. 103).

Much as Marxism regarded the subjective values and ideas of the individual as the vehicle for class position and economic forces, Lacan regarded experience as linguistically embedded in cultural fads (the "imaginary") and social laws (the "symbolic"). The conventional individual subject, the patient as he ordinarily experiences himself, is dispersed in the analytic process so that unconscious meanings, the linguistic meanings that preexisted him and struggle to speak through him, can be clearly heard. The distinction between speech and language is very important here. The analytic process endeavors to make it possible for a more authentic voice to break through the ordinary constrictions of language.

For Lacan, Freud's greatest methodological contribution, free association, made it possible to see through ordinary conversation, the intended content in the patient's mind (which Lacan called "empty speech"), to the deeper symbolic structures operative in the unconscious ("full speech") (1988a, pp. 50–52). Free association unhinges the patient's speech from ordinary subjectivity, ego concerns, needful attachments to imaginary others. "We try to cut off the moorings of the conversation with the other" (1988a, pp. 174–175). It is this dispersal of the conventional subject that allows the unconscious Subject, the Other, to speak through the patient. In this way something deeper than the ordinary awareness of the subject finds its distinctive voice.

At times Lacan seems to reify language, granting it a kind of transpersonal agency. The patient as presented becomes a puzzle, to be disassembled, so that the real meanings are revealed. The analyst provides "a qualified and skilled translation of the cryptogram representing what the subject is conscious of at the moment" (1988a, pp. 13–14). This translation or decoding is required if the subject's own voice is to be present in speech in the face of the cultural reification of language (John Muller, personal communication). Thus psychoanalysis for Lacan is neither the uncovering of instinctual conflict (as it is for most Freudians) nor the transformation of a relationship (as it is, for example, for object relations theorists), but an exegesis of the unintended meanings (the governing signifiers) in the patient's speech.

The analytic process transforms the patient's relationship to language. The patient is jarred by the analyst's general unresponsiveness and unexpected reactions into an appreciation of the otherness of language, the realization that he is not creating the language he is speaking, but, rather, that language predates him and shapes his experience. Language operates in an "ensemble" that is "anterior to any possible link with any particular experience of the subject" (1977, pp. 63–64).

Since the patient has no privileged position from which to understand the meanings of her speech, it is up the analyst to decipher those meanings. Words carry symbolic meanings that continually shift around, grouping and regrouping according to different principles of combination and selection.[8] In Lacan's approach to language, meaning is found in the relationship of important key words to each other, rather than in the relationship between those words and what they signify. Lacan's understanding of symbolism is in sharp contrast to Loewald's, which proposed a dialectical and mutually transformative relationship between the symbol and the symbolized (for example, the snake and the penis); for Lacan, the symbol or the signifier (the snake) becomes unhinged from the symbolized (the penis), and groups of signifiers (for example, phallic symbols) take on a life of their own. Thus language can be analyzed into underlying chains of signifiers, words grouped around common, intersecting nodal points, which link them to other word chains. Part of the impenetrability of Lacan's work in the decade before his death is due to his use of set theory and topological structures—the increasingly technical, mathematical, and abstract ways he understood language to operate, images such as the Mobius strip and Boromian knot that play, paradoxically, with problems of beginnings and endings, insides and outsides.

The Oedipus Complex and the "Symbolic"

The essential concept through which Lacan connected Freudian psychoanalysis, structural linguistics, and Lévi-Strauss's structural anthropology was his rereading of Freud's account of the Oedipus complex. Lacan portrays the infant's original state of being with the mother in paradisiacal terms, mediated through needs the mother is able to gratify. But this early seamless unity is soon broken by the beginnings of awareness of the separation between self and mother. This disconnection from the mother and the disjointedness of the infant's experience of his body and his mental states reflect what Lacan considered a basic disjuncture fundamental to human experience, a congenital gap. "In man . . . this relation to nature is altered by a certain dehiscence at the heart of the organism, a primordial Discord" (1977, p. 4). This gap gives rise to Desire, by which Lacan meant much more than sexual impulse or demands for the satisfaction of needs. Desire is ultimately insatiable, because desire is born of the longing to heal the gap, to repair the disjuncture, to attain an impossible (imaginary) recollection, to be at one with mother and nature once again.

The first desire for each of us is the longing to be the phallus for the mother. Phallus here refers not to the literal penis but the object of the mother's desire. The child wants to be everything for the mother; the child desires to fulfill, by himself the totality of the mother's desire. What stands in the way of this fulfillment is the father. The father lays claim to the mother; the father has the phallus that is the object of the mother's desire; the father lays down the Law that severs the union of child and mother and regulates their exchange. The child cannot be the mother's phallus, and, therefore, he or she is castrated.

In this retelling of the Oedipus story, desire is only minimally concerned with the sexual impulses Freud emphasized; Lacan used *desire* to refer to a longing for a kind of existential reparation, perpetually unfulfillable, "eternally stretching forth towards the *desire for something else*" (1977, p. 167). Castration is the underlying state for both sexes, unrelated to the possession or lack of a literal penis. The renunciation of the child's sexual ambitions and dyadic unity with the mother is established through the father's presence, which stands for the regulating, organizing, symbolizing functions of language itself. Lacan is speaking not just of the actual person of the father, but the "name of the father." By naming the father, the mother ruptures the imaginary union between the child and herself and establishes the "symbolic" order. Through the naming of the father, the child becomes informed of the presence of the father and his phallus that preceded the child, that, in fact, made the birth of the child possible; the child is thereby inducted by the mother into the lawful social order of regulations and symbolic relationships.[9]

Lacanian Analysis

What is the product of a Lacanian analysis like? Because of Lacan's elusiveness and because of his central concern with the seductive dangers of compliance with the analyst's own ideals and values, this question is more difficult to answer than with other schools of psychoanalytic thought. Certainly, a Lacanian analysis would not aim at removing symptoms, improving relationships, or consolidating a more coherent and resilient sense of self. Yet Lacan did provide occasional hints at what he expected to be accomplished.

First, the analysand would live in a state philosophers describe as "being" or "existence" rather than in the ego-consciousness with which he began.[10] His ego, while not exactly withering away (as in some varieties of Eastern enlightenment), would seem less substantial, more transparent, less a self-conscious focus of concern.

For the subject, the uncoupling of his relation to the other causes the image of his ego to fluctuate, to shimmer, to oscillate, renders it complete and incomplete. So that he can recognize all the stages of his desire, all the objects which have given consistency, nourishment and body to this image, he has to perceive it in its completeness, to which he has never had access. (1988a, p. 181)

Second, the analysand would have a very different sense of his relationship to language. Rather than experiencing himself as the creator and agent of the language he generates, he would experience himself as a vehicle through which speaks his unconscious and the linguistic matrix of which he is a part. He learns that his own lines are simply a portion of a larger text (the "Discourse of the Other").

This passion of the signifier now becomes a new dimension of the human condition in that it is not only man who speaks, but that in man and through man *it* speaks . . . that his nature is woven by effects in which is to be found the structure of language, of which he becomes the material, and that therefore there resounds in him, beyond what could be conceived of by a psychology of ideas, the relation of speech. (1977, p. 284)

The surrealists, who shaped much of Lacan's experience of the unconscious, were interested in phenomena such as automatic writing, whereby one surrenders oneself to writing without conscious control or intent, and meaning emerges. Analogously, Lacan seems to have envisioned a kind of automatic living, in which unconscious gestures and speech emerge directly, bypassing the distorting effects of ego and object-relatedness. Lacan's own flamboyant, theatrical lifestyle (see Schneiderman, 1983) was taken as a prototype by his disciples for a creative, heroic subjectivity, released from its conventional constraints through the analytic process. "Creative subjectivity has not ceased in its struggle to renew the never-exhausted power of symbols in the human exchange that brings them to the light of day" (Lacan, 1977, p. 71).

Third, the analytic process as redefined by Lacan would result in a different relationship between the subject and his own desire. Desire is not renounced in favor of a more rational and mature perspective; rather, by being named and recognized, desire is more fully owned. Analysis does not generate freedom—one remains caught in the constraints of the symbolic order and one's own particular history and destiny. Analysis makes possible a fuller embracing of one's destiny as one's own. Thus a Lacanian analyst would not push the patient Michael toward a more adaptive or consistent approach to women or marriage, but a realization that what drives him is the power of his longing for recognition as the object of desire for the

Other. Eventually, love (as distinct from a desire to be loved) may be possible, but this would require, Lacan hinted, a renunciation.

> Man can adumbrate his situation in a field made up of rediscovered knowledge only if he has previously experienced the limits within which, like desire, he is bound. Love, which, it seems to some, I have downgraded, can be posited only in that beyond, where, at first, it renounces its object. (1978, p. 276)

Lacan and Feminism

Lacan has played a crucial and, in some sense, deeply ironic role in the relationship between psychoanalysis and feminism. One way of reading Lacan would render him almost a caricature of the most phallocentric features of classical Freudian thought. Lacan placed the highest value on the phallus as the signifier extraordinaire, the centerpiece of the symbolic order. Although he was generally careful not to equate the phallus with the literal penis, he believed men and women have a very different relationship to the phallus, which "signifies what men (think they) *have* and what women (are considered to) lack" (Grosz, 1990, p. 125).

Another reading of Lacan (and, through him, of Freud) regards him as freeing psychoanalytic concepts from the destiny of anatomy and making it possible to understand gender in purely cultural, linguistic terms. Thus Juliet Mitchell argues, following Lacan, that Freud was not prescribing but describing the patriarchalism that saturated the language of Western cultures; in this reading, Lacan's interpretation of the pervasiveness of underlying symbolic gendered meanings in language becomes the most effective basis for a radical, feminist critique of Western culture. Some of the most important contemporary feminist writers have built on Lacan's analysis of language and the imaginary and symbolic realms. Some (like Juliet Mitchell) have stayed within the bounds of Lacan's depiction of the inescapability of patriarchy; others (like Julia Kristeva and Luce Irigaray) have attempted to work from Lacan's analysis to generate more directly feminine forms of experience and meaning.

CONCLUSION: VARIETIES OF REVISIONISM

In their efforts to preserve and revise Freud's contributions, Kernberg, Schafer, Loewald, and Lacan each developed a distinct strategy. To return to the metaphor with which we began this chapter, it is as if Kernberg has taken Freud's mansion and found ways to greatly expand and extend it. The living quarters of the original structure (drive theory, psychosexual development) have been preserved intact, but new wings (borderline and narcissistic phenomena) have been added alongside, and a new foundation (primitive object relations) has been dug underneath.

Schafer has divided Freud's mansion between those rooms that are hopelessly out of date (drive theory metapsychology), to be preserved as a museum, and those rooms, the central living spaces that were used most frequently (the basic clinical concepts), to be modernized and redecorated. Unlike Kernberg, who has preserved Freud's drive theory by regrounding it in a different foundation, Schafer has set up partitions between what he regards as the dated, anachronistic features of Freud's metapsychology and its vital, clinical core.

The approach taken by both Loewald and Lacan is as if the new heir, in rummaging through the closets, discovered that his benefactor had a passionate, secret hobby no one really knew about. The mansion, which everybody had regarded in only the most obvious ways, actually served to house a very different set of interests and purposes. So Loewald and Lacan, each in his own way, went about redefining and fundamentally realigning the realms and structures of Freud's system to reflect more accurately its true purpose (for Loewald, an elegant and intricate theory of object relations; for Lacan, the discovery of the linguistic nature of the unconscious), which they regard as having been there all along.

Through these various means, Kernberg, Schafer, Loewald, and Lacan each were able to maintain their identifications as Freudian, but assimilate a good deal of the innovation generated in the schools that defined themselves more radically: interpersonal psychoanalysis, Kleinian theory, object relations theories, and self psychology.

A key common element in several of the major revisionist Freudian strategies has been the debiologizing of Freud. In contrast to Kernberg, who attempted to modernize the biological underpinnings of psychoanalysis, Schafer, Loewald, and Lacan all translated Freud's quasi-biological concept of drive into other terms. In the hands of these theorists, all of Freud's basic clinical concepts (such as the Oedipus complex) were recontextualized and understood in quite different terms: for Schafer, as a story line, a narrative form; for Loewald, as a rich account of the dialectical interplay between past and present relationships; for Lacan, as an exposition of the determinative role of language and socio-symbolic structures in shaping experience.

These debiologizing, revisionist accounts of Freud have made Freudian theory more relevant and interesting vis-à-vis developments in other intellectual disciplines. Classical psychoanalysis claimed too much for itself. By assuming that it was tapping the biological bedrock of the psyche, psychoanalytic interpreters of other disciplines often presented their understandings in what contemporary philosophers call "foundational" terms, as if psychoanalysis could see into the deepest, underlying meanings of all human productions: literature, history, the arts, and culture in general. Contemporary psychoanalytic commentators tend to make more modest claims for psychoanalysis, as one way to tell the story of human experience, as one way through which the meanings that are generated in the lives of individuals and cultures can be traced, understood, and appreciated.

8

CONTROVERSIES IN THEORY

Let us admit that psychoanalysis, for the time being, is a rather untidy discipline, still finding its way.

—Hans Loewald

In formal logic, a contradiction is the signal of a defeat: but in the evolution of real knowledge it marks the first step in progress towards a victory. This is one great reason for the utmost toleration of a variety of opinion.

—Alfred North Whitehead

Critics often dismiss psychoanalysis as if it were an integrated, homogeneous point of view. To the casual observer, psychoanalysis may indeed appear to be a more or less singular school of thought, alongside other comprehensive psychological traditions such as behaviorism, existentialism, and so on. And surely, there are beliefs and principles to which virtually all psychoanalytic theorists and clinicians do subscribe: the complexity of the mind, the importance of unconscious mental processes, and the value of a sustained inquiry into subjective experience. However, as the preceding chapters have demonstrated, contemporary psychoanalysis has become quite complex and varied. Rather than a cohesive school of thought, contemporary psychoanalysis might be more accurately characterized as a university unto itself, with many different theories and areas of knowledge coexisting in an intricate and complicated relationship with one another.

In fact, at present it is very difficult to find any psychoanalyst who is really deeply conversant with more than one approach (e.g., Kleinian, Lacanian, ego psychology, self psychology). The literature of each school is extensive and each clinical sensibility finely honed, presenting a challenging prospect to any single analyst attempting to digest it all. To complicate matters, cross-disciplinary courses have not been popular at this university. Psychoanalytic ideologies tend to inspire deep passions among their adherents that have sometimes impeded a constructive exchange of ideas. These controversies are inspired by political issues (which institute using which theory can lay claim to be truly psychoanalytic?), issues of clinical efficacy (which theory inspires a therapeutic application that is deeply curative?), and issues of loyalty (competing allegiances to different founding mothers and fathers). Only recently has "comparative psychoanalysis" emerged as a field of study in its own right.

The preceding chapters have explored the diversity of psychoanalytic ideas theory by theory, considering each school in terms of its own history, basic principles, and clinical applications. En route, we have briefly noted some of the general issues that cut across the different schools. In this chapter and the next, we focus on these controversies themselves—some of the basic problems that all psychoanalytic systems have had to struggle with. This perspective will highlight the interrelationships of the various schools and the way the internal debates within psychoanalysis tend to reflect larger battles and currents in Western intellectual history. We will see that these common issues have both unified and divided the various schools of psychoanalytic thought, creating puzzles that have been explored through continually deepening dialectics of contrasting ideas and emphases.

TRAUMA OR FANTASY: WHAT IS THE CAUSE OF PSYCHOPATHOLOGY?

If we had to select the controversy that has most divided psychoanalytic theorists and clinicians, the single issue that has given rise to the most impassioned, strident, and sharply contrasting beliefs, there is only one candidate, and there are no close seconds. That issue concerns the cause of psychological disorders: Is psychopathology the result of trauma, healthy development thrown off course by destructive events and actual experiences? Or is it the result of the misinterpretation of early experience due to the warping impact of early childhood fantasy? Psychoanalysts are not alone in struggling with this problem. The psychoanalytic debate between proponents of trauma and proponents of fantasy is a reflection of the much broader philosophical debate concerning nature vs. nurture that has raged throughout the history of Western thought.

In tracing the controversies currently dominating psychoanalytic discourse, one often finds both sides of the debate in the different positions Freud argued, often with great incisiveness and certainty, at different points in the development of his thinking. Freud's momentous shift in 1897 from the theory of infantile seduction to the theory of infantile sexuality began to define the debates that are ongoing among current analytic theoreticians.

Freud's first approach to psychopathology, the seduction theory, emphasized the causative impact of nurture—the shaping of the mind by experience. Given the average range of expectable experience, Freud believed, the mind does not become embattled and generate the hysterical and obsessional neuroses that plagued the early patients he treated. Trauma creates affects and thoughts that simply cannot be integrated. The adult who had a normal, nontraumatic childhood is able to contain and assimilate sexual feelings into a continuous sense of self. The adult who experienced a precocious sexual seduction as a child suffers with memories and feelings incompatible with the central mass of thoughts and feelings that constitute his or her experience. Psychic disorders are a direct consequence of experiences that cannot be assimilated.

Freud never subsequently denied that some children are abused and that some neurotics were abused as children. But in 1897 he did abandon the seduction hypothesis as, in itself, a causative account of neurosis, and thereby shifted from an emphasis on nurture to an emphasis on nature. This became the definitive "Freudian" point of view. All adults suffer from conflictual sexual impulses, Freud decided, not just those who had been molested as children. Sexuality does not become problematic only when introduced precociously; there is something in the very nature of human sexuality that is problematic, generating inevitable, universal conflicts. Actual experiences never became unimportant in psychopathology, but their role shifted for Freud from the causative agent itself to a factor that either aggravates or ameliorates a problem predating all actual experience: the conflictual nature of the drives themselves.[1] In this view, psychopathology is not an intrusion from the outside but distortion of what is inside. This view of mental disorder emphasizing nature—the universality of conflictual drives and the Oedipus complex—dominated classical psychoanalysis, and is often mistakenly identified as representing contemporary psychoanalysis in general.

Freud's exploration of infantile sexuality and the classical emphasis on the inevitable conflictual nature of instinctual drives eventually provoked a whole generation of relational theories that swung back to the other side of the dialectic, emphasizing experience once again.[2] The key feature of this shift was the redefinition of "trauma" from a single, cataclysmic childhood event (like a sexual molestation) to parents' chronic failure to meet the psychological needs of the developing child. The importance of this redefinition can be seen dramatically in Winnicott's concept of impingement, and we will consider it as a prototype for a way of thinking that has characterized this entire generation of psychoanalytic theorizing.

The delicate beginnings of personal experience in the infant can be sustained, Winnicott suggested, only in the protective "holding environment" created by the solicitous attention of the ordinary "good-enough" mother. By meeting the infant's needs and actualizing his spontaneous gestures, the mother buffers him from all intrusions, both external and internal. He is free to do what he needs to do—float along in the state of "going-on-being" and await the spontaneous emergence of personal impulses. The mother can fail the child in many ways: by allowing external stimulation to reach painful levels, by intruding into the base state of drifting quiescence, or by allowing the child's internal needs to build to frustrating levels. In Winnicott's terms, all these failures result in impingement—the failure to protect the delicate state necessary for psychological growth and health.

Winnicott's understanding of the way experience can become traumatizing is quite different from Freud's. Trauma for Winnicott is not just the introduction of something dramatically negative, frightening, and noxious (e.g., precocious sexual stimulation); it is most fundamentally the failure to sustain something positive—the necessary conditions for healthy psychic development. Thus M. M. R. Khan (1963) termed Winnicott's theory of the disturbing impact of a lack of good-enough mothering a theory of "cumulative trauma," resonating with Freud's earlier seduction hypothesis, but in a different fashion.

This shift back to the nurture side of the dialectic has been characteristic of the broad spectrum of postclassical theorizing: object relations theories (Fairbairn and Guntrip as well as Winnicott), ego psychology (in the increasing emphasis on maternal care from Hartmann to Spitz to Jacobson and Mahler), and self psychology (in the traumatizing impact of empathic failures).[3] In all these models, elements of Freud's original pre-1897 seduction theory have been revived in a new and much more subtle and sophisticated form. The child is not traumatized by a sexual event, per se; the child is traumatized by parental character pathology. Because of the parents' inability to provide what is necessary, because of the interfering impact of the parents' own difficulties and anxieties, the child is distracted from the delicate project of becoming a person. Instead, attention becomes prematurely diverted to survival, to the parents' needs, to self-distorting adaptation to the external world.

In intellectual realms outside psychoanalysis, the traditional stark polarity between understandings based on nature and those based on nurture now seems simplistic. The very concept of "nature" is understood by many as a human (and therefore cultural) construct (cf. Butler, 1990). What is regarded as given or natural by one society may be regarded as taboo by another. Even animal "nature" is understood differently by succeeding generations. It is argued that our ideas about the natural world, like all our ideas, need to be understood as constructions and reflections of our current social context. Conversely, "nurture" can no longer be regarded in the omnipotent fashion of previous centuries. The intractability and ubiquity of human misery despite impressive technological progress, the backlash of ecological disaster despite campaigns to conquer nature—these developments suggest that human fate is not entirely within our control, that we are bound by our physiology, the limitations of our current perspective, the constraints of the world in which we find ourselves. Nature and nurture are now generally regarded less as distinct, separable causes and more as interactive, mutually created sets of processes.

Similarly, although the dialectic between trauma and fantasy, between an actual past and an invented past, still shapes much of the debate in current psychoanalytic literature, the polarity of the positions has softened and their interrelationships are more complexly conceived.

On the nature side, Freud initially developed the concept of instinctual drive (in its particular psychoanalytic form) when he lost faith in the reliability of his patients' memories of seduction. Not all these memories were true, he came to believe. If these events had not actually happened, the psychic reality of these memories must have been generated autonomously, from *within* the mind of the child. Thus the drive concept was designed specifically to locate processes independent of actual, external events; drives are autonomously arising, internal pressures. Freud depicted the id, the repository of the drives, as actually sheltered from the external, interpersonal world and never in direct contact with it—all contact between the id and the outside world is mediated through the ego.

Contemporary drive theorists (modern psychoanalytic authors who have chosen to build on Freud's metapsychology) regard the drives as very much affected by the external, interpersonal world. Contemporary Freudian theorists such as Loewald and Kernberg (see chapter 7), and Jacobson before them (see chapter 2), regard the drives not as simply acting *on* the external world, but as originally shaped in interaction *with* the external world through the parents' manner of caregiving, providing gratifications, frustrations, and so on. In this way, nurture is seen as built into nature from the beginning.

On the nurture side, the original formulations of relational theorists like Sullivan, Fairbairn, Winnicott, and Kohut tended to attribute psychopathology almost exclusively to external factors—varieties of parental inadequacy. Whatever was natural to the infant was portrayed as good, as the "true" self which, if encouraged and not interfered with, would develop in an integrated and nonconflictual fashion. The causes of psychopathology were located squarely in failure of nurturance (in Winnicott's phrase, "environmental insufficiency").

Contemporary relational theorists (modern psychoanalytic authors who have chosen to build on relational rather than drive concepts) tend to take inherent, internal factors much more into account, not regarding them as drives per se, but as temperamental traits such as excitability, sensitivity to pleasure and pain, and so on. These more recent authors (e.g., Daniel Stern, Joseph Lichtenberg) depict early development less in terms of a healthy infant either facilitated or failed by parents and more in terms of complex interactions through which children and caregivers either fit or do not fit with each other. Individuals are seen as having differing sensibilities and rhythms. A parent whose caregiving style might be quite effective with one child might encounter enormous difficulties with another. Parenting, in this view, is shaped in the context of the inherent temperamental features of both parent and child. In this way, nature is built into nurture from the beginning.

The nature–nurture controversy continues to stimulate new thinking in the psychoanalytic literature; each side of the fantasy–trauma dialectic has been challenged and enriched by the other. And important differences still remain. This has been well demonstrated recently in the positions taken around the reemergence of interest in the very problem that originally led Freud to first propound his seduction theory: childhood sexual abuse.

Contemporary Freudian approaches grant much more importance than Freud did (after he abandoned the seduction theory) to the impact of actual abuse itself. As the title of Leonard Shengold's book *Soul Murder* (1989) suggests, the actual abuse and subsequent obfuscating disclaimers are regarded as having a pernicious and destructive impact on development. Yet, consistent with Freud, the mechanism through which the actual abuse is understood to be so traumatizing is in its augmenting and exacerbating the preexisting sadomasochistic impulses connected with the Oedipus complex and primal scene fantasies (of parental intercourse), naturally arising in all children. Cure, for Shengold, rests ultimately on the release from repression of the child's own fantasies and wishes.

Treating Adult Survivors of Childhood Sexual Abuse (1993), by Jody Messler Davies and Mary Gail Frawley, provides an overlapping but distinctly different approach to the same problem, from the relational side. The most important issue for these and other relational authors is the actuality of the experience itself and the difficulty patients have in knitting together their necessarily dissociated experiences, their wrenchingly discrepant identifications with parents they both loved desperately and were tormented and terrified by. Davies and Frawley also differ from more popular authors such as Jeffrey Masson (1984), who regard survivors of abuse through the simplistic lens of victimology and deny any importance of active fantasy altogether. Davies and Frawley believe that while the child may be a passive victim of the original sexual abuse, the child's subsequent active elaboration of his or her situation through various fantasies, including reparative longings for magical helpers and identifications with the abuser himself, is also a complex aspect of the problem.

For Shengold, psychological cure and freedom lie in acknowledgment of the wish "I wanted this to happen and secretly enjoyed this." For Davies and Frawley, psychological cure and freedom lie in the articulation, containment, and eventual integration of discordant relationships and self-experience: "The father whom I loved (and became like) was also the father who cruelly abused and exploited me (in the way I in turn often abuse others)."

For Shengold, the starting assumption is that incestuous fantasies are universal and incestuous relationships largely imagined; the burden of proof is on the patient to convince the analyst that abuse took place. The greatest danger is for the analyst to validate and thereby collude in what are the patient's fantasies. For Davies and Frawley, the starting assumption is that abused children are most fundamentally damaged in the destruction of their reality-testing and capacity to deal with their experiences in a coherent and integrated way. The analyst begins with a readiness to believe the patient, unless she is given reason not to. The greatest danger is for the analyst to invalidate, and thereby collude in the patient's denial of, her own experience. An additional danger is posed, however, by the analyst's simply declaring that the patient was abused, encouraging a premature foreclosure of the patient's struggle to come to a personal resolution by sorting through confusing, often contradictory images of self and other, fantasy and reality, that are the outcome of trauma. The goal is for the patient to come to believe in the integrity of her own mind.

Fantasy or trauma? Although both are increasingly taken into account by most contemporary theorists, the choice between the two still provides an alternative set of emphases, different centers of gravity, for current analytic thinking.

Freud's vision of nature "red in tooth and claw" played a central historical role in the creation of modern consciousness by toppling the traditional view of human beings' having been specially created by a designer, in his own image. Freud's postulation of a raw, primitive wellspring of human intentions was inspirational to generations of artists, social scientists, and social critics in the first half of the twentieth century, in their efforts to break out of the confining, ethnocentric features of established Western thought, with its Platonic–Christian emphasis on rationality and control.

By positing a primitive, instinctual core within each of us, Freud provided a powerful hedge against adaptation, social convention, and compliance with traditional norms. Thus, the cultural historian Ann Douglas, in her study of modernism, *Terrible Honesty* (1995), argues that Freud was the most important intellectual presence in the crucible of modernist sensibility generated by the convergence of white and black subcultures in Manhattan in the 1920s. The sense of primitivism evoked by Freud's instinct theory, a fascination with beasts as reflective of a naked, pulsing natural force, provided the conceptual scaffolding for the revolt against Victorian conventions both in the arts and in social mores more generally. And from the very beginning of psychoanalysis, the quest by the individual for his own deeply personal meaning, his own authentic voice, has been at the heart of the clinical process.

However, from our current perspective, the very vision of nature that Freud established as an antipode to social and historical convention was itself a social and historical convention of Freud's own time. The images of animals that Freud and his contemporaries generated in the flush of the Darwinian revolution, creatures driven by rapacious sexuality and aggression, do not much resemble animals as understood by contemporary zoologists. In part, Freud used animals as a projection screen for a portrayal of human frustrations and rage in a society that too often squelched individual energies and twisted them back against themselves.

Post-Freudian psychoanalysis proposes a less definitive account of nature. The infant's experience is understood as powerfully impacted upon from the very beginning by the rhythms, values, and personalities of the caregivers. Views of nature and *our* nature are presumed to reflect, themselves, the social and historical context in which we live. However, post-Freudian psychoanalysis is no less fundamentally subversive vis-à-vis social conventions than Freud's psychoanalysis was. As we have seen, essential to the contributions of object relations theorists such as Fairbairn and Winnicott, post–ego psychologists such as Erikson, revisionist Freudians such as Loewald and Lacan, and Kohut and subsequent self psychologists, has been the centrality in the analytic process of the development and emergence of the analysand's authentic, personal voice from the internalization of social forces and significant others.

CONFLICT OR ARRESTED DEVELOPMENT: WHAT IMPEDES HEALING?

What is it that impedes psychological growth and healing? Why are people stuck, in their symptoms and in their relationships, with the painful experiences they encountered early in life? Two basic conceptual models, and the creative tension between them, have dominated psychoanalytic thinking about the tenacity of psychopathology; they derive, in part, from the dialectic we have traced between trauma and fantasy in understanding the *cause* of difficulties in living.

Paul, a young man in his twenties, sought treatment for a cluster of problems he had suffered with from early childhood. He was the only child of a fearful, clinging mother and a sickly, distant father who died when Paul was six years old. Although extremely competent and resourceful, Paul was often tortured by a lack of confidence, a sense of continually finding himself in a world he was totally unprepared for. Although Paul had a long history of successes in school and professional pursuits, he felt himself to be an impostor, always in imminent danger of being exposed. A similar dread stalked him socially and sexually. He was able to establish and maintain rich friendships and sexual relationships, but was often at a total loss to know and really feel what others found attractive and valuable about him. Paul was tormented by a sense of sexual inadequacy and had occasional, fleeting bouts of impotence. He often fantasized about other men—stronger, more forceful, with bigger penises—who, he imagined, could suavely perform all the activities with which he struggled shamefully.

The traditional model of psychopathology that dominated classical Freudian psychoanalytic thinking was centered around the concept of conflict. Neurosis was seen as the product of mental warfare, the psyche at odds with itself. The mind is rent by internal conflicts because different aspects of psychic life are not compatible; impulses deriving from childhood sexual and aggressive drives are in conflict with each other and with repressive forces. When this conceptual strategy is applied to the kinds of difficulties presented by a patient like Paul, the following hypotheses are quickly generated:

Paul suffers from pervasive inhibitions regarding sexual and aggressive impulses. He stops himself out of guilt (superego) and anxiety (ego); he doesn't allow himself to know how powerful and effective he really is. He is afraid of what he will do. This material lends itself to a traditional, oedipal narrative: Paul fantasizes himself as an oedipal victor; he won his mother with the death of his father, and this victory left him terrified of his own sexual and aggressive ambitions. He is afraid his sexuality is deadly and systematically disclaims it in order to render himself harmless. He is afraid his aggressiveness and ambition are lethal and systematically disclaims them to make it safe for others to be with him. Through this massive disconnection from his own conflictual powers and energy, he empties himself of any possible sense of self or inner resources. This positive oedipal constellation, a clinician working within a classical framework might speculate, is accompanied by negative oedipal longings; beneath Paul's obsessive fantasies about stronger, bigger men is a passive homosexual longing to assume a feminine position in relation to a powerful, paternal figure. He is not only afraid of his own dangerous powers; he also fears that allowing himself to claim his own potency would necessitate a loss of his longing to be loved by a more powerful man.

In this traditional model, Paul's difficulties in living, his psychopathology, are a consequence of unconscious conflict. He cannot continue to develop as a person and overcome his problems, because his conscious experience is determined by underlying, depleting struggles that he doesn't have access to. What will be of help is the lifting of repression, allowing him to see and understand the underlying conflictual forces generating his psychological paralysis. The awareness of his unconscious conflicts and their origin in his childhood experience will set him free. He will come to understand that his sexuality and his aggression are not as dangerous as they appeared in his fantasy-dominated child's mind; he will come to renounce his childhood longings for both parents as inappropriate to adult, mature love.

The alternative model of psychopathology that has dominated postclassical psychoanalysis proposes the principle of arrested development rather than conflict as the root of difficulties in living. In this view, Paul's fundamental problem is not that he is at (unconscious) odds with himself, but that his early development was thwarted by the absence of certain crucial parental provisions that are required for psychological growth: someone to look up to, someone who enjoyed Paul's way of being a boy, someone who gave his blessing for Paul to become a man in his own right.

This approach to Paul's problems is actually closer to Paul's own conscious theories of his own difficulties. Paul spent his childhood longing for a father he could count on, who could teach him to play baseball and other ways to be a boy and, later, a man. He had the sense that he was different from other men because he had never received whatever it is that boys get from their fathers—a model of masculinity and a paternal blessing to become a man of one's own, opportunities for identifications that would fill out his image of who he was. Paul had never realized, until being in analysis, that the macho figures he compared himself to unfavorably in his fantasies were symbolic representatives of the father he longed for as a boy. In the arrested-development model, Paul's psychological paralysis is seen not as a result of unconscious conflict but of insufficient conditions for growth. What was missing in Paul's developmental past is still missing in him as an adult.

Different postclassical theorists conceptualize this kind of developmental insufficiency in different ways: An ego psychologist might emphasize a deficiency of paternal identifications that offer no outside anchor to aid Paul in an already difficult separation–individuation process; an object relations theorist might highlight a lack of experience of freedom to be and discover himself without the need to be alert to and comply with the wishes of others; a self psychologist might point to a lack of developmentally sustaining relationships in which others were emotionally attuned to and excited about Paul's own emerging self. These are all complex, multidimensional theories. Their common element is the assumption that what underlies Paul's difficulties in living is not conflict but the thwarting of a natural developmental process due to environmental insufficiency. What will help Paul is not insight per se (although all these approaches pursue understanding) but finding a different sort of experience in the analysis itself. None of these theories regards analysis as actually fulfilling parental functions (Guntrip comes closest in describing analysis as involving "reparenting"); rather, the analytic relationship is seen as offering experiences that are analogues of parental provisions, close enough to revitalize stalled developmental strivings and to make possible an awareness and mourning for what was missed earlier.

These are two very different, seemingly incompatible, accounts of the origin of psychological difficulties. Like the choice between trauma and fantasy, they have created a dynamic tension within contemporary analytic theorizing. The most recent analytic literature reveals movements in the direction of a more complex synthesis. Authors who think primarily in terms of conflict increasingly note that a life crippled by long-term conflict results in a paucity of important experiences. Sexual inhibitions based on conflicts, for example, may result in a phobic avoidance of sexual situations and a loss of normal adolescent opportunities to learn about the negotiation of sexual needs in the context of an intimate relationship.

Thus conflicts result in missing developmental experiences. Lifting repressions and creating insight may not in themselves be sufficient to generate new experience.

Conversely, some authors (e.g., Mitchell, 1988, 1993) regard developmental arrests as preserved not just because of a lack of necessary parental provisions, but also because of conflicts over loyalties to parents (Fairbairn's ties to bad objects) and reparative fantasies based on limited childhood options.

For example, Paul's longing for masculine power and a paternal blessing can also be regarded as a reparative hope for a magical, good father, generated out of the severity of Paul's childhood circumstances. He longed for the day that this father would return to initiate him into manhood, a hope that became precious as a magical solution to all his difficulties. One might further view Paul's minimizing self-reproaches as operating in the service of preserving that hope. If Paul were able to connect with his own power and resources as a man, the fantasied father would no longer be necessary; in fact, it would be difficult to preserve the belief in the possibility of such a larger-than-life paternal figure. He would have to accept his status as a separate individual, grappling with life's experience as an ordinary mortal. So the inhibitions and constrictions Paul suffered consciously might also be regarded as the price he paid for preserving a set of conflictual unconscious fantasies. In the words of songwriter David Bromberg, "You've got to suffer if you want to sing the blues." In this view, conflict and arrested development are not independent processes, but continually interactive dynamics: original developmental deficits lead to longings and fantasies that become conflictual; those conflicts in turn result in major obstacles to attaining necessary developmental experiences, which in turn generate more conflictual fantasies.

The central defense in the classical conflict model is repression. Drive-based instinctual fantasies inevitably come into conflict with one another and the regulating functions of the ego. They are necessarily barred from awareness, denied access to action, and buried within the psyche. The arrested-development model is often presented in concert with an understanding of defensive processes centered on *dissociation* rather than repression. Instead of a horizontal split between consciousness and buried impulses, developmental theorists envision a mind rent by vertical splits between different self-states that have not been integrated with one another.[4] Some developmental needs or longings might be understood as operating in the mind in some dissociated form, like a Winnicottian true self split off from a prevailing false-self organization; others might exist more as undeveloped potentials that have never been provided an appropriate facilitating environment. Other theorists (Bromberg, 1993; Davies, 1995; Mitchell, 1993) have developed the notion of dissociation among multiple self-organizations and self-states, created not by unmet developmental needs but by unintegratable, sometimes traumatic, early interactions with significant others. Jody Messler Davies suggests that this shift from drive theories emphasizing repression to relational theories emphasizing dissociation leads to a very different vision of the unconscious:

> Not an onion which must be carefully peeled or an archaeological site to be meticulously unearthed and reconstructed in its original form, but a child's kaleidoscope in which each glance through the pinhole of a moment in time provides a unique view; a complex organization in which a fixed set of colored, shaped and textured components rearrange themselves in unique crystalline structures determined via infinite pathways of interconnectedness. (in press)

As with the nature–nurture controversy, the polarity between conflict and arrested development still constitutes two distinct centers of gravity in theorizing, but has begun to yield more complex syntheses.

GENDER AND SEXUALITY

There is no realm in which theoretical controversy within psychoanalysis has more dramatically reflected larger intellectual currents and cultural changes than in the area of sexuality and gender. Freud's understanding of sexuality and gender was very much a product of *his* time; in the decades following the introduction of Darwinism, it was extremely compelling to think about human sexuality in the larger context of the evolution of species, natural selection, and the survival of the fittest. Similarly, post-Freudian understandings of sexuality and gender are very much a product of *our* time; feminism, the gay rights movement, and postmodernism in general have all had an enormous impact on the way sexuality and gender have been reconceptualized both outside and within the psychoanalytic literature.

But the lines of influence are more complex. Psychoanalytic thinking about sexuality has been influenced by the broader intellectual and popular culture, but psychoanalytic thinking about sexuality has also had a great deal to do with shaping popular understandings. Freud's theory of sexuality *became* the dominant, popular understanding of sexuality in Western culture (Simon & Gagnon, 1973); much of the current feminist thinking about gender and sexuality, both within and outside psychoanalysis, was defined in reaction to Freud's classical theorizing.

Freud had a great many different things to say about sexuality over the course of several decades; a full treatment of these ideas would require a book in itself. However, certain basic, consistent elements of Freud's views came to dominate Western thinking about and experience of sexuality in general. For Freud, sexuality was a wholly natural phenomenon—the most deeply natural phenomenon in all of human experience. Civilization has transformed our lives in many complex ways, but civilization is always working against the dark, bestial pull of our persistent animal nature, dominated by sexuality.

In our time, the distinction between sexuality and gender has been the topic of much discussion. The great emphasis in recent decades on the cultural origins of gender may make it difficult for us, from our current vantage point, to appreciate how fundamental and unchangeable Freud and his contemporaries took gender to be, precisely because of what he understood to be its biological roots. Since Freud took gender so much for granted, as "bedrock," he wrote very little about it as such. Anatomy, as Freud put it, was destiny, and for Freud, gender development was merely a corollary to the development of sexuality.

In Freud's account, boys value their penis above all else, as the instrument necessary to achieve drive gratification. They assume all humans have penises, and the shock involved in the discovery of the anatomical difference between the sexes organizes their major fear throughout life: their fear of losing their penis (castration anxiety) and hence becoming feminized. That fear underlies much of subsequent neurotic conflict. Girls, in Freud's view, similarly assume everyone is alike and, like boys, take the boy's anatomy to be the basic bodily model. The shock of discovering the anatomical difference between the sexes leaves them feeling castrated and inferior. Women, in Freud's view, long for penis substitutes (in the healthiest circumstances, a baby) and only with great difficulty can accept their biologically dictated gender role and its psychological sequelae.

Subsequent analytic theorists have added to and, in many ways, dramatically transformed most features of Freud's understanding of the nature of sexuality and gender. Because loyalty to Freud's libido theory has always served as a political litmus test, however, the radical nature of many of these changes often went unacknowledged. Consider, for example, the place of sexuality in Klein's system.

In chapter 4 we traced the ways Klein substituted a developmental sequence of "*positions*," organizations of internal and external object relations, for Freud's libidinal phases. Sexuality for Klein remained a powerful, natural force, but she saw it as emerging in the context of the child's struggles to integrate love and hate within the paranoid-schizoid and depressive positions. For Freud, whose thinking was grounded in the physical, sexuality was about tension reduction and was pervaded by oedipal struggle. For Klein, the body was also important, but as a source of symbolic meaning, represented in the mind. Sexuality, for Klein, figured primarily as yet another avenue for the expression of what she felt was the basic human dilemma: the integration of loving and hating feelings in the hoped-for demonstration of the reparative power of one's goodness. For Freud, reproduction was an expression of phallic intactness for the boy and narcissistic compensation for the girl, made possible by her acceptance of her fantasied castrated status. For Klein, reproduction offered proof that something could survive and grow internally despite destructive feelings; pregnancy reflected the viability and goodness of one's internal object world.

As broader features of Klein's theoretical system changed, her understanding of the meaning of sexuality and of gender-related roles of sexuality was also transformed. Freud regarded personality as forming around sexuality as its natural, preexisting latticework. Klein and subsequent relational theorists regarded personality as forming around early relationships with others; sexuality inevitably emerges, but it is largely unformed and takes on its meaning within that context.

The past several decades have witnessed a vast and burgeoning literature critiquing and directly challenging Freud's understanding of gender development, proposing alternatives, both psychoanalytic and nonpsychoanalytic. One common element in these diverse and heterogeneous revisions and critiques is the contemporary rejection of Freud's presumption that both sexes assign a higher value inevitably and universally to masculinity, and that one's image of masculinity should provide the baseline in reference to which femaleness is considered. Once these two basic premises were challenged, a fuller reconsideration of gender, in fantasy, in psychological makeup, and in social processes, became possible.

Contemporary psychoanalysis is rife with accounts of gender development and the very nature of gender itself. They can be roughly grouped according to conceptual strategies.

The counterpart to Freud's classical biologizing was the classical culturalism that emerged in the 1930s and 1940s in the work of Karen Horney, Clara Thompson, and other interpersonal authors. Prefiguring contemporary feminist literature, they saw gender as most fundamentally a cultural creation—roles were established by the assignment of social meanings to biological differences. Thus, for Thompson, a woman's wish for a penis was best understood not as an expression of inevitable, anatomically mandated inferiority; such a wish "is but demanding in this symbolic way some form of equality with men" (1942, p. 208), who occupy the dominant position in the culture.[5] In a fashion that prefigures some of the psychologist Carol Gilligan's widely read empirical work (1982, 1992), Thompson saw the most problematic phase for girls not at the oedipal period, in the perception of anatomical differences, but in adolescence, in the perception of differences in social constraints and power. Gender characteristics, in this model, reflect cultural conditions. Thus, Thompson suggested, because of economic disparities and the use of seductiveness as an understandable compensatory commodity, "woman's alleged narcissism and greater need to be loved may be entirely the result of economic necessity" (p. 214).

A very different approach to gender has surfaced in recent years based on what might be considered a neo-biological model. In contrast to the pure culturalists, these authors revive Freud's strategy of deriving gender from universal fantasies about anatomical realities. They believe Freud was right about anatomy being destiny, but that he simply misread the way anatomy destines us.

Janine Chassequet-Smirgel (1988) and other French Freudians, for example, argue that Freud's phallocentrism was not just wrong, but a motivated error, defending against a deeper universal truth: the dread and denial of the fantasied preoedipal mother and her cloacal, devouring vagina. This dread provides the deeper explanation for the pervasive appearance of oedipal issues. Penises are valuable because they allow escape from the enveloping threat of the preoedipal mother. The classical concept of castration anxiety is thus most deeply understood not as a dread of losing the organ itself, but of succumbing to engulfment. Girls fantasize obtaining a penis through oedipal intercourse; they will steal the father's penis. The anatomical possession or lack of a penis thus destines an individual to one or another set of options and resources in dealing with a common preoedipal dread.

But the game of reading destiny from anatomy can be played in many different ways. Erikson (1950), for example, regarded male genitalia as orienting boys to external space and female genitalia as orienting girls to internal space. Boys build towers to explore the productive and reproductive expansion and penetration their body is destined for; girls build protective enclosures to explore the productive and reproductive containment and nurturing their body is destined for. In contrast to Freud, Erikson assumed that the little girl experiences her internal space as a fertile presence rather than as an absence. Irene Fast (1984) claims that both men and women are destined by their anatomy to envy the prerogatives of the other: girls will envy a boy's penis, and boys will envy a girl's child-bearing capacity.[6] Thus the body has been invested with many more meanings than those Freud proclaimed as "bedrock."

In contrast to these biologically based views, a kind of developmental essentialism has been developed by writers like Gilligan, Jean Baker Miller, and Judith Jordan, who are particularly concerned with the underrepresention of female gender in developmental studies. Here the *origins* of gender differences are stressed less than the fundamentally different *sensibilities* that are believed to correspond to them. Freud, again using his conclusions about men's moral attitudes and functioning as a baseline, had decided that women lack a strong superego and hence are deficient in moral values. In Freud's account, the male superego is established under the threat of castration anxiety, which forces the boy to abandon his oedipal ambitions, but little girls experience themselves as already castrated, and thus have less motivation to keep infantile instinctual impulses in check; consequently they have less energy available for the sublimation that fuels higher-level organization and pursuits. Gilligan's (1982) groundbreaking work rescued what she argues is a distinctively female set of values from what had been regarded as simply an insufficiently developed male consciousness. And Miller and Jordan suggest that women are, because of temperamental and developmental factors, more attuned and related to other people. "Women typically demonstrate more emotional/physical resonance with others' affective arousal than do men" (Jordan, 1992, p. 63).

A closely related but also quite different strategy results from what might be termed a developmental constructivist model, which regards gender differences, pointedly, not as essential, but as an artifact of social structures, most particularly inequalities in male–female participation in child rearing. Thus, the feminist writer Nancy Chodorow suggests, "gender difference is not absolute, abstract or irreducible; it does not involve an essence of gender. Gender differences, and the experience of difference, like differences among women, are socially and psychologically created and situated" (1980, p. 421). Chodorow feels that in many ways, the primacy of female caregivers has made things easier for girls, because they do not have to renounce, as boys do, their primary identification with the mother in developing a gendered identity. Yet Chodorow stresses her belief that these differences are artifacts of cultural inequalities, not essential to male–female differences.

Similarly, Jessica Benjamin (1992) argues that essentialists like Jordan have simply reversed the values in the culturally created polarization of gender, by elevating femininity and deprecating masculinity. Benjamin advocates a creative tension between assertion (which comes more easily for boys in our society, with its female caregivers) and connection (which comes more easily for girls).

One of the most constant features of theorizing about gender is the perpetual dialectic between biological/essentialist accounts and cultural/constructivist accounts. The former roots gender in some notion of nature or the natural. The latter is based on the postmodern premise that no tension exists between nature and culture because nature, as such, is purely a socially constructed category (Gagnon, 1991, p. 274).

Many of the issues concerning gender in the contemporary psychoanalytic literature are also reflected in the recent intense controversies regarding sexual orientation.

Freud regarded sexual orientation as largely constitutional.[7] In many cases, Freud thought, homosexuality was not primarily defensive or psychodynamically derived and, consequently, changing a patient's sexual orientation was not a proper goal of analytic treatment. This attitude toward sexual orientation was one of the few features of Freud's ideas that the American psychoanalytic mainstream virtually disregarded. As psychoanalysis was taken up into American society, with its prominent homophobic currents, a different kind of biological determinism was established. In the 1950s and 1960s the position that dominated the American psychoanalytic literature was that everyone is constitutionally heterosexual and that homosexuality is a pathological, defensive, phobic retreat from castration fears. Homosexuality was viewed variably in terms of preoedipal fixation, arrested development, narcissistic dynamics, binding mothers, detached fathers, and so on. Analysts were urged to employ a directive/suggestive approach (Bieber, 1965; Hatterer, 1970; Ovesy, 1969; Soccarides, 1968), insisting that homosexual patients renounce their sexual orientation and actively directing the process of conversion to heterosexuality. It is a reflection of the passion of those who shaped this position that the distance it took them from Freud's own views on sexual orientation and the central analytic ideal of nondirectiveness seems to have gone unnoticed.

Since the mid-1980s, the directive/suggestive approach to sexual orientation has been discredited in many quarters of the analytic world. As with gender, neo-biological accounts of sexual orientation have also surfaced. There has been considerable recent interest in the neurophysiology of sexual orientation, with some controversial early studies suggesting differences in brain structure of homosexual and heterosexual males. Richard Isay has been prominent among those who have argued that sexual orientation is fundamentally constitutional and not subject to change, and some radical feminists argue that all women would be naturally bisexual or lesbian if not for compulsory heterosexuality.

On the other hand, most contemporary authors tend to regard sexual orientation, as well as gender, as complex psychological and social constructions, not at all a simple extension of either our anatomically based reproductive capacities or our brain physiology. Once sexuality is unhinged from both constitution and reproductive function, the stark pathologizing of homosexuality is no longer feasible. Conversely, heterosexuality can no longer be regarded as a natural blossoming of human biology, but as something to be explored and explained as well.

EMPIRICISM OR HERMENEUTICS?

Over the past several decades, a great ferment both within scholarly disciplines and popular culture has surrounded the very nature of thinking itself. The heterogeneity of the contemporary world, the proliferation of sensibilities and points of view, the rapid shifts of ideologies and understandings have all contributed to the profound sense of turbulence, relativism, and flux that is often associated with the depiction of our contemporary world as "postmodern."

Even science, the worldview Freud believed in devotedly and that housed all classical psychoanalytic theorizing, has changed in ways Freud could not have predicted. Many philosophers of science are now thinking about the very nature of scientific knowledge differently from the scientists of Freud's generation. For Freud, science was the progressive, incremental accumulation of knowledge, bringing us closer and closer to a complete understanding of and control over nature. For many contemporary philosophers (e.g., those influenced by the work of Thomas Kuhn), science has provided a series of different, discontinuous worldviews, paradigms for solving problems relevant to a particular culture and historical time. There has been considerable debate about whether scientific paradigms are upheld or rejected wholly on the basis of rational choice and empirical evidence, or whether they constitute belief systems of a different sort. Given all this ferment, it is not surprising that the psychoanalytic literature has also been filled with intense debates about the best ways to think about psychoanalysis as a clinical treatment and an intellectual discipline.

What sort of knowledge do psychoanalytic practice and psychoanalytic theorizing generate? One answer to this question is Freud's original answer (1933): Psychoanalysis is an empirical discipline; it produces scientific facts that are testable through clearly defined procedures. Freud always regarded psychoanalysis as a branch of science and the psychoanalytic situation itself as a kind of laboratory environment. The psychoanalytic method was, for Freud, one that allowed an objective investigator (the analyst) access to a realm of nature (the underlying structures and forces in the mind of the patient). Just as competent microscopists looking at a slide should all see the same data, Freud assumed that clinicians properly trained in the analytic method would all arrive at the same interpretive understanding of a patient's free associations. Further, Freud believed that the patient's response to an interpretation provided proof pro or con about its correctness (Freud, 1937b). The immediate verbal agreement or disagreement does not count for much, but a correct interpretation, Freud believed, should lift repressions and thereby open up fresh unconscious material: new, rich associations, confirmatory dreams, insights, and so on.

Freud also believed that psychoanalysis was, in principle, subject to confirmation through empirical evidence outside the analytic situation. He began his career as an experimental neurologist, interested in the physiological correlates of psychological processes. He always believed that physical substances eventually would be discovered corresponding to the psychodynamic concept of libido, anticipating the later discovery of sex hormones. Freud was also optimistic about other kinds of extra-analytic experimentation.[8]

Many contemporary analysts share the belief of Freud and his contemporaries that psychoanalysis is best thought of as an empirical discipline. Because of advances in the philosophy of science, however, the problems of empirical validation for psychoanalysis are now approached in more sophisticated terms. The philosopher Adolf Grünbaum has influenced current analytic discussions of these issues by pointing to the problem of suggestion in the analyst's looking for validation of her interpretations from the patient. Because the analyst herself is now understood to be so embedded in the process (in influencing it both directly and indirectly and also in terms of understanding what is taking place), it is difficult for current scientists to regard the analytic situation as a kind of laboratory or the analyst as simply a neutral observer. Thus, those who regard psychoanalysis in empirical terms tend to look to other kinds of data for confirmation of analytic hypotheses.[9]

Alongside the empirical approach has arisen a very different view that represents the impact on psychoanalysis of the turn toward hermeneutics in other intellectual disciplines. As an introduction to the issues involved in thinking about psychoanalysis in hermeneutic terms, consider the way hermeneutics works in the study of history.

Historians of previous generations believed they were simply providing accurate renderings of "what happened." The Roman empire collapsed. Why? Many hypotheses were possible, and good history consisted of collecting data and finding the hypothesis that best fit the facts. In this sense, history operated as a social *science,* using facts to confirm and disconfirm hypotheses. Each generation of historians had a different understanding of many historical situations (such as the fall of the Roman empire), and the assumption was made by each current group that their understanding best fit the facts and was therefore the most historically accurate.

In recent decades, historians and philosophers of history have begun to find it implausible that these succeeding versions of history represent a closer and closer approximation to some objective truth. It began to become clear that the way history is understood and written has a great deal to do not just with historical facts but also with the current context the historian is operating in. Different *ways* of understanding history (in terms of economics, social forces, aesthetic sensibilities, power, and so on) are arrived at by succeeding generations of historians, and the way history is understood at any given time seems very much a reflection of what that particular generation of historians is like. History is now understood by many as not a simple uncovering and assembling of facts, but as an active process between past and present, involving a selection and arrangement of some facts, from an infinite set of possibilities, to produce one among many possible understandings.

What happened toward the end of the Roman empire? The number of facts are infinite. What is happening this very day in Washington, D.C., or Paris or Tokyo that might affect the fate of nations? It is impossible to generate understandings of historical processes without becoming brutally selective and reductive. One simply cannot look at everything, and what one looks at is greatly determined by who, where, and when one is and what one is looking for. Historians who study the distant past have less data, and the extant material may be largely random or tendentiously preserved by surviving protagonists; it cannot be assumed that the surviving data is the most important in any objective sense.

It is very important to note that the hermeneutic approach to history (interpretive systems rather than an accretion of objective knowledge) does not collapse into relativism. There are many possible interpretations of the decline of the Roman empire—they are not all good history. Good history has to fit with our current understanding of the world and how it operates. Good history has to be consistent with whatever facts have been generated and not contradicted in any clear way by them. Good history has to persuasively account for a great deal of what is known; the more it accounts for, the more compelling the history. Historical explanations for the fall of the Roman empire resting on economic, social, and political dynamics are better history (at this point in time) than explanations relying on extraterrestrial invasion. Thus, there is a big difference between historians and fiction writers. To see history as interpretive rather than simply uncovering does not detach it from reality; rather, it regards reality as knowable through different possible understandings that are partially constructed by the knower.

Thinking about psychoanalysis as a hermeneutic discipline is similar to thinking about history that way. What actually happened in a particular patient's early life? What is actually happening now, both in the session with the analyst and in the patient's life outside the sessions? The answers to these questions are infinite. The facts are infinite. What areas are most important to consider? Which among the innumerable bits of information are most relevant? In many respects the psychoanalyst is in a position analogous to that of the historian or the contemporary political analyst. She confronts an infinite array of possible data and seeks an understanding that, if it is to be helpful at all, must be highly selective and reductive.

An appreciation of the hermeneutic perspective was introduced into psychoanalysis primarily by the philosophers Jürgen Habermas and Paul Ricoeur and the psychoanalysts Donald Spence and Roy Schafer. Spence argued that psychoanalysis deals more with "narrative truth" than with "historical truth." The patient's free associations do not simply contain expressions of underlying dynamics; the patient's associations have to be constructed in some fashion. They are generally assembled, Spence demonstrated, according to the analyst's preconceived theoretical commitments. Spence's answer to the ease with which the patient's associations are infused with the analyst's preconceived ideas has been a kind of radical skepticism, a suspension of theorizing and conclusion-drawing, until much more comprehensive data from actual sessions is made available for study and public argumentation.[10]

Schafer has applied hermeneutics in a very different way. In his view, all psychoanalytic understandings are necessarily reductive and operate along what he has termed "narrative storylines." Each theory has its own preferred way of viewing reality, understanding life; each preselects its own villains, heroes, curative journeys. Psychoanalytic understanding, for Schafer, is fundamentally a narrative process, and unavoidably so. This does not make analytic interpretations random, relative, or fictional. As with good history, good psychoanalytic interpretations must also make sense, pull together as much of the known data as possible, provide a coherent and persuasive account, and also facilitate personal growth. Psychoanalytic narratives are developed in communities of clinicians and tested for their clinical utility over time. But ultimately, competing psychoanalytic interpretations are not going to be adjudicated on purely rational or empirical grounds.

Yet another approach to these issues has been developed by Irwin Hoffman under the label "social constructivism" and by Donnel Stern employing

Gadamer's (in contrast to Habermas's) version of hermeneutics. The analyst's contributions, in this perspective, are generated largely in the dense, dynamic interactions of the transference and countertransference. Continual clinical choices and interpretive understandings arise from the pushes and pulls of the analyst's affect-laden participation with the patient; theory does not operate as a largely independent factor (as it does for Schafer). Theory generally permeates the analyst's experience and sometimes comes later as a post hoc explanation.

Thus, in a fundamental sense, contemporary psychoanalysis has been a method in search of a rationale. Some believe that an updated empiricism can still provide that rationale; others have turned toward hermeneutics for a different kind of framework. Still others have argued that psychoanalysis ought to establish its right to exist as a unique discipline unto itself, without having to ground itself in any other frame of reference (see Greenberg, 1991, chap. 4; Schwartz, 1995). Charles Spezzano (1993, drawing on Richard Rorty's critique of "foundationalism"), for example, has argued that psychoanalysis has generated demonstrably useful understandings of human experience that stand on their own terms. Such a view does not necessarily diminish the importance of empirical findings of various sorts as a source for fresh ideas and relevant considerations, but it does eliminate empirical validation as the ultimate adjudicator of psychoanalytic truth.

9

CONTROVERSIES IN TECHNIQUE

If treatment as written about seems so discursive and intellectual and neat and cool, perhaps treatment as it happens really works on the basis of what every psychotherapist feels daily: personal push and pull; nameless, theory-less, shapeless, swarming interaction.

—*Lawrence Friedman*

Each of us really understands in others only those feelings he is capable of producing himself.

—*André Gide*

We will introduce the major contemporary controversies in analytic technique through the actual experiences of a candidate in psychoanalytic training, as he encountered the clinical problems and choices in his work with a patient we will call Harvey.

Harvey, an artist of considerable skill but limited accomplishments, had sought treatment for a variety of problems involving constrictions and inhibitions in his ability to commit himself to his work, his personal relationships, and his sexuality. Harvey's first analyst, who seemed to have an ego psychology orientation, had seen him for five years before retiring. The analysis had helped Harvey feel better about himself and had brought a moderate symptomatic improvement. He had been very dedicated both to the analyst, whom he greatly admired, and the work itself, in which he had become deeply absorbed. Harvey was fascinated with psychoanalysis and read widely in the psychoanalytic literature. He had taken up psychoanalytic concepts as a kind of philosophy of life, and used the technical language with great facility. Although his analyst had given him considerable warning about his impending retirement, Harvey was quite distraught when the end of the treatment arrived. He took about a year to mourn the loss, a time period that had been suggested by the analyst, and then decided to seek treatment again. Because he wanted to be in analysis several times a week, which he now would have trouble affording on a private basis, he applied to the clinic of a psychoanalytic training institute, where he would be seen as a training case by a candidate there.

The candidate who began seeing Harvey quickly assumed he was an ideal training case. Most of the patients who came to the clinic had not been in analysis before. Most were conflicted about being in treatment and "resistant" in obvious ways. They had no sense of what analysis might offer them and were appropriately skeptical about the process. Harvey, on the other hand, was deeply committed to psychoanalysis and had firm convictions about what it had done and might continue to do for him. He was also very accomplished as an analytic patient. In some ways he was more knowledgeable and seasoned than his analyst-in-training.

In working with his other patients, the analyst often found himself not quite knowing what to do: when to speak, what to say, where to focus. In working with Harvey, he often felt he knew just what to do, what to focus on, what to say at any particular time. Both analyst and patient felt that this second analysis seemed to pick up just where the previous one had left off, scarcely missing a beat.

Harvey's understanding of himself, generated in the first analysis, centered almost exclusively around his relationship to his mother, a very bright, creative woman who had struggled with severe depressions her whole life. Following the birth of Harvey's immediately older brother, she had become paralyzed with depression and was hospitalized for several years. During that time she was largely immobile and virtually mute. According to the account Harvey was able to elicit from her several decades later, his mother decided she would have another child, and that decision reanimated her, enabling her to return to her life outside the hospital. She did in fact give birth again, to Harvey, and mothering him became the focus of her life. Harvey's father was somewhat involved with the family's several older children but always left Harvey to his wife's ministrations. As a child, Harvey knew nothing of his mother's severe psychological problems and hospitalization, which were kept as family secrets, but he always sensed that there was something deeply disturbed and extremely fragile about her. He became a very good son to her, surrendering himself to her overprotective, extremely anxious care.

Harvey and his first analyst understood Harvey's various psychological difficulties as stemming from his overly close, constricting relationship with his mother and his oedipal fear of disapproval and punishment by his father. He was afraid to really develop himself fully in any direction for fear that his mother (both as a real person and as an internal presence) would feel abandoned by him and in turn abandon him, ejecting him from the position of her valiant and valued savior. His relationship with the analyst was understood by the two of them as involving, most fundamentally, a father transference: he often felt abandoned and neglected by the analyst in ways he had with his father, and sometimes enjoyed fantasies of being the analyst's special, favorite patient, a position he never felt he had with his real father. A great deal of time was spent, during the sessions, excavating feelings and memories from early childhood involving his loneliness, his sense of having been neglected by his father and appropriated by his mother, and the ways these experiences made him anxious and fearful in his current life.

Harvey's second analysis seemed to be developing along similar lines. The exploration of Harvey's childhood continued in a seemingly productive fashion. The relationship to this second analyst also seemed organized around a sense of the analyst as a longed-for, idealized father figure, sometimes experienced as remote and abandoning, sometimes bestowing a very precious attention.

However, about three years after it began, Harvey's second analysis took a dramatic turn, and the issues that arose bear directly on many of the major controversies regarding analytic technique that current analytic authors struggle with and debate.

Harvey had given some indications that his experience of this analytic relationship was more complicated than it appeared. When Harvey was angry and disappointed about something the analyst did or did not do, he would express that anger with biting, sarcastic humor: perhaps the analyst was not a candidate at the institute at all; perhaps he was the janitor who had been sweeping the office, who had picked up Harvey's folder and called him, impersonating an analyst. Attempts to work with the feelings and concerns suggested by such fantasies always proved impossible, however. Harvey would accuse the analyst, when he tried to take such fantasies seriously, of lacking a sense of humor.

Also, the analyst, now with increased experience working analytically with more patients, began to realize that the feeling of great competence and wisdom he generally got from working with Harvey was not to be taken for granted; upon reflection, he realized it had a lot to do with the way Harvey operated in the sessions. Unlike many of his other patients, Harvey always seemed to have interesting things to talk about, aspects of his experience he had begun reflecting on before the session, and invariably there was some important feature Harvey had not noticed, which allowed the analyst to make an important contribution. The analyst's input was always greatly appreciated and productively elaborated. Harvey was also a prolific dreamer. In contrast to the dreams of his other patients, which were often confusing and obscure, Harvey's dreams were unfailingly accessible. There was always something useful the analyst could say about them. Further, as the analyst became more interested in the subtle features of their interaction, he began to realize that there was a consistent rhythm to the way Harvey presented material. He would tell a dream and provide interesting associations; then he would pause, cueing the analyst that it was time for him to say something, and it was generally clear just what needed to be said. Whatever the analyst offered would be well received and conscientiously elaborated. It was beginning to seem less puzzling why the analyst felt himself to be so much more talented as an analyst with Harvey than with his other patients.

But these observations about their relationship did not prepare the analyst for the events to follow.

One day Harvey was in a good mood, speaking about some recent experiences and associating to them in an animated fashion. The analyst made an occasional comment here and there. Suddenly Harvey began talking in an extremely pressured, anxious fashion. It was clear that something dramatic had happened to change his mood—he seemed quite frightened. The analyst noted the change and asked what had happened. Harvey denied that anything had happened. The analyst felt sure *something* had happened and explained why. Harvey continued his denial at first, but, under the analyst's insistent pressure, eventually allowed that yes, something had happened, but that he was not going to talk about it.

The analyst had no idea of what was going on, but it felt so odd, almost spooky, that it seemed crucial not to just let it pass. So he pressed Harvey on why it was important not to talk about what had happened. Harvey was at first determined not to explain why he could not talk about what had happened. Then he began to sob; he assured the analyst that even though the analyst might *think* he wanted to know, he really did not. Eventually the analyst was able to elicit the following explanation:

In one of the analyst's brief comments, he had used a word that Harvey had never heard before. Harvey was afraid that the analyst had made up this word (a schizophrenic "neologism"), that it did not really exist. This terrified him, because Harvey had been privately harboring concerns for some time that the analyst was quite disturbed. Harvey felt sure that the analyst would be horrified to know that his craziness was visible to Harvey, who felt very protective of the analyst. It seemed that everything depended on Harvey never letting on that he knew how disturbed the analyst really was. By getting so visibly upset, Harvey had failed the analyst miserably; by telling the analyst about it, he feared he was damaging the analyst and destroying the possibility of continuing the treatment.

It took several weeks for the two of them to talk enough about Harvey's fears so that he felt safe enough to explain his anxieties more fully. Harvey's sarcastic joking about the analyst as impostor had always had some truth to it, even though he never fully allowed himself to think directly about it. He had had the fleeting fantasy that the analyst was not a janitor but a person who himself had suffered from severe psychological dysfunction and, perhaps, had been hospitalized. The analyst had dealt with his problems, Harvey further imagined, by going into the mental health field. Harvey had sensitively picked up various pockets of anxiety and depression in the analyst over the years, and this had led him to the conviction that the analyst still suffered from severe difficulties, which he kept at bay by working to help others.

Further, Harvey had the notion that he was the analyst's favorite patient, the patient who helped him feel most competent, most like a professional, least crazy. This made Harvey feel very special. Only *he* knew the analyst's secret, and the very fact that he never let the analyst know that he knew his secret was part of the way he demonstrated his love and support for the analyst. What was most important to the analyst, Harvey believed, was to be able to feel that his problems were hidden and that he was really being perceived as competent and professional. To his horror, Harvey had let the analyst know he knew the analyst's secret. He was terrified that this would destroy the analyst's confidence, that this vocational rehabilitation project would collapse, that the analyst would withdraw, and that Harvey would be abandoned.

As the two of them talked about Harvey's beliefs about the analyst, Harvey, with his analytic sophistication, kept reminding the analyst that this whole story, in fact, must have nothing to do with the analyst. It was transference, Harvey insisted. His mother had been crazy. His mother had been a kind of impostor as a mother, using her helping role to keep herself organized and functional. Through his devotion to his mother and his terror of abandonment, he had kept *her* together by being her good son. All these ideas and feelings that were experienced toward the analyst must be transferred from his experience of his mother.

PAST VS. PRESENT

According to the classical theory of the analytic process, Harvey was essentially right. The analytic situation is conceived of as a medium through which mental content *inside the patient* can become manifest. Harvey's childhood problem was his mother; Harvey's problem is still his mother. His conflicts and inhibitions in living all derived in various ways from his childhood attachment to and fantasies about her. In this view, all the content that arises in the analytic situation is generated from the mind of the patient, displaced from the patient's past.

In this traditional model, the psychoanalytic process operates as a kind of time machine, taking the patient back, experientially in the transference, to his childhood struggles. The analyst is like the operator of the time machine, hidden behind the control panel. Her only significant input is in conducting the procedure properly. It does not matter who she herself is, or what she is like.

Classical technique, when practiced with sophistication and skill, does not of course just involve the patient and analyst talking *about* the past. If revisited exclusively through discussion, the patient's experience of the past may have an intellectual quality, with the issues remaining abstract and not being deeply felt and relived. Further, Freud found that the most central childhood problems regularly surface not in discussion but in disguised form in the analytic relationship. It is too disturbing for the patient to feel he wants to murder his beloved father; the feeling first becomes accessible in relation to the analyst. It is too disturbing for the patient to feel sexually attracted to his mother; in a last-ditch effort, the resistance disguises the feelings as current impulses toward the analyst. Although initially encountering transference as an obstacle, Freud came to feel that the displacement of forbidden impulses and fantasies onto the person of the analyst is essential in helping the patient to experience and work through the issues as lived and deeply felt realities rather than intellectual abstractions and memories.

When Harvey insisted that he really did not believe the analyst to be crazy, that it was his mother's craziness that was the problem, he was both right and wrong (in the classical model). He was right that ultimately he had displaced his experience of his mother onto the person of the analyst. We would assume, unless there was dramatic evidence to the contrary, that the analyst was not crazy. Whatever small bits of difficulties or awkwardness Harvey had picked up in the analyst would be regarded as inconsequential hooks that allowed his displaced childhood experiences to take hold. Like the innocuous waking experiences that get distorted in dreams, which provide necessary access for repressed childhood wishes, the patient's observations about the analyst are distortions that make it possible for their childhood experiences, which are really about their early caretakers, to come to light.[1]

Yet Harvey seemed to be using this understanding (correct, according to the classical model) for defensive purposes. It was palpably clear that when the analyst would allow Harvey to claim the issue had only to do with his mother, Harvey's anxiety would sharply diminish (along with the analyst's anxiety). In the classical model, the analyst should not move too quickly to the actual, historical context. The experiences *need* to be lived in the present.[2] So good classical technique in this kind of situation would dictate that the analyst encourage Harvey to keep the focus on his anxious fantasies about the analyst's craziness, all the while believing that, in good time, they would be recontextualized within the historical setting and relationships to which they actually applied.

An alternative, interactional approach to the analytic process and the transference has gained increasing prominence in recent years.[3] Rather than regarding the analytic situation only as a theater for playing out the past (via the present), the interactional model positions the patient as also firmly engaged in the present (using what he has learned from the past).

People acquire their preferred forms of relating to others from repetitive early experience. They are likely to approach the analyst with anticipations based on past relationships, and to weave what they observe about the analyst into their habitual forms of interacting. Thus the patient's experience of the analyst is not likely to be simply a whole-cloth displacement from earlier relationships. The patient (in this model more actively involved in the present) is likely to have observed a great deal about the analyst and to have constructed a plausible view of her (based on the patient's own past and his typical ongoing organization of experience).

Consider Harvey in terms of this contemporary interactional approach. His most important relationship throughout his childhood was with his mother. He learned that people in authority, people one depends on, may not be what they seem. While appearing strong and commanding, they may in fact be quite shaky and brittle; while taking care of you, they may in fact need you to take care of them. Harvey's important relationships later in life were also constructed along these lines. His wife was a woman of considerable accomplishments whom he greatly admired. Yet he worried that she was fragile, and he tended to keep a great part of his own experience quite hidden from her, thinking of her as having such rarefied sensibilities that she could not endure what he came to feel were his demonic passions. He never really got angry at her.

So, in analysis, it made sense for Harvey to maintain his characteristic vigilance vis-à-vis his analyst's weaknesses and vulnerabilities. Harvey had learned a great deal about complexities in the ways people present themselves; he had become adept at making people he depended on feel safe in his presence. He was alert to their frailties, gracefully supported them, and then adroitly helped them to believe that their problems were invisible.

According to the interactional model, it would be a mistake for the analyst to assume that Harvey's observations about the analyst's anxieties and depression were distortions. From his life experience, one would assume that Harvey knew a great deal about struggles with anxiety and depression. To make a blanket assumption that Harvey's experience of the analyst as crazy was a transferential displacement of his experience of his mother is problematic on several counts:

1. It arbitrarily establishes the analyst as the judge of reality and presumes that there is only one way to see something accurately. (This is much more questionable in our time than in Freud's, because of the movement toward understanding truth in interpretive, hermeneutic terms, discussed in chapter 8.)

2. It contributes to undermining the patient's own sense of reality, encouraging him to abandon his own perspective and compliantly surrender to the analyst's presumably superior vision. It eliminates the possibility that Harvey has developed particular sensitivities that allow him to notice things that others, including the analyst, do not.

3. It is likely to be experienced by the patient as a repetitive reenactment of some of the most warping features of his earlier relationships. For the analyst to insist (or even to agree with Harvey's plea) that Harvey's experience of him as crazy is a distortion, displaced from his experience of his mother, is, ironically, to be acting quite like the mother. It communicates to Harvey a closed attitude toward his observations and perceptions and an unwillingness to explore his concerns. It is very likely to confirm Harvey's suspicions that the analyst is, indeed, fragile and in need of careful protection.

Thus, in the contemporary interactional approach, the patient is assumed to be living in the present according to strategies learned from the past.

Good technique would necessitate an in-depth exploration of Harvey's observations about the analyst, tracking the way he put them together to come to the conclusions he did, letting Harvey become very familiar with what he notices in others and how he processes these observations. Harvey will have to come to learn not that the analyst is without craziness, but that whatever craziness the analyst suffers from is different from Harvey's mother's, that it does not require the loving (and hateful) sacrifice of Harvey's own authentic experience to maintain a connection.

INTERPRETATION VS. RELATIONSHIP

What is it that actually makes change possible for the patient? Freud said many different things about the analytic process, but he was always clear on what he felt was the central mechanism of change: the lifting of repression through insight produced by interpretation. The patient's problems are the result of repression; cure entails the release of impulses, fantasies, and memories from repression. The analyst interprets both the content of the repressed and also the ways the patient is defending against that content. It is important that the analyst get it just right, because the patient has great incentive to avoid coming to terms with the truth of what it is she is repressing. In this classical conception, near misses glance off the conflicted, hidden content; they are actually welcomed by the resistance because to accept them temporarily takes the pressure off and allows the patient to continue to avoid the real problem. A well-timed interpretation is introduced into psychic ground that is well prepared: the analyst has worked slowly, from the surface down, only interpreting material that the patient is capable of recognizing as belonging to him at any given moment.

From a classical perspective, Harvey's transference onto the second analyst of the constellation of feelings relating to his mother's mental illness suggests that even though Harvey had attained intellectual understanding in his previous analysis of some features of his early dynamics, genuine insight had not taken place; the central repressed features were still repressed. So technique informed by the classical model would use the newly emerging transference feelings toward the analyst as a guide to uncovering the remaining hidden features of the earlier relationship with the mother: secret oedipal triumph, castration fears, and so on.

Strachey and the Superego

Challenges have arisen over many decades to Freud's understanding of insight as the basic therapeutic leverage in analysis. One of the most incisive was developed by James Strachey in the early 1930s, and the clarity of his argument makes it a still useful framework for considering various contemporary positions on the therapeutic action.

Strachey pointed out that Freud's contributions on technique (based on the principle of interpretation leading to insight) had been written in 1910s. Freud introduced the concept of the superego in 1923, greatly enriching our understanding of psychodynamics, but did not revise his theory of technique to take the superego into account.

What difference would the concept of the superego make? Freud had conceptualized repression as a struggle between two forces, the repressed content and the defenses. When the analyst makes an interpretation, he describes both sides of this struggle to the patient. (In Harvey's case, "You felt yourself to be sexually triumphant vis-à-vis your mother because your father left you an open field, but you could not allow yourself to know about this consciously because you thought, and still think, it was dangerous.")

With the superego, Freud was introducing a powerful ally of repression. Repression is instituted and maintained not just because the forbidden impulses are dangerous (the ego's concern) but because the child thinks they are wrong, evil, bad (the superego's concern), Freud believed. What happens to the superego when the analyst makes his interpretation? If the forbidden impulses are released from repression but the superego is untouched, Strachey reasoned, the cure would be only temporary, because the unchanged superego would in time pull the still forbidden impulses back into repression. (Harvey would briefly acknowledge his sexual possession of his mother, but, because he still considered such feelings to be so objectionable, he would soon repress them once again.)

So, Strachey argued, for analysis to be effective, it had to have a permanent impact on what Freud was now calling the superego. How might this work?

Strachey was working in England in the years immediately after Melanie Klein's arrival and was able to draw on some of her new thinking to explore Freud's concept of the superego, in particular her emphasis on projective and introjective processes.[4] To understand how the superego might change, Strachey suggested, consider how it is maintained under ordinary circumstances. A person enters a new situation; his expectations are determined by his past experience, which has been internalized in his superego. Thus, if we consider Harvey's attachment to his mother as reflecting avoidance of oedipal issues, we might explain this avoidance as follows. Harvey assumes that new people he meets (such as his analyst) would find objectionable his sexual fantasies regarding his mother, just as he expected that his father would find them objectionable. (In Kleinian terms, he projects his superego, or archaic internal objects, onto the interpersonal field.) It is important to note that Strachey assumed, as did Freud and Klein, that the parental images enshrined in the superego are not simply accurate renderings of the actual parents, but also include reinternalizations of the child's own aggression, projected onto the parents. Harvey's rage toward his father would have boomeranged, making the father feel even more dangerous and threatening to him.

Since people generally find what they are looking for, new experiences are regularly processed according to habitual expectations. Thus Harvey would find various clues suggesting that, in fact, his new acquaintances *are* as moralistic and condemnatory as he experienced his father as being. Further, people often act in a way that provokes precisely the reactions they are expecting. These new experiences are then internalized, reinforcing the original expectations. (The superego figures are reintrojected into the superego.) In this way, the superego remains generally unchanged and is continually reinforced.

There must be something in the psychoanalytic method, Strachey reasoned, that enables not just the release from repression of unconscious material, but a disconfirmation of the patient's deepest expectations (a disruption of the cycle of projection/introjection), resulting in an alteration in the superego itself. This happens, Strachey decided, not in anything the analyst purposely intends, but in the ordinary process of making transference interpretations. When the analyst says to the patient, "The feelings and attitudes you are experiencing with me are actually the feelings and attitudes you experienced long ago with your parent," he is also strongly conveying another, implicit message: "I am a different person from your image of your parent; I do not feel and believe these things you are attributing to me." Thus, while the explicit message in the interpretation is the uncovering of something in the patient's past, the implicit message is the establishment of the analyst as a different sort of person in the present (breaking the projective/introjective cycle through which the superego is maintained). It is this double impact, bridging past and present, Strachey felt, that makes transference interpretations the truly mutative leverage in the analytic process.

Thus, Strachey suggested, patients would not change simply because of the release from repression of impulses and fantasies; they would change because they would develop different attitudes toward themselves, drawn in part from a different cast of characters who would arise in their internal world, who, while holding to values and expectations, would be less rigidly demanding, more understanding of human foibles and temptations. That change in attitude would come from taking in some features of the actual relationship with the analyst. Strachey himself felt the analyst did not have to do anything special for that to happen, just make transference interpretations. But Strachey opened up the question that has occupied many subsequent theorists and clinicians: How does the analyst become a different sort of object, leading to different kinds of internalizations? What is it in the relationship between patient and analyst that makes this possible?

Transformations in the Analytic Relationship

Several major approaches to this question have developed, and the arguments among these positions and their complex cross-fertilizations constitute a good portion of the current analytic literature.

British object relations theorists, Freudian ego psychologists, and self psychologists share a common belief that superego formation associated with oedipal-phase resolution and the acquisition of values, standards, and self-expectation is not the only point of access whereby internalization of others takes place. From the moment of birth, the child's whole being has developed in the context of experiences with others. The analyst, then, has the potential to be taken in as a different sort of object in many ways, partially by virtue of her serving certain key parental functions. The patient is stuck because a normal growth process has been thwarted due to inadequate parental provision of a holding environment, mirroring, an empathic milieu, opportunities for separation–individuation and rapprochement, and so on. What is curative in the analytic relationship is the analyst's offering some form of basic parental responsiveness that was missed early on.

A major fork in the road of this developmental line of thought has occurred. Some theorists have argued that the analyst does not have to *do* anything different from what he did when he thought he was just elucidating the patient's past. Many developmentalists regard normal analyzing not as an absence (as did Strachey[5]) but as a presence, as actually providing missing parental responsiveness in the particulars of their analytic functioning. In this view (e.g., Pine, 1985), the very activities of reliable attendance, careful listening, and thoughtful interpreting are usually similar enough to attentive parenting to reanimate the stalled developmental process.

The other path at the fork is taken by those theorists who argue that the analyst sometimes *has* to do something different from ordinary listening and interpreting, to create, in the analytic situation, real experience that evokes the specific missed provision of childhood. To establish oneself as different from the traumatizing parent, it may be necessary to be more available to patients in some fashion, to respond to their needs in a more individualized way. As we noted in chapter 5, Winnicott suggested an approach with more disturbed patients whereby the analyst bends the environment around the patient's spontaneously arising wishes and gestures; Kohut (chapter 6) advised mirroring responses to patients with specific kinds of disturbances in self-formation. Whereas the analyst operating out of the classical theory of technique is always (rightfully) concerned with not gratifying the patient because to do so would be to lose an opportunity for insight, the analyst operating out of this more developmentally grounded approach is always (rightfully) concerned with not retraumatizing the patient.

Another approach to the curative features of the analytic relationship, developed in the interpersonal tradition, regards the analyst's response to the patient as organized not along parent–child lines but rather along adult-to-adult lines. Erich Fromm was an important influence here. As both an existentialist and a Marxist, Fromm felt that one of the deepest problems in contemporary life was a profound dishonesty, both with oneself and with others, the squelching of authentic experience in order to adapt to social conventions. People lie to themselves and one another all the time, Fromm believed, and one of the deepest needs for the patient who seeks psychoanalytic treatment is for an honest response; what is curative in the analytic relationship, what is internalized in a freeing way, is precisely the capacity for a more authentic honesty and engagement.

Consider these various understandings of the analytic relationship as alternatives (in terms of both the kind of intervention and how one would understand the analyst's involvement and impact) available to Harvey's analyst at the point where the transferential issues became dramatically explicit.

In one line of intervention, the analyst might make interpretations first about Harvey's defense against experiencing the feelings toward the person of the analyst: "Right now the person you are worried is crazy and fragile, who needs propping up and the sacrifice of your own independence and self-development, is me, and you are having a lot of trouble allowing yourself to stay with that experience." Eventually, as Harvey was able to experience the disturbing feelings more fully, in a less intellectualized way, an interpretive shift to the historical origins of the transference would take place: "This whole constellation of feelings between you and me is a reanimation of the simultaneously overstimulating and terrifying fusion you felt with your mother, in which you were, at one and the same time, her savior and helpless victim. And, unconsciously, your life is still organized around this pact with her."

Assuming this sequence was effective in productively engaging Harvey in further inquiry, analysts from different orientations would likely understand its therapeutic action quite differently.

According to the classical theory of technique, the analyst is generating insight into the patient's past and releasing from repression unconscious conflictual wishes, facilitating the fully emotional engagement of these issues by initially enlivening them in relation to the person of the analyst.

According to Strachey's reconceptualization, in addition to generating such insight the analyst, in the very process of making such interpretations, is disconfirming Harvey's assumption (superego projection) that the analyst is like Harvey's internalized image of his mother. Implicitly, the analyst is communicating "I am not crazy like your mother; she could not listen openly to you like this without becoming crushed herself. She could never comfortably consider how you felt about her; she was not able to offer you these kinds of noncondemnatory understandings."

An analyst with a more developmentally based approach would, in all likelihood, take issue with the confrontational quality of this particular line of intervention. Such an analyst might speculate that its effectiveness, however, was made possible by the patient's having already used other deeply restorative features of the analytic relationship. The analyst's careful listening, nonretaliatory interest, and active pursuit of Harvey's feelings and concerns had provided fundamental self-confirming parental responses that his mother's psychopathology had made impossible. This allowed Harvey to take in the crucial implicit communication in the analyst's interventions. The analyst had empathically grasped Harvey's deep fear of retraumatization, the consequence of his painful experience of his parents' unreliability in supporting his development. This fear manifested in Harvey's self-protective vigilance with the analyst, his continually orchestrating the analytic experience rather than allowing himself to rely on the analyst.

Or Harvey's analyst might feel that it would be necessary and useful to *do* something different besides making standard transference interpretations.

From a developmental approach, he might feel that Harvey had missed any real experience of stability and availability on the part of a caregiver. He might feel that becoming a different sort of object from the mother would require a careful attention to tentative expressions of Harvey's own needs, perhaps in terms of allowing extra sessions and phone contacts, or encouraging his curiosity about the person of the analyst, and so on. Perhaps the establishment for Harvey of the analyst as a different sort of person from his mother would require not just an implicit disconfirmation but active encouragement of carefully chosen quasi-parental experiences with the analyst.

Alternatively, in a more interpersonal approach, Harvey's analyst might feel called upon to transcend a more interpretive stance by engaging Harvey more actively and directly. The analyst's aggressive, insistent pursuit of

Harvey's reactions was already a step in this direction. Further extensions might involve a more open discussion of the analyst's experience of what it was like for him to have Harvey treating him as so fragile.

Freud believed that because the core of psychopathology was the repression of conflictual, infantile impulses, which sought disguised gratification from the analyst in many different forms, it was essential for the analyst *not* to give the patient any gratification, because gratification allows the impulse to be discharged rather than be remembered, thought about, and renounced. American Freudian technique, in particular, took on a marked austerity. Casual interactions with a patient—such as responding to questions, friendly conversation, divulging any personal information—were all strictly forbidden; they could easily satisfy needs and longings that the patient would consequently never come to articulate. If one can pilfer a little cash every now and then, one may never be forced to rob a bank! According to this American classical model, only frustration makes analytic insight possible.

This clear dichotomy between gratification and frustration is not possible for contemporary analysts who understand their patient's problems not just in terms of repressed conflicts but also in terms of aborted development and attachments to old object relations.

COUNTERTRANSFERENCE

The development of different concepts of countertransference throughout the history of psychoanalytic ideas has been remarkably parallel to the development of analytic thinking about transference.

We have noted that Freud at first regarded transference as a most unwanted obstacle. The task of the analysis, as he had first conceptualized it, was memory work—to reach as quickly as possible the repressed childhood memories, impulses, and fantasies. Along the way, something else happened: the sudden development of intense feelings toward the analyst, which inevitably disrupted the work of the analysis. The analyst became an enemy or a potential lover, and the analytic work no longer seemed important to the patient. Gradually, however, in trying to understand the nature of these disruptive transferences, Freud realized that they were not unrelated to the patient's childhood dynamics, the object of the analytic search. In fact, Freud came to believe, the patient's transferential feelings toward the analyst, properly understood, represented the emergence of repressed feelings toward early childhood figures, displaced onto the person of the analyst. Rather than an obstacle in the way of the work, the transference became a powerful vehicle for advancing the process.

Ideas about countertransference have followed an identical course, a half step behind. Freud and the earliest generations of analysts envisioned the ideal demeanor of the analyst as calm and objective: "evenly hovering attention" was the phrase Freud used. The transferential material produced by the patient, even if it was directed at or seemed to be about the analyst, really had nothing to do with the analyst. She was merely the operator of the time machine who, in a caring yet rational fashion, interpreted the experiences that were emerging and reset them into their original historical context. What if the analyst were to find herself feeling intense, passionate love or hate toward the patient? This should not be happening, and if it was, something was wrong. This was countertransference (a mirror image of the patient's transference)—the displacement of feelings from the *analyst's* past onto the analytic situation. While the patient's past was relevant to the subject matter of the analysis, the analyst's past was not. So countertransference was regarded as an obstacle, an intrusion into the analytic process. The analyst either was enjoined to rid herself of it through self-analysis or to return to her own psychoanalyst for help.

Over the past several decades a radical shift in thinking about countertransference has taken place in all schools of analytic thought. This rethinking has accompanied the more general shift in psychoanalytic concepts from the one-person framework of classical analytic theory to the two-person framework within which most contemporary analytic theorizing operates. The pioneers of this approach to countertransference were Ferenczi, Racker, and the interpersonalists.

As we noted in chapter 3, Sullivan regarded the basic unit of mind as an interactive field rather than as a bounded individual. Different people evoke different kinds of responses in each other; a person does not have a static "personality" that is carried around and displayed across all interpersonal situations. Different dimensions of the person (including the person of the analyst) are evoked in different situations, which are mutually generated with the others in that situation. (This does not mean, of course, that personality is infinitely malleable and simply generated from scratch on the spot!) Although Sullivan himself was conservative and cautious about the kinds of experiences he considered useful for the analyst to allow herself in interaction with the patient, Fromm felt that the analyst's frank and honest reactions were just what the patient needed to know about and understand. Why does the patient's life always evolve into the same, repetitive tangles with people? What is he doing to perpetuate his difficulties? Rather than driving them underground through a contrived kind of "professionalism," Fromm believed that the analyst should value personal reactions to the patient (professionally constrained and not acted upon) as containing crucial analytic data. Fromm believed that people in our society rarely speak truthfully to each other about how they actually feel about each other. A major hope of many patients on entering analysis is that they will finally find someone who will speak frankly with them about what they are like, how they affect others, and what goes wrong between them and others. Traditional analytic reserve is disastrous in these circumstances, Fromm felt; a judicious and constructive disclosure of the analyst's personal feelings and reactions might be essential.

Second-generation interpersonalists extended this use of the counter-transference in many ways.[6] The analyst was considered to be a part of the interactional field that patient and analyst were trying to understand. The patient's repetitive interpersonal difficulties were bound to have an impact on the analyst; the interactional patterns that developed between analyst and patient were bound to reflect the past patterns in the patient's family. Therefore, the analyst's experiences of and with the patient were regarded as a key domain of the analytic process. Rather than an obstacle, they were considered a vehicle for advancing the analytic work.

Other schools of analytic thought, each in its own language and through its own concepts, have similarly come to find countertransference to be a valuable tool.

The Kleinians, through recent extensions of the notion of projective iden-tification, have come to regard the analyst's experience as the central site where the patient's dynamics are to be discovered and recognized. Object relations theorists tend to regard countertransference as a key device for gaining access to the repetitive self–object configurations of the patient's internal world. Some Freudians have come to regard countertransference as unavoidable, even if not terribly helpful (Martin Silverman, Sander Abend); other Freudians have come to see in the analyst's countertransference instructive enactments of the patient's dynamics and jointly created reenact-ments of the patient's interpersonal past (Judith Chused, Theodore Jacobs). Although Kohut himself was quite conservative with regard to counter-transference, some second-generation self psychologists (especially Robert Stolorow and his collaborators) have increasingly looked to the counter-transference as an important source of information regarding repetitive (as well as selfobject) transferences.

Although increasing interest in countertransference and the shift to a more interactive perspective on the analytic process have been quite wide-spread, analytic authors differ with respect to the way the analyst's coun-tertransference is best utilized. Let us return to Harvey and his analyst to illustrate these different options.

What was the analyst's general emotional response to Harvey? At first, he found himself gratified by the work, perhaps too gratified, for a while, to notice that Harvey was involved in making him feel especially competent and wise. The analyst had begun the analysis with considerable anxiety about his own competence, which Harvey undoubtedly picked up on. There was something deeply reassuring about the sagacity that Harvey's manner of being an analytic patient ceded to the analyst. Then, when he discovered Harvey's carefully guarded doubts about his sanity, the analyst felt anxious and exposed. How much of his own neurotic conflicts had been detected by Harvey's acute sense of other people's problems? Finally, as the extent of Harvey's dedicated caretaking became known, the analyst felt both moved and patronized. Harvey's protectiveness felt both like a profound form of love and a subtly contemptuous superiority.

What is to be made of these countertransference reactions? In previous generations, they would have been regarded as inappropriate; they would have probably remained unnoticed and uncertainly undeveloped.[7] Contemporary analytic clinicians might work with them in several different ways, and the different positions can be best organized around two closely related questions: Why is the analyst feeling this way? And what is to be done about it?

Why does the analyst have these feelings?

Some would say that the analyst's reactions are ordinary, common responses to the sort of interpersonal positions and pressures Harvey set up. Virtually anyone would feel this way with Harvey. (It was in this sense that Winnicott used the term "objective countertransference.")

Others would say that Harvey and his analyst have participated in a reenactment of Harvey's relationship with his mother. The analyst's motives in the reenactment are not terribly important; what is crucial is the playing out of the past.

Contemporary Kleinians would say that the analyst's experiences are a more complex result of the patient's projective identifications. Harvey fears for his own fragile sanity. He is unable to simply resolve this fear, so he projects it into the analyst, where he takes care of it at a safe distance. It has little to do with the analyst, who has become largely a container for dissociated features of Harvey's experience.

A more fully two-person approach to countertransference would extend the focus on what Harvey is doing to the analyst to the question of what responsive chords this strikes in the analyst.[8] Harvey's search for and nurturance of the analyst's vulnerabilities and craziness are likely to elicit from the analyst pieces of his own experience that correspond to Harvey's projections. We all have vulnerable, crazy parts, this line of thought would go; the analyst's countertransference reflects not just a shallow, ordinary social reaction but the way Harvey, like all patients, gets under the analyst's skin, evoking dynamics that are difficult for even the best-integrated analyst. In this view (e.g., Winer, 1994), any deeply engaged analysis is likely to evolve into crises in which both analysand (in the transference neurosis) and analyst (in the countertransference neurosis) are implicated. The heart of the work is understood to entail precisely the struggle of both parties to work their way constructively out of this crisis.

Some recent authors have suggested that the analyst should not be the only one consulted about the countertransference. All of us have a less than complete understanding of our own dynamics, and the patient may often be able to pick up features of the countertransference that the analyst's own defenses (counterresistance) block him from becoming aware of. Thus some theorists (e.g., Hoffman, Aron, Blechner) have stressed the utility of extended explorations of the patient's experience of and hypotheses about the analyst's experience. Many patients grew up feeling their perceptions of their parents were forbidden and dangerous. They have learned to discount their own often discerning observations and consequently feel mystified about what happens between themselves and others. The permission for the patient to truly explore and encounter the analyst as an other can sometimes serve as a precondition for the patient to learn to become comfortable with his own experience.

What is to be done with the analyst's feelings? Probably the most important dividing line in current approaches to using countertransference is around the question of whether the analyst's reactions ought to be in any way divulged to the patient, an intervention termed "disclosure."

Many authors take the position that the utility of countertransference lies in the information it provides regarding the patient's side of the interaction. By exploring his own feelings, the analyst gathers clues to what the patient might be feeling and doing. If the analyst notices twinges of irritation in himself, he might speculate about the patient's awareness of that irritation resulting in a wariness the patient seems to display around him. If the analyst discovers a sexual excitement in the patient's presence, she might learn something about an unnoticed erotic dimension of the patient's demeanor.

In the classical model of technique, the rationale for the injunction against disclosure on the part of the analyst was quite clear and persuasive: The analyst's feelings had nothing to do with anything except his own problems. For the analyst to have strong feelings one way or another (violating neutrality) was bad enough; for the analyst to express those personal feelings would compound the problem. It would muddy the blank screen upon which the patient projects his transferences; it would contaminate the process. The analyst should remain silent except when interpreting the underlying meaning of the patient's associations.

However, as we have noted, most contemporary analysts now regard the analyst's experience as quite relevant to what she and the patient are struggling to understand. Therefore, the contemporary discussion about disclosure reflects new concerns and levels of complexity. One common concern is that the focus be kept at all times on the *patient's* experience, not the analyst's. Even though the countertransference may be an important tool for understanding the dynamics of the patient's transference, for the analyst to speak openly about her feelings can deflect the inquiry away from an indepth exploration of the meaning of their interaction *to the patient*. Further, to say that the countertransference may contain useful information is not to say that it is oracular (Racker, 1968, p. 170); the analyst may very will be absorbed with issues and problems of her own. Many clinicians who find a two-person framework useful look to the countertransference for hypotheses about the patient that need other confirming evidence from the patient's side of the experience. In addition, those who emphasize the importance of exploring the *patient's* experience of the analyst's participation point out that the analyst may sometimes not be in the best position to know what she has been doing and why. Because the analyst is not transparent to herself, disclosing her account of her own experience may defensively foreclose an exploration of the patient's sometimes more discerning perceptions (see Greenberg, 1991; Hoffman, 1983). Finally, Kernberg (1994) has argued that a scrupulous adherence to the technical principle of nondisclosure is an essential condition for the analyst to feel free enough to explore her own countertransference fantasies in a way that will become useful to the patient through the analyst's interpretations. If the analyst had the option of disclosing or not, she might feel less free to allow herself her more intimate fantasies.

Concerns about the analyst's motives for revealing countertransferential feelings are often expressed in the warning against "countertransference confessions." As the term suggests, disclosure of the analyst's feelings may well serve the purpose of confessing guilt on her part, which is likely to make it difficult for the patient to fully explore his own feelings.

Let us make some of these options more concrete by considering an analyst who is ten minutes late beginning a session. The patient is angry. Should the analyst tell the patient his thoughts about the reasons for and possible motives underlying the lateness? Should the analyst apologize? The more conservative approach to countertransference disclosure is based on the assumption that any disclosure is likely to impede or undercut the patient's expression and exploration of his own feelings about the lateness, which, after all, is the fundamental business of the analysis.

Other authors and clinicians argue for the utility of selective countertransference disclosures. No one recommends continual revelation of the analyst's experience, which would be both impossible and, even if possible, counterproductive. However, many contemporary analysts feel that, judiciously chosen, countertransference disclosures in some situations can be both necessary and very helpful. Perhaps in our example of the analyst who is late, the exploration of his own experience reveals an increasing irritation about the patient's own chronic tardiness. The analyst's disclosure of his thoughts about both his own and the patient's lateness might relate to power struggles in the patient's family involving waiting and longing and promises that were never kept, early experience that now shapes his way of involving himself with others. Contemporary relational analysts (e.g., Greenberg, 1991; Hoffman, 1994; Mitchell, 1988; Maroda, 1991, 1993) regard experience as pervaded by repetitive self–other configurations established in early significant relationships that are likely to appear in the analysis through transference–countertransference interactions. Disclosure can provide both the analyst and the analysand with crucial material for understanding.

For many patients, depending on their background and dynamics, the laconic style of classical analysis can feel quite dangerous, not at all neutral or reassuring. At intense moments, when the patient has the sense that the analyst is, indeed, deeply involved, lovingly or hatefully, technical opaqueness and a refusal to discuss what is taking place can be experienced as mystifying, arbitrary, and defensive. (Remember the beseeching of the wizard in *The Wizard of Oz* for Dorothy to "pay no attention to the man behind the curtain.") In our example, a patient who, as a child, was treated as inconsequential by significant adults may very well experience the analyst's unexplained lateness not as good technique but as a new edition of callous and disrespectful treatment. On the other hand, the analyst's actually expressing distress, both at his own lateness and at being kept waiting by the patient, might open up a heretofore closed area in the patient's life, a longed-for but defensively disavowed wish that someone could actually care whether he was present or not, that a more neutral, interpretive approach would preclude. The more recent analytic literature is filled with examples of the selective disclosure of the analyst's experience enhancing the authenticity and collaborative spirit of the analytic relationship, resolving sticky impasses and deepening the process, often opening up previously inaccessible areas in the patient's experience.

Those analysts who have adopted a more expressive and openly interactive style tend to emphasize the patient's developing a *new* object relationship with the analyst as a necessary condition for the old, transferential relationship to be given up. Whereas Strachey thought the analyst merely needed to make interpretations to become a new object, many analysts now feel that the analyst often needs to do something more active and directly engaging to make her presence more palpable and her emotional involvement more effective.

For example, as Harvey struggled with his habitual mode of establishing close connections with important others, now discernible in the analytic relationship as well, it was hard for him to imagine being important to the analyst in any way other than as his rescuer. If the analyst really did not need Harvey to hold him together, what significance could he have for the analyst at all? During this extended exploration, the analyst at times felt himself quite moved by Harvey's dedication and told him so. He found it touching that Harvey could want to help him so much that he was willing to sacrifice his own life if he felt it would make the analyst feel competent and whole. (Of course, Harvey also resented doing this and felt he really had no compelling alternative.) Later in the analysis, Harvey suggested that there was something important and liberating for him in feeling he had mattered to and moved the analyst, which helped him feel better about renegotiating their relationship along lines that allowed him less fusion and more autonomy.

PSYCHOANALYSIS AND OTHER TREATMENTS

Not surprisingly, all the controversy in theory and technique we have been tracing in these final two chapters has been accompanied by great ferment over the very definition of psychoanalysis and its relationship to other psychological treatments.

Freud and his European contemporaries practiced psychoanalysis in a fashion that was flexible and often quite informal. Treatment sometimes lasted only a few months; many patients returned at brief intervals. Freud interacted with his patients in many different ways, from didactic to hospitable.

Psychoanalysis in the United States took on a very different tone. Partly as a result of its medicalization (which Freud [1927] himself opposed), partly as a result of the need to define it in contrast to other psychotherapies, many of which were derivatives of psychoanalysis (Friedman, 1988), "orthodox" Freudian psychoanalysis in the United States became quite formalized, and the role of the analyst extremely ritualized and often remote. Psychoanalysis was defined according to a narrow set of criteria: a minimum of four sessions a week, the use of the couch from the very beginning, and an anonymous, largely silent, interpretive analyst. These conditions were felt to be necessary to allow for the full development of the patient's transference neurosis, the trip in the analytic time machine back to the patient's past.

The last several decades have brought dramatic changes in the ways psychoanalysts work with patients. There have been two major sources for these developments.

Some of the modifications in analytic practice have been brought about by the developments in theory we have traced throughout this book. As various psychoanalytic schools of thought have moved, in different ways, in the direction of a two-person framework, the analyst has come to be regarded as having an inevitable impact on the process, no matter what she does. The patient is not seen as simply reliving the past, but as reacting, to one degree or another, to his present experience. An approach that makes one patient feel safe and "held" may make another feel endangered. Conditions that encourage one patient to deeply engage her inner experience and her past may cause another to flee. Therefore, many analysts now work in a variety of ways: one or two sessions a week, as well as three or four; the patient sitting up or lying on the couch; an active, occasionally confrontational style, sometimes expressive and somewhat self-revealing, as well as a more silent, interpretive style; and so on. Some analysts combine analytic techniques with other therapeutic modalities, such as behavioral therapy techniques (Frank, 1992, 1993; Wachtel, 1987) family therapy, group therapy, social intervention (Altmann, 1995), and so on.

A second set of influences on analytic practice has been the product of social, economic, and political forces outside psychoanalysis itself. Three or four sessions a week is expensive. During the 1960s and 1970s, when a relatively small percentage of the population sought psychological treatment, some of that cost was defrayed by insurance coverage. As more people became aware of their need for psychological help of various sorts and as the concern about skyrocketing health costs increased, psychoanalysis came under attack as cost-inefficient, a luxury rather than a necessity. Defenders of psychoanalysis on pragmatic grounds (e.g., Gabbard, 1995) have noted the considerable research suggesting that the psychological well-being psychoanalysis often achieves markedly decreases the individual's need for other costly treatment for physical disease, addictions, and alcoholism. These issues are now hotly contested, as the American political system is in the process of rethinking its priorities in the areas of health care and psychological care. The impact of these social and economic processes on practicing psychoanalysts has been to broaden the practice of most clinicians beyond traditionally structured formal analysis.

Should shorter treatments, less frequent sessions, and face-to-face work still be considered psychoanalysis? Or should the term *psychoanalysis* be reserved for the traditional, formal analytic setting, and the term *psychotherapy* be used in relation to the wide range of modifications now being practiced?

There has been a great deal of debate in the literature about how psychoanalysis, in contrast to psychotherapy, should be defined. Gill (1994) has argued that the formal, "extrinsic" criteria—three or four sessions a week, the couch, and so on—should themselves not be the basis for calling a treatment psychoanalytic; for Gill, what is definitive of psychoanalysis are the "intrinsic" criteria: the depth of the process and the systematic exploration of transference–countertransference issues. Some argue that a true analytic process of in-depth work with transference phenomena cannot happen with one or two sessions a week, or without the couch, or in treatments of short duration. Others (including Gill) argue that the deepest dynamic issues and transference–countertransference interactions can emerge in many different circumstances, if the analyst is willing to focus on and engage them. The debate goes on and will go on for some time.

We have thus come full circle, ending with the same question we asked at the beginning, "What is psychoanalysis?" Our hope is that the reader will be better able to appreciate the breadth and depth of psychoanalysis as a system of thought or, rather, as a collection of various subsystems of thought.

Freud himself defined psychoanalysis in different ways at different times. One of the most widely cited (1914b) was his statement that what makes a treatment psychoanalytic is an emphasis on transference and resistance. The problem (and the virtue) of this definition is, as we have seen, that the very ways analysts understand both transference and resistance keep changing. One thing has not changed, however. Psychoanalytic theories radiate in different directions from a common, core commitment to a sustained, collaborative inquiry into the complex textures of human experience, established in the interplay between past and present, actuality and fantasy, self and other, internal and external, conscious and unconscious.

We hope the reader will develop his or her own views concerning the question of what makes a clinical treatment distinctly psychoanalytic, by reflecting on the time, the intensity of mutual effort, and the courage required: for Gloria to develop the capacity to make choices and commitments, for Angela to emerge from behind her wall, for Fred to tolerate greater intimacy with his wife, for Emily to understand the isolating impact of her self-sufficiency, for Rachel to knit together her worlds of feces and flowers, for

Charles to find other ways to feel connected to his parents besides episodic depressions, for Jane to emerge from her self-monitored prison, for Peter to enter his experiences rather than observe them at a measured distance, for Doris to tolerate and enjoy silence and solitude, for Eduardo to feel fully human and self-sufficient rather than his mother's puppet, and for Harvey to reclaim himself from a life held hostage by the compulsive need to create and care for psychological invalids. In our view, clinical psychoanalysis is best defined not in terms of the furniture employed, the frequency of the sessions, or a set of rules of conduct. Clinical psychoanalysis is most fundamentally about people and their difficulties in living, about a relationship that is committed to deeper self-understanding, a richer sense of personal meaning, and a greater degree of freedom.

NOTES

PREFACE

1. Fred Pine (1985) has provided an impressive catalogue of the considerations leading to the masking of innovation in psychoanalytic thought:

   The awesome power of Freud as mentor and of one's own analyst similarly; the need for referrals, which leads to caution in what one presents about one's work to the world; the ease with which the motives of revisionists can be interpreted in this field (i.e., the resort to ad hominem argument) and the "timelessness of teaching," that is, the tendency to teach what we were taught rather than what we ourselves have come to think or do. (pp. 26–27)

CHAPTER 1. SIGMUND FREUD AND THE CLASSICAL PSYCHOANALYTIC TRADITION

1. Many philosophers, poets, and psychologists, before and during Freud's lifetime, had described ideas and feelings that operated outside of awareness (see Ellenberger, 1970).

2. The long delay between Breuer's treatment of Anna O. and his joint publication with Freud on hysteria was due in part to the traumatic fashion in which that treatment ended. Anna O. developed an erotic transference to Breuer, manifesting itself in a hysterical pregnancy, which shook Breuer considerably and led to his abandonment of the field and a reconcentration on his work as internist. These events were disclosed only many years later, when the psychoanalytic notions of transference and countertransference (see chapter 9) had become advanced enough to make such devel-

opments understandable and workable (too late for Breuer, however).

3. Breuer's collaboration with Freud ended shortly after the publication of *Studies on Hysteria,* at least partially because of Freud's controversial turn toward sexuality in exploring the origin of hysteria.

4. Jeffrey Masson (1984) attacked Freud's motives for abandoning the seduction theory, which, Masson claimed, had to do with Freud's scurrilous efforts to cover up parental abuse of children and medical abuse (particularly by Fliess) of patients.

5. This model was thoroughly characteristic of the science of Freud's day, which drew extensively on Newtonian physics and Darwinian biology in constructing an understanding of both living creatures and inanimate objects in terms of matter, forces, and motion. Freud's instinct theory is traditionally separated into two distinct dimensions: a psychology of sexuality, self-preservation, and aggression and a metapsychology that concerns the distribution and regulation of psychic energy and dynamic forces. There is considerable controversy about how independent these two dimensions are from each other (see Gill & Holzman, 1976).

6. The "phallic" phase is still pregenital because, although the child's sexuality is centered in the genitals, Freud believed that the three- to four-year-old has no understanding of two different genders or the complementarity of male and female genitalia. Freud posited that at this point, children believe the penis and clitoris are equivalent and assume all people to be anatomically similar. Freud's concepts of gender development and their subsequent revisions will be considered in chapter 8.

7. Many commentators regard the horrifying events of World War I, the beginnings of Freud's own protracted struggle with cancer, and the death of his favorite daughter, Sophie, as all contributing to his growing pessimism.

8. Later social critics, such as Herbert Marcuse (1955) and Norman O. Brown (1959), who drew heavily on Freud's concepts in their critique of social convention, necessarily emphasize Freud's earlier instinct theory, where the absence of repression can be envisioned as constructive, not disastrous.

9. In subsequent chapters we consider the work of those theorists who have introduced major innovative lines of psychoanalytic theorizing: some (such as the Freudian ego psychologists) retaining Freud's basic model but departing in a significant fashion, some (such as Fairbairn and Winnicott) retaining Freud's language but altering his basic premises, some (such as Loewald, Schafer, and Lacan) greatly developing certain dimensions of Freud's vision and minimizing others. Important contributions have also been made by authors who have sharpened and extended the basic framework Freud established. Among the most significant of these authors are Jacob Arlow (1985, 1987), Charles Brenner (1976, 1982), and William Grossman (1992).

CHAPTER 2. EGO PSYCHOLOGY

1. For a fuller consideration of this issue, see David Shapiro's *Neurotic Styles* (1965), which offers a brilliant analysis of how character, perception, cognitive style, and a general approach to living can all be correlated with one's preferred defensive operations. Wilhelm Reich further developed Anna Freud's work on defenses in the influential *Character Analysis* (1936). Later in his career Reich veered off from the psychoanalytic mainstream in developing his theory of "orgone" energy.

2. Remarkably, this is precisely how Wilfred Bion (1955) described what it was like to be the object of someone else's projective identifications (see chapter 4). We might speculate that this experience of Angela's came about because she found herself so often used by her mother to house her mother's own projections.

3. It was later discovered that these failure-to-thrive infants suffer from an actual deficiency of growth hormones that are activated by physical and emotional stimulation provided by caregivers.

4. While one might note the possible symbolic meaning of six-year-old Stanley's equation of a baby with an animal trapped in a cage, Mahler did not directly address this issue. For her, the ability to draw abstract connections requires a perceptual reliability in concretely perceiving similarities and differences, a capacity that she felt was absent in this troubled child (see Mahler, 1968, p. 94).

5. The ego psychology emphasis on the role of maternal failings in psychopathology has troubled feminist writers, who take issue both with the exoneration of the father from the role of equal responsibility in a child's early development, as well as with the rather self-less depiction of the female-as-mother that it seems to advocate as necessary for a child's healthy development (cf. Benjamin, 1988). The father's role in the process of separation–individuation was in fact given some attention by ego psychologists. The father was seen primarily as having a crucial role in offering the child a connection *outside* the symbiotic relationship with the mother, thus bolstering the child's move toward greater autonomy and his involvement in the outside world. Greenson (1968) further explored the special challenge to the boy in establishing his male gender identity, needing to disidentify from the sameness he had experienced in the symbiotic union with mother. His concomitant crucial identification with father was, Greenson felt, enhanced by the boy's experience of solid motives for this identification, such as the father's being involved with the boy and appealing to him, as well as by the father's being valued by the mother.

6. This conceptualization of libido and aggression was prefigured by Freud (1940, p. 148) in his description of the aims of libido (to bind together) and aggression (to undo connections). For Freud, however, the final *aim* of aggression was the destruction of life.

7. Present-day researchers, in a conclusion that evokes an interesting resonance with this early formulation, suggest that endorphin pathways are
established during the first year of life in response to various kinds of emotional experiences between the child and her caregivers. Thus if the child's
early experiences are traumatic, the release of endorphin, the body's opi-
ate, is physiologically linked with pain and anxiety, so that in adult
patients who hurt themselves (self-mutilators), the pain seems to produce
a chemically mediated sedation (Van der Kolk, 1988).

8. The emphasis in ego psychology on preoedipal issues did not preclude
oedipal conflicts; what became fundamental in patients like Angela, however, was not the oedipal conflict itself, so much as the way in which this
inevitable drama became filtered through the existing preoedipal dynamics. In this dream, for example, we see how the longing for a man, a possibly oedipal representation, is filtered through preoedipal merger imagery.
The oedipal punishment, then, is not castration but psychic disappearance.

9. This idea of Jacobson's may derive from Melanie Klein's concepts of splitting and depressive anxiety, developed in the 1930s (see chapter 4). These
ideas are developed further in the work of Otto Kernberg (see chapter 7).

10. While the ego psychologists enriched the dynamic understandings of
masochism in important and useful ways, releasing the concept from its
position of psychic inevitability, they did less to address Freud's equally
disturbing conclusion about masochism: that it is a fundamental psychic
orientation of the female self (see chapter 8 for additional considerations).

11. Adrienne Harris (1995) has observed that "no psychoanalytic study of
female aggression can fail to comment on the social dimension of this
problem" noting the profound "psychic consequences, conscious and
unconscious, of thwarted and conflicted ambition and aggression" that
can give rise to "multi-generational histories" of problems with rage and
aggression in women. In this regard, one wonders whether aggression
would have been such an all-consuming psychological problem for Angela
if her mother had not had to contend with the disrupting and repressive
impact of cultural and religious gender role expectations that so disrupted
her own life.

12. In choosing to discuss only specific contributions of a small handful of
people, we have tried to articulate the basic building blocks of the ego psychology tradition, particularly as it contributes to the progression of psychoanalytic thought in a more general way. The tradition of ego psychology was collectively built on the work of many writers. They include:
Phyllis Greenacre, Rudolf Loewenstein, Helene Deutsch, Grete Bibring,
Kurt Eissler, Ralph Greenson, Joseph and Ann Marie Sandler, Anni
Bergmann, Martin Bergmann, Fred Pine, and Paul Gray.

CHAPTER 3. HARRY STACK SULLIVAN AND INTERPERSONAL PSYCHOANALYSIS

1. Sullivan did not specify the mechanisms whereby anxiety in the caregivers is picked up by the baby, and even in an era of highly sophisticated research into infancy, the workings of this process remain somewhat obscure. The phenomenon is familiar to anyone who has spent any time around babies, however. Some people are "good" with babies and some are not, although people who are not sometimes get better as they get more comfortable and relaxed. See Beebe and Lachmann (1992) for important work in mutual affective regulation between mother and infant.

2. Karen Horney's reformulation of basic Freudian concepts in terms of cultural influences and social processes bears a great similarity to Fromm's. Horney (1885–1952), Sullivan, and Fromm are often grouped together as "culturalists" or "neo-Freudians." There seems to have been considerable mutual influence among the three until personal and political factors in the 1930s created a rift between Horney and Fromm, leading her to establish the American Institute for Psychoanalysis to teach her point of view. (Fromm, Sullivan, and Thompson all were key figures in the development of the William Alanson White Institute, which has remained since then the center of interpersonal psychoanalysis.) Horney's critique of the classical, phallocentric Freudian approach to female development played a key role in the later understanding of gender and development within the interpersonal school.

3. Many interpersonal authors have contributed to this tradition, including: Bromberg (1983, 1991, 1993), Ehrenberg (1992), Feiner (1979), Hirsch (1984, 1987, 1994), Levenson (1972, 1983), Stern (1987, 1990, 1991), Tauber (1979), Wolstein (1971).

4. This central contribution in the work of Freud, Klein, and Winnicott is explored in Ogden (1994).

5. Sullivan's depiction of the self-system strikingly anticipated Jacques Lacan's understanding of the ego as a narcissistic, illusory construction (see chapter 7).

CHAPTER 4. MELANIE KLEIN AND CONTEMPORARY KLEINIAN THEORY

1. Freud's theories of early mental life had been derived from extrapolating backward in his work with adult neurotic patients. Freud had himself never treated children. In the case of "Little Hans," Freud supplied Hans's father, who served as a sort of informal analyst for his son, with psychoanalytic interpretations.

2. The recent efforts of Elizabeth Bott-Spillius have gone a considerable way

toward making Kleinian theory known and understandable to those outside the Kleinian psychoanalytic world.

3. In some contemporary applications of Klein (e.g., Aron, 1995; Mitchell,
   1988), the "goodness" and "badness" of the breast are derived, in contrast
   to Klein's intrapsychic account, from actual gratifications and deprivations. The flowers and shit people, for example, might be understood to
   derive initially, at least in part, from actual loving and protective vs. callous and abusive treatment by Rachel's caregivers.

4. The kind of clinical material from which such a hypothesis is drawn might
   be the not infrequent claim of certain patients that the analyst could easily have given in the first session all the interpretations made over the years
   of the analysis, but meted them out gradually to maintain power and
   financial control over the patient. Some analysts, in their grandiosity, also
   believe in this fantasy.

5. Sullivan depicted this kind of process in a strikingly similar fashion
   (although in very different language) in the security operation he termed
   specious ideals, whereby one puts considerable distance between oneself
   and one's disowned impulses (e.g., aggressive feelings) by taking the high
   moral ground (e.g., joining an antiviolence society), opposing those very
   impulses in others.

6. Recent infant research has found a powerful tendency toward affective
   contagion between mothers and infants (Stern, 1985; Tronick & Adamson, 1980).

CHAPTER 5. THE BRITISH OBJECT RELATIONS SCHOOL: W. R. D. FAIRBAIRN AND D. W. WINNICOTT

1. Psychoanalytic ideas develop in dialectic swings. The overcorrection for
   Klein's omission of the actual mother has sometimes led, in post-Kleinian
   object relations theorizing, to a tendency to blame the mother.

2. In 1920, Freud tried to explain these phenomena by proposing a death
   instinct, operating "beyond the pleasure principle," manifesting itself in
   the tendency of the mind to preserve and return to earlier states and, ultimately, nonexistence. This was not a solution to the problem of the repetition compulsion many analysts found particularly useful.

3. More contemporary authors whose work derives from the independent
   group's tradition include: Masud Khan, Nina Coltart, Christopher Bollas,
   John Klauber, Adam Phillips, Neville Symmington, and Patrick Casement.

4. Ferenczi fell out of favor with Freud because of what appears to have been
   a complex amalgam of personal, conceptual, and political differences. A
   fuller story of this important schism in the history of psychoanalysis has
   only recently been made possible with the publication of Ferenczi's clinical diary and the Freud–Ferenczi correspondence. See Aron and Harris

(1993) for a thoughtful and balanced consideration of Ferenczi's enormously influential role in the history of psychoanalytic ideas.

CHAPTER 6. PSYCHOLOGIES OF IDENTITY AND SELF: ERIK ERIKSON AND HEINZ KOHUT

1. Erickson's work had many features in common with the culturalist perspective of Harry Stack Sullivan, Erich Fromm, and Karen Horney.

2. David Rapaport, the most important historian and explicator of ego psychology, noted that for Hartmann the id remained as it did for Freud, unalterable by environmental influences; for Erikson, however, there was no sector of the psyche that was inaccessible to social influences (1958, p. 620).

3. Not all analysts agreed with Freud about the analytic inaccessibility of more severely disturbed patients. Eventually, the concepts of "psychotic transferences" and "borderline transferences" were developed to depict the particular kinds of involvement with the analyst that typify the transferences of patients with severe forms of psychopathology.

4. A historian who posthumously edited Kohut's correspondence has proposed that Kohut drew on his own experiences as inspiration for Mr Z (Cocks, 1994). The analyst's use of self-experience to comprehend the workings of the psyche has been a fundamental feature of psychoanalysis since Freud's earliest writings, where his own self-analysis provided him with crucial understandings. Psychoanalytic historians have convincingly demonstrated the resonance between psychoanalytic theories and the cultural context and personal struggles of their authors. (See, for example, Stolorow & Atwood, 1979, which discusses the lives of Freud, Jung, Reich, and Rank from this perspective.)

5. As we noted in chapter 1, the classical approach to dream interpretation was to regard the dream, as it was reported by the dreamer, to be of little import. This "manifest content" of the dream was felt to cover over the analytically crucial dream-generating dynamics which could be accessed only through the patient's additional associations to discrete dream elements, which were then interpreted by the analyst, revealing their deeper meaning. Within self psychology, the manifest content of the dream was given increased attention. It was viewed as a potential communication to the analyst representing the state of the patient's self (referred to as "self-state dreams") as in this case, where Eduardo's description of himself as his mother's puppet seems to graphically capture his internal sense of self as fragile, inhuman, and controlled. See Fosshage (1987, 1989) for a fuller discussion of dream analysis within self psychology.

6. See A. Ornstein (1974) for an interesting discussion of this topic. Issue has been taken with Kohut's depiction of transference as "found" rather than

created by the analyst's particular way of organizing the clinical material. See for example, Schafer (1983) and Black (1987) for a fuller discussion of the philosophical dilemmas and analytic blind spots created by viewing the transference in this way.

7. These reformulations of the nature of transference are closely related to the understanding of transference developed within the interpersonal tradition and, especially, in the contributions of Merton Gill, which we will explore in some detail in chapter 9.

8. Constraints of space prevent us from discussing the valuable contributions of: Michael Basch, Arnold Goldberg, Ruth Gruenthal, and Paul Ornstein.

CHAPTER 7. CONTEMPORARY FREUDIAN REVISIONISTS: OTTO KERNBERG, ROY SCHAFER, HANS LOEWALD, AND JACQUES LACAN

1. See, for example, Harold Bloom's account (1973) of the manner in which major poets systematically misread the work of their major predecessors.

2. For an approach that attempts to integrate various features of Kohut's and Kernberg's approaches to narcissism and aggression, see Mitchell (1988, chaps. 7 and 8; 1993, chap. 6).

3. A great deal of Schafer's critique of classical psychoanalysis and some of his suggested solutions were prefigured by the existential philosophers and existential psychologists: for example, Rollo May and Leslie Farber.

4. It should be noted that any effort at a clear and systematic summary of Lacan's ideas is by definition anti-Lacanian.

5. Muller and Richardson (1982) offer a wonderful description of Lacan's style:

> The elusive-allusive-illusive manner, the encrustation with rhetorical tropes, the kaleidoscopic erudition, the deliberate ambiguity, the auditory echoes, the oblique irony, the disdain of logical sequence, the prankish playfulness and sardonic (sometimes scathing humor)—all of these forms of preciousness that Lacan affects are essentially a concrete demonstration in verbal locution of the perverse ways of the unconscious as he experiences it. (p. 3)

6. Lacan's account of the creation of the self within the imaginary is remarkably similar to Sullivan's account (drawing on the social psychology of George Herbert Mead) of what he called the "self-system" generated through "reflected appraisals" of others (see Greenberg & Mitchell, 1983, chap. 4). Like Lacan, Sullivan came to feel that this self generated through mirrored perceptions of others is largely adaptive and serves security needs at the expense of a richer, more satisfying existence.

7. Because he gives no weight to an agent of subjectivity, Lacan's system

might be seen in Ogden's framework as lacking any authentic depressive position, lived largely in a paranoid-schizoid world in which one is acted on by external forces (signifiers).

8. Lacan argued that Freud's discovery of the use of condensation and displacement in dream formation was an anticipation of the more general principles of metaphor and metonymy in later structural linguistics.

9. Lacan took Lévi-Strauss's approach to anthropology as a model for his own rereading of Freud. Lévi-Strauss cited linguistic principles as the basis for underlying social structures; similarly, Lacan recontextualized Freudian account of the culmination and renunciation of infantile sexuality in terms of the induction of the child into a determinative linguistic matrix.

10. Lacan drew heavily on both Heidegger and Sartre (see Muller & Richardson, 1982, for an excellent analysis).

CHAPTER 8. CONTROVERSIES IN THEORY

1. Freud understood nature and nurture as operating in a complementary fashion. The more constitution played a part in any individual, the less conflictual experience was required to create a fixation. The less constitution played a part, the more conflictual experience was required (see, for example, Freud, 1905b, pp. 170–171).

2. The term *relational* was used by Greenberg and Mitchell (1983) to highlight the common theoretical framework underlying interpersonal psychoanalysis, British school object relations theories, and self psychology.

3. Klein and subsequent Kleinian theorists are the major exception to this generational shift. The Kleinian approach to the origins of psychopathology retains an almost exclusive emphasis, even more than that of classical Freudians, on inborn instinctual drives.

4. See, for example, Kohut (1971). In some sense, this represents a return, in a much more sophisticated form, of Breuer's notion of altered states of consciousness underlying hysterical systems.

5. A recent joke reflects the relationship between the anatomical and social in ironic terms: Following a sex-change operation, Joe, now Jane, is asked by his male friends "Which cut hurt the worst?" as they offer graphic visions of the surgery. "The cut in salary," answers their friend sadly.

6. Horney (1926) wrote of womb envy in men.

7. Freud termed homosexuality a perversion, because he considered only heterosexual genital intercourse to be the "normal" sexual organization. In the Freudian lexicon, perversions are pregenital fixations caused either by constitution (an overabundance of one or another component drive) or conflict.

8. Freud's intense interest in Jung (which ended in great animosity by 1913) was based partially on his hope that the word-association test Jung had

developed would provide experimental evidence confirming psychoanalytic concepts. See Kerr (1993) for an absorbing and insightful account of the relationship between Freud and Jung.

9. A vast array of empirical approaches has been tried. Some study actual analytic sessions (with audio- or videotapes), subjecting them to linguistic analyses of various sorts (Dill and Hoffman, Gerhardt and Stinson). In this work, the analyst is considered part of the data to be understood, not an external, objective observer. Others study outcome data, looking at the longer-range impact of different kinds of therapy with patients. Others conduct experimental tests of specific theoretical concepts—for example, using tachistoscopes and subliminal perception to study various hypotheses concerning repression (Silverman, Lachmann, and Milich).

10. Because of his belief in ultimate empirical validation, Spence's position has been understood by some critics as not reflecting a truly hermeneutic stance (Sass & Woolfolk, 1988) and as a "lapsed positivism" (Bruner, 1993).

CHAPTER 9. CONTROVERSIES IN TECHNIQUE

1. In Freud's theory of dream formation, unconscious infantile impulses pressing for recognition piggyback onto *day residue,* concrete fragments of conscious experience from the previous day, to gain access into the preconscious and thereby become available for representation in the dream.

2. The once popular term *transference neurosis* concerns the belief that in order for childhood dynamic issues to be fully worked through, the patient's problems must become so powerfully reanimated in the treatment that the analyst and the treatment itself become the patient's central preoccupation and source of discomfort.

3. This model was introduced in the seminal contributions of Heinrich Racker, Edgar Levenson, and Merton Gill, and further developed in the writings of, among others, Joseph Sandler, Irwin Hoffman, Jay Greenberg, Stephen Mitchell, Phillip Bromberg, Lewis Aron, Owen Renik, Donnel Stern, and Charles Spezzano. In somewhat modified form, it is found in the progressive, contemporary Freudian literature (Theodore Jacobs, Judith Chused), in the more interactional versions of self psychology (Robert Stolorow, James Fosshage), and in some of the contemporary Kleinian literature (Betty Joseph, Elizabeth Bott-Spillius). See Hoffman (1983) for an early history of and incisive commentary on the emergence of this point of view.

4. Strachey's suggestion that the superego must change in order for analysis to have long-term effects parallels the importance that Anna Freud gave to alterations in the ego. Both were writing in the early 1930s. Anna Freud dealt with ego functions, Strachey with internal objects. This difference in conceptualizing the crucial scene for internal transformation was later

expanded into the divergence between the ego psychology tradition and the object relations tradition.

5. Strachey emphasized throughout that the analyst should never do anything other than give interpretations.

> It is a paradoxical fact that the best way of ensuring that [the patient's] ego shall be able to distinguish between phantasy and reality is to withhold reality from him as much as possible. But it is true . . . he can only cope with reality if it is administered in minimal doses. And these doses are in fact what the analyst gives him, in the form of interpretations. (1954, p. 350)

6. Among this second generation were Levenson, Singer, Tauber, and Wolstein.

7. See Abend (1986) for an account of the way the classical approach to countertransference led to a widespread sense of shame on the part of analysts about their own inevitable reactions toward patients.

8. This approach was pioneered by Racker and Searles and has been further developed by Hoffman, Greenberg, Mitchell, Tansey and Burke, Ogden, Aron, Maroda, and others.

REFERENCES

Abend, S. (1986). Countertransference, empathy and the analytic ideal: The impact of life stresses on analytic capability. *Psychoanalytic Quarterly, 55,* 563–575.

Abraham, K. (1921). Contributions to the theory of the anal character. In *Selected papers of Karl Abraham* (pp. 370–392). London: Hogarth, 1973.

Altman, N. (1995). *The psychoanalyst in the inner city.* Hillsdale, NJ: Analytic Press.

Arlow, J. A. (1985). The concept of psychic reality and related problems. *Journal of the American Psychoanalytic Association, 33,* 521–535.

Arlow, J. A. (1987). The dynamics of interpretation. *Psychoanalytic Quarterly, 56,* 68–87.

Aron, L. (1991). The patient's experience of the analyst's subjectivity. *Psychoanalytic Dialogues, 1,* 29–51.

Aron, L. (1992). Interpretation as expression of the analyst's subjectivity. *Psychoanalytic Dialogues, 2*(4), 475–508.

Aron, L. (1995). The internalized primal scene. *Psychoanalytic Dialogues, 5*(2), 195–238.

Aron, L., & Harris, A. (Eds.). (1993). *The legacy of Sandor Ferenczi.* Hillsdale, NJ: Analytic Press.

Atwood, G., & Stolorow, R. (1984). *Structures of subjectivity: Explorations in psychoanalytic phenomenology.* Hillsdale, NJ: Analytic Press.

Bacal, H. (1985). Optimal responsiveness and the therapeutic process. In A. Goldberg (Ed.), *Progress in self psychology* (Vol. 1, pp. 202–227). Hillsdale, NJ: Analytic Press.

Bacal, H. (1995). The essence of Kohut's work and the progress of self psychology. *Psychoanalytic Dialogues, 5,* 353–356.

Bacal, H., & Newman, K. (1990). *Theories of object relations: Bridge to self psychology.* New York: Columbia University Press.

Balint, M. (1937). Early developmental states of the ego. In *Primary love and psycho-analytic technique*. New York: Liveright, 1965.

Balint, M. (1968). *The basic fault*. London: Tavistock.

Barringer, F. (1988, July 18). In the new Soviet psyche, a place is made for Freud. *New York Times*, p. 1.

Bass, A. (1993). Review essay: *Learning from the patient*, by Patrick Casement. *Psychoanalytic Dialogues, 3*(1).

Beebe, B., & Lachmann, F. (1988). Mother–infant mutual influence and the precursors of psychic structure. In A. Goldberg (Ed.), *Frontiers in self psychology* (Vol. 3, pp. 3–25). Hillsdale, NJ: Analytic Press.

Beebe, B., & Lachmann, F. (1992). A dyadic systems view of communication. In N. Skolnick & S. Warshaw (Eds.), *Relational perspectives in psychoanalysis*. Hillsdale, NJ: Analytic Press.

Beebe, B., & Lachmann, F. (1994). Representation and internalization in infancy: Three principles of salience. *Psychoanalytic Dialogues, 11*, 127–166.

Benjamin, J. (1988). *The bonds of love: Psychoanalysis, feminism, and the problem of domination*. New York: Pantheon.

Benjamin, J. (1992). Discussion of Judith Jordan's "The relational self." *Contemporary Psychotherapy Review, 7*, 82–96.

Bergmann, M. S. (1973). *The anatomy of loving*. New York: Columbia University Press.

Bieber, I. (1965). Clinical aspects of male homosexuality. In J. Marmor (Ed.), *Sexual inversion: The multiple roots of homosexuality*. New York: Basic Books.

Bion, W. R. (1955). Group dynamics: A re-view. In M. Klein, P. Heiman, & R. E. Money-Kyrle (Eds.), *New directions in psycho-analysis* (pp. 440–477). London: Maresfield Reprints.

Bion, W. (1967). Notes on memory and desire. In E. Bott-Spillius (Ed.), *Melanie Klein today* (Vol. 2, pp. 17–21). London: Routledge, 1988.

Black, M. (1987). The analyst's stance: Transferential implications of technical orientation. In *Annual of Psychoanalysis* (Vol. 15). New York: International Universities Press.

Blanck, G., & Blanck, R. (1974). *Ego psychology: Theory and practice*. New York: Columbia University Press.

Blechner, M. (1992). Working in the counterransference. *Psychoanalytic Dialogues, 2*, 161–180.

Bloom, H. (1973). *The anxiety of influence*. New York: Oxford University Press.

Bloom, H. (1986, March 23). Freud, the greatest modern writer. *New York Times Book Review*.

Bollas, C. (1987). *The shadow of the object: Psychoanalysis of the unthought known*. New York: Columbia University Press.

Bowlby, J. (1969). *Attachment and loss: Vol. 1. Attachment.* New York: Basic-Books.

Bowlby, J. (1973). *Attachment and loss: Vol. 2. Separation: Anxiety and anger.* New York: BasicBooks.

Bowlby, J. (1980). *Attachment and loss: Vol 3. Loss: Sadness and depression.* New York: BasicBooks.

Brenner, C. (1976). *Psychoanalytic technique and psychic conflict.* New York: International Universities Press.

Brenner, C. (1982). *The mind in conflict.* New York: International Universities Press.

Bromberg, P. (1980). Empathy, anxiety and reality: A view from the bridge. *Contemporary Psychoanalysis, 16,* 223–236.

Bromberg, P. (1983). The mirror and the mask: On narcissism and psychoanalytic growth. *Contemporary Psychoanalysis, 19*(2), 359–387.

Bromberg, P. (1989). Interpersonal psychoanalysis and self psychology: A clinical comparison. In D. Detrick & S. Detrick (Eds.), *Self psychology.* Hillsdale, NJ: Analytic Press.

Bromberg, P. (1991). On knowing one's patient inside out. *Psychoanalytic Dialogues, 1*(4), 399–422.

Bromberg, P. (1993). Shadow and substance. *Psychoanalytic Psychology, 10*(2), 147–168.

Brown, N. O. (1959). *Life against death: The psychoanalytic meaning of history.* Middletown, Conn.: Wesleyan University Press.

Bruner, J. (1993). Loyal opposition and the clarity of dissent. *Psychoanalytic Dialogues, 3,* 11–20.

Butler, J. (1990). *Gender trouble: Feminism and the subversion of identity.* New York: Routledge.

Casement, P. (1991). *Learning from the patient.* New York: Guilford.

Chassequet-Smirgel, J. (1988). *Female sexuality.* Ann Arbor: University of Michigan Press.

Chodorow, N. (1980). Gender, relation, and difference in psychoanalytic perspective. In C. Zanardi (Ed.), *Essential papers on the psychology of women.* New York: New York University Press, 1990.

Chodorow, N. (1989). *Feminism and psychoanalytic theory.* New Haven, CT: Yale University Press.

Chused, J. (1991). The evocative power of enactments. *Journal of the American Psychoanalytic Society, 39,* 615–639.

Cocks, G. (Ed.). (1994). *The curve of life: Correspondence of Heinz Kohut, 1923–1981.* Chicago: University of Chicago Press.

Coles, R. (1970). *Erik H. Erikson: The growth of his work.* Boston: Atlantic/ Little, Brown.

Coltart, N. (1992). *Slouching towards Bethlehem . . .* New York: Guilford.

Davies, J. (in press). *Psychoanalytic dialogues.*

Davies, J., & Frawley, M. (1993). *Treating adult survivors of childhood sexual abuse.* New York: BasicBooks.

Dimen, M. (1991). Deconstructing differences: Gender, splitting and transitional space. *Psychoanalytic Dialogues, 1*(3), 335–352.

Douglas, A. (1995). *Terrible honesty: Mongrel Manhattan in the 1920s.* New York: Farrar, Straus & Giroux.

Eissler, R., & Eissler, K. (1966). Heinz Hartmann: A biographical sketch. In R. Loewenstein, L. Newman, M. Shur, & A. Solnit (Eds.), *A general psychology: Essays in honor of Heinz Hartmann* (pp. 3–15). New York: International Universities Press.

Ehrenberg, D. (1992). *The intimate edge.* New York: Norton.

Ellenberger, H. (1970). *The discovery of the unconscious.* New York: Basic-Books.

Erikson, E. (1950). *Childhood and society.* New York: Norton.

Erikson, E. (1958). *Young man Luther.* New York: Norton.

Erikson, E. (1959). *Identity and the life cycle: Vol 1. Selected papers, Psychological issues.* New York: International Universities Press.

Erikson, E. (1968). *Identity: Youth and crisis.* New York: Norton.

Fairbairn, W. R. D. (1952). *An object-relations theory of the personality.* New York: BasicBooks.

Fairbairn, W. R. D. (1994). *From instinct to self: Selected papers of W. R. D. Fairbairn* (Vols. 1–2) (E. F. Birtles & D. E. Scharff, Eds.). Northvale, NJ: Aronson.

Farber, L. (1976). *Lying, despair, jealousy, envy, sex, suicide, drugs, and the good life.* New York: BasicBooks.

Fast, I. (1984). *Gender identity: A differentiation model.* Hillsdale, NJ: Analytic Press.

Feiner, A. (1979). Countertransference and the anxiety of influence. In L. Epstein & A. Feiner (Eds.), *Countertransference.* New York: Aronson.

Feiner, K., & Kiersky, S. (1994). Empathy: A common ground. *Psychoanalytic Dialogues, 4,* 425–440.

Felman, S. (1987). *Jacques Lacan and the adventure of insight.* Cambridge, MA: Harvard University Press.

Ferenczi, S. (1988). *The clinical diary of Sandor Ferenczi* (J. Dupont, Ed.). Cambridge, MA: Harvard University Press.

Fogel, G. (1989). The authentic function of psychoanalytic theory: An overview of the contributions of Hans Loewald. *Psychoanalytic Quarterly, 58,* 419–451.

Fosshage, J. (1987). Dream interpretation revisited. In A. Goldberg (Ed.), *Frontiers in self psychology* (pp. 161–175). Hillsdale, NJ: Analytic Press.

Fosshage, J. (1989). The developmental function of dreaming mentation: Clinical implications. In A. Goldberg (Ed.), *Dimensions of self experience* (pp. 3–11). Hillsdale, NJ: Analytic Press.

Fosshage, J. (1992). Self psychology: The self and its vicissituedes within a relational matrix. In N. Skolnick & S. Warshaw (Eds.), *Relational perspectives in psychoanalysis*. Hillsdale, NJ: Analytic Press.

Fosshage, J. (1994). Toward reconceptualizing transference. *International Journal of Psycho-Analysis, 75*, 265–280.

Fosshage, J., & Loew, C. (Eds.). (1987). *Dream interpretation: A comparative study* (Rev. ed.). Costa Mesa, Calif.: PMA.

Fraiberg, S. (1977). *Every child's birthright: In defense of mothering*. New York: BasicBooks.

Frank, K. (1992). Combining action techniques with psychoanalytic therapy. *International Review of Psychoanalysis, 19*, 57–79.

Frank, K. (1993). Action, insight and working through: Outline of an integrative approach. *Psychoanalytic Dialogues, 3*(4), 535–578.

Freud, A. (1936). *The ego and the mechanisms of defense*. London: Hogarth.

Freud, A. (1966). Links between Hartmann's ego psychology and the child analyst's thinking in psychoanalysis. In R. Loewenstein, L. Newman, M. Shur, & A. Solnit (Eds.), *A general psychology: Essays in honor of Heinz Hartmann* (pp. 16–27). New York: International Universities Press.

Freud, A., Nagera, H., & Freud, W. E. (1965). Metapsychological assessment of the adult personality: The adult profile. *Psychoanalytic Study of the Child, 20*, 9–41.

Freud, S. (1900). *The interpretation of dreams*. SE, Vols. 4 & 5, pp. 1–626.

Freud, S. (1905a). *Fragment of an analysis of a case of hysteria*. The standard edition of the complete psychological works of Sigmund Freud (J. Strachey, Trans.). London: Hogarth, Vol. 7, pp. 1–122).

Freud, S. (1905b). *Three essays on the theory of sexuality*. SE, Vol. 7, pp. 125–245.

Freud, S. (1908). "Civilized" sexual morality and modern nervous illness. SE, Vol. 9, pp. 177–204.

Freud, S. (1912). The dynamics of transference. SE, Vol. 12, pp. 99–108.

Freud, S. (1913). On beginning the treatment (Further recommendations on the technique of psychoanalysis). SE, Vol. 12, pp. 121–144.

Freud, S. (1913). *Totem and taboo*. SE, Vol. 13, pp. 1–164.

Freud, S. (1914a). On narcissism: An introduction. SE, Vol. 14, pp. 67–102.

Freud, S. (1914b). On the history of the psycho-analytic movement. SE, Vol. 14, pp. 1–66.

Freud, S. (1914c). Remembering, repeating and working through. SE, Vol. 12, pp. 145–156.

Freud, S. (1915). Instincts and their vicissitudes. SE, Vol. 14, pp. 111–140.

Freud, S. (1916). Some character types met with in psychoanalytical work. SE, Vol. 14, pp. 311–333.

Freud, S. (1920). *Beyond the pleasure principle*. SE, Vol. 18, pp. 1–64.

Freud, S. (1923). *The ego and the id*. SE, Vol. 19, pp. 1–66.

Freud, S. (1927). *The future of an illusion*. SE, Vol. 21, pp. 34–63.

Freud, S. (1930). *Civilization and its discontents.* SE, Vol. 21, pp. 59–145.

Freud, S. (1933). *New introductory lectures on psycho-analysis.* SE, Vol. 22, pp. 1–182.

Freud, S. (1937a). Analysis terminable and interminable. SE, Vol. 23, pp. 216–253.

Freud, S. (1937b). Constructions in analysis. SE, Vol. 23, pp. 255–270.

Freud, S. (1985). *The complete letters of Sigmund Freud to Wilhelm Fliess, 1887–1904* (J. Masson, Trans. & Ed.). Cambridge, Mass.: Harvard University Press.

Freud, S., & Breuer, J. (1895). *Studies on hysteria.* SE, Vol. 2.

Freud, S., & Ferenczi, S. (1992). *The correspondence of Sigmund Freud and Sandor Ferenczi* (E. Brabant, E. Falzeder, & P. Giampieri-Deutsch, Eds.). Cambridge, MA: Harvard University Press.

Friedman, L. (1988). *Anatomy of psychoanalysis.* Hillsdale, NJ: Analytic Press.

Fromm, E. (1941). *Escape from freedom.* New York: Avon.

Fromm, E. (1947). *Man for himself.* Greenwich, CT: Fawcett.

Gabbard, G. (1995). *Psychotherapy, cost effectiveness, and cost offset.* Oral presentation, W. A. White Institute, New York, NY, April 7.

Gagnon, J. (1991). Commentary. *Psychoanalytic Dialogues, 1,* 373–376.

Gay, P. (1988). *Freud: A life for our time.* New York: Norton.

Gerhardt, J., & Stinson, C. (1995). "I don't know." Resistance or groping for words? The construction of analytic subjectivity. *Psychoanalytic Dialogues, 5.*

Ghent, E. (1992). Process and paradox. *Psychoanalytic Dialogues, 2*(4), 135–160.

Gill, M. (1982). *The analysis of transference* (Vol. 1). New York: International Universities Press.

Gill, M. (1994). *Psychoanalysis in transition.* Hillsdale, NJ: Analytic Press.

Gill, M., & Hoffman, I. Z. (1982). A method for studying the analysis of aspects of the patient's experience of the relationship in psychoanalysis and psychotherapy. *Journal of the American Psychoanalytic Association, 30,* 137–168.

Gill, M., & Holzman, P. (1976). *Psychology vs. metapsychology.* Psychological Issues, Vol. 14, #4, Monograph 36, International Universities Press.

Gilligan, C. (1982). *In a different voice.* Cambridge, MA: Harvard University Press.

Gilligan, C. (1992). *Meeting at the crossroads.* Cambridge, MA: Harvard University Press.

Gray, P. (1994). *The ego and analysis of defense.* Northvale, NJ: Jason Aronson.

Green, M. (Ed.). (1964). *Interpersonal psychoanalysis: The selected papers of Clara M. Thompson.* New York: BasicBooks.

Greenberg, J. (1991). *Oedipus and beyond: A clinical theory.* Cambridge, MA: Harvard University Press.

Greenberg, J., & Mitchell, S. (1983). *Object relations in psychoanalytic theory.* Cambridge, MA: Harvard University Press.

Greenson, R. (1965). The working alliance and the transference neurosis. In *Explorations in psychoanalysis* (pp. 99–224). New York: International Universities Press, 1978.

Greenson, R. (1967). *The technique and practice of Psycho-analysis.* New York: International Universities Press.

Greenson, R. (1968). Disidentifying from Mother. *International Journal of Psychoanalysis, 49,* 370–374.

Greenson, R. (1974). Transference: Freud or Klein? In *Explorations in psychoanalysis* (pp. 519–540). New York: International Universities Press, 1978.

Grosskurth, P. (1986). *Melanie Klein: Her world and her work.* New York: Knopf.

Grosskurth, P. (1991). *The secret ring.* Reading, MA: Addison-Wesley.

Grossman, W. (1992). Hierarchies, boundaries, and representation in the Freudian model of mental organization. *Journal of the American Psychoanalytic Association, 40,* 27–62.

Grosz, E. (1990). *Jacques Lacan: A feminist introduction.* New York: Routledge.

Grotstein, J. (1987). Making the best of a bad deal: A discussion of Boris' "Bion revisited." *Contemporary Psychoanalysis, 23*(1), 60–76.

Gruenthal, R. (1993). The patient's transference experience of the analyst's gender: Projection, factuality, interpretation of construction? *Psychoanalytic Dialogues, 3,* 323–341.

Grunbaum, A. (1984). *The foundations of psychoanalysis.* Berkeley: University of California Press.

Guntrip, H. (1969). *Schizoid phenomena, object relations and the self.* New York: BasicBooks.

Guntrip, H. (1971). *Psychoanalytic theory, therapy and the self.* New York: BasicBooks.

Guntrip, H. (1975). My experience of analysis with Fairbairn and Winnicott. *International Review of Psychoanalysis, 2,* 145–156.

Habermas, J. (1968). *Knowledge and human interests.* New York: Beacon.

Harris, A. (1991). Gender as contradiction. *Psychoanalytic Dialogues, 1*(2), 197–224.

Harris, A. (1995). Envy and aggression: The hidden dilemmas in women's ambition. Paper presented at the winter scientific meeting of the Postgraduate Psychoanalytic Society, New York, January 28, 1995.

Hartmann, H. (1939). *Ego psychology and the problem of adaptation.* New York: International Universities Press.

Hartmann, H. (1964). *Essays on ego psychology.* New York: International Universities Press.

Hartmann, H., Kris, E., & Loewenstein, R. (1946). Comments on the formation of psychic structure. *Psychoanalytic Study of the Child, 2.*

Hartmann, H., Kris, E., & Loewenstein, R. (1951). Some psychoanalytic comments on culture and personality. In G. B. Wilbur & W. Muensterberger (Eds.), *Psychoanalysis and culture*. New York: International Universities Press.

Hatterer, L. (1970). *Changing homosexuality in the male*. New York: McGraw-Hill.

Hirsch, I. (1984). The rediscovery of the advantages of the participant-observation model. *Psychoanalysis and Contemporary Thought, 8,* 441–469.

Hirsch, I. (1987). Varying modes of analytic participation. *Journal of the American Academy of Psychoanalysis, 15,* 205–222.

Hirsch, I. (1994). Countertransference love and theoretical model. *Psychoanalytic Dialogues, 4,* 171–192.

Hoffman, I. Z. (1983). The patient as interpreter of the analyst's experience. *Contemporary Psychoanalysis, 19,* 389–422.

Hoffman, I. Z. (1987). The value of uncertainty in psychoanalytic practice. *Contemporary Psychoanalysis, 23*(2), 205–215.

Hoffman, I. Z. (1991). Discussion: Toward a social-constructivist view of the psychoanalytic situation. *Psychoanalytic Dialogues, 1,* 74–105.

Hoffman, I. Z. (1992). Some practical implications of a social-constructivist view of the psychoanalytic situation. *Psychoanalytic Dialogues, 2,* 287–304.

Hoffman, I. Z. (1994). Dialectical thinking and therapeutic action in the psychoanalytic process. *Psychoanalytic Quarterly, 63,* 187–218.

Hofstadter, D., & Dennett, D. (1981). *The mind's I: Fantasies and reflections on self and soul*. New York: BasicBooks.

Horney, K. (1926). The flight from womanhood. In K. Horney, *Feminine psychology*. New York: Norton, 1967.

Horney, K. (1937). *The neurotic personality of our time*. New York: Norton.

Irigaray, L. (1977). The sex which is not one. In C. Zanardi (Ed.), *Essential papers on the psychology of women*. New York: New York University Press, 1990.

Isaacs, S. (1943). The nature and function of phantasy. In M. Klein, P. Heimann, S. Isaacs, & J. Riviere (eds.), *Developments in psychoanalysis*. London: Hogarth, 1952.

Jacobs, T. (1991). *The use of the self*. New York: International Universities Press.

Jacobson, E. (1964). *The self and the object world*. New York: International Universities Press.

Jacobson, E. (1971). *Depression*. New York: International Universities Press.

Jordan, J. (1992). The relational self: A new perspective for understanding women's development. *Contemporary Psychotherapy Review, 7,* 56–71.

Joseph, B. (1989). *Psychic equilibrium and psychic change*. London: Tavistock/Routledge.

Jung, C. (1933). *Modern man in search of a soul*. New York: Harvest.

Kernberg, O. (1975). *Boarderline conditions and pathological narcissism*. New York: Jason Aronson.

Kernberg, O. (1976). *Object relations theory and clinical psychoanalysis*. New York: Jason Aronson.

Kernberg, O. (1980). *Internal world and external reality*. New York: Jason Aronson.

Kernberg, O. (1984). *Severe personality disorders*. New Haven, CT: Yale University Press.

Kernberg, O. (1994). Love in the analytic setting. *Journal of the American Psychoanalytic Association, 42*(4), 1137–1158.

Kerr, J. (1993). *A most dangerous method: The story of Jung, Freud and Sabina Spielrein*. New York: Knopf.

Khan, M. M. R. (1963). *The privacy of the self*. New York: International Universities Press.

Kirsner, D. (1982). Self psychology and the psychoanalytic movement: An interview with Dr. Heinz Kohut. *Psychoanalysis and Contemporary Thought, 5*(3), 483–495.

Klauber, J., & others (1987). *Illusion and spontaneity in psychoanalysis*. London: Free Association Press.

Klein, M. (1932). *The psycho-analysis of children*. London: Hogarth.

Klein, M. (1935). A contribution to the psychogenesis of manic-depressive states. In *Contributions to psychoanalysis, 1921–1945*. New York: McGraw-Hill, 1964.

Klein, M. (1940). Mourning and its relation to manic-depressive states. In *Contributions to psychoanalysis, 1921–1945*. New York: McGraw-Hill, 1964.

Klein, M. (1957). *Envy and gratitude and other works: 1946–63*. New York: Delacorte, 1975.

Kligerman, C. (1985). The memorials for Heinz Kohut, M.D., October 31, 1981. *The annual of psychoanalysis* (pp. 9–15). New York: International Universities Press.

Kohut, H. (1959). Introspection, empathy and psychoanalysis. *Journal of the American Psychoanalytic Association, 7*, 459–483.

Kohut, H. (1971). *The analysis of self*. New York: International Universities Press.

Kohut, H. (1977). *The restoration of the self*. New York: International Universities Press.

Kohut, H. (1979). The two analyses of Mr. Z. *International Journal of Psychoanalysis, 60*, 3–27.

Kohut, H. (1984). *How does analysis cure?* Chicago: University of Chicago Press.

Kohut, H. (1994). *The course of life: Correspondence of Heinz Kohut, 1923–1981* (G. Cocks, Ed.). Chicago: University of Chicago Press.

Kohut, H., & Wolf, E. (1978). The disorders of the self and their treatment: An outline. *International Journal of Psychoanalysis, 59*, 413–425.

Kris, E. (1951). Ego psychology and interpretation in psychoanalytic therapy. In C. Thompson (Ed.), *An outline of psychoanalysis* (pp. 77–93). New York: Random House, 1955.

Kris, E. (1952). *Psychoanalytic explorations in art.* New York: International Universities Press.

Kristeva, J. (1981). Women's time. In C. Zanardi (Ed.), *Essential papers on the psychology of women* (pp. 374–400). New York: New York University Press, 1990.

Kristeva, J. (1986). *The Kristeva reader* (T. Moi, Ed.). New York: Columbia University Press.

Kristeva, J. (1992). *The samurai.* New York: Columbia University Press.

Kronold, E. (1980). Edith Jacobson 1897–1978. *Psychoanalytic Quarterly, 49,* 505–507.

Lacan, J. (1977). *Ecrits: A selection* (Alan Sheridan, Trans.). New York: Norton.

Lacan, J. (1978). *The four fundamental concepts of psychoanalysis* (Jacques-Alain Miller, Ed., Alan Sheridan, Trans.). New York: Norton.

Lacan, J. (1988a). *The seminar of Jacques Lacan: Book I: Freud's papers on technique, 1953–1954* (Jacques-Alain Miller, Ed.; John Forrester, Trans.). New York: Norton.

Lacan, J. (1988b). *The seminar of Jacques Lacan: Book II: The ego in Freud's theory and in the technique of psychoanalysis, 1954–1955.* (Jacques-Alain Miller, Ed., John Forrester, Trans.). New York: Norton.

Lachmann, F., & Beebe, B. (1992). Representational and selfobject transferences: A developmental perspective. In *New therapeutic visions: Progress in self psychology* (Vol. 8, pp. 3–15). Hillsdale, NJ: Analytic Press.

Lachmann, F., & Beebe, B. (1994). Representation and internalization in infancy: 3 principles of salience. *Psychoanalytic Psychology, 11*(2), 127–166.

Lachmann, F., & Stolorow, R. (1987). Transference—The organization of experience. In R. Stolorow, B. Brandschaft & G. Atwood (Eds.), *Psychoanalytic treatment: An intersubjective approach.* Hillsdale, NJ: Analytic Press.

Laing, R. D., & Esterson, A. (1970). *Sanity, madness and the family.* Harmondsworth, Middlesex, England: Penguin.

Lasch, C. (1978). *The culture of narcissism: American life in an age of diminishing expectations.* New York: Norton.

Levenson, E. (1972). *The fallacy of understanding.* New York: BasicBooks.

Levenson, E. (1983). *The ambiguity of change.* New York: BasicBooks.

Lichtenberg, J. (1983). *Psychoanalysis and infant research.* Hillsdale, NJ: Analytic Press.

Lichtenberg, J. (1989). *Psychoanalysis and motivation.* Hillsdale, NJ: Analytic Press.

Little, M. (1985). Winnicott working in areas where psychotic anxieties predominate: A personal record. *Free Associations, 3,* 9–41.

Loewald, H. (1980). *Papers on psychoanalysis.* New Haven, CT: Yale University Press, 1980.

Loewald, H. (1988). *Sublimation.* New Haven, CT: Yale University Press.

Lorenz, K. (1966). *On aggression.* New York: Harcourt, Brace & World.

Mahler, M. (1966). Notes on the development of basic moods: The depressive affect. In R. Loewenstein, L. Newman, M. Schur, & A. Solnit, Eds., *Psychoanalysis: A general psychology* (pp. 152–168). New York: International Universities Press.

Mahler, M. (1968). *On human symbiosis and the vicissitudes of individuation.* Vol. 1. *Infantile psychosis.* New York: International Universities Press.

Mahler, M., Pine, F., & Bergman, A. (1975). *The psychological birth of the human infant.* New York: BasicBooks.

Marcuse, H. (1955). *Eros and civilization.* Boston: Beacon.

Maroda, K. (1991). *The power of countertransference.* Northvale, NJ: Jason Aronson.

Masson, J. (1984). *The assault on truth: Freud's suppression of the seduction theory.* New York: Farrar, Straus & Giroux.

May, R. (1969). *Love and will.* New York: Norton.

May, R., Angel, E., & Ellenberger, H. (1967). *Existence.* New York: Simon & Schuster.

Mehlman, J. (1972). The "floating signifier": From Lévi-Strauss to Lacan. In *French Freud; Structural Studies in Psychoanalysis, Yale French Studies, 48,* 10–37.

Messer, S., Sass, L., & Woolfolk, R. (Eds.) (1988). *Hermeneutics and psychological theory: Interpretive perspectives on personality, psychotherapy and psychopathology.* New Brunswick NJ: Rutgers University Press.

Michels, R. (1988). The future of psychoanalysis. *Psychoanalytic Quarterly, 57,* 167–185.

Mitchell, J. (1975). *Psychoanalysis and feminism.* New York: Vintage.

Mitchell, S. (1988). *Relational concepts in psychoanalysis: An integration.* Cambridge, MA: Harvard University Press.

Mitchell, S. (1993). *Hope and dread in psychoanalysis.* New York: BasicBooks.

Modell, A. (1984). *Psychoanalysis in a new context.* New York: International Universities Press.

Muller, J. (1995). *Beyond the psychoanalytic dyad: Developmental semiotics in Freud, Pierce and Lacan.* New York: Routledge.

Muller, J., & Richardson, W. (1982). *Lacan and language: A reader's guide to Ecrits.* New York: International Universities Press.

Ogden, T. (1982). *Projective identification and psychotherapeutic technique.* New York: Jason Aronson.

Ogden, T. (1986). *The matrix of the mind.* Northvale, NJ: Jason Aronson.

Ogden, T. (1989). *The primitive edge of experience.* Northvale, NJ: Jason Aronson.

Ogden, T. (1991). An interview with Thomas Ogden. *Psychoanalytic Dialogues, 1,* 361–376.

Ogden, T. (1994). *Subjects of analysis*. Northvale, NJ: Jason Aronson.

Oliner, M. (1988). *Cultivating Freud's garden in France*. New York: Aronson.

Ornstein, A. (1974). The dread to repeat and the new beginning. *Annual of Psychoanalysis, 2,* 231–248.

Ovesy, L. (1969). *Homosexuality and pseudohomosexuality*. New York: Science House.

Panel (1978). Survey of psychoanalytic practice 1976; some trends and implications. S. E. Pulver, Reporter. *Journal of the American Psychoanalytic Association, 26,* 615–631.

Perry, H. S. (1982). *Psychiatrist of America: The life of Harry Stack Sullivan*. Cambridge, MA: Harvard University Press.

Phillips, A. (1988). *Winnicott*. Cambridge, MA: Harvard University Press.

Phillips, A. (1993). *On kissing, tickling and being bored*. Cambridge, MA: Harvard University Press.

Phillips, A. (1994). *On flirtation: Psychoanalytic essays on the uncommitted life*. Cambridge, MA: Harvard University Press.

Pine, F. (1985). *Developmental theory and clinical process*. New Haven, CT: Yale University Press.

Pine, F. (1991). *Drive, ego, object, self*. New York: BasicBooks.

Pizer, S. (1992). The negotiation of paradox in the analytic patient. *Psychoanalytic Dialogues, 2*(2), 215–40.

Plottel, J. (1985). Jacques Lacan: Psychoanalyst, surrealist and mystic. In J. Reppen (Ed.), *Beyond Freud: A study of modern psychoanalytic theorists*. Hillsdale, NJ: Analytic Press.

Racker, H. (1968). *Transference and countertransference*. New York: International Universities Press.

Rapaport, D. (1958). A historical survey of psychoanalytic ego psychology. In *The collected papers of David Rapaport* (M. Gill, Ed.). New York: BasicBooks, 1967.

Reich, W. (1929). The genital character and the neurotic character. In R. Fliess (Ed.), *The psychoanalytic reader*. New York: International Universities Press, 1948.

Renik, O. (1993). Analytic interaction: Conceptualizing technique in light of the analyst's irredicible subjectivity. *Psychoanalytic Quarterly, 62*(4), 553–571.

Ricoeur, P. (1970). *Freud and philosophy: An essay on interpretation*. New Haven, CT: Yale University Press.

Rosenfeld, H. (1987). *Impasse and interpretation*. London: Tavistock.

Samson, H., & Weiss, J. (1986). *The psychoanalytic process: Theory, clinical observation and empirical research*. New York: Guilford.

Sandler, J. (1976). Countertransference and role-responsiveness. *International Review of Psychoanalysis, 3,* 43–48.

Sass, L., & Woolfolk, R. (1988). Psychoanalysis and the hermeneutic turn: A critique of *Narrative truth and historical truth*. *Journal of the American Psychoanalytic Association, 36,* 429–454.

Schafer, R. (1968). *Aspects of internalization*. New York: International Universities Press.

Schafer, R. (1976). *A new language for psychoanalysis*. New Haven, CT: Yale University Press.

Schafer, R. (1978). *Language and insight*. New Haven, CT: Yale University Press.

Schafer, R. (1983). *The analytic attitude*. New York: BasicBooks.

Schafer, R. (1992). *Retelling a life*. New York: BasicBooks.

Schafer, R. (1994). The contemporary Kleinians of London. *Psychoanalytic Quarterly, 63*(3), 409–432.

Schneiderman, S. (1983). *Jacques Lacan: The death of an intellectual hero*. Cambridge, MA: Harvard University Press.

Schwartz, J. (1995). What does the physicist know? Thraldom and insecurity in the relationship of psychoanalysis to physics. *Psychoanalytic Dialogues, 5*, 45–62.

Searles, H. (1979). *Countertransfereance and related subjects*. New York: International Universities Press.

Searles, H. (1986). *My work with borderline patients*. Northvale, NJ: Jason Aronson.

Seligman, S., & Shanok, R. (1995). Subjectivity, complexity and the social world: Erikson's identity concept and contemporary relational theories. *Psychoanalytic Dialogues, 5*.

Shapiro, D. (1965). *Neurotic styles*. New York: BasicBooks.

Shengold, L. (1989). *Soul murder*. New York: International Universities Press.

Silverman, L., Lachmann, F., & Milich, R. (1982). *The search for oneness*. New York: International Universities Press.

Silverman, M. (1985). Countertransference and the myth of the perfectly analyzed analyst. *Psychoanalytic Quarterly, 54*,(2), 175–199.

Simon, J., & Gagnon, W. (1973). *Sexual conduct*. Chicago: Aldine.

Singer, E. (1965). *Key concepts in psychotherapy*. New York: Random House.

Soccarides, C. (1968). *The overt homosexual*. New York: Grune & Stratton.

Sorenson, R. L. (1994). Ongoing change in psychoanalytic theory: Implications for analysis of religious experience. *Psychoanalytic Dialogues, 4*, 631–660.

Spence, D. (1982). *Narrative truth, historical truth*. New York: Norton.

Spezzano, C. (1993). *Affect in psychoanalytic theory and therapy: Towards a new synthesis*. Hillsdale, NJ: Analytic Press.

Spillius, E. (1988). Introductions to *Melanie Klein Today* (Vols. 1–2). New York: Routledge.

Spitz, R. A. (1946a). Hospitalism: a follow-up report. *Psychoanalytic Study of the Child, 2*, 113–117.

Spitz, R. A. (1946b). Anaclitic depression. *Psychoanalytic Study of the Child, 2*, 313–342.

Spitz, R. A. (1957). *No and yes: On the genesis of human communication*. New York: International Universities Press.

Spitz, R. (1965). *The first year of life.* New York: International Universities Press.

Stern, D. (1985). *The interpersonal world of the infant.* New York: BasicBooks.

Stern, D. B. (1987). Unformulated experience. *Contemporary Psychoanalysis, 19*, 71–99.

Stern, D. B. (1990). Courting surprise. *Contemporary Psychoanalysis, 26*, 452–478.

Stern, D. B. (1991). A philosophy for the embedded analyst. *Contemporary Psychoanalysis, 27*(1), 51–80.

Stolorow, R., & Atwood, G. (1979). *Faces in a cloud: Subjectivity in personality theory.* New York: Aronson.

Stolorow, R., & Atwood, G. (1992). *Contexts of being: The intersubjective foundations of psychological life.* Hillsdale, NJ: Analytic Press.

Stolorow, R., Brandschaft, B., & Atwood, G. (1987). *Psychoanalytic treatment: An intersubjective approach.* Hillsdale, NJ: Analytic Press.

Stolorow, R., & Lachmann, F. (1984/1985). Transference: The future of an illusion. *Annual of Psychoanalysis* (Vols. 12–13, pp. 19–37). New York: International Universities Press.

Strachey, J. (1934). The nature of the therapeutic action of psychoanalysis. In M. Bergmann & F. Hartman (Eds.), *The evolution of psychoanalytic technique* (pp. 331–360). New York: BasicBooks, 1976.

Strozier, C. (1985). Glimpses of a life: Heinz Kohut (1913–1981). In A. Goldberg (Ed.), *Progress in self psychology* (Vol. 1, pp. 3–12). Hillsdale, NJ: Analytic Press.

Sullivan, H. S. (1938). The data of psychiatry. In *The fusion of psychiatry and social science.* New York: Norton, 1964.

Sullivan, H. S. (1940). *Conceptions of modern psychiatry.* New York: Norton.

Sullivan, H. S. (1950). The illusion of personal individuality. In *The fusion of psychiatry and social science.* New York: Norton, 1964.

Sullivan, H. S. (1953). *The interpersonal theory of psychiatry.* New York: Norton.

Sullivan, H. S. (1956). *Clinical studies in psychiatry.* New York: Norton.

Sutherland, J. D. (1989). *Fairbairn's journey into the interior.* London: Free Association Books.

Tansey, M., & Burke, W. (1989). *Understanding countertransference: From projective identification to empathy.* Hillsdale, NJ: Analytic Press.

Tauber, E. (1979). *Countertransference reexamined.* In L. Epstein & A. Feiner (Eds.), *Countertransference.* New York: Aronson.

Thompson, C. (1942). Cultural pressures in the psychology of women. In C. Zanardi (Ed.), *Essential papers on the psychology of women.* New York: New York University Press, 1990.

Tronick, E., & Adamson, L. (1980). *Babies as people: New findings on our social beginnings.* New York: Collier.

Turkle, S. (1978). *Psychoanalytic politics: Freud's French revolution.* Cambridge, MA: MIT Press.

van der Kolk, B. (1988). The trauma spectrum: The interaction of biological and social events in the genesis of the trauma response. *Journal of Traumatic Stress, 1,* 273–290.

Wachtel, P. (1987). *Action and insight.* New York: Guilford.

Winer, R. (1994). *Close encounters: A relational view of the therapeutic process.* Northvale, NJ: Jason Aronson.

Winnicott, D. W. (1958). *Through paediatrics to psychoanalysis.* London: Hogarth.

Winnicott, D. W. (1965). *The maturational process and the facilitating environment.* New York: International Universities Press.

Winnicott, D. W. (1971). *Playing and reality.* Middlesex, England: Penguin.

Wolf, E. (1976). Ambience and abstinence. *Annual of Psychoanalysis, 4,* 101–115.

Wolstein, B. (1971). *Human psyche in psychoanalysis.* Springfield, IL: Charles C. Thomas.

Zetzel, E. R. (1956). Current concepts of transference. *International Journal of Psycho-Analysis, 37,* 369–376.

Zetzel, E. (1958). Therapeutic alliance in the analysis of hysteria. In E. R. Zetzel (Ed.), *The capacity for emotional growth* (pp. 182–196). New York: International Universities Press, 1970.

NAME INDEX

Abend, Sander, 245
Abraham, Karl, 86, 176–77
Adler, Alfred, 21
"Anna O." (Bertha Pappenheim),
  3–5, 156, 255–56*n*2
Aron, L., 247

Bacal, Howard, 167–68
Balint, Michael, 113, 134–36
Barringer, F., *xix*
Bateson, Gregory, 60, 143
Beebe, Beatrice, 166–67, 259*n*1
Benedict, Ruth, 143
Benjamin, Jessica, 222, 257*n*5
Bergman, Martin, 48
Bernheim, Hippolyte, 2
Bieber, I., 223
Bion, Wilfred, 102–8, 257*n*2

Blechner, M., 247
Bloom, Harold, *xix,* 262*n*1
Blos, Peter, 142
Bollas, Christopher, 260*n*3
Bott-Spillius, Elizabeth, 259–60*n*2
Bowlby, John, *xix–xx,* 113–14, 134,
  136–37
Breton, André, 193
Breuer, Josef, 3–5, 255–56*n*2
Bromberg, David, 217
Bromberg, P., 74, 84, 218
Brown, Norman O., 256*n*8
Burlingham, Dorothy, 142
Butler, J., 210

Charcot, Jean-Martin, 2–3
Chassequet-Smirgel, Janine, 221
Chodorow, Nancy, 22

283

SUBJECT INDEX

adaptation, 34–42, 136, 143–44
adhesiveness of libido, 114–15
adolescence, 11, 17, 221
affect: contagion of, 105–6; isolation of, 27; management of, 17–19; perception of, 50; pleasure vs. pain, 174. *See also specific affects*
agency, 180–83
aggressive drive, 4, 18–19; ego psychology, 30–32, 52–53, 55–56; Kleinian theory, 88–89, 94–95, 100; vs. libidinal drive, 48–49, 95–99; sign of vulnerability, 164; social impact on female, 258n11
aim-inhibited drives, 14, 39
ambition, in self-realization, 164
anal character, 176–77

anal eroticism, 14
anger. *See* aggressive drive
anthropology, 170–71
anxiety: castration, 15, 219; as defense, 232–33, 235; interpersonal view, 65–77, 259n1; Kleinian view, 88–94; in object relations, 130–31; stranger, 42; in transference, 7–8, 54
archaeology, influence on Freud, 1–2
arrested development, 214–18
attachment theory, 136–38
attacks on linking, 104
autonomy, 37–38, 41, 52

castration anxiety, 15, 219
catharsis, 4
character. *See* personality

287